I0805080

Praise for

Goose Creek
A Definitive History
Volume Two
Rebellion, Reconstruction and Beyond

Dr. Heitzler's outstanding two-volume history of Goose Creek demonstrates a sincere love for this unique Lowcountry community. Dr. Heitzler has skillfully uncovered a wide variety of public and private records to tell the multiple stories that make Goose Creek special. Teachers and students of South Carolina history should find this book to be an invaluable resource that will stand as *the* definitive history of Goose Creek for many years to come.

Donald O. Stewart
Project Director, Teaching American History in South Carolina
South Carolina Department of Archives and History

Mike Heitzler's most interesting and readable history is an extraordinary gift, not only to the current and future residents of Goose Creek, but also to the people of this region and all of South Carolina. The sense of place that comes with knowledge of our past can help us build a better future and Mike Heitzler has splendidly given us a vivid understanding of a special place in South Carolina.

Joseph P. Riley Jr.
Mayor, City of Charleston, South Carolina

Michael J. Heitzler has spent four years compiling his wonderful two-volume history of Goose Creek, a community that fundamentally shaped the early political, agricultural and social history of South Carolina. Using in-depth research and analysis, the author has crafted one of the state's finest local histories, which will be of great interest to both scholars and laymen.

W. Eric Emerson, PhD
Executive Director, South Carolina Historical Society

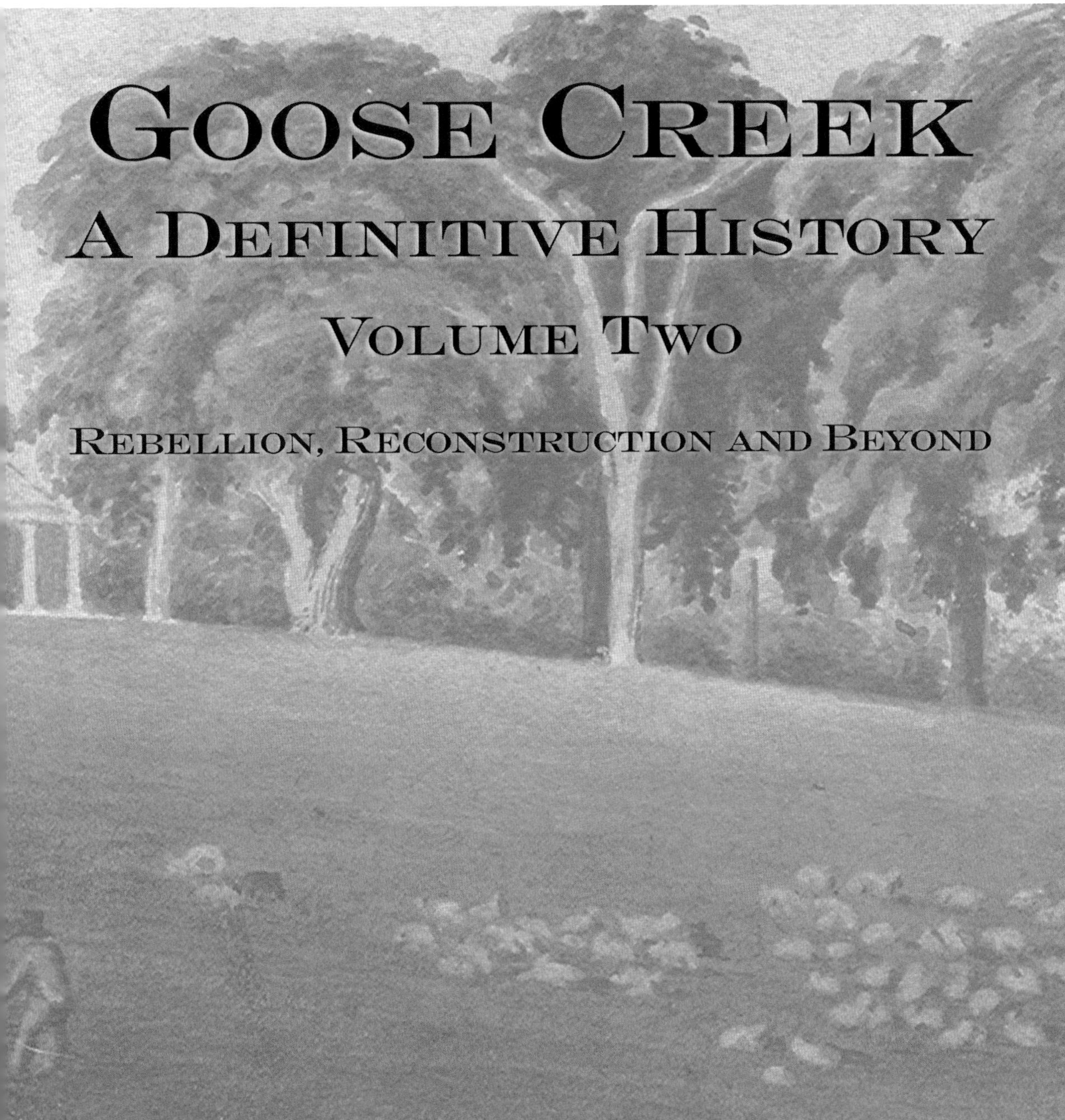

Goose Creek

A Definitive History

Volume Two

Rebellion, Reconstruction and Beyond

Michael J. Heitzler

Edited by Nancy Paul Kirchner

The History Press

Published by The History Press
Charleston, SC 29403
www.historypress.net

Copyright © 2006 by Michael J. Heitzler
All rights reserved

Front cover image: The charter members of the Pineview Baptist Church in July 1961.
Back cover image: The photograph shows Geneva Varner Clark and her three sons in 1938 standing near their home in Varner Town. The house was located approximately half a mile north of Carnes Cross Roads. The photograph was taken by Marion Post Wolcott. *Courtesy Library of Congress.*
Title page: "The Elms" Goose Creek, South Carolina, The country seat of Ralph Izard Esquire. Painted by Thomas Middleton, 1811. Courtesy of the South Carolina Historical Society.
Facing page: An unidentified boy sitting on a fallen section of the Elms Plantation main house in 1930. *Courtesy Library of Congress.*
Following page: Twin lion heads grace the grand entrance lawn between the double drive to Medway Plantation. The photograph was taken March 15, 2005. *Author's collection.*

First published 2006
Manufactured in the United States
ISBN 978.1.59629.056.3

Library of Congress Cataloging-in-Publication Data

Heitzler, Michael J. (Michael James), 1947-
Goose Creek, South Carolina : a definitive history 1670-2003 / Michael J. Heitzler ; edited by Nancy Paul Kirchner.
p. cm.
Includes bibliographical references (p.293) and index.
ISBN 978-1-59629-056-3 (alk. paper)
1. Goose Creek (S.C.)--History. I. Kirchner, Nancy Paul. II. Title.
F279.G66H447 2005
975.7'91--dc22
2005014513

Notice: The information in this book is true and complete to the best of our knowledge. It is offered without guarantee on the part of the author or The History Press. The author and The History Press disclaim all liability in connection with the use of this book.

All rights reserved. No part of this book may be reproduced or transmitted in any form whatsoever without prior written permission from the publisher except in the case of brief quotations embodied in critical articles and reviews.

The publisher regrets an error in Volume One, page 192, plat 7.12.

The partial plat represents Woodstock Plantation.

To you, my neighbors, across town and near,
Who I have known forever, or have yet to meet.
All of you bring truth to the old axiom,
"There's no place like home!"

Contents

Acknowledgements and Credits

This work would have been impossible without the assistance and encouragement of many who shared my love and enthusiasm for Goose Creek. I appreciate the kindness of Goose Creek City Council for authorizing municipal staff to provide assistance copying and acquiring many municipal documents for research, as well as reading and editing the initial drafts. I especially appreciate the scrutiny of city councilman Mark Phillips who edited some of the final draft. His analytical training as an engineer kept the document logical and simple throughout. I am thankful to many friends such as Richard Hanf, Scott Reid, Deidre Brown, Wendy Schulz, Diane Crawford, Lanora Rogers and Barbara Ash who read sections of the manuscript and wrote editorial suggestions. No help has gone unappreciated.

I thank John Tienken, chief executive officer, and Jerry Stafford, reproduction specialist, of the South Carolina Public Service Authority (Santee Cooper) for digitizing the Henry A.M. Smith plats facilitating their use in several chapters. I also thank Captain Gary Edwards, commanding officer, and Terrence Larimer, natural resource supervisor, at the Naval Weapons Station, Charleston, for their kindness and patience while showing me many historical relics in the restricted sections of the military property.

I also acknowledge the kindness and skilled assistance of the staff of the South Carolina Historical Society, the South Carolina Department of Archives and History and the United States Library of Congress for their assistance in searching and granting permission to reproduce illustrations, plats, maps, photographs and drawings. I also thank the skilled personnel at the Goose Creek and Moncks Corner branches of the Berkeley County Library and the South Carolina Room of the Charleston County Library for their patience and kindness.

My appreciation extends to Frances Etling Roberson for searching her private collection of family photographs and permitting me to use several of them. I also thank Mrs. Caroline Cohen for graciously allowing me to use a copy of a selected Charles Fraser art piece.

I offer my sincerest gratitude to Linda Sineath, dear friend and colleague, who sat by my side for dozens of hours and consistently found ways to improve the English sentence. What we sowed during those hours of toil heaped a bounty upon the content of this book and my understanding of friendship.

Finally, I thank Nancy Paul Kirchner for editing the book. She teaches English at the College of Charleston. As an enthusiastic editor, she worked with a well-stocked toolbox and the experience to aptly employ each instrument. That she did without exception. She brought clarity to the Goose Creek story and prepared the end product for public scrutiny.

List of Illustrations

Drawings and Figures

Maps

Photographs

Photograph 1.5: The photograph shows the Springhill Methodist Church. The photograph was taken April 4, 2003, by the author.
Photograph 1.6: The photograph shows the Wassamasaw Baptist Church.
Photograph 2.1: The photograph shows the front view of St. James, Goose Creek Church. The photograph is in the personal collection of the author.
Photograph 2.2: The photograph shows a bas-relief figure of a pelican feeding three hatchlings.
Photograph 2.3: The photograph shows the interior of the church with the stairway, pulpit and sounding board in the center.
Photograph 2.4: The photograph shows a church window decorated with a masonry cherub face and wings.
Photograph 2.5: The photograph shows a granite cross that marks the location of the French Huguenot Church in St. James, Goose Creek Parish.
Photograph 2.6: The photograph was taken near the beginning of the twentieth century. It shows discoloration around the front door caused by moisture.
Photograph 2.7: The photograph shows several cemetery markers at the sight of the St. James Chapel of Ease and Bethlehem Baptist Church in Strawberry.
Photograph 2.8: The photograph shows the Groomsville Baptist Church.
Photograph 2.9: The photograph shows the Izard hatchment displayed on the face of the St. James, Goose Creek Church balcony.
Photograph 3.1: The photograph shows the one-room schoolhouse at Medway Plantation.
Photograph 3.2: The photograph shows a one-room schoolhouse for Negro Children in the vicinity of today's Highway 17A near Carnes Crossroads in 1938.
Photograph 4.1: The photograph shows the general store at Wassamasaw. It was built in 1880.
Photograph 4.2: This photograph shows a farm near Charleston at the end of the nineteenth century.
Photograph 4.3: The photograph shows a phosphate processing plant in Goose Creek.
Photograph 4.4: The photograph shows the Dallas Van Buren Carnes House located at Carnes Crossroads where Highways 176 and Alternate 17 intersect.
Photograph 4.5: The photograph shows the 37-Mile House.
Photograph 4.6: The photograph shows a person walking alongside a horse, rider and buggy on the shaded avenue approaching the Oaks entrance gate near the end of the nineteenth century.
Photograph 4.7: The photograph shows St. Paul's Church.
Photograph 5.1: The photograph shows the Goose Creek Bridge circa 1904.
Photograph 5.2: The photograph shows an automobile on the State Road in Goose Creek circa 1925.
Photograph 5.3: The photograph shows four unidentified children on the front porch of the *Stephen Williams House* in 1930.
Photograph 5.4: The blurred photograph shows a man at a trunk gate in a Goose Creek rice field between 1901 and 1905.
Photograph 5.5: The photograph shows Geneva Varner Clark and three of her sons in 1938.
Photograph 5.6: The photograph shows people fishing on a bridge at Ancrum Creek circa 1904.
Photograph 5.7: The photograph shows four members of the Wassamasaw Tribe.
Photograph 5.8: The photograph shows a clay-lined well, oven and a crane hoist.
Photograph 5.9: The photograph shows the Clark brothers at their home in Varnertown.

Photograph 7.1: The photograph shows incumbent city council members Lagette Shiver, Doreen Davis and Calvin Woods when they picked up petitions to run for re-election in 1984.
Photograph 7.2: Goose Creek Police Chief Harvey Becker is shown with the Goose Creek police force in 1989.
Photograph 7.3: The photograph shows a line of citizens outside the Goose Creek recreation center on Old Moncks Corner Road three days after Hurricane Hugo struck leaving coastal South Carolina without power.
Photograph 7.4: The photograph shows the pavement, rooflines and overhead power and communication lines that characterized the commercial center of Goose Creek.
Photograph 7.5: The photograph shows the mayor and city council at the dedication ceremony of The Marguerite Brown Municipal Center.
Photograph 8.1: The postcard photograph shows the St. James, Goose Creek Church and graveyard near the time of the ghostly tale.
Photograph 8.2: The photograph shows a small boy holding a large key at the side door of the Goose Creek Church.
Photograph 8.3: The photograph shows the tomb where Elizabeth Ann Smith is buried.
Photograph 8.4: The photograph shows a vision of a head, face and torso of a person dressed in white in the center of the window.
Photograph 9.1: The photograph shows Canada geese feeding on the great lawn at the Marguerite H. Brown Municipal Center.

Plats

Plat 1.1: The drawing depicts "Baxter's House."
Plat 1.2: The partial plat shows Harmon's House and cleared land situated near Black Tom Bay in 1853.
Plat 2.1: This partial plat shows the location of the French Church marked as "Remains of French Church."
Plat 2.2: The partial plat shows the St. James, Goose Creek "Chapel of Ease" near the 23-Mile House on the Moncks Corner Road.
Plat 4.1: The plat was drawn by Langdon Cheves in 1918 from an 1872 survey and is shown below as an overlay on a section of the City of Goose Creek as it was in 2003.
Plat 4.2: The plat shows 228 acres owned by John Donnelly Sr. and John Donnelly Junior in 1831.
Plat 4.3: The partial plat was drawn from a survey made by T.J. Mellard in 1872 showing the lands owned by Henry A. Middleton.
Plat 5.1: The plat shows the Otranto Railroad Depot at the intersection of the Atlantic Coastline Railroad and Otranto Road.
Plat 5.2: The plat shows the Ingleside Mining Co. consisting of 1,639 acres contiguous to the Southern Railroad.
Plat 5.3: The partial plat shows the twenty-five-acre tract purchased by the United Methodist Church at Casey [Caice].
Plat 7.1:The plat shows the planned downtown as envisioned by the City of Goose Creek Economic Development Committee in 2002.

Tables

Table 7.3: The table shows traffic counts, rates of increase and projected volumes for the major thoroughfares in the City of Goose Creek.
Table 7.4: The table shows the household incomes of families in various increments in 1990 and 2000 and the change in dollars and percent.
Table 7.5: The table shows the population of various racial groups in 1990 and 2000 and the percent of difference.
Table 7.6: The table shows the distribution of different age groups in 1990 and 2000 and the percent of difference.
Table 7.7: The table shows the projects and associated costs in the Goose Creek Redevelopment Area also known as the Tax Increment Financing (TIF) District.

Preface

Here is the second volume of the two-volume *Goose Creek: A Definitive History*. Volume I, *Planters, Politicians and Patriots*, describes the successes and failures of Goose Creekers during the perilous frontier period, the heady plantation era and the episodic decades leading to the American Revolution. Volume I also traces the ownership of the parish lands, which were the foundation of the social, economic and political order of the seventeenth and eighteenth centuries. The prevailing belief was that land ownership was the best foundation for efficient order and this belief was the genesis of South Carolina culture from which enduring systems and institutions evolved.

Volume II: Rebellion, Reconstruction and Beyond describes the economic, social and political systems, as well as the local institutions that emerged within the context of land ownership. It explains the systemic transitions that occurred as the large estates were subdivided into smaller and smaller farms and finally into suburban lots for residents and businesses of the twentieth century. The successes and failures of the evolving institutions depended upon the bounties from the farms and forests of semi-tropical Carolina. Here, the people and their emerging local governments, churches and schools met the challenges of shifting markets and changing racial attitudes. They were tested by civil war and reconstruction during the nineteenth century and endured social and political revolutions forced upon them as residents of the "New South" during the twentieth century.

Ultimately, in 1961, a handful of citizens in this seasoned section of South Carolina created a new municipality that they named the, "City of Goose Creek." The small city was erected upon a shaky foundation, but in its persistence for more than four decades, it has emerged as one of the premier municipalities on the South Carolina coast. Today, the greatest challenge to Goose Creekers is the protection of their land, forests and waters that have sustained the community for more than three centuries and the safeguard of the tranquil lifestyles that have long characterized their little corner of South Carolina.

Chapter I
Revolution to Rebellion
1783–1865

At the close of the Revolutionary War, the Patriots were victorious and a wave of optimism swept the nation, but along with independence came grave responsibilities for the young government of the United States of America. The economic foundation of the new nation was badly weakened by its separation from the British Empire and by the destruction of war. The South suffered from depressed prices, unmarketable products, soil exhaustion and an unprofitable slave system. All indicators portended an ominous economic future, and while South Carolinians sought solutions to these persistent problems, Thomas Jefferson spoke of freeing his slaves and predicted with confidence the natural death of the institution of forced servitude that Goose Creekers had depended upon since the earliest years of settlement.

Upon returning to Goose Creek, the planter-patriots found damaged plantations and daunting poverty. The warring sides vandalized many of the plantations, and the properties that were not intentionally damaged were debilitated through neglect and in dire need of repair. Sadly, the new American government could offer little assistance, and although requests for recompense were sent to England, no help returned. In 1784, commissioners traveled to England to seek payment for slaves and other property taken by the evacuating British army. William Logan of Goose Creek was one of the South Carolina commissioners, but his long voyage to England and troublesome negotiations netted no compensation, requiring Goose Creek to face their postwar problems unaided.[1]

The war punctuated years of economic decline that began during the waning decades of the eighteenth century and continued into the next. The large estates and vast fortunes dwindled and never resurrected so that sixty years after the end of the war, Edmund Ruffin, the southern agricultural reformer, described Goose Creek, "as much a scene of desolation as any."[2] A few diversified estates persevered by producing rice, bricks and lumber in the eastern section of the parish. Toward the mid-century, limited non-agricultural employment opportunities became available, but the period witnessed the demise of the grand agricultural plantations in the eastern section and the emergence of less affluent farms and estates in the central and western parts. As these sections emerged as viable economies for smaller landowners and yeoman farmers, leadership shifted westward as planters, such as John Willson of Wassamasaw became relatively wealthy and rose to political prominence on the local and State level. His home, built shortly after the Revolutionary War on one of the largest and more productive farms in the central parish, is shown in Photograph 1.1. Notwithstanding, most

Photograph 1.1 The photograph is entitled, "House on the Road to Columbia" in the *Johnson Scrapbook, Volume 1*. An additional notation states "Built just after the Revolution by the grandfather of Rev. John O. Willson." *Courtesy South Carolina Historical Society, Charleston, South Carolina.*

of the Goose Creekers who moved into these sections remained only marginally successful until the trials of the Civil War, and the eradication of slavery caused total economic collapse.

The Changing Parish

Shortly after the Revolutionary War and during the early decades of the nineteenth century, the habits of many Goose Creek planters changed as the parish evolved from a community of large prosperous estates to an economy based upon the production of marginally successful plantations and farms. During this period, many of those with resources moved out of the eastern section of the parish, abandoning the unhealthy and increasingly unsafe environments. One Goose Creeker recalled that after the Revolutionary War, highway robbery and horse stealing were so common that "persons rarely ventured to travel the Goose Creek road without arms."[3] In addition to wanton crime, malaria plagued the eastern section. The early planters built homes along the rivers and creeks that provided convenient cultivation of the rice and indigo, but the wet swamplands bred malaria-infested mosquitoes that caused serious illness or death. During the hot summer months, the planters believed that a gas, which they called "miasma," rose from the mud and stagnant water and caused a fever with chills. They were not aware that infected mosquitoes caused malaria and did not understand how many of their African slaves were genetically endowed to resist the illness. As a consequence of those predictable summer fevers, more planters spent the warmer months in well-drained pine forest communities such as Summerville and Pinopolis or near the ocean breezes of Charleston and the Sea Islands and would not return to the countryside until after the first frost. James Withers and James Graham were two of several Goose Creek planters who spent entire summers on Sullivan Island.[4]

By the beginning of the nineteenth century, the plantation high society that long characterized the eastern third of the St. James, Goose Creek Parish was replaced by absentee landowners, less affluent planters, tenants and African American slaves. As more families evaded the summer fevers, overseers were employed to manage the slaves and care for the land during most of the year. Some of the Goose Creek properties were kept by wealthy owners as investments or mere country retreats and it became common practice for the families of landowners to return to their rural estates near Thanksgiving to hunt and fish, enjoy the winter holidays, rekindle acquaintances with the hired and enslaved help, and stay until the land was planted. But, the affluent families departed in late May or early June to return to their principal residence in Charleston or on high and dry ground in the vicinity. Consequently, among the 154 heads of households counted in the parish census of 1810, there were 36 new families not present twenty years earlier. Most of these additional heads of households were overseers who settled on the old estates in the eastern section. Table 1.1 lists 19 overseers in the eastern parish in 1809 according to the *Directory for the District of Charleston Comprising the places of residence and occupation of the White Inhabitants of the Following Parishes to wit…St. James, Goose Creek in 1809, (Directory).*[5]

The overseers became increasingly more important to the Goose Creek society and economy. In some cases, the overseers owned slaves and worked them side by side with the landowner's. For example, overseers William Browning, William Campbell, Joseph Cantey and Andrew Dehay shown in table 1.1, owned 129, 137, 69 and 6 slaves respectively.[6] These overseers were the heads of relatively wealthy households who managed and resided upon someone else's land, but most of the overseers were less wealthy with fewer or no slaves. Also, there were an increasing number of "free colored" overseers during the nineteenth century. By 1830 there were 61 emancipated African American Goose Creekers, some of which were employed as farm workers and overseers with varying levels of responsibilities.[7] By the turn of the nineteenth century, approximately 40 percent of the landowners in the eastern section used white overseers. Table 1.2 lists the 27 planters (60 percent) who did not employ white managers.

Table 1.1: The table lists the names of selected landowners and their white overseers, as well as the location of the plantation taken from the *Directory of the White Inhabitants of the Charleston District in 1802*. The directory is among the collections of the South Carolina Historical Society, Charleston, South Carolina.

Name of Overseer	Name of Landowner	Location at Mile Marker/Road
James Brown	Levi D. Wigfall	21/Moncks Corner Road
Aben Bagnell	Henry Middleton Smith	19/Moncks Corner Road
John Brecker	Charles Smith	18/State Road
William Browning	Beltzer (no first name)	14/State Road
John Burbridge	Henry Deas	21/Moncks Corner Road
William Cambell	John Ball	22/Moncks Corner Road
Joseph Cantey	George Smith	21/Red Bank Road

Name of Overseer	Name of Landowner	Location at Mile Marker/Road
Andrew Dehay	David Deas	22/Moncks Corner Road
Durand (no additional name)	William Johnson	23/Red Bank Road
Daniel Dorcham	A. Edwards	20/State Road
S. Fawksworth	Thomas Baldric	8/State Road
John Huff	Samuel Mazyck	18/Back River Lower Road
William Lewis	Samuel Prioleau	21/Lower Back River Road
Stephen Minus	Charles Tennant	26/Red Bank River Road
John Morris	William Johnson	23/Red Bank River Road
Archibald McKelpin	William Allen Deas	13/State Road
William Powell	Beltser (no first name)	22/State Road
Phillip Perry	(name not listed)	9/State Road
Russel Willson	Harriet Horry	18/Red Bank Road

Some of these planters such as Benjamin Paul Williams, John Bowen and James Withers were well-to-do owners of large relatively successful estates. These men also owned homes in Charleston where they spent the unhealthy warmer months of the year. It is likely that they, as well as others on the list employed "free colored" overseers or relied upon their own bound help to manage the lands in their absence. During these decades, it became increasingly common for landowners to assign the management of their estates to the skillful care of trusted slaves. By the nineteenth century, some slave families had lived many generations on the estates and were trusted members of the household.

Table 1.2: The table lists planters in the eastern parish that did not employ white overseers according to the *Directory*.

Name of Planter	Location at Mile Marker/ Road
John Bridley	24/road unknown
John Bowen	21/Red Bank Road
Nicholas Burrbridge	26/State Road
John George Brindley	23/road unknown
John Brailsford	9/Goose Creed Road
Richard Burbridge	25/State Road
Jonathan Burbridge	25/State Road
Mary Cannon	20/road unknown
Daniel Driggers	21/State Road
Benjamin/ Catherine Fuller	15/St. Andrews
John Grooms	26/Moncks Corner Road
Jacob Huff	22/Moncks Corner Road
James Headwright	22/road unkown
Captain George Keckley	25/road to Dorchester
Michael Keckley	20/road to Dorchester

Name of Planter	Location at Mile Marker/ Road
John Moreton	26/road unknown
Samuel Marion	21/road unknown
Mary McBride	22/road unknown
Archibald McCume	20/road unkown
Tilman Plat	21/State Road
John Philbing	10/Goose Creek Road
(no first name) Poppinham	20/road to Dorchester
Thomas Screven	8/Goose Creek Road
Lewis Thompson	20/road unkown
Bejamin Paul Williams	22/Moncks Corner Road
James Winter	35/State Road
Elisha Walden	24/road unkown

Not surprisingly, oral tradition tells of black servants who managed white owned plantations in Goose Creek and were loved and respected by the landowner's family. Some of these managers were assertive black women who carried the title of "Maum." Maum Katy Brown was one such slave who became an indispensable plantation matriarch. Her gravestone is found today on a rise off Longridge Road near its intersection with Wassamasaw Church Road and is shown in photograph 1.2. The stone inscription states:

Maum Katy Brown
Died 1899
Lived Over Eighty Years

Maum Katy Brown resided in the parish before and after emancipation, and earned the title of "Maum" from those who loved her and provided the gravestone. The title "Maum" is probably the

Photograph 1.2 The photograph shows the burial site of Maum Katy Brown in a small cemetery on Longridge Road less than one mile from the Wassamasaw Baptist Church. The photograph was taken March 20, 2002. *Author's collection.*

local derivation from "mom" and follows the interesting African tradition of using familial titles to show respect. Since the earliest days of settlement, the local African and Euro Americans in South Carolina used terms of endearment such as "auntie" and "sissie" for "aunt" and "sister" among African American communities.[8] Even the familiar "good old boy" name of "Bubba" meaning brother, likely follows the African pattern for a familial term of endearment.

John Carmille's petition reflects the situation forced on some slave owners when complex social relations and genuine affection resulted in slaves socially evolving from human property to loved family members. Carmille petitioned the South Carolina General Assembly to free his slave mistress and their three children. When his petition was denied, he circumvented the denial by establishing a special trust that deeded Henrietta, his slave mistress and their children, Charlotte, Francis and Nancy to George Pringle and Philip Chartrand under specified conditions. The conditions stated that the "Negroes above named...work out their own maintenance and support;...to take for their sole use and benefit, all such money as they might obtain for their labor." In return the slave family would pay one dollar a year to Pringle and Chartrand as their part of the work contract. For true compensation, Carmille deeded two additional slaves to Pringle and Chartrand. By the same agreement those slaves provided the labor to support the slave mistress and her children until the youngest child reached twenty-one years of age. At that juncture the two additional slaves could be sold with the return divided equally between Henrietta and her children.[9] To shore up this arrangement, Carmille bequeathed his estate, which included a house and lot in Charleston and 111 acres of farmland in Goose Creek, to Henrietta and her children. In his will he also asked the executors to petition the General Assembly to free his slave family within fifteen years of his death, or failing that to send them to a state where they could be freed.

After his death the terms of the agreement were challenged in court but the South Carolina Court of Appeals interceded to uphold the terms of the trust. The court action alarmed the General Assembly who responded to Carmille's victory by enacting additional laws the following year that precluded similar future manumissions.[10] Understandably, some white and black Goose Creekers were sorely challenged to adhere to the strict racial codes, but in spite of love or money the State leadership was determined to safeguard the old social order even as the maintenance of that prevailing social order increasingly fell to the charge of non-landowning overseers of both races.

Under the increasing guidance of white and black overseers, planting remained the primary industry throughout the nineteenth century. The list of main exports sent through the port of Charleston in 1783, the year the formal peace treaty was signed that ended the War, included rice, corn, hides, naval stores and lumber products. Other than the absence of indigo, the list of export items was unchanged by the war and the market destinations remained the same as well. Goods were shipped to Great Britain, France, Amsterdam, Rotterdam, Bremen, Hamburg, French West Indies, British West Indies, Dutch West Indies, Madeira, Havana and some U.S. ports.[11] Even though the type of goods and their destinations were mostly unchanged, the lack of a subsidy by the British Empire brought on fierce competition, which caused the demand for American goods to falter so that the amount of exports fell sharply.

As a state in the new Republic, South Carolina no longer enjoyed the benefits of the British Empire. Before the Revolution, a British bounty on indigo and naval stores made businesses profitable for many Goose Creekers and the bounty on rice production provided unprecedented advantages to Goose Creek and Cooper River rice planters. Without these bounties, successful competition in the open world market was insurmountable for most South Carolinians. To make matters worse for some, the new methodology of water culture for rice production caused Goose Creek to lose most of its attraction to rice farmers.

The year of final peace between the colonies and England was also the year that the Goose Creek planter, Gideon Dupont, introduced the water-culture method of rice production. In 1783, he introduced the method of overflowing fields with water at specific tidal intervals. This method gave Carolina rice planters a great advantage despite the absence of the British bounty. For nearly one hundred years, Carolina rice was a highly profitable commodity on the world market, but the new labor saving methodology depended upon tidal influenced rivers and creeks. Consequently, inland rice lands in Goose Creek such as Thorogood and Liberty Hall Plantations became less lucrative and most planters looked beyond the limited tidal lands on Goose Creek, such as Otranto and White Hall Plantations to invest in more lucrative expanses along the Cooper, Wando, Santee Rivers and elsewhere.

Except for a few planters who worked lands along the tidal influenced reaches of Back River and Goose Creek, the tidal rice culture methodologies offered little advantage to most Goose Creek planters. Notwithstanding, the significant labor saving benefits of tidal rice culture in other sections of the State were noted in 1810 when Gideon F. Dupont Jr. petitioned the government for compensation for his father's work.[12] This invention was one of a few agricultural advancements made in South Carolina in the years following the Revolution, so that agriculture remained generally unaltered in Goose Creek and elsewhere. The brute conditions of slavery and the lack of innovation persisted as noted by Goose Creek landowner Timothy Ford when he wrote in his diary in 1784, "the number of slaves supplies the almost total want of instruments of husbandry; & the dint of muscular force the want of invention."[13] Such conditions remained the prevailing work norm for many more decades.

Slavery in Goose Creek, once the basis for plantation economy and society, was no longer as profitable without the availability of the British Empire's markets for agricultural goods. However, regardless of the wish of Thomas Jefferson to end slavery, emancipation was not in the foreseeable future. The introduction of Eli Whitney's cotton gin, ten years after the peace with England, made southern short-staple cotton extremely profitable. This agricultural revolution brought prosperity to many sections of the South and cotton was grown on most Goose Creek farms, but its cultivation only provided a few extra dollars and no long-term economic benefits for the parish.

The once-rich plantation land that provided an abundance of rice, indigo and foodstuffs was exhausted because Goose Creekers planted the land for more than a hundred years without applying fertilizers or crop rotation. As early as 1750, Reverend Robert Stone wrote that Goose Creek lands were wearing out and that some inhabitants had departed in search of better soils.[14] By the 1790s, the land was not fertile enough to grow much of any crop and was especially ill suited for cotton. Cotton requires nutrient-rich soil, as was in the virgin bottomlands of the Gulf States, and never produced fortunes in Goose Creek even after the introduction of fertilization made the effort more worthwhile.

The production of naval stores, once a profitable commodity needed for the British Navy, was no longer a money-maker, and any profit from livestock or corn production was barely enough for the maintenance of the household. By the turn of the nineteenth century, a few successful estates on deep water, baked clay and floated the brick along with lumber to Charleston markets, but most of the old plantations that once produced fortunes were relegated to absentee management or subdivided into smaller tracts that produced decreasing returns. Consequently, resourceful planters spent less time working their worn Goose Creek lands and supported fewer local businesses. As a result, during the first years of the nineteenth century, the local economy supported only fifteen non-agricultural entrepreneurs including tavern keepers, millers and carpenters and remarkably, these numbers dwindled even more in the succeeding two decades before rebounding near mid-century. Table 1.3 lists Goose Creekers involved in non-agricultural occupations in 1802. The information derived from the *Directory* and the 1810 Federal Census shows the size of families among non-planters ranged up to ten members with some families working as many as thirty-four slaves, but notably, six of the non-planting residents listed in the 1809 directory were not recorded in the census count one year later. Their absence suggests that non-planting occupations were transient. It also suggests that paying jobs for carpenters, doctors, innkeepers and others that depended on income from planting dwindled markedly in the early nineteenth century. Non-agricultural employment became increasingly rare and unemployment became a common concern.

Unemployment received some relief in 1792 with the construction of the Santee Canal. Economical transportation was a requirement for a sound agricultural system prompting a long-standing interest in cost-effective water transport. Earlier requests were made to the new state government to cut navigation channels through the marsh, but a much greater navigation project was envisioned for the Cooper River. The Cooper River system was a superb network of fresh-water rivers, streams and deep tidal creeks and it was almost a perfect means of water travel from the plantations to the market. Twenty years earlier, a Commons House committee reported favorably on a plan for a canal from the Santee River to the headwaters of the Cooper River, but it was not until 1786 that a canal company was chartered. Upon completion, the canal was twenty-two miles long and four feet deep with locks to raise and lower the water levels. Some notable Goose Creekers, such as planters Aaron Loocock and Ralph Izard, bought stock in the Santee Canal Company. Both of these men were among the increasing number of absentee Goose Creek landowners. Aaron Loocock owned a profitable mercantile business in Charleston and Izard cultivated prosperous investment connections with the New York Delancey family.

Table 1.3: The table lists Goose Creekers who were employed in non-agricultural livelihoods, according to the *Directory*, *as* well as, supplemental information from the 1810 census.

Name	Occupation	Mile Marker/Road	No. in Family According to the 1810 Census	No. of Slaves According to the 1810 Census
Mary Bell	Tavern Keeper	22/Moncks Corner Road	1	16
Lewis Brecker	Tavern Keeper	18/State Road	9	7
Jacob Brecker	Blacksmith	18/State Road	10	7
Mary Brown	Tavern Keeper	20/State Road	0	5
Thomas Burrbridge	Miller	26/State Road	7	9

Name	Occupation	Mile Marker/Road	No. in Family According to the 1810 Census	No. of Slaves According to the 1810 Census
Edward Brailsford	Physician	20/road unknown	not in census	not in census
Alexander Burn	Carpenter	10/Goose Creek Road	not in census	not in census
John Hinds	Tavern Keeper	17/State Road	not in census	not in census
Samuel Huff	Tavern Keeper	25/State Road	7	3
M. Jackson	Tavern Keeper/ Deputy Sheriff	23/Moncks Corner Road	not in census	not in census
James Reardon	Tavern Keeper	23/Moncks Corner Road	6	1
Charles Tennant	Physician	21/Red Bank Road	5	34
Benjamin Tyler	School Master	17/State Road	not in census	not in census
William Tate	Carpenter	10/Goose Creek Road	not in census	not in census
John Wilson	Physician	30/State Road	1	24

The Santee Canal was an exciting idea, but the channel was expensive to maintain and sometimes operations ceased when drought lowered the water levels. Consequently, it was never profitable but nevertheless, its construction temporarily relieved the dire economic problems of Goose Creek. The construction project needed labor, and Goose Creek landowners were eager to hire out their bound men and women for annual payments that returned more than the same amount of manpower produced working the worn plantation fields.

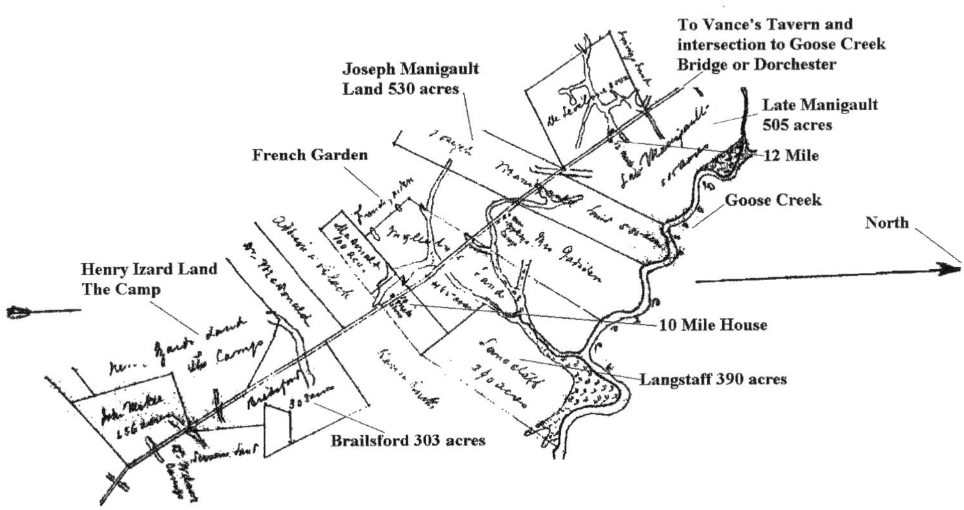

Map 1.1 The partial plat is titled "The Goose Creek Road from the Ten Mile House to Vance's Tavern with the relative situations of the plantations." Henry Ravenel drew the plat in 1826. Henry A.M. Smith traced the original and the manuscript labels were added for this publication because much of the script on the plat is difficult to read. The plat is among the Henry A.M. Smith collection on deposit with the South Carolina Historical Society, Charleston, South Carolina.

Later in 1818, the South Carolina General Assembly authorized a board of internal improvements to manage $1,000,000 for the construction of roads and canals. This large amount of money was four times greater than the typical annual budget for such programs and instigated opposing political interests. Unfortunately, the political competition scuttled most of the improvement initiatives, but not before Goose Creekers brought seven petitions to the state government for canals from 1786 to 1819. The final request for a Goose Creek canal project was presented twenty-six years later in 1845, but like the petitions that came before, it was never funded.

Goose Creekers persisted to find opportunities to hire out their slaves to work on internal improvement projects. Petitions for public canal projects included schemes to cut marshland on Goose Creek, float produce through inland swamps to Back River, bring farm products along the Wassamasaw waterway to the Ashley River, transport agricultural products from Four Hole Swamp to the Edisto River and use a lottery to fund selected canals including one near Strawberry (See appendix I for a listing and description of the petitions for canals). Finally, thirteen residents petitioned the General Assembly in 1845 to connect the Edisto River with the Ashley in an effort to make the transportation of goods via waterways to the Charleston market less expensive. Clearly many citizens of the parish envisioned grandiose schemes that could connect many parts of the parish by waterway to Charleston, and could also employ the slaves that were increasingly less profitable.[15] But, because none of the requests for canals were funded and the Santee Canal failed to meet the expectations of its investors, the State abandoned these initiatives and substituted road projects to answer the call for less expensive transport of agricultural goods.

One such road project was the construction of the State Road to traverse the St. James, Goose Creek Parish from east to west by way of Wassamasaw and to connect Charleston's port and markets to thousands of inland farms. On March 2, 1786, a petition to the State House requested turnpikes and tolls on the Goose Creek Road from Charleston to Wassamasaw. This action was the continuation of earlier efforts to improve the support of the main road through the parish, but similar to the initiatives that preceded this petition, the consistent maintenance of the road remained insufficient. About the same time, residents of the parish petitioned the State government for other road projects in their sections and by the time of the Civil War, as many as ten petitions to connect farms to rail and market centers and to assume the expense of road maintenance were submitted to the General Assembly (See appendix II for a listing and description of the petitions for improved roads).

Henry Izard, Chairman of the St. James, Goose Creek Road Commission asked in 1807 for an improved system of keeping roads in repair. He complained that the current system of assessing contiguous landowners unfairly placed increasingly more expense and responsibility on those living closer to Charleston. He argued that those in the most distant neighborhoods kept the roads in repair only for their own use, while the landowners closer to Charleston kept the roads in repair for themselves as well as all the users in every more distant neighborhood. He requested that a toll system be arranged so that those using the road paid in proportion to the amount of distance traveled.[16]

The State Road (today State Highways 52 and 176) was originally built as a toll road. It began in Charleston and traversed the entire length of the St. James, Goose Creek Parish to Holly Hill. From Holly Hill it continued to Cameron, Saint Matthews and Columbia. From Columbia it continued west to Saluda Mountain in the Greenville District.[17] In 1823, the State Legislature took possession of the State Road and initiated a toll system, but many travelers complained that the tolls were too high and avoided the fees by bypassing on poorly maintained local paths. Nonetheless, there is much evidence that the road was heavily used through Goose Creek and that most travelers paid the tolls from the Goose Creek Bridge to Charleston because there were no other ways to pass through that low and wet section.

Henry Ravenel drew map 1.1 in 1826 that shows much of the neighborhood along the Goose Creek Road, as well as to the proximity of the land to the Goose Creek waterway. The purpose of the map was to regulate the cutting of timber used for road repair, but this section of the State Road also shows that many of the larger tracts were subdivided by 1826, which indicates increased density of population and a greater need of the roadway. A petition to the State Judiciary Committee also attested to the heavy use of the byway. Four years before the Ravenel map was drawn a petition was presented to the committee to prohibit private households from selling liquor without a license along that section of roadway. Samuel Prioleau, chairman of the committee, reported that the road was heavily used and that the private families were "too near the public highway to avoid entertaining travelers and too poor to do so gratis."[18] Consequently, the petition to prohibit was denied.

Though the toll system that replaced the unfair and impractical methodology of assessing contiguous landowners for road upkeep was somewhat successful along the Goose Creek section, the collections never fully paid the expenses for road maintenance nor did it meet the demands of all discriminate users as attested by the following entry in a travel diary:

> *After traveling a few miles we entered on the State Road to Columbia & over the Goose Creek Bridge. Other materials failing, they have split small logs in half & have lain them bridge fashion, the flat side upward & covered them with a few inches of clayey sand. As the chairs or gigs of this country have no springs, this kind of road keeps your bodies in a perpetual quiver, & you are left to apprehend that your brains may be shaken out of place or addled. Yet it must be acknowledged that the road is much improved, especially for waggoners, from its former state when the wheels used to sink deep into the sand. Such is the state turnpike, & the toll is duly collected at the proper distances so that you have the pleasure of being well shaken & paying for it, half of which pleasure you enjoy on a northern turnpike.*[19]

In 1829, not long after this traveler's bumpy ride, the lower half of the public road from Charleston to Columbia was completed, and the Goose Creek Bridge was replaced. The new bridge was a substantial covered structure, two hundred feet long, with wooden floor planking, brick abutments at both ends and a heavy wooden support in the middle. The roof was covered with cypress shingles to delay weathering.[20] It was a significant public works success and one of several transportation improvements completed during the first half of the nineteenth century. During this period the parish road commissioners dutifully coordinated local and state funding to construct roads, causeways and bridges, and to repair, improve and maintain the roadways. They also consistently worried, debated and complained about the lack of state support. A report to the State Legislature in 1851 from Levy F. Rhame, Chairman of the St. James, Goose Creek Parish Road Commission explained the difficult responsibilities of the Goose Creek commissioners and appealed for greater assistance for the "exceptionally long and difficult road maintenance." He explained that the commission was responsible for forty-four miles of State Road with heavy bridging, embankments, causeways, ditching and draining.[21] The commissioners undertook this troublesome responsibility without compensation and some served many years. They are listed in appendix III.

Better roads to the hinterlands, along with deteriorating health and soil conditions in the eastern section, resulted in the central and western sections of the St. James, Goose Creek Parish becoming retreats of opportunity for yeoman farmers. The State granted land in those sections to 101 farmers from 1792 to 1860. The awards for land in the mid and upper parish often consisted of about 500 acres, though many were larger and some even consisted of 1,000 acres or more resulting in a mean size of 744 acres. The records of these land holdings identified the farmers and their acreage during that time and are shown in appendix IV. According to the *Directory* and as listed in appendix V, no landowner in those sections used white overseers, suggesting that the newly arrived families to the central and western sections worked their land year-around with their own family members and slaves.

Parishioners in the central and western sections were among those who petitioned for canals or better roads.[22] Early in the nineteenth century, Goose Creekers from the western section circulated a petition to establish a road to Charleston. Fifty-five members of the Wiggins, Bunch, Murray, Carr, Luis, Rast, Meeks, Warnock, Hart, Crawford and Platt families submitted a petition to the General Assembly to protest the closing of a road in the upper parish.[23] The Ballentine, Murray, Jones, Brabham, Murray, Bunch, Mallard, Carn, Hill, Seabrook, Dehay, Cannon, Varner, Clark, Singletary, Baylor, Jones, Dehay, Driggers, Hart, McKewn and Packer families, residing in the central section of the parish near Wassamasaw, signed a petition to establish a byway to intersect the State Road at the 29-mile marker.[24]

The end of British rule coincided with the decline of prosperity in the eastern section of the parish and the emergence of viable farms in the central and western sections. These economic, social and demographic adjustments were reflected in church affiliation and attendance. Religious zeal for the Church of England greatly declined after the Revolutionary War. As a result, many of the Anglican ministers were recalled to England and those who stayed found their congregations smaller and less prosperous. To fill the spiritual void, other protestant congregations, such as the Methodists and Baptists expanded.

Methodists came to the parish as early as 1786. Reverend Francis Asbury followed the State Road to Wassamasaw where he encountered floodwaters. To avoid the high water, he proceeded east on Longridge Road and "planted the seeds of old Appii Church."[25] Here and in most sections, families worshipped without an ordained minister. Groups of families with no church or minister gathered to sing hymns, read the Bible and enjoy fellowship because affiliation with a church group was important to most. Thomas Hilton was one settler in the western section of the parish who found land and a church community.[26] He arrived at Sandridge in the upper parish near the end of the eighteenth century but does not appear on the Federal Census until 1820. He acquired 297 acres where he reared an extended family, some descendents of which continue to reside on the property today.[27] His name appears on the *Class Book for the Society at Harry's Meeting House Commencing January 1st, 1807 Cypress Circuit* (*Class Book*). The *Class Book* lists the names of families who worshipped without a minister at "Harry's Meeting House." The listed names were members of the Myers, Truelin (?), Carr, Gelzer, Harry, Williams, Tedder, Rudd, Whaley, Singletary, Bradwell, Smith, Hodges, Rumph, Barrow, Mims, Peasley, Bowman,

Photograph 1.3 The photograph shows West Williams (1792–1868), a Methodist minister and prominent planter in the St. James, Goose Creek Parish. The photograph was taken from *Historic Ramblin's Through Berkeley* by Russell Cross.

Hall, Faulling, King, Disto, Lyons, Helton, V(B)allentine, Crawford, Brabham, Clark, Hilton and Browning families. Interestingly, the 1807 list also indicated that five African Americans were charter members.[28]

Methodists also worshipped under a brush arbor at Spring Hill in Sandridge as early as 1800. This sharp knoll rises above a fresh water spring in Four Hole Swamp near an important stagecoach route called Gaillard Road. This road was built and maintained as the principal route from Charleston westward prior to the construction of the State Road. Two acres of property were donated for the use of the church and a more permanent log structure replaced the brush arbor in 1814. Methodist circuit preachers provided monthly services in this log church, which featured a partition to divide the interior for separate white and black worship during the same service.[29]

In 1846, Reverend Stephen Williams built a new home at Sandridge to escape the malaria that killed his entire family.[30] When his home was completed, he challenged the congregation to build a church to replace the log structure. The challenge was met and the new church was completed in 1841. Today worshipers gather on the same hill above a plentiful artesian spring to worship in a newer church built in 1951. The earliest date recorded in the church cemetery is 1809, marking the burial place of one of Reverend Williams' children, but worshipers from as early as the colonial period rest on the grounds. Families with members at this final resting place include the Russel, Hilton, Saulisbury, Hutto, Grooms, Ayers, Chubb, Thompson and Williams families. Nearby, on State Road stands the *Reverend Stephen Williams House,* which has been beautifully renovated and remains an active family home today.

Photograph 1.4 The photograph shows the Stephen Williams House, which was built in 1846 for the minister of the Springhill Methodist Church. The photograph was taken April 4, 2003. *Author's collection.*

Photograph 1.5 The photograph shows the Springhill Methodist Church. The photograph was taken April 4, 2003. *Author's collection.*

More Methodist churches were established including one in the summer village of Cypress Swamp and at New Hope. Also, the John Kiser Church stood on Calamus Pond Road, and the Lebanon Church stood above Patrick's Creek Road. The first Charleston Methodist camp meeting at Goose Creek was led by John Colinsworth in 1814.[31] The *South Carolina Advocate* of April 2, 1841, reported the burning of the Cooper River Campground, which was also known as the "Goose Creek Methodist Camp" near the confluence of Goose Creek to the Cooper.[32]

The Wassamasaw Baptist Church originated soon after the Revolutionary War and was built at the old colonial site of the St. James, Goose Creek Parish Chapel of Ease and School. The Reverend Ralph Bowman was the first pastor and Senator Robert Thornley and Thomas Blackman were two of the more prominent early members.[33] Later, Richard Furman engaged in Baptist missionary work in Goose Creek and other areas near Charleston setting the stage for the church leaders who followed. One such follower was Reverend Matthew McCullers who came to Wassamasaw when a revival was in progress in 1804. Soon after, he traveled the short distance to Strawberry in the eastern parish and stayed to serve the Baptist congregation there.[34] With the help of Mrs. Hepzibah Townsend, Reverend McCullers expanded the congregation at Strawberry to sufficiently support the Bethlehem Baptist Church until his death in 1817.[35] For many years this church was referred to as Bethlehem Baptist, but in 1855, John J. Singletary, "church clerk" requested a Charter of Incorporation from the State of South Carolina. Therein the Bethlehem Baptist Church in Strawberry was officially titled "St. James Baptist Church." It was granted a Charter of Incorporation that authorized it to hold real and personal wealth not to exceed $50,000.[36] By mid-century, fourteen houses of worship

Photograph 1.6 The photograph shows the Wassamasaw Baptist Church. It was founded in 1784, and the present church was constructed in 1882. The photograph was taken March 20, 2002. *Author's collection.*

were established throughout the parish including nine Methodist, four Baptist and one Presbyterian Church.[37] Churches continued to accommodate 80 to 500 people with an average of about 230 per congregation until the turmoil of civil war displaced neighborhoods and scattered the families.[38]

As health and economic conditions debilitated the plantation society that characterized the eastern parish during the colonial era, the old semi-aristocratic order all but disappeared as farmers and protestant church congregations in the central and western sections replaced the landed gentry and the established Church of England. As planters and farmers worked their new lands in Wassamasaw, Longridge, Sandridge and nearby areas, wealth and political leadership shifted. These new leaders joined ranks with the remaining owners of diversifying estates in the older sections to shape local policy and make the difficult political decisions in the decades leading to the Civil War. In hindsight, conflict appeared inevitable because along with the significant social, economic and demographic shifts that occurred in St. James, Goose Creek Parish during the first half of the nineteenth century, the agricultural system continued to depend on slave labor and foreign markets, both of which were increasingly challenged by a leadership in Congress that was expanding with representatives from new states who opposed slavery and supported taxes on imports.

Political and Economic Preludes to the Civil War

On May 25, 1787, a quorum of fifty-five representatives from twelve states convened in Philadelphia to form a new constitution for the United States. Severe economic problems threatened to destroy the nation that, in the absence of strong federal leadership, was floundering in the world market and at home. The national tax system, the public debt and the nation's credit presented difficult challenges. Symptoms of the economic crisis were exemplified a year earlier when impoverished Massachusetts, backcountry farmers protested in Shay's Rebellion. The need for national leadership was paramount. Fortunately, President George Washington with a new Constitution provided much of that guidance.

In 1787, representatives from each state went to Philadelphia and agreed to submit a new Federal Constitution to each state for ratification. The *State Gazette* of South Carolina on June 2, 1788, reported that a special convention of South Carolinians considered the document and ratified it on May 23 of that year. All of the Goose Creek conventioneers including Ralph Izard, Peter Smith, Benjamin Smith, Gabriel Manigault, William Smith, John Parker Jr. and John Deas Jr. voted for ratification. Soon after, the House of Representatives selected two men to conduct elections for six representatives from the St. James, Goose Creek Parish. The two Goose Creek commissioners, Robert Eccles and John Hutchinson conducted an unchallenged election after which, Alexander Moultrie declined to serve and was replaced by Thomas Middleton. Middleton was sent to serve a two-year term in the House of Representatives for the new Republic along with Goose Creekers Ralph Izard Sr., George Flagg, John Baddeley, William Johnson, Captain James Stevenson and Peter Smith. All but one of the new representatives were landowners from the old eastern sector of the parish. James Stevenson, one of the first representatives elected under the new Constitution, was a planter who resided on 1,300 acres in Wassamasaw that he had received through a South Carolina land grant in 1785. His election was an early indication of the impending shift of political leadership westward during the nineteenth century, but subsequent elections to

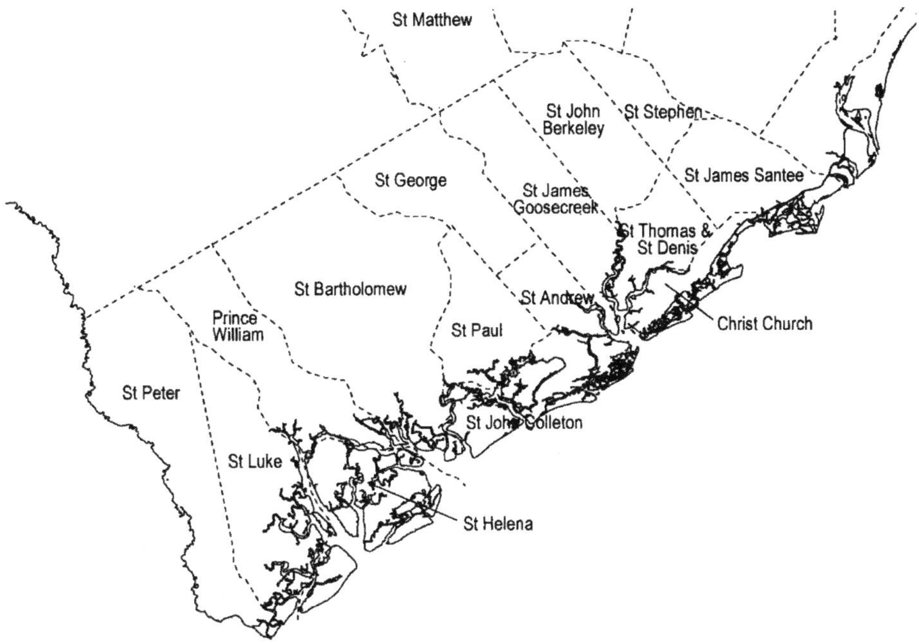

Map 1.2 The map shows selected South Carolina election districts in 1790. The map was taken from *Biographical Directory of the South Carolina House of Representatives*, by Walter Edgar and Louise Bailey.

the House during that decade, selected Representatives solely from among the established owners of land in the aging eastern sector. These landowners were sons and grandsons of old Goose Creek families who retained family holdings in the parish but who usually resided in Charleston. They were:

> 1785–1786: William Smith, Gabriel Manigault, Ralph Izard, Alexander Garden Jr., John Parker Jr. William Johnson and Peter Bacot received equal votes and John Baddeley was elected but died in 1786.
>
> 1787–1788: John Deas Jr., Ralph Izard Sr., Gabriel Manigault, John Parker Jr., Peter Smith and William Laughton Smith.
>
> 1789–1790: John Deas Jr., Peter Gray, Ralph Izard Sr., Gabriel Manigault, Peter Smith and William Smith.

There were no provisions in the Federal Constitution for political parties, but politicians soon divided into the Federalist camp or the Jeffersonian-Republican camp. William Laughton Smith of Button Hall Plantation was Alexander Hamilton's spokesman in Congress and was known as the "Federalist's Federalist." Smith was rewarded for his political loyalty when he was made one of the first directors of the Bank of the United States and minister to Portugal and Turkey. The Federalist

Party enjoyed a great amount of influence for about ten years and Smith's personal and professional alliance with fellow Goose Creekers Gabriel Manigault and Ralph Izard greatly enhanced his clout until the wane of the Federalist Party resulted in the election of Thomas Jefferson and the fall of William Smith from political favor. Consequently, Smith was recalled from his duties abroad and after touring Europe for two years returned to Charleston.[39]

As the nation established a firmer foothold, the state followed suit when in May of 1790, a convention met in Columbia to adopt a constitution for South Carolina. Delegates from St. James, Goose Creek Parish, were Aaron Loocock, John Deas, Peter Gray, Nathaniel McCants, William Allen Deas, James Smith and Thomas Parker.[40] Some of the election districts established by the State Constitution are shown on map 1.2 and the names of Representatives from Goose Creek who served as members of the House of Representatives and Senate are given in appendix VI. The first session of the State General Assembly commenced January 3, 1791. All Goose Creek representatives serving in the first session hailed from the eastern section of the parish, but Robert Thornley, captain under Francis Marion in the Revolution was elected to serve in the House a year later and continued to serve South Carolina until he died as a member of the State Senate in 1805. He planted more than a thousand acres at Wassamasaw and was one of the first of a long line of central and western parish political leaders. Beginning with him and Elish Mellard from Wassamasaw who was elected in 1800, until Lewis E. Connor in 1865, more than 50 percent of the twenty-seven residents elected to the South Carolina House of Representatives from the St. James, Goose Creek Parish resided in Wassamasaw or farther west. The trend was more pronounced among those elected to the State Senate. Eight (75 percent) of the twelve Senators elected from the parish to the South Carolina Senate from 1800 to the end of the Civil War were farmers in the central or western sectors.

The State leadership confronted mounting political problems before the end of the eighteenth century, and early in the nineteenth century symptoms of discontent with some federal policies were revealed during protest meetings in Goose Creek. An emerging issue that was contested until the outbreak of the Civil War was the extent of sovereignty South Carolina would exercise within the Republic. Federal policies regarding national internal improvements, tariffs and slavery were in the political forefront of the parish and elsewhere and the Goose Creek people were as active in their rejection of federal authority as they were rejecting the proprietors and royal ministers during the colonial era.

Tariffs were taxes on imports that were imposed to protect young and inefficient northern industries. Although the tariffs made the cost of American manufactured items competitive with those from England, the Southern merchants, many with new cotton interests and growing commercial ties with the textile magnates of England, were much in opposition. Southerners consumed many imported manufactured goods and resented the higher prices of imports resulting from the tariffs. Southerners became more alarmed in 1828 when the Federal Congress imposed an unusually high nation-wide import tax. Southerners referred to the 1828 tariff as the "Tariff of Abominations" and several Southern states protested formally. In South Carolina the flags were lowered to half-mast, and one South Carolinian protested during an eloquent speech, "Let the New England beware how she imitates the old."[41] The people of Goose Creek were infuriated too. They were part of the old South, one of the least flourishing sections of the young nation, and felt increasingly betrayed by Congress.

The Northeast was reaping profits from tariff-protected industries; the West was experiencing rapid population growth with accompanying prosperity, and the new Southwest was producing shiploads of cotton. The old South was impoverished and the leaders, right or wrong, blamed the economic woes on what they perceived to be unfair federal practices. The people of Goose Creek joined the statewide protests.

Goose Creek citizens held a protest meeting against tariffs at the Wassamasaw Chapel in 1821. Captain Nathaniel Lawrence presided, with Cashwell Mims acting as secretary. John N. Davis, Thomas Blackman, Dr. John Williams, Thomas West, John Shuler, Isaac Bradwell, S. Shingler, Captain A. Gillon and Colonel William Mellard were chosen to serve on a resolution committee. These men produced a document with a preamble and seven resolutions that appeared in the *Charleston Mercury,* October 15, 1821. The preamble expressed the frustration of the residents to "encroachments of the general government upon the authority and sovereignty of the states" and further rejected the "passing of the tariff imposing duties, not for the purpose of revenue, but for the protection of manufacturers, to the…ruin of our commercial and agricultural interests." The resolutions that followed restated their beliefs in states' rights including the tenant that the Federal Constitution derived its authority from the collective states not the collective inhabitants of the states. The resolutions further expressed resentment that Congress overextended its authority when it taxed all citizens through tariffs or other means to build roads and canals. In retaliation, the assembly resolved to rely upon their own resources by making and wearing homespun clothing and unifying in opposition to the unfair laws and in support of their State Legislature.

As a result of a series of such meetings throughout the state, two political parties emerged in South Carolina, both of which opposed the tariff but differed in their methods. The States Rights and Free Trade Party (States Rights Party) wanted complete nullification of the tariff laws even at the risk of rebellion and war. The Union and States Rights Party (Union Party) was not in favor of complete nullification. What resulted in 1832 was a hotly contested general election that was closely scrutinized and ended after hearings before the appropriate committee of the House of Representatives challenged voters' residency and qualifications.[42] Surprisingly, John N. Davis, Senator and J.L. Strohecker, Representative, two Goose Creek Union Party candidates were elected to the Legislature.[43]

St. James, Goose Creek was one of only 11 electoral districts in the State where the Unionists elected all of their candidates.[44] This interesting political phenomenon is revealed when the election results are examined in light of the 1828 tax returns and the 1830 census count. Goose Creek planters owned large numbers of slaves and appeared to be dependent upon that institution for economic survival. Thus, one would reasonably expect the voters to send the nullification candidates to the General Assembly. Remarkably, according to the 1828 tax records, 64 percent of the residents of Goose Creek owned at least one slave and the 1830 census revealed a 79 percent ownership, but in 1832, only 40 percent of the Goose Creek voters supported the nullification candidates.[45] The unusual result at the polls suggests that many voting Goose Creekers were not as committed to slavery as the high percentage of slave ownership may suggest. The fact that many Goose Creek landowners in the eastern section had diversified their interests may explain this election phenomenon. Although the planters kept ownership of their Goose Creek lands and thus retained voting rights, many resided and invested their fortunes elsewhere, including within some Northern states. The unexpected electoral support for the Unionists may reflect the opinions of those Goose Creek planters who had diversified their interests beyond the parish and State lines and subsequently developed some kindred interests with the northern elite.

Nevertheless, Nullifiers won statewide, and after the election, the governor called for an extra session of the legislature to meet with the newly elected members. Three days later a bill was passed that called for a convention of delegates to which Goose Creek sent Isaac Bradwell Jr. and George H. Smith. An Ordinance of Nullification was passed at the convention with all Goose Creek delegates voting in favor.[46] Soon after, the fear of Federal retaliation caused special provisions to be taken for home defense and all officers (except legislators) were required to take an oath of allegiance to the new ordinance.

The Union Party protested against the Nullification Ordinance and the Oath of Allegiance and began to organize military companies loyal to the President of the United States, while the Nullifiers established arsenals and military depots.[47] The entire affair became increasingly ominous until it was quieted for a short while by a compromise tariff. Nevertheless, the specter of civil war remained and became provocative years later when the tariff issue resurfaced.

It was about this time that Northern abolitionists began to strengthen their ranks and called for an end to slavery. The inhumanity of slavery, which many Southerners perceived as a necessary evil, caused the emergence of antislavery societies throughout the nation. Northern abolitionists intensified their social reform movements in the 1830s and 1840s, and additional momentum was gained during this period when the slaves were freed in the British Empire. Some extremists, such as William Lloyd Garrison, greatly alarmed the slave-dependent South when in his militant newspaper, *The Liberator*, he made a frontal assault on Southern slave owners by attacking them as individuals and as a group.[48] Consequently, as the abolitionist movement gained momentum, the Southerners, bound to the institution by tradition and dependency, held fast. This was the beginning of a thirty-year verbal battle that would finally culminate in civil war and emancipation.

The Southern states retaliated by organizing defenses in opposition to the abolitionists and possible Northern aggression. The slavery issue was the gravest concern in the Carolina Lowcountry because less than 25 percent of the population was white, and the economy depended on forced labor. The Goose Creek people were adamantly supportive of slavery because the small farmers in the central and western parish, as well as those on the aging plantations in the eastern section, had struggled against adverse economic conditions for decades and were in no position to abandon an inexpensive source of labor. Also, the institution was sanctioned since the arrival of the earliest settlers and had been long rationalized, but slave rebellion or the success of Northern abolitionists would cause economic collapse. More than 64 percent of the white Goose Creekers owned slaves in 1820 and fourteen "Free persons of color" kept bound workers during the antebellum period.[49] The largest non-white slaveholder was the African American, Lamb Stevens who planted the old De La Plaine Plantation in Ladson with thirty slaves in 1850 and fifteen slaves in 1860. Slavery was a moral conundrum, but more importantly it was perceived by South Carolinians as a necessity that if surrendered would spell economic doom and social chaos.

Table 1.4: The table shows the number and percentage of white and slave populations in Goose Creek.

Census Year	No. of Whites	No. of Slaves	No. of Free Colored	Percentage of Population in Slavery
1820	1,221	4,192	86	76
1830	1,788	6,904	61	79
1840	1,627	2,403	101	58

Anxieties heightened when slave conspiracies were detected in nearby Charleston, and worries of slave rebellions frequented the minds of Goose Creekers throughout the 1820s. At that time the overall percentage of the population in bondage increased slightly above 76 percent and although the 1824 tax returns for Goose Creek show a dip in slave ownership, the numbers increased to 79 percent by 1830. That year the average slaveholder depended upon nine bound souls.[50] Slave rebellion would spell disaster for the white community, so in response, concerned citizens attended a meeting in Summerville in August of 1835 to vent their ire and denounce the actions of the Northern abolitionists.[51]

As a follow-up to the Summerville assembly, Goose Creek and Dorchester citizens met at the Cypress Camp Ground on September 9, 1835, near Wassamasaw to hear the report from the Summerville August meeting. At that assemblage the citizens again resolved to resist the activities of the "northern fanatics." In response some Goose Creek neighborhoods established committees of vigilance. Such committees were not new to the parish because some sections had supported vigilante type committees for years in response to the threat of slave rebellion. Groups such as the Charleston Neck Rangers provided armed patrols long before the threat from the abolitionists.[52] For example, twelve years earlier in 1823, a state committee reviewed a petition from the widow of James C. Martindale, owner of Brick House Plantation near the 12-mile marker on the Goose Creek Road. She requested payment for her husband's expenses during a slave insurrection the previous year. Upon his discretion, James C. Martindale purchased 119 muskets and bayonets for use by the Charleston Neck Rangers. No slave uprisings occurred, and the Rangers never used the weapons, but the idea of vigilante action remained an accepted practice.[53] Communication was slow and unreliable, and because the abolition question was so upsetting, committees were established in each neighborhood to keep the people informed. The September 18, 1835 edition of the *Charleston Mercury* reported that Isaac Bradwell, Esq., Chairman, and Captain Thomas Mims, J.J. McCants, J. Smith, Dr. J. Wilson, John Inabinit, C. Mims, Dr. R.H. Jones, John Cockfield, Wm. Riggs, Richard Minus, Dr. Bradwell, John Plat, B. Earnist, R. Chinnus were appointed as a committee of vigilance with R. Stephenson as the secretary.

Most of the significant landowners, all of whom depended upon slave labor, are shown on map 1.3 entitled, *Copy of a Plan of Mr. Fred A. Ford...*[54] The map describes much of the St. James, Goose Creek Parish in 1840 during the difficult decades leading to the Civil War. The name "McCollie" appears on the Moncks Corner Road at the 22-Mile-House along with "Miss Keith." "William Bell," "Gaillard Stoney" and "Tennents" are shown on Back River. "Dr. Graves," "Mrs. Sturgis," "Thos. Dixon," "Charles Graves," "Vidal" and "Dr. Desel" are noted near Foster Creek. James Vidal owned Howe Hall and Charles Desel owned Liberty Hall Plantation at that time. "Cannon," "T. Gadsden," "Caren," "Benjamin Gadsden," "Jas. Johnson," "William Tennent," "Ravenel," "Mrs. Brown,"

Map 1.3 The partial map is titled "Copy of a Plan of Mr. Fred A. Ford compiled in 1840 by him From the original C.P. Copied in January 1841." The map is among the H.A.M. Smith plat collection and in possession of the South Carolina Historical Society, Charleston, South Carolina.

"Malone," "Wood" and "George Henry Smith" are shown as heads of households residing along the banks of Goose Creek.

According to the slave schedule of that year, Charles Graves owned 62 slaves, H.G. Prioleau owned 61, John Parker owned 58, Charles Tennent owned 42 and Barbara Poppenheim owned 33 slaves. The two who owned the most slaves in the parish were Walter Izard with 105 and the estate of W. Liston with 106 slaves. Goose Creekers owning more than 50 slaves at that time were Charles Wilson, John Wilson, W.B. Salvone, M. Connors, E. Mallard, T. Cline, T. Raval, William Riggs, Eloza Riscoun, Anna Rowal, the Estate of R. Matthews, Caleb Wall, M. Jenkins, Robert Winter, the Estate of George Robertson, Henry Smith, George Chisolm, C. Winthrope, M. Jones and H.G. Prioleaiu.[55] Clearly, Goose Creek landowners depended upon an enslaved workforce in 1840.

Throughout the antebellum period some Goose Creekers worked one hundred or more enslaved hands. Men such as Thomas Blackman, Benjamin Green and Walter Izard each worked more than one hundred slaves for three or four decades and some kept even larger forces.[56] John Ball's plantation account book for the years 1831 to 1841 shows that he managed more than six hundred slaves on four Cooper River Plantations: Comingtee, Stoke, Kensington and Midway in the parish of St. Johns, Berkeley.[57] His Back River Plantation account book showed that he kept far fewer slaves in St. James, Goose Creek Parish, but nevertheless he was one of the wealthiest Goose Creekers of the antebellum era.[58]

The percentage of enslaved Goose Creekers dropped slightly during the decades immediately leading to the Civil War, and then rose a little prior to 1860, but no significance is indicated by the minor shifts. What appears to be meaningful is the number of slaves possessed by each owner during the same period. As the war years approached, fewer planters owned slaves as is shown by the statistical record of slave holdings for the years 1830 and 1860 in appendix VII. The records reveal that fewer Goose Creekers owned slaves in 1860 than in 1830 and that the percentage of Goose Creekers who owned no slaves increased from 16 percent in 1830 to 40 percent in 1860. These numbers suggest that slave labor became less affordable during the first half of the nineteenth century and the costs rose beyond the means of most Goose Creekers as the war years approached. The change in slave ownership also suggests a widening disparity in wealth between the rich and poor that resulted in fewer whites amassing sufficient capital to purchase and keep expensive human workers. Interestingly, the reduction in slave ownership also accompanied expanded interests in commercial, industrial and other non-agricultural occupations that were supported by the wage labor system. Diversified occupations beyond the farm began to displace increasingly unaffordable slave labor with white and a few black wage earners prior to the Civil War. Sadly, however the diversification of the economy did not occur sufficiently or early enough to diffuse the white furor that was associated with the prospects of slave emancipation.

The number of Goose Creekers in non-agricultural livelihoods increased toward mid-century when the greater number of year-round families residing on smaller agricultural units needed doctors, lawyers, teachers, mechanics, mill operators and craftsmen to support their marginally self-sufficient farms. Occupations continued to diversify when non-agricultural livelihoods such as carpenters, blacksmiths, mechanics, surveyors, wheel-rights, woodcutters, capitalists, toll gatekeepers and pump menders emerged. By 1860, the average $3.00 monthly wage was as much or more than most could earn working their own fields and a typical day laborer could earn $.50 a day with board

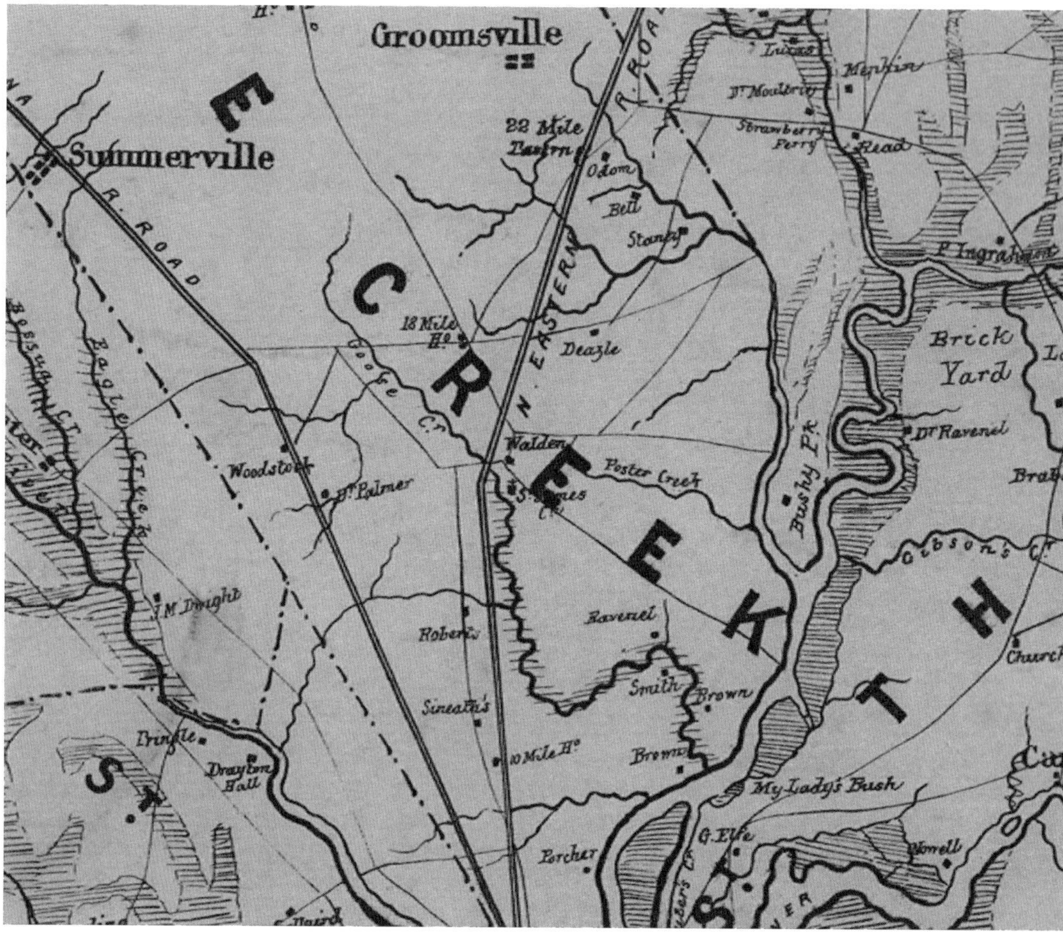

Map 1.4 The Evan's and Cogswell Map of South Carolina shows the eastern section of the St. James, Goose Creek Parish in 1861. ***Courtesy Library of Congress.***

and $.75 without. Skilled workers such as carpenters brought home $1.50 daily, while women were compensated with a $2.00 weekly wage for domestic work if they lived on-site. By 1840 most Goose Creekers continued to farm, but fourteen residents pursued occupations as doctors, lawyers and teachers and fourteen more were engaged in navigation and trade. By mid-century, Thomas Mims, George Smith, Henry Nichols and James Hughes were Goose Creek schoolteachers and Thomas L. Gilson and Tamil Hamilton were physicians. William Mellard was a surveyor, and William Bunch made and repaired shoes. Others were painters, plantation managers, coach makers, watchmakers, coal burners and turpentine distillers. Elmo Browning was a magistrate and Cashwell Mims was a "capitalist" (money lender).

The employment diversification continued to the eve of the war with men such as James Hughes, John Gadsden, M.E. Woode and Nelson Joiner teaching school and others earning livelihoods as watchmakers, shoemakers, coachmakers, pump tenders, mill operators and medical doctors. There were as many doctors in Goose Creek during the two pre-war decades as were during the most prosperous colonial period with doctors John Watson Jr., Thomas L. Gibson and Tamil H. Hamilton practicing medicine in 1850 and I.B. Varner, L.B. Gilmore, H.J. Abbott, L. Fissions and O.C. Rhame practicing ten years later.[59]

Although occupations based upon wage labor expanded, slave labor remained the basis of the Goose Creek economy. Twenty years after the Ford Map (map 1.3) was drawn and one year before the first shots of the Civil War were fired upon Fort Sumter in Charleston Harbor, there were 357 families residing on 215 parish farms with more than half of these families owning at least one of the 3,946 slaves in the parish.[60] On the eve of the conflict the largest slave owners were John Willson with 202 slaves, William Bell with 160 slaves, J.S. Tennent with 129 slaves, P.G. Stoney with 120 slaves, Charles Graves with 101 slaves and Henry Manigault with 80 bound souls. There were also small farmers like Lewis Poppenheim, Mary Bunch and Francis Bunch who kept 15, four and two slaves respectively.[61]

The Evans and Cogswell Map shows the location of some properties and landowners in Goose Creek in 1861 and indicates the importance of slavery in Goose Creek in the year the war began. Every landowner noted on the map owned varying numbers of slaves. Two of the largest slave owners, "Bell" and "Stoney" are shown on the headwaters of Back River, but moderate and small size owners such as "Walden," "Roberts," "Palmer," and "Sineath" are listed along the road and railways. "Mrs. J. Odum" appears on the 1860 slave schedule with 15 slaves, and "Ravenel," "Smith," and "Brown" are names of moderate size owners on Goose Creek near the Cooper River.

By 1860, it is obvious that Goose Creek had fully evolved from a large plantation-dominated economy to one of smaller and less efficient plantations and farms that required a more diversified labor force and support system. The 215 farms in 1860 were almost three times the number operating seventy years earlier, due to the settling of lands in the central and western parish, as well as the subdivision of some of the larger tracts in the eastern section. Thus, the typical farm in 1860 consisted of only 650 acres and was valued at merely $2,400. The smaller and less efficient parish farms produced a combined output of only 1,600 bales of cotton and 733,487 pounds of rice in 1859. Their combined value fell to slightly more than half a million dollars ($523,975) because smaller farms were less efficient, yielded smaller returns and were not nearly as self-sufficient as their larger predecessors. Expensive labor forced smaller farmers to delimit the number of tillable acres to merely 15 percent of their holdings, and the smaller farms required the isolated families to rely upon the remaining 85 percent of unimproved property for fuel logs, fence timber, building lumber, grazing pasture and water reserves. But remarkably, the reduced returns from the smaller farms accompanied the development of the non-agricultural livelihoods that were needed to support smaller agricultural units. No longer would single versatile plantation settlements support their own carpenters, coopers and blacksmiths as were typical during the heady colonial era.[62]

Even the largest and most prosperous plantations in 1860 were no longer self-sufficient but depended on the community support of public roads and service providers. The production of the most valued properties is capsulated in table 1.5. The table lists the forty-four (21 percent) of the properties with values from $4,000 to $20,000.

Table 1.5: The table lists the farms and plantations in St. James, Goose Creek Parish in 1860 valued at $4,000 or more with the corresponding production, as well as location and number of slaves according to the 1860 Agricultural Census, Census Report, Slave Schedule and miscellaneous land records.

Name of Owner	Name or Location of Plantion	Acres	Slaves	Value in Dollars	Heads of Cattle	Bushels of Corn	Bales of Cotton	Pounds of Rice
Dr. O.C. Rhames	Grove Hall	1,300	11	8,000	19	250	0	0
J.H. Poppeneim	Persimmon Hill*	1,700	16	5,000	24	500	15	600
Thomas Winter	Wassamasaw	650	16	4,000	14	100	0	0
T.F. Mims	Four Hole	1,460	3	5,000	28	600	2	300
William Mims **	Four Hole	1,000	3	5,000	26	900	17	600
Frederick Shuler	Wassamasaw	5,700	100	8,000	206	1,500	9	0
Thomas Ray	Dean Swamp	4,170	N/A	10,000	205	1,500	9	0
Lewis E. Conner	Western Parish	1,000	30	6,000	12	900	44	1,800
Esta. William Mellard	Rum Neck/ Dean Swamp	960	28	6,000	40	800	15	2,400
Jacob Wiggins	Four Hole/ Spring Hill	1,300	33	5,000	18	500	13	300
S.W. Williams	Wassamasaw	1,688	26	5,000	23	1,000	21	1,200
Martha Heards	N/A	500	25	4,000	38	500	0	600
P.G. Stoney	Medway	3,400	100	20,000	60	600	0	175,000
Dr. C. Tennent	Parnassus	3,005	130	16,000	57	500	60 wool	1,500
Alfred Shuler	Wassamasaw	1,625	9	5,000	22	700	20	1,500
John Browning	Cypress Swamp	450	17	4,000	66	700	0	1,800
Dr. J. Murray	Wassamasaw	1,150	53	6,000	100	1,800	10	1,200
J.B. Earneash (Earnest)	Upper Parish	1,850	N/A	8,000	80	1,500	7	3,000
J.E. Heape	Poppenheim's "Wee John"	1,300	29	7,000	65	1,000	18	0
William Whaley	Gaillard Road at 37 Mile Marker	2,300	16	9,000	85	700	2	2,400
T. West	N/A	1,280	18	6,400	50	500	4	1,200
William Bell	Back River	6,000	160	20,000	80	3,000	0	300,000
Charles Graves	Brick Hope	1,600	80	4,500	20	400	0	0
Thomas Gantt	Wassamasaw	3,000	23	7,000	38	300	0	0
P.J. Porcher	Otranto	800	60	10,000	15	1,000	16	84,000
Thomas Ledbeder	N/A	870	15	6,000	100	700	0	1,810
Mrs. Charles Brown	Mt. Pleasant/ Palmettoes	2,380	80	20,000	125	1,200	0	1,800

Name of Owner	Name or Location of Planttion	Acres	Slaves	Value in Dollars	Heads of Cattle	Bushels of Corn	Bales of Cotton	Pounds of Rice
Esta. H. Smith	Bloomfield	1,700	15	15,000	50	150	0	0
John Henon	N/A	620	25	10,000	2	200	0	0
William Sineath	12 Mile House	250	5	7,000	37	200	0	0
C. Cose (Vose)?	The Oaks	1,350	No Record	6,000	305	700	0	0
Caswell Heart	N/A	800	24	5,000	71	1,000	18	0
J.P. Bunch	N/A	630	10	5,000	44	350	21	1,200
J.S. Tennent	Red Bank	990	41	12,000	38	30	0	4,000
E. Geddings	The Elms	1,800	71	15,000	60	1,500	11	3,000
T.R. Waring	Southern Half of Otranto	700	45	5,000	35	750	50	0
D.M. Winter	Wassamasaw	665	20	4,000	39	600	1	0
Esta. Dr. J. Willson	Wassamasaw Tract at 30 Mile Marker	5,370	203	10,000	400	2,000	40	2,000
Joseph Crawford	Black Tom Bay	3,450	50	5,300	54	1,300	23	0
WIlliam Smith	Button Hall	1,300	26	4,000	85	1,000	0	0
J.P. Devaux	N/A	800	40	12,000	50	1,500	90	0
Dr. D.D. Graves	Marrington	1,860	101	10,000	40	500	0	50,000
Ben Gadsden	Cedar Grove	900	59	5,000	45	800	0	5,000
John Murray	Longridge	1,190	52	5,000	62	1,200	0	1,800

*John F. Poppenheim owned the property that was later named Persimmon Hill and is a residential area today.
**William Mims tax return in 1825 showed that he owned 1,300 acres and twelve slaves (S.C. Archives 1824 Tax Returns Number 2303).
Additional notes: Henry Manigault appears on the 1860 slave schedule with twenty-six slaves, E.S Mickell is recorded with sixty-two slaves and Josiah McKewn is recorded with thirty slaves but none of these names appear on the 1860 agricultural census.

The most valued estates belonged to Charles Brown, William Bell and Peter Gaillard Stoney. These old tracts were situated on Back River and Goose Creek, but nearly half of the wealthiest farms in 1860 were in the middle or upper sections. Eleven of the wealthiest farms were situated in Wassamasaw and Cypress Swamp in the mid section, and seven were situated in the upper section at Four Hole Swamp, Dean's Swamp and the vicinity. Interestingly, the most successful planters continued to produce impressive amounts of rice. South Carolina rice was valued worldwide, but stiff competition required that labor costs be mitigated by the use of tidal rice culture. Thus, Back River planters such as P.G. Stoney and William Bell, as well as Cooper River planters D.D. Graves and J.S. Tennent took advantage of the daily tides to flood, irrigate and drain their fields. Also, P.J. Porcher was able to employ tidal influences as far upstream as Otranto. Limited inland rice production remained possible without tides on some lands near fresh water reserves at Wassamasaw, Cypress, Dean and Four Hole Swamps.

Successful plantation owners during the first half of the nineteenth century were multitalented and diversified the production of the plantation to stay in business. William Bell and Peter Gaillard Stoney produced large numbers of bricks along with their impressive harvests of rice. From March to October the slaves cultivated and harvested rice as well as corn, potatoes, peas, peanuts, oats and livestock. During the winter months both planters operated two of the largest brick factories in the state.[63] Remarkably, Peter Stoney shipped 594,000 bricks in a ten-month period, from 1852 to 1853.[64] A Medway overseer's daybook reported that well-planned division of labor contributed to successful brick making. The book recorded that twelve slaves produced 6,000 bricks in one day on October 12, 1852:

> *2 hands digging clay; 1 hand carting clay to pit; 1 hand filling pit; 6 hands cutting wood, hauling wood, moulding bricks; 1 hand putting out fire; 1 hand loading bricks under shed.*[65]

The baked bricks were loaded on Stoney's sloop and sailed down Back River and the Cooper to Charleston. A large, approximately thirty feet long, iron boiler that weighs nearly fifteen tons remains hidden in the forests at Medway Plantation today. It is likely that this remnant is an old boiler used to generate steam and drive a brick-making machine that "beat" and mixed clay.[66]

Charles Graves was a neighbor of Stoney and a brick maker on nearby Foster Creek. Graves made daily entries in his journal, which described the diversification required to manage a successful plantation. He commented daily in his journal about the weather, field preparation, planting and harvesting of oats, potatoes, corn, rice, peas and more. He inventoried green bricks, as well as those ready for market, mended fences, cleared trees and hauled trash. He was a skilled bricklayer and brickbaker and he owned a sloop that he kept at his landing on Foster Creek to float his bricks and crops to market. The efficiency of his slaves at moving bricks onto a boat was indicated in Graves' journal entry for January 12, 1855. He noted, "sloop arrived at 1 oclock [*sic*] loaded her with 11,500 Gray Bricks and started her for town at 2½ oclock [*sic*]."[67] His uncle, physician Daniel DeSaussure Graves, resided nearby at Brick Hope Plantation. Both men pooled their resources and regularly assisted each other.[68]

The Back River and Foster Creek brickbakers also raised cattle. William Bell and Peter Gaillard Stoney kept herds of one hundred or more head. Other successful farmers such as Murray, Shuler and Willson at Wassamasaw, Vose at the Oaks, Brown at Mt. Pleasant and Ray at Dean Swamp used abundant water reserves and grazing pastures to keep large herds of one to four hundred head.

The diversification of some larger plantations and the increase of non-agricultural occupations accompanied the expansion of the paid labor system in Goose Creek. In addition to the brick factories owned by William Bell on Back River, Gaillard Stoney of Medway, Charles W. Graves and A.D. Graves at Brick Hope, two other factories owned by Charles Tennent of Red Bank baked bricks and George Smith made gray, brown and red bricks on Goose Creek. All of the brickyard owners used horses, mules and oxen to mix the clay, worked slaves to carry wood, stack bricks, load the sloops, and employed six to twenty paid laborers to perform varying functions from cutting firewood to timing the ovens. The typical salary amounted to $7.00 a month, but this salary usually consisted of a $.37 daily wage with lodging, or a $.50 daily wage without lodging. A carpenter or similar skilled laborer earned $ .75 a day while a laborer paid $2.50 weekly for room and board.[69]

Some of the larger and more diversified plantations operated sawmills for their own use, but small private entrepreneurs also began operating mills. By mid-century there were four sawmills, one of which used a thirty-horsepower steam engine. The others used animals to supply the power, and all used slave labor along with seven to twenty white wage earners.[70] On the eve of the Civil War, paid laborers increasingly augmented slave labor so that by 1860, the parish sawmills and brick bakeries together employed more than ninety men.[71]

Since 21 percent of the estates in the parish were valued at $4,000 or higher, most Goose Creekers owned one of the remaining 171 smaller and less valuable farms that held average values of $860.00. Those farms ranged from 50 to 500 acres with a mean size of 270 acres. As did the owners of the larger tracts, the small farmers usually tilled only 15 percent to 20 percent of the land and left the remaining property unimproved. The mean amount of improved acres was less than 50 acres per unit with more than 225 acres untilled. Like the larger estates, unimproved lands provided wood, grazing grasses, or irrigation reserves, but irrigation on the smaller Goose Creek farms was insufficient for successful rice production. Little or no rice was grown on the smaller farms in 1860, but the family and their slaves on the typical Goose Creek farm produced a wide variety of food, always relying upon corn as food for the family and field workers and fodder for the animals. Pigs and poultry and usually more than thirty heads of cattle were raised on the smaller farms each year. The farmer relied upon free-range feeding supplemented with grains or food residuals and byproducts such as corn blades and rice straw. Usually one bale or less of cotton was produced each year per farm and that small amount of cotton along with a few head of cattle provided whatever currency could be earned at market. The selected small farms used to derive the findings are listed with accompanying production figures in appendix VIII.

The homesteads of lesser value in the parish were usually situated away from navigable water and reliable water reserves but were always situated on or near passable roads. These farms were dependent upon roadways to carry the limited products to market, but they generally retained an isolated and partly self-sufficient lifestyle independent of significant social or market centers. The typical antebellum farmhouse in Goose Creek was built of wood and featured roofs of shaved wooden shingles, chimney made from brick or clay and wattle and foundations made from brick or heart-pine stump footings. Wattle chimneys were constructed by stacking and overlaying split wood and pushing fist-sized balls of clay into the openings between the layers. The wattle chimney was finished by spreading clay over the exposed wood and allowing the heat of the first fire to bake the clay.

Typical examples of small farms were situated on both sides of the State Road from the 20-mile marker at Thorogood to the 28-mile marker at Wassamasaw. Some of these farms were located near Crowfield Plantation and Carnes Crossroads in the eastern section of the parish, and included the farms worked by John F. Drose (Droze) who owned two tracts of 283 and 318 acres. Others were Archibald Harmon's with more than 900 acres, Elisha Driggers whose tract contained 296 acres, and Daniel Baxter who farmed 233 acres. Plats of these properties provide good descriptions of the use of the land and some, albeit limited, description of rural residential architecture of this period. A frontal view of "Baxter's" farmhouse is provided on an 1853 plat

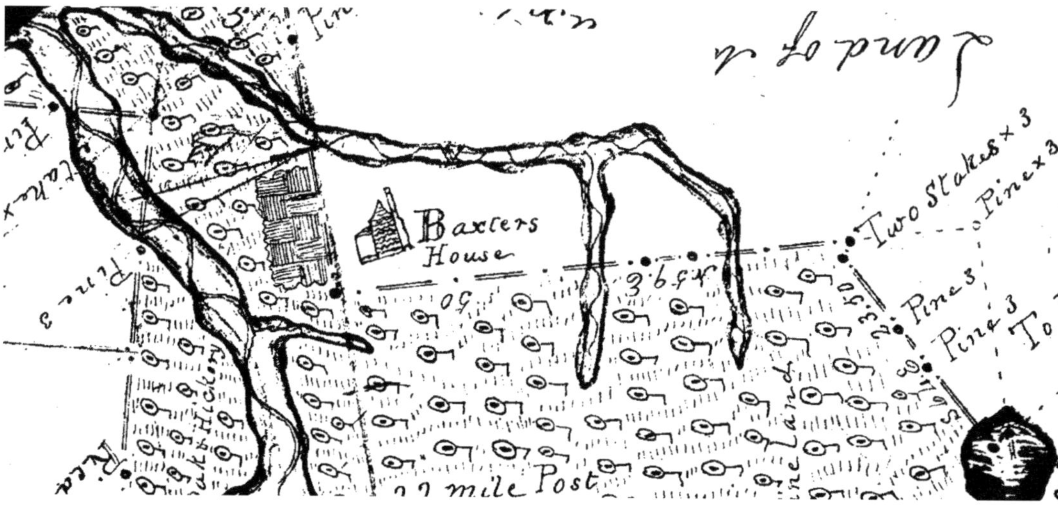

Plat 1.1 The drawing depicts "Baxter's House" and was taken from a plat showing Old Barns Plantation, which was made from a survey by Thomas Joyner in 1850. The plat is among the Hutchinson Papers in the collections of the South Carolina Historical Society, Charleston, South Carolina.

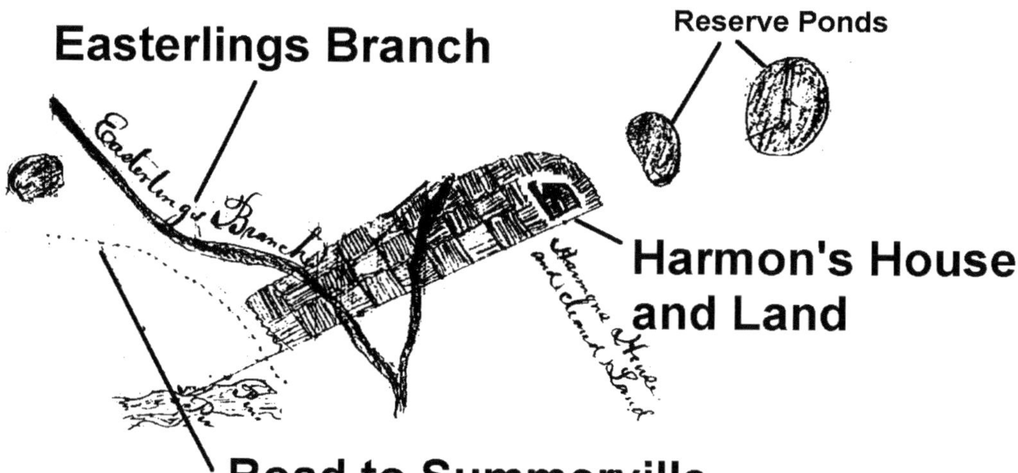

Plat 1.2 The partial plat shows Harmon's House and cleared land situated near Black Tom Bay in 1853. The plat was drawn from a survey made by Samuel Joyner. The tract consisted of 918 acres northwest of where the intersection of State Highways Alternate 17 and 176 is today. The manuscript words were added to this publication for clarity. The plat is on deposit with the South Carolina Archives.

drawn by Thomas Joiner. The farmhouse is situated on high ground near tilled fields.[72] A side view of the same house is shown on an 1850 plat of Old Barn's Plantation, which includes some of Baxter's farm.[73] Thus the plats provide two views of the same farmhouse. The 1850 plat shows details of Baxter's house and describes a wooden, one story house that featured a pitched roof, covered porch and chimney.

Plat 1.2 shows the property of Archibald Harmon in 1853. The layout of this farm was remarkably similar to others in the area. Except for slight variances in the overall number of acres, all farms featured tilled and untilled lands, ponds for water reserves, access to local roads and a single or 1½-story home with porch and fireplace. The full plat shows that Harmon's farm contained 918 acres near Black Tom Bay west of Carnes Crossroads near Nettles Road and a lesser road that led to Summerville. The lesser road is likely the same route followed by South Carolina State Highway 17 Alternate today.[74]

The farms were nearly self-sufficient, but a sheriff was needed to enforce the laws in each neighborhood, and an area magistrate was required to manage the local courts. The magistrates who kept law and order during the unsettled decades leading to the Civil War are listed in appendix IX. The social and economic conflicts that contributed to war furor also instigated crimes and civil disorder. Consequently, many of the problems confronted by the magistrates emerged from political angst caused by the rivalry of competing political groups, the fear of abolitionists' ideologies, vigilante behaviors springing forth from loosely controlled committees of "safety and correspondence," and a changing economy that caused troublesome labor unrest.

Political disputes and labor strife sometimes converged during the 1850s. In 1850, the State Legislature authorized an election to select delegates to a convention in Columbia for consideration of abolition issues. Delegates to the convention from St. James, Goose Creek were West Williams and Isaac Bradwell Jr.[75] Protest meetings, which hinted at secession, became common throughout the parish because most of the farmers and planters depended on slave labor, and the concept of emancipation was unthinkable. As a result, a summer meeting was held in St. James, Goose Creek Parish in 1851 that produced another resolution, this time to defend slavery at all costs. The temperament of the general population was becoming increasingly desperate.[76]

The Southern states seceded from the union for a multitude of reasons, but slavery and tariffs, two issues so deeply rooted in Southern economics, were the main causes of War. The secession that led to the war, known in the South as "The War for Southern Independence," threatened to divide and weaken a nation that had endured the struggle and resulting problems of its own independence 90 years earlier. Political influence in Congress shifted away from the South and threatened the system of slavery that the Southern economy depended upon. The settling of the west brought anti-slavery congressmen from the new states to Washington, and Harriet Beecher Stowe's masterpiece book, *Uncle Tom's Cabin,* placed popular support firmly behind the anti-slavery movement in most parts of the nation. The South was in a desperate situation, and the people of Goose Creek reacted adamantly by insisting that abolitionist thought not be tolerated. In 1850, a Northern emigrant to Goose Creek was arrested for disturbing the peace by "preaching abolitionists doctrine."[77]

On September 16, 1851, a large meeting of the citizens of the parish of St. James, Goose Creek met at the Wassamasaw Chapel. Colonel T.B. Earnest called the meeting to order and the assembly elected the Honorable John Willson as chairman and J.J. Browning and George C. Smith as secretaries. They resolved to cooperate with all of the slave-holding Southern states in resisting the encroachment of tyranny by "maintaining our just rights." They pledged trust and confidence in others who, with themselves, were threatened by a common danger. During the same meeting, the members resolved that it would not be proper or in good faith for South Carolina to secede alone. Reminiscent of the rebellious days of the American Revolution, a Committee of Safety and Correspondence for the parish was appointed. Reverend Stephen Williams, Reverend West Williams, Benjamin Godfrey, George Crawford, Thomas Mims, William McWilliams, Colonel Thomas J. Mellard, Captain S.C. Warnock, W.B. Thomas, Albert Clark, Hamilton Hart, William Martin Sr., William Whaley, J.J. McCants, Colonel J.B. Earnest, J.J. Browning, G.C. Smith, H.T. Browning, Reverend A.G. Sims, J.T. Crawford, Honorable John Willson and John Lawrence were appointed to the committee.[78]

An incident in 1855 took the issue of slavery off the minds of the people for a while. The first railroad strike in the state occurred in Goose Creek between the Northeastern Railroad and its workers. The workers marched to Charleston armed with clubs and pistols where they met resistance at the city limits from the sheriff and some concerned citizens. They returned to the railroad construction site where the strike soon ended when twenty-four of the workers were arrested and held on riot charges.[79]

Attention returned to the abolitionists when a convention was called in 1860 in Columbia for statewide delegates to consider the encroachment of the Northern abolitionists and secession from the Union. John N. Shingler and C.P. Brown arrived from Goose Creek but returned to Charleston when the convention moved there because of a threat of smallpox.[80] In December 1860, 169 conventioneers met at St. Andrew's Society Hall where the Ordinance of Secession was read to a politely silent crowd and approved by a unanimous vote. The twenty-two words that affected the lives of every Carolinian announced: "The Union now subsisting between South Carolina and other States, under the name of the 'United States of America' is hereby dissolved."[81] These words turned Charleston into a joyous celebration and paper sheets were tossed from the windows of the *Charleston Mercury* newspaper office, which read, "The Union is dissolved." Flags waved, cannons roared, and people screamed the news throughout the streets. Military companies organized immediately, arms were gathered and the most popular toast was "Damnation to the Yankees."[82]

The War

Almost all able-bodied white males in Goose Creek rushed to volunteer. Most reported for duty with the Charleston Battalion and later embarked by train with that battalion to join with the Army of Northern Virginia, under the command of Robert E. Lee.[83] One man who quickly volunteered was Carlston William Vose, Captain of the Goose Creek Company attached to the 18th Regiment. He was proprietor of the 18-mile House, but he was too old to serve and thus remained at his store during the conflict.[84] His son, John George Vose did join the Confederate Army and participated in numerous engagements. He vividly remembered the excitement after the proclamation of secession:[85]

> *I got up about 9 o'clock at night and found the whole family making a flag of a Palmetto tree and the words "Southern Republic" sewed on under the tree. You see, the state had just seceded! That flag was*

hung across the road in front of Pa's store the next morning and I expect it was one of the first flags of the Confederate States.[86]

Other Goose Creekers in the Charleston Battalion were W.A. Zimmerman, J.S. Sineath, William Sinkler, N. Sinkler, W.H. Cannon, William Tennant, Charles Tennant, E.S. Tennant, W. Williams, James Withers, George Brown and William Wilson.[87] Peter Gaillard Stoney, owner of Medway Plantation and six of his sons fought with the confederacy.[88] One son, I. Dwight Stoney was cited for gallantry and promoted from Private to Second Lieutenant because of his actions during a furious engagement defending Petersburg, Virginia.[89] Many more Goose Creekers enlisted to protect their homes and sense of order, but as the war years droned on, little action was seen in Goose Creek.

Two rail lines from Charleston that traversed the St. James, Goose Creek Parish and were vital strategic connections to the other sections of the state were not important objectives of the Union Army. Even late in the war, when General William T. Sherman's soldiers marched from Savannah, Georgia, to Columbia, South Carolina, they went by way of Orangeburg and merely skirted the St. James, Goose Creek Parish. Thus, except for raiding parties sent to protect the federal flank, the Union Army avoided Goose Creek until the last months of war.

Map 1.5 The Johnson and Browning Map shows St. James, Goose Creek Parish and Berkeley County in 1861.

On one occasion, a large raiding party camped behind the Black Creek Baptist Church in the Sandridge section. The raiders scavenged what they needed from the countryside and moved on.[90] Although no engagements occurred within the parish, Confederate General Edward J. Dennis supervised the construction of an earthen fortification on property owned by the Williams family near Dean Swamp to stop any "Yankees" from using the Gaillard or State Road to travel to Columbia. The fortification was never used but it was later named *Dennis' Confederate Fort.*[91]

Although no Civil War battles were fought in Goose Creek, the people suffered its effects. In April 1861, President Lincoln issued a proclamation stating that a blockade of the Southern ports was in effect. At first this was only a paper blockade with no actual effect, but eventually the "Stone Fleet," closed Charleston Harbor. The Stone Fleet was so named because the ships were loaded with granite and sunk by the Union Navy to prevent the flow of water traffic.

The blockade resulted in a shortage of almost everything and touched the lives of all Lowcountry residents. By early 1862, there was a shortage of shoes and prices on everything rose with the depreciation of Confederate money. In 1863, when the common monthly pay was $3.00, corn was selling for $2.25 a bushel and bacon was $1.00 a pound. By 1864, the price of corn had almost doubled and bacon increased to $5.00 a pound, butter $6.00 a pound, sugar, $1.00 a pound and a pair of boots reached $250.00. Eventually most items were not available at any price.[92]

In response to shortages, the *Charleston Mercury* newspaper printed a plea from the Confederate Congress in March, 1863, for all Carolinians to forego the production of cotton and tobacco, and plant only foodstuffs in anticipation of a lengthy engagement. Food shortages affected the war effort in Charleston because it was difficult to transport enough food to the city when most of the agricultural manpower was displaced to lines of defense.

The men remaining in the Goose Creek countryside drilled as the South Carolina 18th Regiment Militia but the militia seldom consisted of more than forty-five to fifty males between the ages of seventeen and fifty and was not a formidable force. Table 1.6 shows that only forty-five men of enlistment age served in 1864 and each of the four parish militia companies were thinly manned and composed mostly of males too young or old for regular service. Furthermore, most of the remaining men of enlistment age were exempt from regular service due to disabilities or because they were slave overseers, railroad workers, or blacksmiths and were essential to the wartime economy that depended on productive slaves and operable rail lines.

As the war slugged on, fewer women remained in the countryside. Most took refuge in the city and many worked gallantly in its defense. On one occasion, the confederate captain at Fort Moultrie called upon the women of Charleston to produce several thousand cartridge bags in twenty-four hours. The women worked late into the evening to meet the challenge, and the bags made from petticoats and pillowcases were delivered.[93]

Near that time, the *Charleston Daily Courier* warned of an impending Union invasion of the Lowcountry and three Goose Creek men, Keith Brown, B. Rhame and C.W. Graves were appointed to procure slaves to reinforce the Charleston Neck breastwork to thwart invasion of the city by land.[94] The *Charleston Mercury* reported an order to all slave owners in selected parishes, including Goose Creek, to deliver 20 percent of their slaves with spades or shovels and three days ration to rail depots for transport to Charleston where they would labor for thirty days.[95]

Table 1.6: The table shows the *Return of Men Liable Under the Recent Call* for each of the four-militia companies in the St. James, Goose Creek Parish on September 1864. The records concerning the 18th Regiment of South Carolina Militia are among the papers of the Adjutant and Inspector General Office no. 43/679 at The South Carolina Historical Society, Charleston, South Carolina.

Name of Company	Goose Creek Company	Wassamasaw Company	Four Hole Company	Dean Swamp Company
Name of commander	Captain Philip Porcher	Captain Wiggins (no first name)	Captain William Cummings	Captain I.A. Varn
Number ages 16–17 years	1	14	2	4
Number ages 17–50 years	18	14	0	13
Number 50 and older	22	information not available	information not available	information not available
Number disabled	3	information not available	information not available	11
Number exempt for reasons other than disabilities	8	information not available	information not available	2

In addition to procuring slaves to work on defense details, Goose Creekers served on the *Board of Soldier's Relief*.[96] Charles W. Graves, John Earnest, James E. Heape, Joseph Crawford, John T. Browning, George C. Owens, West Williams, John A. Varn, E.G. Shuler, T.C. Warnock, James Wiggins and Thomas Ray supervised the disbursements of support to destitute families. The *Board of Soldier's Relief* provided increasingly meager support to families who struggled without breadwinners. More than 90 Goose Creek families, or 26 percent of the total, relied upon relief, and the board reported in March of 1863 that the support for the "pressing needs" of the families was "too small." The report signed by T.C. Warnock, showed a steady increase in the number of needy families, a decreasing amount of available dollars, and the correlating reduction in the amount of relief paid to each.[97] The waste and consumption of war, as well as the effects of the blockade greatly limited available necessities, but the absence of the able bodied men was felt most grievously.

By February 1865, the cause was hopeless and Confederate Brigadier General Pierre Gustav Toutant Beauregard ordered the evacuation of Charleston. As the Union Army marched in, the Confederates destroyed the Goose Creek Bridge by fire to slow their pursuit.[98] Some rebels marched through Goose Creek to the Moncks Corner Road, but most of the evacuating army traveled by steamer up the Cooper to Strawberry Ferry and then marched to Cordesville, where they boarded railcars that carried them to an assembly point in St. Stephens in upper Berkeley County.[99] Within days of the Confederate retreat, Union soldiers repaired the Goose Creek Bridge and proceeded north, followed by streams of reinforcements arriving daily by train at Otranto Station.

Several dozen African American Union soldiers camped in the cold rain under the grand trees of the Oaks Plantation on the evening of February 27, 1865 while Henry O. Marcy, a Union Army Surgeon, and the other white officers of that unit enjoyed dinner, piano music and a dry bed in the main house.[100] Two days later, as parties of soldiers reconnoitered the parish, Marcy embarked with seven mounted men to forage at Medway Plantation. The diary kept by him during his few days in Goose Creek explains, to a large extent, the challenges of the landowners and slaves as the Union soldiers visited each plantation, and with force and persuasion replaced the old southern order based on slavery with a new untested arrangement that was exhilarating to newly emancipated slaves, but terrorizing to the landowners.

At Medway Plantation, Marcy and his riders encountered a cohort of "bitter rebels"[101] consisting of 18 women and children of the Stoney family under the care of one disabled son-in-law. To avoid confrontation, Mrs. Stoney patiently greeted the raiders and soon after invited all of them to dinner. Marcy accepted on behalf of his men and later noted in his diary that he was ill inclined to confront the "attractive" women at Medway.[102] After dinner, Mrs. Stoney informed the surgeon that in recent days her "niggers had become unruly and she feared trouble" if he did not impose his authority and order the servants to remain at work in the fields. He hesitantly agreed to try, and at her request, more than 150 slaves assembled before the veranda to listen to the Army Surgeon. After a fifteen-minute oration explaining the benefits of remaining with the land during trying times, he greeted each emancipated man, woman and child with a handshake as they passed by his place on the veranda. He admitted to his hostess that in spite of his best efforts he feared his brief oration was unlikely to reverse the proclamation of President Abraham Lincoln. The somber mood turned more ominous as all guests retired with the family to the parlor to bid farewells. Clearly, the entire household feared the pending chaos that they believed would accompany the arrival of the black and white Union troops. The arrival of black troops especially emboldened the recently emancipated Africans and dredged forth the nagging fear of slave revolt, which throbbed in the minds of every white landowner since the earliest plantation era.

The seven riders returned to the Oaks Plantation from their foraging trip empty handed but well fed, and that evening the surgeon entered in his diary a vivid description of the newly freed souls who assembled before him at Medway. He penned, "The gathering would have made a fair subject for a painter," and described his audience as:

> *People of all ages and sizes-clothed in all sorts of garments from the ordinary homespun to whole suits made of old carpets and blankets-nearly all stood with heads and feet bare, and very few were clothed sufficiently warm to prevent them from suffering.*[103]

In the following days, the emancipated African Americans at Medway walked off the plantations as did most throughout Goose Creek, and desperate landowners searched for refuge. Some Federals rode rail lines to Moncks Corner and others marched west along the State Road where the Wassamasaw Church was occupied as a dry and warm hospital for Northern soldiers.[104] As that winter waned, Union troops steamed up the Cooper and Back River on gunboats to pillage the plantations, and African American army units foraged as well. These assaults forced the Cooper and Back River white families to seek refuge in the relative safety of occupied Charleston rather than suffer the chaos and dangers of the countryside. So when John Stafford Stoney was relieved of Confederate duty and arrived home to Medway, he found the slaves scattered, his house burned to the ground, and his family missing. In anguish he hurried to Charleston to search for his loved ones and found them safe at the Ball's townhouse. There he learned that his wife and children, fearful of restless slaves and Yankee gunboats, had embarked upon their "brick sloop" with two neighboring families, the Fitzsimmons and Balls, and sailed to the safety of the union occupied city.[105] The homecomings were similar for J.S. Tennent, a Calhoun Guardsman who returned to a ransacked house at Parnassus Plantation and William Williams, a Sumpter Guardsman who walked for weeks to his overgrown homestead at Wassamasaw. But other fighters from Wassamasaw were not as fortunate and never returned home.

J.C. McKewn was the Captain of the Wasamassaw Cavalry when it entered Confederate service in 1862. That summer it was ordered to Virginia and with other companies formed the Second South Carolina Regiment, commanded by General M.C. Butler. The regiment remained at the front, taking many casualties until the spring of 1864 when it was ordered home to recruit horses and men.[106] The unit's blue and white silk flag was lost in Virginia. It featured a palmetto tree and the motto, "The brave may fail, but never yield" along with the words "Wassamasaw Cavalry."[107] The flag as well as many Goose Creek Confederates remained missing, and few of the men who returned to the parish stayed long after the war so that by the turn of the twentieth century, Mary Cannon was the sole Goose Creeker connected to the conflict. She was collecting pension payments for the service of her late husband, George M. Cannon of Company A, Hagood's Artillery.[108]

By the time of the surrender at Appomattox, the parish was in ruin and the people were hungry, frightened, angry and desperate. Post-war recovery would be dreadfully slow partly because there was little sympathy for Charleston in the Northern states. The *New York Tribune* published, "Doom hangs over wicked Charleston,"[109] and a letter from General Holleck in Washington, D.C., to General Sherman suggested, "Should you capture Charleston, I hope that by some accident the place may be destroyed."[110]

Chapter II
St. James, Goose Creek Church
1714–2003

I love your parish, and most of all its romantically situated ancient church...
—E.A. Poyas, *The Olden Times of South Carolina*

The venerable St. James Church is an inseparable part of the long history of Goose Creek. It survived the ravages of time and remains as stately as when it was erected in 1714 on the banks of Goose Creek. It is situated in ancient forests near the Middleton Oaks Estate, across the water from once-spacious Otranto Plantation and approximately 200 yards south of the Goose Creek Bridge. Much of the church's history is contained in the book, *St. James' Church, Goose Creek, South Carolina: A Sketch of the Parish from 1706–1896,* written by church vestryman, Dr. Joseph Ioor Waring in 1897. At the request of the vestry, Dr. Waring prepared a history of the church to raise funds for the care and maintenance of the old building. He expressed his admiration for the remarkable structure when he wrote that it, "is greatly to be doubted whether there is anywhere on this continent another church, chapel, or meeting house more interesting."[111]

For three hundred years church vestrymen, such as Dr. Waring, have maintained the church and its grounds. The church was laid out in 1710 as a forty-by-fifty-foot structure facing west and although services began in 1714, the building was not completed until five years later. Tie rods were inserted through the walls in 1844 to stabilize it, and in 1876 the roof was altered to facilitate the application of a slate cover to improve fire resistance. Metal shutters were added at the same time. Ten years later, the earthquake of 1886 collapsed the western gable and another effort was needed by the vestry to make repairs and save the building from further damage and deterioration. The work of the vestry continued into the twentieth century. Proceeds from Dr. Waring's book sales were used to partially satisfy the cost of installing a fence around the grounds, and renovating the pulpit, reading desk and communion rail. In 1955 reinforced concrete footings were placed under the building to prevent cracking of the foundation. The last project installed a drainage system to channel water away from the building and to lower damaging humidity inside.[112] Today, the vestry continues to preserve the church and because of their work, the ancient place of worship has survived to tell the stories of old Goose Creek.

The church is reminiscent of the Barbadian origin of the first Goose Creek settlers and the building would not seem architecturally out of place if it were somehow transported to Barbados. It is built with brick that are protected with coral colored masonry stucco. It features a hipped roof and large, airy and shuttered windows, all of which are common on the Caribbean islands. There are thirteen arched windows, two side doors and one main entrance. The keystone over each window is decorated with a cherub's face and wings made of stucco and the main entrance is headed with five bas-relief hearts. Above the front door is a plaster model of a mother pelican feeding her hatchlings. This icon is the symbol of *The Society for the Propagation of the Gospel in Foreign Parts* (SPG), the organization, which sent missionaries to the Goose Creek wilderness. The iconic pelican is feeding her young by tearing meat from her own breast; thereby symbolizing the missionary acts of sacrificial charity. The exterior SPG symbol was installed over the door in 1907 to replace the worn original fixture that is stored inside the church.

Inside the church is a small robing room situated under the stairs that lead to the gallery. There are also twenty-four pews of the old square box pattern. The wooden pew box walls are approximately four inches shorter than the original heights because water damage from periodic seepage rotted the bottoms of the boxes and the damaged sections of wood were cut off during a renovation process. The aisles are paved with flagstone and lead to a tall, elaborate central pulpit, which is ascended by winding stairs. According to a recent archaeological study, the pulpit was originally placed in the front southern corner of the church and did not block the view of the church altar. A ceiling hook and remains of a post hole indicate its original position, but there are no explanation for its repositioning to the front center of the room. A large sounding board is located above the pulpit and a small reading desk and communion table stands within the chancel rail. Also within the chancel is the Royal Arms of Great Britain, supported by four Corinthian pillars. The Royal Arms are painted brilliant red, blue and yellow representing the three King Georges and it presents the white horse of the Royal House of Hanover.[113]

Marble tablets bearing the Decalogue, Apostles' Creed and the Lord's Prayer grace each side of the chancel. Memorials displayed on the walls include a testimonial to Colonel John and Mrs. Jane Gibbes, as well as to Ralph Izard and Peter Taylor (see appendix X for the text of the memorials). Located over the main entrance is the gallery, which provided seating for church members who did not own a pew box. A diamond shaped, wooden symbol of the Izard family, known as the family hatchment, is displayed on the face of the gallery. In accordance with English tradition, the hatchment was carried in front of the coffin during the burial procession of the head of the family. After the burial the hatchment was hung inside the church. The Izard hatchment is one of only two in America.[114]

No minister was available to lead religious services in Goose Creek until the first missionary arrived in 1700. Reverend William Corben, A.M., the first missionary, was formerly in service at the Chapel of Bromley, St. Leonard in Middlesex, England. Shortly after he began his work in Goose Creek, the Church of England organized the dynamic and influential SPG that sent churchmen to North America. In 1701, the SPG concluded that more than half of the seven thousand Carolina colonists, not including the African, were without religion and there were no churches or schools outside of Charleston and no teachers except a few much-despised dissenters.[115] In response, it sent Reverend Samuel Thomas as their first missionary to Goose Creek in 1702 to continue the work begun by Reverend Corben who was recalled to England.

Reverend Thomas suffered a miserable voyage to America. In his own accounts of the passage down the English Channel he was "forc'd to lye upon a chest" and was "curs'd and treated very ill

Photograph 2.1 The photograph, taken March 12, 2002, shows the front view of St. James, Goose Creek Church. *Author's collection.*

Photograph 2.2 The photograph shows a bas-relief figure of a pelican feeding three hatchlings. It is the symbol of the Society for the Propagation of the Gospel in Foreign Parts. The photograph was taken March 12, 2002. *Author's collection.*

Photograph 2.3 The photograph shows the interior of the church with the stairway, pulpit and sounding board in the center. The Decalogue and Apostles Creed flank the pulpit. The photograph was taken April 24, 2002. *Author's collection.*

Photograph 2.4 The photograph, taken April 24, 2002, shows a church window decorated with a masonry cherub face and wings. *Author's collection.*

on board."[116] At Plymouth he almost died from illness, but recovered well enough to sail to Carolina where after "12 weeks and 2 days at sea" he arrived in Charleston on Christmas Day, 1702. His purpose was to bring the gospel to the Yemassee Indians, so the SPG decided that he should be "laid out in stuffs for the use of the wild Indians,"[117] but because the Native Americans were hostile at that time, Governor Nathaniel Johnson moved Thomas in with his family at the governor's home at Silk Hope Plantation on the Cooper River near the future site of Strawberry Ferry. Soon he was reassigned to "the care of the people settled upon the three branches of Cooper River."[118]

At that time Goose Creek was the largest and most populated community outside Charleston, and it was there that Reverend Thomas began his earnest missionary work with about 120 families who he believed were "ignorant but well inclined."[119] He made a good impression and the governor and council wrote to the SPG to express their gratitude for the society's work with "our poor infant church in this Province," and their pleasure at the arrival of Reverend Thomas.

Reverend Thomas was the first effective missionary in Goose Creek. He found only five communicants when he arrived, but through his efforts the number increased to thirty-two and he noted that the "heathen slaves in this parish...come constantly to Church." In a letter dated May 3, 1704, he described the congregation "so numerous that the Church could not contain them."[120] Within a year he counted twenty African slaves among his communicants and he believed that all of them were "well understanding the English tongue," and could read and write. He wrote in 1705 that there were a large number of slaves "desirous of Christian knowledge, and many of them can read the Bible distinctly."[121]

Reverend Thomas was determined to stay in Goose Creek and thus sailed to England and returned with his family in 1705. Sadly, he died shortly after returning, but not before he laid a sound religious foundation for his successor.[122] The following year the St. James, Goose Creek Parish was organized by an act of the Assembly and its boundaries were defined. That same year, the SPG sent a native Frenchman, the Reverend Francis LeJau, Doctor of Divinity, to replace Thomas.[123] He was a native of Angers, France, and reared as a French Huguenot, but he had been ordained by the Anglican Bishop of London and came to Goose Creek to officiate at the Anglican Church. At first, as he continued the work of Reverend Thomas to proselytize the Negroes, masters such as Lady Moore, Captain David Davis and Sarah Baker brought their slaves to be instructed and baptized and his good fortune continued when he found a large nearby congregation of Frenchmen that he was eventually able to bring into his fold.

The French were hardy frontiersmen who came to Carolina to escape religious persecution in France and were second only to the English Barbadians in shaping the development of Goose Creek. A French church was built among the Huguenot plantations near the end of the seventeenth century and from 1685 onward, the political influence of the French population increased. The Huguenot settlers in South Carolina were divided into four groups. One group settled at Charleston, another settled at Orange Quarter in the parishes of St. Thomas and St. Denis, while the largest group built plantations on the Santee River, and the smallest group moved to the headwaters of Goose Creek in today's area of Ladson and Sangaree. According to Peter Girard, 31 French Huguenots resided in Goose Creek in 1699, but his list probably excluded women, children and slaves.

As early as 1695, the relatively large group of Goose Creek settlers began to establish a place of worship where their church was known as "L'Eglise francoise qui s'assembl sur Gouscrick," or "the French

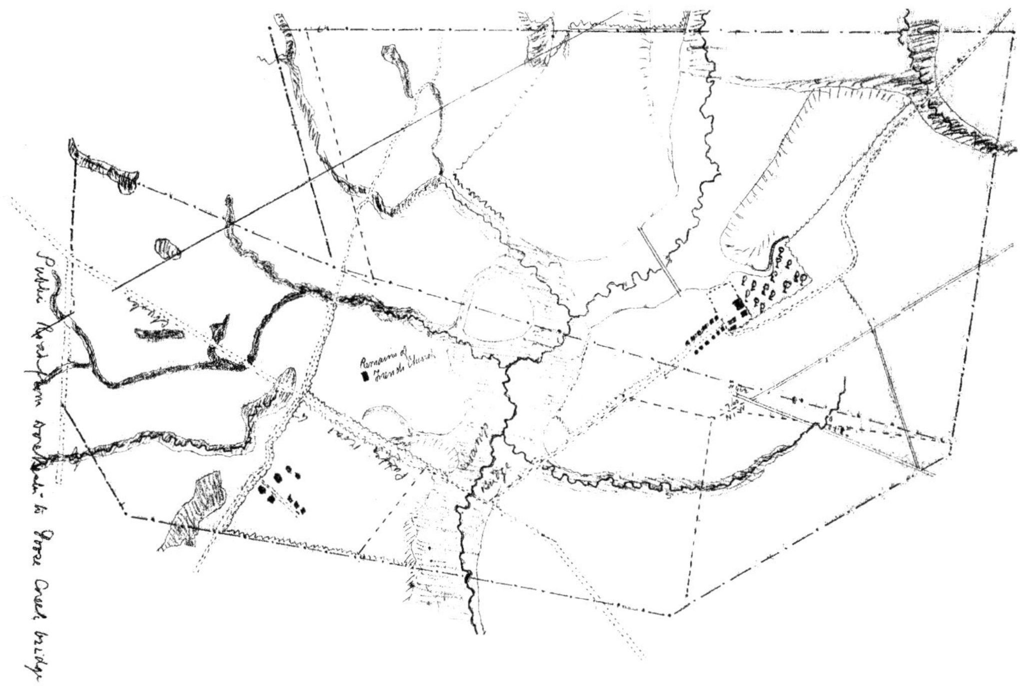

Plat 2.1 This partial plat shows the location of the French Church noted as "Remains of French Church" near the center of the plat. Joseph Purcell drew the plat from a survey in 1791. The plantation settlement is shown on the right half of the drawing and another unidentified settlement is shown on the lower left section. The two public roads to Dorchester intersect near the center left margin in Ladson. The plat was traced by Henry A.M. Smith and is among the collections of the South Carolina Historical Society, Charleston, South Carolina.

Church which meets on Goose Creek." The earliest mention of a French congregation in Goose Creek is found in the will of Anthony Prudhomme dated 1695. He bequeathed a cow and two heifers to the congregation.[124] Another indication of the church is recorded on a plat dated 1785 and drawn by Joseph Purcell, surveyor of the Parker plantation. He designated the site as the "Remains of a French Church." It was located on a tract of 500 acres originally granted to Abraham Fleury S. de la Plaine in 1696.[125]

The French membership apparently owned no land, not even the site upon which the church building stood and the date the church was erected is unknown as well as most of its history. The building was located on the Road to Dorchester about four miles northwest of St. James, Goose Creek Church and one and one-half miles east of Ladson Station. The Huguenot Society of South Carolina, to mark the site, erected a cross of granite in the early twentieth century. The cross is 571 feet northwest of the old road from Ladson to the Goose Creek Bridge.[126] Today a chain linked fence and locked gate protects the location at the end of the paved section of Ancrum Road.

Judge Henry A.M. Smith, a Lowcountry historian, believed that James Gignilliat, who lived in the immediate area of the church, was one of the early ministers or perhaps the only one.[127] Judge Smith visited the site near the close of the nineteenth century and found the remains of a few unmarked graves and some bricks that may have been from the church pillars. The French families

Photograph 2.5 The photograph shows the granite cross that marks the location of the French Huguenot Church in St. James, Goose Creek Parish. The photograph was taken December 2, 2002. *Author's collection.*

Drawing 2.1 The drawing depicts Reverend Francis LeJau.

residing nearby including the Bacot, Boisseau, Dassex or Dasseu, Dupont, Faucheraud, Fleaury, Franchomme, Godin, Guerin, Marion, Porcher, Postell, Trouillart and Verdity probably composed the congregation.[128]

Upon his arrival, Reverend Francis LeJau found that the Anglican parishioners were collecting materials for the construction of a larger church and parsonage. The Church Act was passed in 1706, the same year he arrived and the Church of England became the official state church and the most dynamic religious institution in the colony. In support of this newly sanctioned official church, Benjamin Schenckingh gave a gift of one hundred acres of land. The plat states that one acre was reserved for the church building and the remaining land was to be used in support of the newly arrived minister.[129] Soon, under the leadership of Reverend LeJau, the nearby French families abandoned their little church in Ladson and became active members of LeJau's congregation in Goose Creek.[130]

The larger wooden church was not built on Schenckingh's hundred-acre gift, but it was built on another grant of sixteen acres given by Benjamin Godin. Soon after the wooden church was completed, the Churchwardens and vestry were sworn into service. Oaths were taken by the first church officers, proclaiming the absence of transubstantiation of bread and wine to the body and blood of Christ and the rejection of Papal authority. The church parishioners then met on Easter Monday, in 1707, and elected Reverend Francis LeJau as Rector. The first wardens were Robert Stevens and John Sanders and the first vestrymen were Ralph Izard, George Cantey, Captain James Moore, Arthur Middleton, Captain John Cantey, William Williams and Captain David Deas.[131] That year the parish contained approximately one thousand people of which Reverend LeJau baptized twenty-one children and received thirty-five communicants.[132]

The people of Goose Creek regarded Reverend LeJau highly. He abolished the customary baptismal fee that most were unwilling or unable to pay, and he worked diligently to educate and baptize the black slaves and Native Americans who lived nearby. To show their respect for him, the parishioners subscribed £60 yearly allowance in addition to his regular SPG salary.[133] LeJau was also pleased with his parishioners and he reported to the SPG that they had improved their moral character and were attending services in increasing numbers. He complained, however, that there were "some few atheistical persons, and scoffers at all revelation." Nevertheless, he worked diligently to bring as many into the church as possible including any slave child who was presented by the master. Also, adult slaves could have their children baptized if both parents had been baptized, and later he baptized any slave child if presented by parents, even if only one parent was Christian.

The new minister was appalled by what he described as the most scandalous and common crimes in Goose Creek. He complained that the slaves frequently changed their wives and husbands, which often caused great consternation. He instructed the slaves that Christianity did not allow plural marriages or any changing of spouses and to stress this point, he required slaves to promise during their baptismal proceedings that they would keep their spouse until death. He also instructed the slaves against merriment on the Lord's Day and threatened to refuse them communion if they did not comply. His sincere and careful guidance was apparently successful because, the number of communicants steadily increased. Two years after arriving in Goose Creek, he counted thirty-seven communicants of which five were Negroes and by his seventh year he counted sixty members with five Negro men and two women. According to his letters, the congregation steadily increased during his tenure.

Before the outbreak of the Yemassee Indian War in 1715, Reverend LeJau convinced the SPG to send the first schoolmaster to the parish. This request was the beginning of a long tradition of formal education that was continued by an enthusiastic and growing congregation that soon after increased beyond the capacity of the wooden church. During the last years of Reverend LeJau's service to Goose Creek the handsome brick church that stands today and a parsonage were erected. The new church opened in 1714 to receive seventy white communicants and eight African Americans.[134] Three years later, Reverend Francis LeJau became sick and died after a long and painful illness. He was buried at the front of the chancel where his only son placed a marble tablet over his grave.

After the death of Reverend LeJau, the vestry requested that the SPG send another missionary. They expressed the great loss with the death of their rector and declared that he was a "good, pious and learned minister, by whose doctrine and conversation many have reaped much profit."[135] After his death, Abel Kittleby, Esquire of the Middle Temple, London and Landgrave of Carolina presented a large and beautiful Book of Common Prayer to the parish in 1717, and nearby Anglican ministers temporarily filled the pastoral vacancy until a new minister could be assigned.

In 1719, a resolution was passed by the vestry providing that the first two lower pews of the middle two rows of the Church be used only by the wardens and vestry. A visitor to the church today can recognize these pews by the brass identification plates. The resolution also reserved one pew for Arthur Middleton and his heirs, due to his help with the church construction and his donation of land for the parsonage. Another pew was reserved for Benjamin Schenckingh and Benjamin Godin for their land contributions. Pews were also allocated to Colonel James Moore, Roger Moore, Mrs. Anne Davis, Benjamin Gibbes and John Gibbes.[136] The remaining pews were sold.

The SPG sent Reverend Francis Merry to Goose Creek in 1720 to fill the vacancy left by LeJau's demise, but the vestry disapproved of him and reported to the SPG that "Mr. Merry's behavior is so indiscreet that the parish can not elect him," and "his Excellency Governor Nicholson and all the clergy were very sensible of how he had behaved himself, etc." The SPG recalled Merry and invited Reverend Thomas Marritt to hold services until a replacement arrived.

Soon after, the SPG sent Reverend Richard Ludlam, A.M., in 1723 and he was immediately elected Rector and began a short but renowned tenure. The public treasury paid his yearly salary of £100 in Carolina currency and Reverend Ludlam enjoyed the handsome brick parsonage house near the church and the hundred-acre tract of land that supplied much of his needs. He was well loved and greatly respected by the parishioners.[137] Like his predecessor, Francis LeJau, he spent much of his time converting and teaching the slaves, who were during that early period, still mostly African-born. He reported to the SPG that his parishioners were "sober, well-disposed, and attentive to public worship," and that the people continued to bring their children to be baptized, and that many "devoutly received the Lord's Supper." After five years of service he died twelve days after the demise of his wife in 1721.[138] He and his spouse are probably buried side by side on the grounds of the church and although no grave markers are evident today, he is remembered by his bequeath of approximately £2,000 currency to the establishment of a school for the poor.[139] This is an impressive amount of money. John Harvard's gift to Harvard College was only about £800.

The Society appointed the Reverend Thomas as Reverend Ludlam's successor in 1729 but unfortunately he drowned while embarking from England.[140] Two years after Ludlam's death, the SPG sent Reverend Lewis Jones of St. Helena's Parish to St. James on a temporary assignment and was soon ordered to return to St. Helena's when the Reverend Timothy Millechamp, A.M., was sent by the SPG in 1732 and elected Rector.

It appears that the church congregation weakened significantly during the four-year absence of a regular minister. The church had only occasional services during that period and the congregation decreased. Millechamp complained two years after his arrival that he had baptized only one Negro man and he later reported that there were 2,160 non-baptized Negroes and 20 Indians in the parish that he was not serving. At the same time, he counted 91 white families of which ten were dissenters and on Christmas day in 1742, ten years after his arrival, only 20 white and 2 black communicants attended his service.[141] The apathy in the parish alarmed him greatly, but he did not despair and responded by undertaking many projects to improve the facilities. During his tenure, the energetic minister accomplished many repairs to the church and parsonage and improved the grounds as well. The Commons House of Assembly responded to his appeals by providing £100 in 1735 for church repairs and more for the church ground improvements in 1732. The Common House allocated £500 toward the purchase of a piece of land for a glebe and free school,[142] and £375 to repair the parsonage house.[143]

As the Reverend Millechamp aged he sought remedies to improve his failing health and regain his vigor. He ventured to England in 1738 and again in 1744 for long rests and cures. Upon his 1744 departure he was presented a testimonial from the vestry that recorded his able and pious service to the people of the parish (see appendix XI for the text of the testimonial). His health deteriorated and he was unable to return to Carolina but as he remained away for years he petitioned the Commons House to continue his salary until he regained his strength to return. He was granted one-year salary while he was "absent to cure palsy at waters of Bath."[144] Two years later, however, the vestry wrote to the Bishop of London and the SPG, to complain about the absence of Millechamp and to request a replacement. In the meantime, Millechamp recovered his health and became the rector of the Parish of Colesbourne in the Diocese of Gloucester, England and the SPG relieved him of his mission in Goose Creek.[145] During the four-year absence of a regular rector, services were conducted monthly by neighboring ministers.

Reverend Robert Stone succeeded Millechamp in 1748 and served until his death three years later. He was greatly concerned with the physical well being of his parishioners and reported that he buried eight people in the first nine weeks he was in the parish. Soon after his arrival he reported that the land was unhealthy, but his alarm slowly abated and his enthusiasm lifted as the months passed. Two years later, he wrote with confidence and optimism that conditions had improved and he believed he was doing effective work among the people. Interestingly, he set aside Sunday afternoons to teach and give service to the "Negroes," whose "numbers crowded the Church before and were very off[ensive] to the whites." He was pleased that both the Africans and their masters appreciated his willingness to conduct segregated services.[146]

Reverend Stone died in 1751, and was buried in St. Philips churchyard in Charleston. A year later Reverend Jonathon Copp arrived from Georgia to assume the position in Goose Creek, but the SPG had already appointed Reverend James Harrison, A.M. who was soon elected by the vestry and allocated an extra £340 currency to "purchase a Negro for the use of the Parsonage."

As those before him, Reverend Harrison turned his attention to the education of the parish children. He wrote to the SPG that subscription and the Ludlam Fund had raised enough money through the years to build a schoolhouse and that the need was great in a sprawling parish where many brought their children from as far away as 280 miles to be baptized. He served thirty white and seventeen Negro communicants in 1757 and it seems as if the conditions were improving when William Middleton presented the Decalogue, Apostles' Creed and Lord's Prayer on large marble plaques to be placed on each interior side of the last window of the church.

Reverend Harrison remained optimistic the following year when he reported to the SPG that his congregation continued to serve twenty-six white and twenty black communicants, and that he recently baptized eighteen white children and five adult Negroes. But, only a few years later, according to Reverend Harrison, the numbers fell due to the war with the Cherokee Indians that caused some of the parishioners to depart in search of greater security.[147]

During Harrison's tenure, power of attorney was sent from the SPG to the vestry to allocate the money left by Reverend Ludlam for a school, as well as money left by Peter Taylor in 1765. For this purpose, the Reverend James Harrison, Robert Horne, Benjamin Coachman, and John Parker were appointed attorneys. It was near this time that Reverend Harrison notified the vestry that he intended to resign. In his resignation letter he commented on the great flow of people in that section of the province and the fact that the church and parsonage were located so near the well-traveled road resulting in travelers consistently crossing the creek, visiting the nearby tavern, and pestering him for lodging and entertainment.[148] He wanted no more of that inconvenience and departed before the turbulence of the Revolutionary War. He moved to St. Bartholomew's Parish where several years later he died and was buried.[149]

Reverend Harrison submitted all of the Ludlam Fund accounts to the vestry, which amounted to more than £15,272. Upon his departure, the Reverend Edward Ellington of St. Helena's Parish was elected Rector. In 1778, during the turmoil of war, the vestry was incorporated to enable them, in their words, "effectually to put into execution the trust reposed in the Society for the Propagation of the Gospel in Foreign Parts, by the last will and testament of Reverend Richard Ludlam."[150] A deed dated the same year references a conveyance of twelve acres of land from Henry Middleton to the church vestry that could be used for a school site. The land was presented to the church with Benjamin Coachman and Benjamin Mazyck representing the vestrymen and wardens. The giving and receiving of "a twig and a turf" transferred the small tract.

Reverend Edward Ellington was rector of the church during the chaotic years of the American Revolution. Loyalties were divided and tempers flared when the British occupied Charleston and the parish fell within British lines. During this time, the Reverend preceded to use prayer in the litany for the King of England. One parishioner threatened the priest that if he used the prayer for the King, he would throw his prayer book at his head. The threat did not prevent the reverend from using the prayer the following Sunday, but the promise was kept, and Reverend Ellington was the target of a hurled book. As a result, Ellington refused to hold services until after the war and peace returned to the countryside.

During these disturbing years some churches were converted into garrisons, hospitals or barracks and some were burned, but the British did not harm the little church in Goose Creek because of the presence of the Royal Arms displayed over the altar. The arms remained prominently displayed after the war even amidst the patriotic emotions that prevailed throughout the parish because as one patriot explained, "not the sternest Republican would now wish to see these symbols of regality removed, when it is known that they saved the temple of God from the violence of a mercenary and ruthless soldiery."[151] Also, Reverend Ellington remained a well loved and respected rector. One explained that the reverend was "pious, talented, eloquent, and zealous in his parochial duties" and that he was "one of the most engaging in every social assemblage of that then genteel, hospitable and populous neighborhood."[152]

Reverend Ellington was more than just a good minister. During his tenure the Goose Creek Bridge was razed so that a new one could be constructed. Many were not aware that the bridge was demolished, and upon traveling far, were forced to retrace their paths and traverse on poorly kept roads around the swamps at the head of Goose Creek. The detour was a considerable distance and the Reverend realized the great inconvenience the lack of a bridge caused many travelers. In response, he procured a flat boat, employed men to provide a ferry service and charged a fair crossing fee. When a wagon driver once complained that the fee was too high for the short ferry ride, the priest admitted that he had no authority to charge a fee as there was no act of the Legislature providing for it, but he reasoned also that he was under no obligation to provide the service. The customer begrudgingly paid but still murmured about the short crossing. A few days later, the same man returned and called for a crossing for his wagon and team. Ellington instructed his ferryman, who loaded the wagon and team and proceeded to pole the flatboat up and down the creek until the driver became quite irritated. When the rector called out to ask if he had gotten a long enough ride, the customer quickly agreed.[153]

Reverend Ellington resigned in 1793 and moved to Savannah, leaving the church without a minister for three years, when the Reverend Milward Pogson was elected. Pogson served until his resignation ten years later. As the husband of Miss Henrietta Wragg, he was well connected to an old and prosperous Charleston family and was the first minister ordained in the Diocese of South Carolina.[154] A humorous story about Reverend Pogson tells that the good father could not refrain from his favorite sport of fishing, even on Sundays. One Sunday morning while walking to church carrying his sermon under one arm and his fishing pole on his shoulders, he stopped on the bridge to test his luck. Upon hooking a large trout, he forgot his sermon and allowed the papers to slip into the water. He was unable to retrieve his sermon as it floated away leaving the minister with his trout but no message for his congregation.[155] Near that time, Charles Fraser drew a sketch of the St. James Church, viewed from the parsonage. It shows the church on a slight hill, northeast of the present road and gives evidence of an older road that, according to a Lowcountry custom, led directly to the church door. The sketch also shows a small vestry building where parish business was conducted and coachmen took shelter.[156]

Reverend Pogson's resignation was followed by the election of the Reverend John Thompson, but he served only two years before returning to England in 1801. The early decades of the nineteenth century witnessed the general decline of the parish and Thompson was the last minister to conduct regular Sunday services because many parishioners no longer remained year around. Additionally, the Church of England lost much of its appeal during the post war era.[157] Nevertheless, the vestry provided occasional church services, and supported the education of the children of needy parishioners during the nineteenth century and in these ways remained somewhat active.

In 1825, the Reverend C.P. Elliott, deacon, served as a missionary but became rector the following year. He reported that only four or five communicants lived in the area near the church among seven or eight families. He conducted services every second Sunday to his small congregation until he resigned a year later. Major Edward H. Edwards became church deputy in 1832. He and the vestry added to the treasury collecting $800 for rental of three acres of land to tenant farmers. The lease was transferred from one tenant to another until it reverted back to the vestry. This money, as well as a $500 gift from St. Michael's Church in Charleston, defrayed the expense of installing iron rods to bind the walls and strengthen the roof. Also, the interior was replastered and the roughcasting plaster on the outside was repaired.

As the surrounding forest grew, the Church became well hidden from public view and the target of vandals. Consequently, an 1844 contract repaired the Coat of Arms that was defaced when the lion's tail was stolen, and the beautiful SPG pelican and hatchlings were duplicated and replaced after much effort. Also, about this time, the pulpit stair railing was replaced, the flooring was re-laid and the pews were cut down to remove the rotting lower edges. Finally, the encroaching forest was cut away in 1845, at which time the vestry requested that the church be consecrated for the first time. The church had never been consecrated because a Bishop is required by canon law to perform the rite and there was no bishop in South Carolina during the colonial period.[158] After consecration in April of 1845, Reverend Philip Gadsden, Rector of St. Paul's, Stono and St. Paul's, Summerville provided services until he was replaced by Reverend J.W. Taylor.

Services continued throughout the Civil War and the congregation increased because of the hostilities. The Reverend L. Phillips was the minister of St. Stephen's Church on Anson Street in Charleston. The St. Stephens Church was shelled and greatly damaged by bombardment from the blockading Union Navy. At the suggestion of a member of St. James Church and with the bishop's approval, Reverend Phillips conducted seven services at the Goose Creek church. He also conducted seven services on the plantations for the slaves and baptized twenty-three Negroes. He believed the Goose Creek area was an excellent community for missionary work, but he provided services for only a short period before abandoning the Goose Creek mission.

During the Civil War, the church records and communion silver were lost, and during the turbulent post-war years the church was closed and not reopened until 1876. The Church was damaged considerably during the Reconstruction era and after, and the vestry stayed busy raising funds to repair the wear and tear from natural elements, malicious mischief and the earthquake of 1886.

Toward the end of the nineteenth century, the church was used intermittently, usually for special Easter services. Reverend Robert Wilson, D.D., rector of St. Luke's Church, Charleston, conducted an interesting service in April 1896. The church was filled with many old parish families to witness the dedication of a white marble tablet that was affixed to an interior wall and which reads:

St. James Parish, Goose Creek
Established by Act of Assembly
November 30th 1706.
Organized April 14th 1707.
First Church built about 1707.
Present Church built about 1713.

Church consecrated April 17th 1845.
RECTORS
Rev. Francis LeJau, D.D., 1707–1717.
Rev. Richard Ludlam, A.M., 1723–1728.
Rev. Timothy Millechamp, A.M., 1732–1748.
Rev. Robert Stone, A.M., 1749–1751.
Rev. James Harrison, A.M., 1752–1774.
Rev. Edward Ellington, A.M., 1775–1793.
Rev. Milward Pogson, 1796–1806.
Rev. John Thomson, 1806–1808.

For many occasions, the Atlantic Coast Line Railroad operated a charter train to carry Charlestonians to the old house of worship. Reverend Henry J. Mikell conducted a service with a large congregation in the spring of 1900. The attending vestry members that day were Dr. John Parker, Dwight Stoney, Dr. Joseph I. Waring and Samuel Stoney.[159] Another service was conducted in April 1904 to commemorate the arrival of the first SPG missionary, the Reverend Samuel Thomas. Colonel John P. Thomas, a descendant of the first missionary, delivered the address.[160] Two years later a service was conducted by the Bishop of the Diocese of South Carolina, the Right Reverend Ellison Capers, D.D., commemorating the 200th anniversary of the establishment of the parish of St. James, Goose Creek. At this time the Bishop dedicated a marble tablet in memory of Reverend Richard Ludlam. Two children, who were educated by the Ludlam fund, unveiled the memorial tablet in 1906 that was affixed to the interior wall of the church and read in part that Reverend Ludlam was "Zealous and faithful in the discharge of his Duties" and expressed appreciation for his generosity that educated so many children. Below the inscription appear the names of the wardens, Francis LeJau Parker and Samuel Parker Stoney; and of the vestry, Isaac Dwight Stoney, Joseph Ioor Waring, Samuel Gaillard Waring and Edwin Parsons.

The railroad was the most commonly used method of transportation to the church during the first decade of the twentieth century. Seven train coaches were used for the ride to Goose Creek in 1906 and on another occasion seven hundred people attended.[161] It was a pleasant ride by rail coach, and a short walk over the creek bridge from the Otranto Rail Station. Although, by 1925 the motor car replaced the train, the popularity of the annual service remained.

In 1909, the vestry was composed of Francis LeJau Parker, M.D., and S. Porcher Stoney, as wardens, with Samuel Gaillard Stoney, Joseph Ioor Waring, Edwin Parsons and Francis William Holmes as vestrymen. Professor Francis L. Holmes served on the vestry for many years. He owned Ingleside plantation, located a few miles from the church and was largely responsible for the maintenance of the building during the last decades of the nineteenth century.[162] During these years the church was badly damaged by an earthquake. The front section was destroyed and the walls were badly cracked when the east gable crumbled.[163] The quake also damaged one of the memorial tablets and the Royal Arms over the chancel was destroyed. Restoration began immediately, but the broken Royal Arms seemed impossible to restore until one recalled where a copy could be obtained. Years before, the daughter of Professor John McCrady painted a copy in oils for the use of the New England Historical Society. The painting was obtained, from which a replica was fashioned.[164]

Photograph 2.6 The photograph was taken near the beginning of the twentieth century. It shows discoloration around the front door caused by moisture. The photograph appeared in *Johnson's Scrapbook, Volume 1*, which is among the collections of the South Carolina Historical Society, Charleston, South Carolina.

By the turn of the century the church was in good repair. Through painstaking effort it was returned near to its original condition and appearance, but because forest fires were a threat, the shutters and doors were covered with iron and the roof with slate, which made it almost fireproof. The exterior of the church was again repaired because vandals marred the door with graffiti and carvings,[165] and it was repainted in 1931 in accordance with the sketch by Charles Fraser made 128 years earlier.

Today, access to the old structure is granted only under supervision, and a brick wall with an iron gate protects an intriguing churchyard. Inside the protective brick wall remains one of the oldest, most interesting and informative cemeteries in North America. It is much like an outdoor museum where a great store of local history, literature and art is preserved in the natural, outdoor setting. The Church and its cemetery are recorded on the National Register of Historic Places and thus protected. Consequently, many grave markers from other Goose Creek sites have been moved to this secluded and safer churchyard. Within the protective wall of the cemetery are twenty-seven graves, twenty-six of which are marked with tombstones. These grave markers contain large amounts of historical data with thirty-seven names of deceased parishioners inscribed on the stones. Other parishioners are buried on the grounds or inside the structure according to the memorial plaques affixed to the interior walls of the church. The Reverend LeJau is interred at the foot of the altar. Others, who died more recently are buried outside the protective cemetery wall.

Of the thirty-seven persons buried inside the protected cemetery with grave markers, twenty-one are male and sixteen are female. Three infants and three children are among the thirty-seven. The earliest death recorded by the inscriptions is that of Doctor Robert Broun, Esquire, who died in 1757. Mrs. Mary Mazyck, who died at the age of eighty-two years of age, appears to be the oldest parishioner interred. The tombstone data indicates the average male lifespan was thirty-eight years, and the average female was forty years of age. A visitor entering St. James Church cemetery through the iron-gate will find the testimonial stone to Thomas Bromley immediately to the right. Bromley was buried upon his request on Peter Manigault's Goose Creek estate known as "Steepbrook." Peter Manigault's grandson, Charles moved the stone to the house he purchased from William Drayton at 6 Gibbes Street, Charleston, probably in 1836. The stone remained there until the owner of 6 Gibbes Street, Mrs. F.G. Boggs, moved it to St. James Churchyard. The stone is so worn and weathered that the marble inscription is difficult to read.

Thomas Bromley was an attorney in Charleston and an Englishman by birth. He was a close friend of Goose Creek planter, Peter Manigault and died at Manigault's country home in Goose Creek from an "attack of fever" and was buried on the grounds.[166] Mrs. Manigault's diary stated simply that, "Mr. Bromley died." He was a man of wealth and good taste, and a bachelor who died without heirs. It appears from his epitaph that he enjoyed his friends and merriment (see appendix XII for the text of the memorial inscription and a translation of the Latin).

Standing near the stone of Thomas Bromley is the marker of Dr. Robert Broun. Dr. Broun was buried at St. James Chapel of Ease, which fell into ruin after the Revolutionary War. Dr. Broun's stone was later removed to the protection of the Goose Creek churchyard. William Senkler's infant child is buried next to Dr. Broun. Moving counterclockwise around the church, one finds the grave of Elizabeth Ann Smith. Mrs. E.A. Poyas wrote, "The husband [of Elizabeth Ann Smith] was then thirty four when he became a widower."[167]

Four grave markers were brought to Goose Creek from Windsor Hill, the home of the renowned Moultrie family. The grave marker for General and Governor William Moultrie may be found at St. James Church. General Moultrie was buried in an unmarked spot in the family graveyard at Windsor Hill Plantation. His grave was identified through the laborious efforts of the Huguenot Society of South Carolina and its president, the Reverend Canon Edward B. Guerry. William Moultrie was then re-interred at Fort Moultrie on Sullivan's Island. Most of the grave's remains, including parts of the coffin, are buried at St. James Church, but bone slivers of the General were interred at Fort Moultrie.

St. James, Goose Creek Chapels of Ease

There were two "chapels of ease" in the parish during the early colonial period. The parish was large, many of the people were widely scattered, and transportation was slow and difficult so that chapels were needed to accommodate parishioners living far from the parish church. An account of the Thomas Smith family traveling by road and water to reach the church explains some of the travail. They traveled from their home at Yeamans Hall by carriage until they arrived at the waters of Goose Creek. There they floated the horses and carriage over Goose Creek on a flat boat while the family crossed in a canoe. After arriving on the far side of the creek they traversed several remaining miles again by carriage.[168]

The chapels of ease provided conveniences for distant worshippers. One chapel was situated at Wassamasaw. Not much is known about the location of this little chapel except that it was probably close to a popular watering place for livestock near the present Wassamasaw Baptist Church and cemetery. Reverend Timothy Millechamp of St. James Church reported in 1736 that he administered the sacraments at the Wassamasaw Chapel because the village was too distant for the people to attend the Goose Creek Church. In 1759, Reverend James Harrison reported that he officiated at the Wassamasaw Chapel five or six times a year, and the Henry Mouzon Map published in 1775 depicts a Chapel at Wassamasaw. Today there are no recognizable remains or records that provide any description of the place. It may have been a temporarily arranged meeting house used from time to time for worship, or a small wooden or brick edifice that crumpled and overgrew.

Another chapel was located about seven miles south west of Strawberry Ferry and nearly seven miles from the Goose Creek Church. It was a brick building constructed in the shape of a cross. It was built sometime between 1721 and 1725.No extant record gives the date of construction, but one historian reported that a figure resembling "1721" appeared on one of the bricks and an early road record indicated that the chapel was standing in 1725.[169] Decades later, in 1785, John Deas, Aaron Loocock, Archibald Broun and John Deas Jr. acted as commissioners to receive one acre of land from George Chicken to be laid out in a square from the outside walls of the chapel. Later the property passed to Isaac Dubose. The 1788 plat by Joseph Purcell shows the chapel, in the shape of a cross, set east of the Road to Moncks Corner and south of the 23-Mile House Tract. The plat shows two paths leading from the Moncks Corner Road to the front door of the chapel.

Frederick Dalcho wrote in 1820 that the church had crumpled but that, "There are several tombstones around it; the oldest inscription upon them, that is legible, is 1757." Earlier unmarked

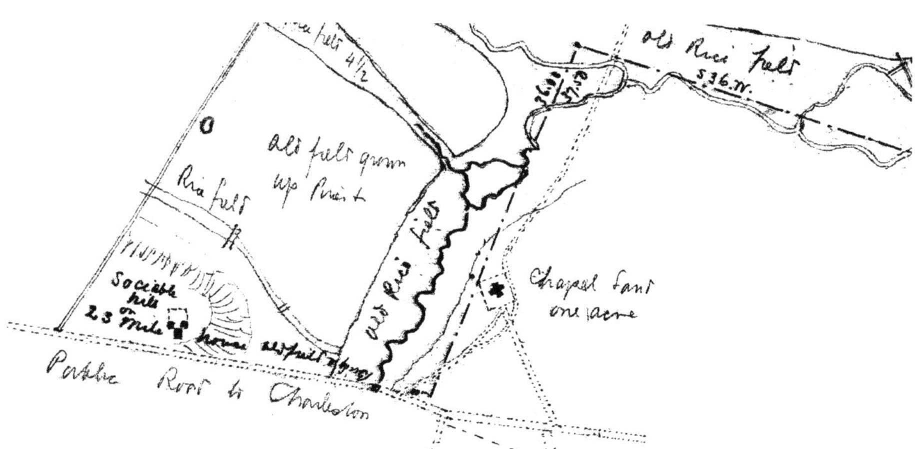

Plat 2.2 The partial plat shows the St. James, Goose Creek "Chapel of Ease" near the 23-Mile House on the Moncks Corner Road. The plat was drawn from a survey made by Joseph Purcell in 1788. Henry A.M. Smith traced the original. The tracing is in the possession of the South Carolina Historical Society, Charleston, South Carolina.

graves are probably situated there. It seems that some of the stones may have been stolen or destroyed. Judge Henry A.M. Smith reported near the turn of the twentieth century that the chapel was probably destroyed during the Revolutionary War but the Joseph Purcell plat shows it as late as 1788, five years after the Treaty of Peace that ended the war.

Today there are eighteenth- and nineteenth-century tombstones, as well as brick and stone box tombs. The Bethlehem Baptist Church was chartered in 1812 and was situated next to the chapel of ease for sixty-eight years. It was renamed "St. James Baptist Church" and "Goose Creek Baptist Church" before it was disassembled in 1888 and carted board by board from the chapel site to property donated to the church by the Groom's family 4½ miles away. The Baptist Church burial ground remains contiguous to the cemetery for the chapel of ease, making distinction between the two places difficult. Many cemetery stones remain among thick forest growth to this day. The grave markers bear the family names of McCullers, Broun (Revolutionary War Patriot), Loocock, Breaker, Readhimer (Revolutionary War Patriot), Lewis, Campbell, Motte, Broughton, Hough, Couch, Deas, Barclay, Hains, Browning, Shier, Haig, Walling and Lynes.

No one knows for certain what happened to the chapel, and there are few remnants from which to glean clues. Many of the scattered bricks were carried off so that when the site was visited by

Photograph 2.7 The photograph shows several cemetery markers at the sight of the St. James Chapel of Ease and Bethlehem Baptist Church in Strawberry. The photograph was taken March 20, 2002. *Author's collection.*

Photograph 2.8 The photograph shows the Groomsville Baptist Church after it was relocated to Groomsville from Strawberry. The twenty- by thirty-foot clapboard structure with six shuttered windows was disassembled, loaded on wagons and rebuilt on its present site in 1888. The photograph was taken June 9, 2005. *Author's collection.*

Mrs. Elizabeth Poyas in the mid 1800s she was unsure of the cause of destruction, but surmised that somehow it had accidentally burned down leaving little except tumbled bricks and cemetery grave markers. She also noted that the "Baptists have a neat wooden church adjoining the ruin, from which they have used a few bricks for their steps."[170] Another account recorded that the remains of John Deas were interred at the site and marked by an engraved stone and that his wife was buried by his side. Sadly, the ruins of the church were plundered some time in the early 1800s and someone stole the grave marker to use as a hearthstone in a nearby "cabin." Steps were never taken to recover it and it remains missing today.[171]

Today, earth covered mounds clearly form the outline of a cross with a north-south orientation that measures approximately thirty feet by thirty feet from each end. Each cross extension is fifteen feet wide and the cross extensions are of equal dimensions. The earthen mounds conceal whole and broken bricks buried under less than an inch of forest groundcover. Also, a neat stack of intact bricks nearby, and another less discernable stack twenty feet distant, are probably remains of two footings upon which the wooden Baptist Church once stood. That little twenty-by-forty-foot wooden structure stands reconstructed today on Groomsville Road.

Few ruins of the Chapel of Ease remain and even the historical highway marker has been removed from its long-standing place along old Highway 52. The lost marker once read:

GOOSE CREEK CHAPEL

HERE STOOD THE CHAPEL OF EASE
OF THE PARISH OF ST. JAMES, GOOSE
CREEK, ERECTED SOME TIME PRIOR
TO 1725.

The St. James, Goose Creek Church is a monument to the labor and love of the Carolinians for their land, families and friends. Economic forces and ravages of war caused the decline of the once prosperous community to the point that the church lost much of its usefulness. Nevertheless, a strong sense of pride for the old house of worship remains and the annual services provide a unique experience in timelessness. The early missionaries left their homes and cast their lots with the frontiersmen in the Carolina wilderness. These ministers were not the dregs of the Anglican Church, but in most cases, were men of learning and ability. Of the eight rectors of the church, one was a canon of St. Paul's Cathedral and earned the Doctor of Divinity degree. Five others earned A.M. degrees.

The country church meant much to the people of Goose Creek during the colonial period because it was more than a place of worship, it was also the political and social center of the parish. Voting was conducted at the church and because it was the established church of the colony, it promoted a

Photograph 2.9 The photograph shows the Izard hatchment displayed on the face of the St. James, Goose Creek Church balcony. The hatchment indicates the importance of the church community to the Izard family and the dedication of the family to the church. The photograph was taken March 20, 2002. *Author's collection.*

strong spirit of loyalty to constituted authority. Sunday was eagerly awaited because it was the day to see neighbors and friends. On Sunday mornings before the service, men gathered near the front door to discuss crops, politics and the latest horse race. During recess between morning and evening prayers, a mid-day meal was enjoyed in picnic fashion beneath the live oak trees nearby. During the mid-1700s, there were often more communicants at the Goose Creek Church than at St. Philips Church in Charleston, but when the trials of the Revolution approached, the patriotic spirit of the American cause stirred the church patrons and divided the membership. The war and the depressed economy that followed steadily reduced the community's wealth and the congregation's numbers until the church fell into disuse after the Civil War. Today the sanctuary is seldom used and mostly ignored, but it remains a monument to the Goose Creek community and a reminder of the spiritual forces that bound families together during the heady colonial era.

Chapter III
Education and Schools
1670–1900

Liberty cannot be perceived without a general knowledge among the people .
—John Adams, second president of the United States

Many Goose Creek settlers were well educated and promoted moral and cultural improvement for themselves and their children soon after they arrived in the Carolina wilderness. There is evidence that literacy was common among many professionals, government leaders and others living in Goose Creek during the colonial period, but there were few schools. The small number of schools during the seventeenth, eighteenth and nineteenth centuries reflected the long standing belief that public education was a charitable gift and that private tutors and private schools were expected to provide the bulk of formal instruction for those who could afford the luxury. Consequently, there was occasional public instruction for poor children scattered throughout the parish, but no public school buildings were erected in Goose Creek until well into the twentieth century and the few private school houses that were erected were church-based and small.

At first, education in Goose Creek had little to do with schools, teachers or books. The earliest instruction for frontiersmen came from Native Americans who taught valuable lessons in hunting, farming, fishing and survival. The father, as head of the household, was responsible for learning frontier lessons and passing them to the boys in the family. Unlike Europe, however, the frontier family was nuclear without extended kinships, because the large extended families were divided by the voyages to the new world. Consequently, the apprentice instructional system provided by many generations of extended families in Europe was left behind in the old world. In addition to the effects of the frontier and the nuclear family, the nature of Goose Creek society greatly influenced the style of education. Goose Creek supported a plantation society that existed without a town center and without centrally located children. It was not practical to establish community schools. Also, most plantations were large, self-sufficient and connected with poor roads and narrow paths. The rivers and creeks provided the most efficient means of transportation and communication, but the parish was sprawling and many settlers lacked access to water transportation. Thus, public schools in Goose Creek remained impractical until the twentieth century. But, the same water system that provided conveniences for some in Goose Creek also made the private schools and tutors in Charleston accessible to the wealthy planters. Because many planters were also Charleston merchants with town houses, it was convenient to educate children there.

From approximately 1730, Charleston boasted a number of private schools for boys and girls of all ages. Charleston provided experienced teachers of language, mathematics, music, dancing and other "polite arts." According to a study of the *South Carolina Gazette*, more than four hundred advertisements relating to schools and schoolmasters appeared in Charleston from 1732 to 1774.[172] Another study identified the myriad subjects offered and the schoolmasters and mistresses who offered their services. According to these studies, students could find coursework in the classic subjects of Latin and Greek as well as the typical curriculum in reading, French and History, but many teachers advertised instruction in fine arts and crafts such as needlework, dance and embroidery, as well as utilitarian course work in bookkeeping, navigation and surveying.

In lieu of sending children to Charleston private schools, the English practice of employing tutors became common among some large planters. A tutor typically resided at Medway Plantation, as well as the old Goose Creek plantation, now known as Yeamans Hall. John Parker, the rich Goose Creek planter who resided at the Hayes plantation, advertised in the *Royal Gazette* for a schoolmaster "who can teach the English Language grammatically."[173] The tutors were usually expected to perform multiple duties, such as keeping the estate accounts, in addition to teaching the children of the household. In a few instances, private schoolhouses were erected. An excellent example is found at Medway. Today, there is a charming little one-room schoolhouse near the plantation home and shown in photograph 3.1, but it is impossible to determine how many children received education at such schools. A plantation school site was a reasonable place for providing education in the rural environment but separate schoolhouses on the plantations in Goose Creek were rare. A part of the main house or the shade of an oak tree was more commonly used for instructional facilities.

During the colonial period, religion and education were inseparable. Consequently, the church facilitated education more than the family or the government. The absence of a town or community center, the isolation of the independent family units, and the gentile culture that evolved from the planter society, discouraged the promotion of public schools. Although there is much evidence that the Goose Creek planters were relatively well educated, the early church missionaries expressed concern about the ignorance of the general population and started schools to improve conditions. The prosperity and relatively dense population of the colonial parish of St. James, Goose Creek drew the attention and continual support of the SPG.[174] The SPG was established as an auxiliary to the Anglican Church and was active in promoting education in all of the southern colonies except Virginia.[175] Their work in Goose Creek resulted in the construction of a church, the appointment of a number of Anglican ministers, the hiring of the first schoolmaster and finally the construction of a church-supported schoolhouse.

The SPG based its missionary programs on the assumptions that education was inseparable from Christianity and that the development of the Negro slave was associated with the success of the master. Consequently, SPG missionaries felt obligated to instruct both races. This instructional principal provided African Americans their first step toward Christianity and literacy, which eventually led to the establishment of their own churches and institutions.[176] Reverend Samuel Thomas began teaching the Goose Creek slaves in 1695 and was so successful that, in ten years, he identified twenty black communicants able to read and write.[177] Some disapproved of his success. Thomas Nairne, an Indian agent, criticized Thomas as misguided and reported that, "All Carolina laughs" at his efforts to convert the "Goose Creek Negroes."[178] Even a fellow church minister, Reverend Stevens, was critical

Photograph 3.1 The photograph, taken in January 1980, shows the one-room schoolhouse at Medway Plantation. *Author's collection.*

of Thomas' work. He wrote that he did not know of Negroes that were being instructed except by, "now and then preaching."[179] Stevens disapproved of the practice of allowing Negroes to possess books and reported unfavorably that the missionary had unwisely presented Bibles and prayer books to the slaves. He believed that the decision, as well as the expense, should be left to the master. In spite of the criticism, Thomas persevered and his early success with the slaves made the SPG aware that Negroes were able to learn quickly and convinced the society to continue the work.

The Reverend Francis LeJau succeeded Thomas. He expanded the missionary efforts, and from an early date expressed to the society the need for schools. He and his wife opened a school at their Goose Creek home where European, as well as African and Native American children were instructed. Contrary to the popular belief of the time, it became increasingly apparent to LeJau that many Negroes wanted education and were capable of learning quickly, but he faced many obstacles. In letters to the SPG, he complained that some masters feared that an educated slave would be rebellious. Thus, many planters refused to send their slaves for instruction but LeJau persevered. He provided weekly instruction to all slaves that were sent to him and he continued to work closely with many plantation masters to gain their trust. He suggested that slave masters choose intelligent male slaves to be trained by him as literate slave leaders. He also recommended that some servants devote themselves to book learning, while others might best be left to crafts and manual skills.[180] His novel idea of student selection based upon abilities was the forerunner to the academic "track" system that became a standard practice in American public schools two hundred years later. Additionally, according to LeJau, it was easier for the Africans to adopt European culture than it was for the Native Americans. He observed that the Native Americans remained aloof and did not respond willingly to instructional efforts.[181] He believed that the Africans more willingly followed directives of the master and thus were better students and that their rich African language and culture easily Americanized.[182]

Convinced that his educational program needed to expand, LeJau requested that the SPG send a schoolmaster to Goose Creek.[183] In 1710, Benjamin Dennis was appointed and arrived a year later but shortly after his arrival Dennis broke his thighbone and became ill. Nevertheless, by 1712 progress was made toward establishing a school. Dennis reported that year that he was well, and accomplished the "tedious work" of establishing a school where he instructed "eighteen scholars, four of which are blacks."[184] Dennis' school served Negro, Native American and Caucasian children. By the end of the first year his enrollment increased to twenty-nine scholars, and the following year his class increased by one.

The Goose Creek schoolmaster received an annual salary of £20 from the SPG and he was supplied with a collection of books including prayer, grammar and reading primer books, as well as "Testoments" [*sic*] and a copy of *Dr. Talbot's Christian School Master.*"[185] Dennis taught his pupils grammar, reading and simple arithmetic, but the bulk of his instructional time was used for teaching the principles of Christianity. The Yemassee War interrupted his success and the school was closed in 1715 when Benjamin Dennis joined the hastily assembled force to defend the province. Later that year, Lieutenant General James Moore discharged him from this service, and Dennis reopened the school with only four pupils.[186] He wrote to the SPG a month later that six more scholars had arrived, but that the trauma of war caused many to move to Charleston for protection. He asked permission to also go to Charleston to teach more pupils and provide greater service to the children, but his request was denied.[187]

Reverend LeJau was worried about the lack of education of the adults, as well as the children and was especially concerned about religious dissenters. To counter the work of the dissenters, he requested that the SPG send "some writings tending to confound atheists and freethinkers," which he received from England several months later. Among the works were several orthodox texts including Cardinal Thomas Wolsey's research countering atheism, as well as studies debunking Deism, "natural" religion and a translation of *Grotius De Veritate.* The Baptists in Goose Creek were few but increasingly worrisome to LeJau. He described the Baptists as "cunning and artful… dangerous only to the ignorant." In light of his gravest concerns, he considered education to be the best vehicle for "true" religious guidance and defense of the colony but few educational advances were accomplished.

All earlier attempts to legislate educational support were failures or meager at best. A law passed in 1695 provided that poor children could be "bound out" as apprentices in order to learn a trade, and become productive citizens.[188] A 1710 Act provided that various bequests, made for the establishment of a free school, be placed under the control of a board of trustees. That act empowered the trustees to build a school and employ a master capable of teaching Latin, Greek and the "useful parts" of mathematics but although the able Doctor LeJau served as a trustee, little was accomplished.[189] Two years later, the Act of 1712 recognized that Benjamin Dennis was specifically in need of financial aid and in support of his work in Goose Creek the legislature set his salary at £100 annually, but the Act of 1712 was much more comprehensive than previous educational laws.

The new law provided that twelve pupils be admitted free of tuition and required others to pay £4 a year. It set a new course of study, which was a progressive change from the traditional Latin grammar programs and was similar to the later academies. This law required the schoolmasters to teach Latin and Greek, and an usher to teach writing, arithmetic and business accounting. The usher's salary of £50 was also paid out of public funds.

Additionally, the Act of 1712 authorized the vestry in each parish to use as much as £12 from public funds to build a schoolhouse and £10 per year to supplement the master's salary.[190] The law also granted the vestry of St. James Church the authority to nominate two or more persons to be overseers of the poor of the parish and to apprentice impoverished youngsters until they became of age. The Act of 1712 appears to have been well conceived for the times, but in actuality it provided few additional educational benefits in Goose Creek because it perpetuated the common belief that public schools were charitable institutions. Schools for the poor were never successful because of the stigma of accepting charity.

Nine years later, the Act of 1721 established a judge for the St. James, Goose Creek Parish at Wassamasaw and empowered him to set qualifications for schoolmasters and to pay the schoolmasters £25 annually. The judges were empowered to select ten poor students to be taught free of charge. This act assigned schools to Wassamasaw and Goose Creek, but no money was allocated to build schoolhouses. A year later, another act gave the justices authority to purchase land, erect free schools and assess the property and slaves in each parish for the support of its schools but to no avail.[191] Seven years later, however, in 1728, Landgrave Thomas Smith of Yeamans Hall contributed forty acres of land for the use of a free school in Wassamasaw. He named Isaac Porcher, Cornelius Dupre, Francis Cordes and Abraham Dupont as school trustees. Other Goose Creekers, such as William Adams, Isaac Porcher, Roger Saunders, Cornelius Dupre, Peter Porcher, Abraham Dupont and Francis Cordes made financial contributions to pay a schoolmaster.[192] School sessions began in Wassamasaw, but no schoolhouse was erected.

Colonial South Carolina did not enact laws to establish schools for all children, such as was done in New England, and because class lines were distinctly drawn, the children of the rich and poor were never expected to attend the same institutions. Consequently, the efforts of the South Carolina Assembly to advance literacy followed class distinctions. The General Assembly passed the first library procedural rules in North America. Anyone could check out a book, but was required to deposit three times the book's value to guarantee its timely return. Thus, only those with money to spare could legally check out a library book. Regardless of the strict checkout rule the system failed. The rules were not enforced and the books in the St. James, Goose Creek Parish library (St. James Church Rectory) disappeared. By 1720, there were no parish libraries in operation in the colony and the General Assembly made no further efforts to establish more.[193]

Early in the eighteenth century, there were approximately one thousand residents in the St. James, Goose Creek Parish. Education was meager, but because of generous contributions from individuals, Goose Creek led the colony in providing free instruction.[194] In 1728, Goose Creek Pastor, Reverend Richard Ludlam died.[195] He bequeathed all of his estate to the SPG in trust, "for erecting and maintaining a school for the instruction of the poor children of this parish."[196]

Fourteen years later no school was standing, but more than £5,927 was collecting interest at 10 percent annually, and there were unsold lands that could add to this total. Still there was not enough to build a school and maintain it, so the money remained invested while the vestry solicited more contributions. In 1744 another solicitation effort garnered £2,220 in pledges from 56 parishioners. These parishioners promised varying amounts of money over a three-year period with eleven parishioners promising up to £300. A total of £6,660 was promised toward the construction of a schoolhouse. Appendix XIII shows the narrative of the circulated paper, the names of the parishioners and the promised contributions.

The list of contributors appears as a "Whose Who" list of the parish in 1744. William Middleton of the Oaks, Peter Taylor of Bloomfield, Zachariah Villeponteaux of Parnassus, Benjamin Mazyck of Howe Hall, John Parker of the Hayes and Henry Izard of the Elms were a few of the Goose Creekers on the distinguished list. Still no schoolhouse was erected, and only small amounts of progress were made through the years.

Twelve years after the solicitation drive, Reverend James Harrison informed the Society that the subscription for the schoolhouse was raised; land bought and bricks made and Reverend Harrison urged the Society to continue its work toward erecting a school. Progress was slow. Nine years later, in 1765, Rev. Harrison again wrote to the Society to transmit the accounts of Reverend Ludlam's legacy. Harrison informed the Society that the parish amassed £200, which the vestry promised to contribute if the Society consented to the vestry plan for supervising the teacher, the curriculum and assessing the effectiveness of the program. The SPG consented and a successful church school opened with this arrangement.[197] Adding to the support of the Goose Creek school was a bequest from Peter Taylor in 1765. He gave the vestry £100 for the erection and maintenance of a school after his death. His bequest was held at interest for a school to educate the poor children of the parish.

The vestry was incorporated in 1778 to execute the trust left by the last will and testament of Reverend Ludlam.[198] Reverend Harrison was leaving the parish and submitted all the accounts belonging to the Ludlam Fund to the vestry. At that time the account had a total of £15,272 and 2 shillings but the fund had depreciated considerably during the Revolutionary War. The British damaged properties, and valuable slaves were stolen, but enough money remained in the account to erect a brick schoolhouse. The date of the construction is unknown, but Henry Smith visited the schoolhouse site and observed its ruins near the end of the nineteenth century and reported that the brick schoolhouse was built sometime between 1765 and 1770. He noted that the site was, "about a mile to the north-east along the road that passes in front of the church."[199]

A second schoolhouse was erected approximately thirty years later. Henry Smith recorded in his notes that land was purchased and a "red brick" schoolhouse was erected about 1800. [200] In 1814, Mrs. Rebecca Smith bequeathed a legacy to Reverend Benjamin Tyler, schoolmaster of the "Ludlam School," but her generosity was insufficient to keep the school open.[201] The church membership declined after the Revolutionary War and in spite of individual efforts and generosity, the school was sold in 1828 to Charles Graves.[202] Afterward, the building was used for a dwelling and remained standing as late as 1852. It later fell into ruin and was overgrown with bushes and trees but the foundation could be traced during the first decade of the twentieth century.[203] According to a plat drawn in 1888, a school stood in the proximity of the church, at the intersection of Snake and Red Bank Roads. This is probably the site of the school built circa 1765–80 and probably on the twelve-acre school tract given by Henry

Middleton for "a twig and a turf." Today, that school site is opposite the Goose Creek Rural Fire Department.[204]

During the nineteenth century, the State of South Carolina augmented the St. James Church vestry's efforts to provide free education throughout the parish. In 1811, an *Act to Establish Free Schools Throughout the State* provided educational opportunities in the parish on an intermittent and limited basis for the next 55 years. In accordance with the 1811 Act, the people of the St. James, Goose Creek Parish were entitled to three school commissioners. The law required that the number of school commissioners be equal to the number of members sent to the House of Representatives from each election district. The primary elements of reading, writing and arithmetic were imparted in these schools. Any child was entitled to attend free of tuition, but in case of an overload, preferences were always given to orphans or children of poor parents. Preference to the poor in the 1811 Act doomed the plan to failure. During the tenure of the law, those with resources used private schools and the poor generally refused to accept the stigma that came with the receipt of charity.

The year after the 1811 Act, the St. James, Goose Creek School Commissioners petitioned the General Assembly for authorization to "bind out" as apprentices any children educated by schools "erected for the poor."[205] This petition states that schools were to be "erected." The commissioners probably envisioned that schools would eventually be built, but there is no evidence of public school construction at that time.

School commissioners were appointed by the legislature to serve three-year terms and to oversee the schools in each district. The commissioners appointed teachers, scheduled the time and place of instruction, reported to the legislature and petitioned the General Assembly annually for school funds.[206] The commissioners received an annual state allocation of $300 per school, which was used to employ teachers at the salary of $25 a month and to provide periodic instruction throughout the parish.[207] Both men and women were employed to teach and one, James P. Hughes accumulated a $2,000 estate after instructing more than twenty years.[208] The teachers changed locations during the year and from year to year, to provide educational opportunities to varying sections of the parish. Most school terms spanned three to six months at any one location, but a few schools stayed in session from nine to twelve months. Class size varied widely with enrollments ranging from one to thirty-nine students.[209]

The commissioners oversaw as many as thirty-nine school sites that spanned from Four Hole Swamp in the western section, Wassamasaw in the central, to Groomsville and Goose Creek in the eastern sections of the parish. Some schools were reported by name, and an identification number accounted for others. This reporting practice and the fact that some commissioners used similar identifying names on the reports such as, Targate, Target, Tarhill and Tarkiln, may have led to errors. These four names may refer to the same school or to four different locations resulting in more or fewer than thirty-nine different sites. Regardless of the interpretations of the reports, it is evident that the sites were many, changed often and rarely remained at the same place two consecutive years. Public schoolhouses were not constructed but various buildings were used instead. For example, the Gasquette Meeting House was used in 1836 and in 1856, a chapel, a church and a building, which was formerly a tavern, were used.[210] The number of students served annually varied widely as well. The St. James, Goose Creek Parish served sixty-five children in three schools in 1829, and sixty-six students in two schools in 1831,[211] but nine years later there were only twenty-seven children attending one school.[212]

The state legislature provided oversight of the Ludlam money and in 1827 school commissioners were appointed to investigate the status of the fund and to determine the amount of money available for educating poor children.[213] As a result, the church vestry decided to establish two schools, one in Groomsville in the lower part of the parish, and the other at Wassamasaw Chapel.[214] Two schoolmasters were employed at $300 annually, the same as public school teachers and students were usually if not always from poor families. During this time one visitor to the Groomsville School noted that a young teacher was employed to instruct, "a few scholars from the lower class."[215] The other church school at Wassamasaw was established on 40 acres of land donated by Landgrave Thomas Smith a hundred years earlier.[216] The school was located in the same vicinity as the Wassamasaw Chapel of Ease where the Wassamasaw Baptist Church is situated today.

Bernard E. Bee, Chairman of the Goose Creek vestry, submitted a report to the state legislature in accordance with the Act of 1827. His interesting report explained that the two vestry schools, one at the central and one at the lower part of the parish, were so located partly because the state's free schools were all situated in the upper parish and by arranging the church schools as they were, all parish sections could be served. He explained that the schools operated with "respectable teachers," and the vestry was satisfied with school results, but was disappointed with some parents who failed to send their children regularly. Eighteen children attended the lower school at Groomsville of which nine who attended regularly, could write legibly and were advanced in arithmetic. Twelve of the sixteen students assigned to the central school at Wassamasaw attended regularly but others attended "scarcely at all." Those who attended regularly progressed well and could read the Testament, United States History and other literature. They learned grammar and advanced arithmetic, including compound subtraction. Interestingly, the vestry report expressed their desire to continue operating the schools from the same two locations, rather than moving from place to place each session as the legislature preferred. Chairman Bee explained "no other possible good could come from a traveling school than that of spreading the knowledge of the alphabet over the parish." He asked permission to remain at least five years in the same location.[217]

The vestry made annual reports to the legislature after 1843, explaining the appropriate use of the Ludlam money. Caswell Hart, Ellis Shuler, James Wiggins, J.B. Rhame, W.S. Sineath and William Whaley were parish school commissioners during this period.[218] In 1847, the vestry elected trustees to supervise their schools, but because they provided inadequate oversight, the Reverend C. Wallace was asked to review operations. As a result, he recommended instructional changes and new books. According to Wallace's report, William Waterland, a teacher at the Wassamasaw School, was progressive in at least one instructional area. He made a particular point of teaching English grammatically, and it seems that he was the first to do so in America.[219]

In the 1840s, '50s and '60s the state commissioners and church vestrymen continued to coordinate their educational resources to serve as many children as possible, but in spite of their best combined efforts, some residents regularly traveled to schools in Charleston that they believed better served their children. This practice became so common that a number of citizens petitioned the general assembly in 1846 to ask that they be excused from paying the toll on the State Road.

They claimed that they traveled frequently to Charleston due to "poor health and educational facilities," in Goose Creek.[220]

During the two decades leading to the Civil War, the Goose Creek vestry managed to educate approximately 20 percent of the children in the parish. In 1850, six schools served 203 students with enrollments ranging from 25 to 30 students per school.[221] Two of these schools housed only girls and two were operated and funded entirely by the Goose Creek vestry. Four years later, ten schools were operating but beginning in 1854, schools were listed as either free or assisted. Six of the ten schools were "assisted," which meant that partial tuition was provided, but each student was expected to pay four dollars a quarter, which removed some of the stigma associated with charity.

Beginning in 1854, the vestry used Ludlam's money to help some students pay tuition and by the end of that decade, the vestry paid $200 to the St. James Academy for the purpose of sending twelve scholars tuition-free.[222] The St. James Academy was public and the only academy in the parish during this period and thus the only place where post elementary instruction was available in the parish. In 1859, the parish schools served 244 children with 192 attending state-supported schools and 52 attending church supported schools.

During these years the Goose Creek vestry usually supported two schools. They paid the annual teaching salaries and expended a little more than twenty dollars yearly for supplies at each facility.[223] For many years during these decades, George C. Smith taught 20 to 30 students each term in the Wassamasaw School, sometimes referred to as the "upper school," and Henry Nichols taught 20 to 30 scholars at the Groomsville School sometimes known as the "lower school."[224] At the end of the decade (1859), 225 students attended schools in the parish. Church-supported elementary schools served 40 children and 72 children attended one of the four public elementary schools. One academy instructed 35 students and three high schools served 78 students.[225]

During the 1860s, the vestry continued to use the $14,531 of Ludlam money to support its programs. The vestry invested the money in bank, railroad and stock shares to maintain their church schools until the Civil War. The number of church schools expanded from two to three during this time and they continued to pay tuition for needy parish youth to attend the academy. The vestry educated fifty-seven scholars in 1860 including nineteen scholars at Thorogood School, sixteen at Wassamasaw School, ten at Groomsville School and twelve students were sent to the St. James Academy. The 1860 report is the only mention of the school at Thorogood, suggesting that it operated for only a brief period.[226]

Efforts were made during the decades after the Civil War to retrieve some poorly managed church money and use it for school support. Isaac W. Hayne, the South Carolina Attorney General, reported in 1854 that the state had proceeded against Bernard Bee to recover money borrowed by him from the Ludlam Fund.[227] General Bernard Bee gave 4,605 acres of land in the Milan Land District in Texas to the vestry for payment of a bond debt of $3,379 borrowed by him from the Ludlam Fund.[228] During the confusion of the Civil War, much of his Texas land was taken by settlers or was confiscated for taxes. In 1873, the vestry attempted, but was unable to recover the property. Consequently, they retained a legal firm in Texas. A large portion of land was recovered in 1882, but after paying legal fees equal to one half of the value of the land, the church received only $5,000, which was invested in the Ludlam Fund.[229]

The vestry eventually stopped its support of the church schools, but continued to use the Ludlam money as intended. Children received tuition assistance after 1872. Some students received Ludlam money to attend Porter Academy, Pinopolis Academy, The Confederate Honor College and Union College. Union College was in Schenectady, New York but the other schools were local. Such scholastic assistance continued until 1925.[230]

The free school system of education that began in 1811 ended shortly after the close of the Civil War, when the state governor vetoed the funds appropriated for the schools. At that time, the Federal Congress created the Bureau of Refugees and Freedmen and Abandoned Lands and charged it with the control of all matters relating to the welfare of the emancipated African Americans. Brigadier General Rufus Saxon was responsible for South Carolina during the Reconstruction era. He immediately undertook the "schooling for the blacks" and according to one source the, "freedmen themselves early evidenced a passionate longing for learning."[231] Unfortunately, the Freedmen's Bureau funds for education were so limited that private organizations were expected to recruit and pay teachers but no privately funded schools appeared in Goose Creek as they did in places such as Charleston, Aiken, Beaufort and Mt. Pleasant.[232]

Whites did not appear to oppose education of the emancipated blacks, but they were increasingly opposed to the type of education for the freedmen. They resented the northern teachers who used the classroom to "belittle the south, to preach social equality, and to instill ideas in Negroes that made for ill feelings between the races."[233] White opposition to education for Negroes was at first ineffectual and uncoordinated, but by 1867, due largely to the emergence of blacks as a political force, antipathy among the whites became widespread and aggressive. Assistant Federal Commissioners reported "an alarming increase" in "outrages" and crimes as a result of political tensions. Consequently, the opportunities enjoyed by black children who attended school for a few years following the war declined noticeably after 1867.[234]

Photograph 3.2 The photograph shows a one-room schoolhouse for Negro children in the vicinity of Highway 17A near Carnes Cross Roads in 1938. *Courtesy Library of Congress.*

In 1870, more than half of the population in the parish could not read and a larger number could not write.[235] This high percentage of illiteracy is understandable because the emancipated Africans were assessed for literacy for the first time. In spite of lifetimes of ignorance and illiteracy, the 1870 census indicated that many black children in Goose Creek attended school. All three of Isaac Brown's children attended. Isaac Brown was merely a farm laborer, but his children Ben, Frank and Moultrie attended school along with eight-year-old Bella Glover, Laura, Wesley and Henry Pringle and Jane, William, Nancy and Plenty Johnson. The census indicated that children attended lessons if they lived close enough to walk to school. No transportation was available and many resided too many miles from their lessons to attend at all.

The state's public schools received little political support after the Civil War because of the long-standing practice of the wealthy using private education, and the post-war burden of educating thousands of children of the emancipated blacks. Thus, public education became even more unpopular among the white political leadership and the meager system failed further. Trained staff became woefully rare. In the 1880s, citizen groups complained about the inadequacy of the public school system in Berkeley County and criticized low teacher salaries as one reason that few skilled educators remained.[236] The statewide situation was no better. Walter Edgar, state historian wrote, "Illiteracy was a scandal." By 1890, almost half of the state population older than ten years could neither read nor write.[237] Few schools and poorly trained teachers resulted in a deplorable state of public education in Goose Creek, as well as other Berkeley and South Carolina communities.

The State Constitution of 1895 sanctioned segregated schools. Article 2, section 7, stated that "Separate schools shall be provided for children of white and colored races, and no child of either race shall ever be permitted to attend a school provided for children of the other race." The tradition of private education for all but the poor, the forced emancipation of a race of South Carolinians that in many communities far outnumbered the whites and the resentment toward northern infringement into the school curriculum, eliminated any remaining political support for public schools. Shortly after the enactment of the constitution in 1895, the poll tax law that was used for many years to fund public education was repealed. Without this tax there was no reliable support for schools and public education in South Carolina disappeared. Consequently, the public system of education in Goose Creek remained wanting and relatively unchanged for almost a hundred years after the Civil War. The schools changed little until the 1950s and '60s when the Federal Civil Rights Laws were enforced. As a result, the enforcement of the progressive Civil Rights Laws along with an influx of people with new business interests and resulting prosperity lifted the public expectations for education in Goose Creek.

Chapter IV
Reconstruction and Beyond
1865–1900

The Emancipation Proclamation freed the slaves and spawned hope for thousands of Goose Creek African Americans, but the journey from bondage to full citizenship required another century of progress in humanity and civil rights. After the slaves were freed, the white establishment found ways to return black Goose Creekers to a status of servitude that made the pursuit of freedom a daily struggle for black Americans and a moral conundrum for white Americans. In response, the post–Civil War Federal Administration tried to reconstruct the South by enforcing constitutional amendments that freed the slaves and granted male suffrage, but southern white resistance to reforms prevented black Goose Creekers from fully contributing to the revitalization of the flawed society and broken economy. These failures greatly delayed rebuilding the political and social systems that had long been an anachronistic embarrassment to the southern states.

Goose Creek had long been an African American community. The proportion of black to white people shifted from time to time, but African Americans always comprised at least 70 percent of the population from the earliest frontier period until the last decades of the twentieth century. Black Goose Creekers made their contributions in bondage during the first two hundred years, as small farmers for the next century, and finally, during the most recent four decades, in partnership with the white community. Because black and white Goose Creekers were not acculturated during the decades following the Civil War, the differences between the two groups remained distant. But, in spite of the failure of the political and economic system to unify the races in the struggle against common obstacles, it was a time of personal triumph for many black Goose Creekers who continued to suffer discrimination, but enjoyed more control over their personal destiny than during any previous period. In contrast, this was a time of uncertainty for white Goose Creekers who attempted to rebuild the failed, but familiar political system of the pre-war era.

The problems of post-war Goose Creek were formidable. The economy was crippled, the infrastructure was destroyed and thousands of emancipated African Americans sought their place in a new social order that offered few employment opportunities. The brick and lumber industries ceased operations during the Civil War and the conflict destroyed agriculture.[238] Farm production diminished to a small fraction of what it had been before hostilities. Most of the fields lay fallow, 60 percent of the livestock were missing and much of the agricultural tools and infrastructure, such as plows, wagons and barns were stolen or destroyed. The emergence of non-agricultural employment opportunities and the return of productive farmers to the land required the revival of business, capital investments, and the timely repair of the infrastructures, but immediate improvement was hopeless because the bridges and roads that were essential to economic revival were all destroyed or greatly damaged.

Confederate forces destroyed the Goose Creek Bridge by fire to slow Federal troop movements. The Union Army rebuilt it with loblolly pine saplings that soon decayed, so that shortly after the conflict, the bridge was no longer reliable. In addition to the Goose Creek Bridge, all of the major overpasses along the State Road, including the ones over Wassamasaw Swamp, Dean Swamp and Sandy Creek needed extensive repair or replacement. The Goose Creek Road Commissioners complained that the State Road had fallen into such ill repair that it was impassable in many places and to further exacerbate the situation, use of railroads caused the toll system to be "unproductive." Consequently, the commissioners fumed that the state unfairly and unrealistically expected the Goose Creek people to effect the needed renovations without sufficient funding or available workforces. John F. Poppenheim, Chairman of the Goose Creek Road Commission, complained that the white population had mostly immigrated outside the parish leaving only a few scattered and impoverished farmers to shoulder the expensive responsibilities, and available road crews were too lightly manned to accomplish the extensive repairs.[239]

Federal financial aid could have repaired the infrastructure and stimulated agricultural production by improving the vital links between the farms and markets, and federal money could have infused much-needed dollars into the stagnant economy, but desperately needed assistance never arrived. Furthermore, the economy was weakened by the development of "sharecropping" and "crop lien" systems of finance. These systems emerged because soon after the war hard-pressed creditors began demanding interest and principal payments on mortgages. As a result, many indebted farmers were forced to sell tracts of land in order to finance cultivation of the remaining acres or to lease their land to tenant farmers or sharecroppers. Under the tenant and sharecropping systems, land was not sold, but divided into many smallholdings, resembling little farms, but actually remaining parts of single plantations. These transitions caused a drastic shift in land use and ownership resulting in many Goose Creekers becoming renters and landowners for the first time. It also resulted in extremely wasteful and damaging use of the topsoil, because small plots were productively inefficient and could not realistically support proper crop rotation or erosion controls.

Jim Crow and the KKK

The pre-war, white-dominated society was lost forever, but nevertheless white southerners sought the return of the social and political order that was stripped away. One way to return to the previous order was through the use of the state legislature. The white leadership enacted laws designed to return the African American to a subservient position. These laws were referred to as "black codes" and were given a moniker that referenced a popular minstrel show character called "Jim Crow." The so-called "Jim Crow" laws appeared to be racially neutral, but in reality were designed to suppress black citizens. To many, the white actors in the minstrel shows who painted their faces black represented the new codes that appeared equitable, but were based on racial disguise. The Jim Crow laws appeared in the South Carolina Constitution of 1865, which failed to give blacks the right to vote and imposed racial qualifications to serve in elected office.

Blacks wielded no political means to counter the Jim Crow laws, one of which required "persons of color" who came into the state to enter into a work bond with two free holders. Thus, bondage similar to slavery was required for all new "colored" immigrants. Additionally, the law required servants to never leave the free holders premises without the permission of the "master," and to assist "their masters in the defense of their own person, family or property." Additionally, no person of color could become an artisan, mechanic or shopkeeper unless he obtained a license from the judge of the district court that cost a hundred dollars or more. Consequently, as a result of the 1865 State Constitution, black Goose Creekers found their status similar to their servitude condition prior to the Civil War. In response, the United States Congress passed the Reconstruction Acts in 1867 to counter the post war arrangement in South Carolina and other southern states and to force the south to reform into more equitable societies.

The Reconstruction Acts created military districts, protected voter registration, and allowed political conventions to pass new state constitutions. The progressive South Carolina Constitution enacted by the black political conventions of 1867 and 1868 included the fourteenth amendment, which enfranchised both races and thus provided for universal adult male suffrage. It also established segregated public schools, social welfare programs, increased property taxes with exemptions for small landowners, and a homestead provision that prevented land seizure because of debt. After the conventions, the state legislature ratified the new state constitution and the fourteenth amendment to the Federal Constitution, which allowed the State of South Carolina to soon be readmitted to the United States of America. South Carolina rejoined the union with a majority of African American voters and a black majority of Representatives in the State House who soon enacted additional state laws to extend the newfound freedoms and rights, which included the creation of the South Carolina Land Commission to fairly distribute acreage to the newly freed farmers.

A progressive labor contract system was established in South Carolina under the influence of the Reconstruction Government, the South Carolina Land Commission and the Freedmen's Bureau. This labor contract arrangement allowed an African American to "have land, and turn it and till it by their own hands." African Americans also gained the right to end contracts and establish new agreements with other plantations. As a result, the African Americans in South Carolina enjoyed more freedom and rights than ever before, which caused grave fears and concerns among the white population. Nonetheless, the federal lawmakers felt little sympathy for the defeated white rebels, and sent army officers south, not to protect the whites, but to keep the new order and enforce the new rights and freedoms for all South Carolinians.

Under the provisions of the Reconstruction Act, the defeated southern states were divided into five military districts. South Carolina was assigned to District 2, under the command of General Daniel E. Sickles. Captain F.W. Liedtke was assigned to oversee the people of Goose Creek. Captain Liedtke's primary responsibility was to assess the labor contracts that existed between landowners and farm workers in order to ensure that the working relationship complied with the new state constitution. He was also expected to settle disputes and deliver aid and support where needed, but the conditions in Goose Creek greatly challenged him. Captain Liedtke was gravely concerned with starvation and disease that wracked the moribund society. He reported that smallpox was so pervasive that it "interferes with planting" and that the people were so unclean and "careless in their habits," that he did not expect the conditions to improve.[240] The dire situation was evident at

Parnassus Plantation where after emancipation the slave settlement degraded into chaos. A brief period of celebration ensued after which, most workers wandered off and those that remained perished from disease and starvation. The returning son of the landowner found the slave village deserted except the remains of one poor elderly man who had been left behind to die. His body was found in the empty "potatohouse," wracked with small pox, decimated from starvation and "in his hands were a few stringy roots he had gnawed at."[241] Within a year the main house at Parnassus burned to the ground.[242]

Such scenes were not uncommon in Goose Creek and Captain Liedtke pleaded with the white landowners during these confused times to provide food and care to the emancipated workers and thus continue some aspects of the paternalistic relationship that existed prior to emancipation. Liedtke was especially worried about the freed workers who left the land and thus could no longer rely upon the security typically provided by the white landowner. The "peculiar institution" of slavery, with the responsibilities of the master to the slave and visa versa, persisted somewhat after emancipation when some planters advanced available foodstuffs to starving workers in exchange for their labor. Other landowners resisted the new social order causing unnecessary suffering and distrust. One Goose Creek landowner, who abandoned his Spring Grove Plantation for the relative safety of Charleston, wrote that the "whole moral character of the people have changed." He complained about the "lazy Negroes from the countryside," but he also accused members of his race as being "old fogeys, crowing about things that will never happen," because the "old things have passed away and all things are new." He continued, "The people here are worse than Yankees...everyone for himself and for nobody else."[243] Where the emancipated African and the white landowner refused to agree upon some sort of work arrangement, the fields remained unplanted and harvests ungathered. In these cases, bitterness grew and lawlessness prevailed, spawned from fear, cruelty and desperation.[244]

Examples of lawlessness and disorder in Goose Creek were common and exemplified the challenges faced by military reconstruction officers. Ely Faulk, a white man, entered into a heated quarrel with Peter Marang, a black man, at the Mt. Holly rail station over two missing barrels of turpentine that belonged to Faulk's employer. As the black man ran from the scene, Faulk fired two shots. The shots missed the target but the Goose Creek military officer brought charges against Faulk for firing the weapon and appealed to the magistrate for enforcement. The magistrate set a $500 bail until trial, but released Faulk upon the promise of his employer to pay the bail. Faulk left the area, the employer refused to pay, and the case never came to trial. Another incident occurred in Wassamasaw when John Wesley, a black man driving a heavily loaded wagon met Ann Fielder driving a light buggy on a narrow path. Both refused to let the other pass. The black wagoner was brought before P.M.C. Earnest, the brother of the female buggy driver and the white magistrate for the Wassamasaw area. The black man was locked in a Charleston jail for 2½ months without a trial, was never allowed to present witnesses and was released without a hearing. There were many instances of failed justice reported in Goose Creek during this period, suggesting a pattern of inequity when dealing with white on black crimes or black on white crimes.[245]

The unfair justice meted by some magistrates in Goose Creek resulted from the fury felt by most white leaders statewide. White Carolinians were not prepared to allow what they termed a "radical" system of governance. Many white Goose Creekers resisted the laws promising equity and freedom to blacks and refused to accept as legitimate, the government of South Carolina based upon the

1868 state constitution. White resistance grew and eventually personified as white controlled local law enforcement cadres. These white controlled bands appeared in the form of nightriders and vigilantes, and although no level of government authorized them, they became effective in advancing the political agenda of most whites in South Carolina.

One example of semi-organized resistance occurred near Carnes Crossroads. On the State Road, about five miles west of the Goose Creek Church was a tollgate situated near a house. During Reconstruction, a body of U.S. troops in route from Charleston to Columbia encamped in the field by the tollgate. They were awakened all night by occasional shots fired into their tents from different directions. Shanghai Riggs was responsible for the harassment of the Federal soldiers. Riggs was a six-foot, eight-inch tall man from the western part of the parish of who it was said, "you could not get him into the confederacy, but after he was captured and conscripted, you could not get him out of the Confederacy."[246] Later he organized the white men of his neighborhood into a band of nighttime raiders. One testimony claimed, "by his terror to the Negroes, he saved many-a-white family from destruction during the reconstruction period."[247] The Ku Klux Klan (KKK) grew out of this type of local fear and sadly, nightriders remained active in many southern communities during Reconstruction, and raids and rallies ensued in Goose Creek for another hundred years.

In response to the terror movement that spread throughout the state, the governor organized a state militia to counter the growing white insurgency. The whites countered with local hunting clubs that became well organized, well armed and effective enforcement arms of the political bodies known as "Democratic Clubs," which were organized to concert the white community against the federally supported "radical" black government. Club members resolved not to hire blacks associated with the new government and complained that radical black political party members kept many whites and blacks from voting at the southern polls. Nevertheless, emboldened by their freedom and supported by northerners, African Americans dominated politics until near the end of Reconstruction in 1877.

Political rallies were tumultuous during the years of Reconstruction and bitter feuds were common between Republicans (mostly black) and Democrats (mostly white), but nevertheless, South Carolina was readmitted to the Union in 1868 amidst the political turmoil. And within eight years after readmittance, the whites overcame black political control and elected their choice, Wade Hampton, as governor in 1876.

In September of that year, the *Charleston News and Courier* favored the white Democrats and reported on a political rally at Strawberry Landing near Goose Creek. Strawberry was a black Republican stronghold with approximately 650 black voters and 25 whites. The Republicans accepted a Democrat challenge at the podium, and large numbers of Republicans and Democrats met for the rally. The so-called "Radical Republican stronghold" was invaded by cheering Democrats, many of who steamed up the Cooper River from Charleston on the Ship M.S. Allison. Arriving on horseback to lend support to the outnumbered Democrats were members of the Hampton Social Mounted Club of Goose Creek, the Mt. Pleasant Mounted Club and the Goose Creek Cavalry. The Hampton Mounted Club consisted of 30 men under the command of Captain George M. Tharin. Major Huguenin commanded 25 mounted men from the Mt. Pleasant club, and Major Barker led the riders from Goose Creek. At the rally the mounted clubs were confronted with hundreds of bystanders and some people were armed with muskets, rifles, shotguns, swords and bayonets, but Major Barker,

Photograph 4.1 The photograph shows the general store at Wassamasaw. It was built in 1880. The photograph was taken in April 2003. *Author's collection.*

boldly instructed his riders to keep the peace and prevent anybody including any "colored" person from being intimidated.[248]

The newspaper report alleged that some black citizens desired to join the Democrats, but were threatened by the black Republicans and Major Barker's self assigned mission saved the day by protecting the black men who wanted to join the Democratic Party. The meeting at Strawberry was threatening with heated words by various speakers but the event culminated in a loud crash when the speaking platform collapsed. Fortunately, no injuries resulted from the crash and no riots ensued. Some contended that Barker was able to keep the peace because he had recently purchased 25 navy revolvers for his mounted men, making his band the most formidable force at the rally.[249]

Another formidable group in the parish was the Wassamasaw Mounted Club that was the enforcement arm of the Centennial Democratic Club of St. James, Goose Creek. The first meeting of this group occurred in September 1876, with C.W. Sanders as secretary and T.S. Browning as the Captain.[250] The mounted clubs provided a layer of government for a white population who felt disenfranchised and impotent during the Reconstruction Era and the clubs provided unofficial law enforcement by keeping the white communities armed and independent of the black Republican political party and state government. Photograph 4.1 shows the Wassamasaw General Store that was build during this period and where the club occasionally met.

Frequent political rallies occurred in Goose Creek during these decades as the white population struggled to reassert and then keep its dominance. One rally began as a typical debate, but erupted into a shouting match. The Charleston newspaper reported that a group of blacks appeared with clubs and a few guns, which they had hidden in an old abandoned house. The news account may not have told both sides of the story but a riot did erupt, during which many people were injured and a few died. As such events became more commonplace throughout the state, Republican Governor Chamberlain tried to disband the rifle and mounted clubs, but he had little success because the clubs enjoyed a great deal of popular support among the white population and white people's faith in the state government did not return until Governor Wade Hampton was elected in 1876, one year before the end of Federal Reconstruction. Hampton replaced the so-called radical trial judges with Democrat ones, including the appointment of Judge H.H. Murray in the St. James, Goose Creek Parish.[251]

General Wade Hampton was the Democratic candidate for governor again in 1878 and in his support many people from Goose Creek attended a Democratic rally in Bonneau in October. The Goose Creek Democrats boarded the train at Mt. Holly Station and stopped nearby at Strawberry Station to embark club president, Dr. O.C. Rhame and members of the Strawberry Democratic Club for a cheering ride to Bonneau. Remarkably, Hampton was popular among many African Americans in Strawberry and dozens of them accompanied the predominantly white group. They all wore red ribbons, red shirts and red pieces of cloth to signify unity and to bolster their presence in a parish that was dominated by African American Republicans.

The State conducted a census three years before the Bonneau rally and counted 23,142 citizens in the St. James, Goose Creek Parish.[252] The census was extremely exaggerated because the count included many people residing outside of the parish, but the figures accurately revealed a nearly four to one black-to-white ratio in Goose Creek and its vicinity.[253] Understandably, because of the large African American majority, the black Republicans carried the Berkeley precincts that year, but the Democrats carried the state as a whole and the redshirts returned Governor Wade Hampton to Columbia.[254]

Tenants, Sharecroppers and Miners

During the tumultuous post war political period and later after the return of the so-called "Conservative" government, whites found opportunities to suppress the emancipated blacks and to discard their new rights and freedoms. One example of black suppression resulted from the demise of the wage labor system. Much to the disadvantage of the black farmer, the wage labor system succumbed to the tenancy system, which bound the poor farmer unrelentingly to the land.

Table 4.1: The table describes three types of tenancy. The table is courtesy of Michael Trinkley, Chief Executive Officer of The South Carolina Chicora Foundation, Columbia, South Carolina.

Tenancy Type	Landlord Provides	Tenant Provides	Landlord Receives
cash renter	land, house, fuel	labor, animals, equipment, seed, fertilizer	fixed amount of cash or crop
share tenant	land, house, fuel, ¼ or ⅓ fertilizer	labor, animals, equipment, ¾ or ⅔ fertilizer	¼ or ⅓ of crop
share cropper	land, house, fuel, equipment, animals, seed, ½ fertilizer	labor, ½ fertilizer	½ of crop

Under the tenancy system, a farmer could rent land for cash or a part of the production. Both types of tenancy made black land ownership difficult because white landowners did not pay a wage to the farm laborer and thus the laborer was unlikely to ever amass sufficient currency to purchase any amount of property.

Unfortunately, the "share crop" system was commonly used and with this arrangement the farmer kept one-third of the crop, gave one-third to the landowner, and one-third to the supplier of seed and fertilizer. There were arrangements that varied from the one-third split shown in table 4.1, but the table shows the typical tenancy arrangement in South Carolina after the Civil War. The sharecropper suffered other disadvantages. The state's lien laws gave priority to lenders, usually owners of the general stores, for debt repayments. The laws permitted those farmers who controlled their own crops to take out liens, thus, the tenant farmer could borrow money, but the sharecropper could not. Later the law granted the landowner first share of the crop for debt repayment before the lender, and a later version required the lender, usually the general store owner, to report debts and payments to the landowner, if requested.[255] Consequently, the network of legal controls and local agreements kept many poor farmers bound indefinitely to the land not greatly different from most pre-emancipation arrangements.

Attaining a small plot of land was a big achievement for a Goose Creek black man, but even if such a feat was possible, he was unlikely to get crops planted unless a merchant advanced the seed, as well as capital for equipment, and money for necessities such as food and clothing. All of the grocery stores, mills, factories and mines in Goose Creek were owned and operated by Euro-Americans before the war and for at least seventy years after.[256] Thus, African American Goose Creekers were at a distinct disadvantage, but all Goose Creekers suffered to some extent due to the scarcity of capital to purchase necessities and pay wages. Consequently, many Goose Creek estates were sold in pieces to pay taxes, purchase equipment and buy everyday requirements. Eventually much of the Goose Creek land was divided into smaller holdings.

The economic system that existed prior to the war was badly flawed, but it was considerably more robust and diverse than what immediately followed the hostilities. The emerging brick and lumber industries buoyed the pre-war economy and expanded the wage labor system for whites but these businesses collapsed as a result of the hostilities that freed the inexpensive slave labor force. The lumber industry eventually recovered, but the brick industry never again produced bricks as inexpensively as it did with slave labor, and the impoverished consumers after the war could no longer afford to build with baked clay. As a result, significant demographic shifts occurred when fewer professional and skilled workers could earn a living in Goose Creek and were forced to depart the parish. Those few whites that remained were primarily farmers, but some worked on the railroad or in the emerging phosphate industry and a few found employments with the woefully scarce wage paying occupations, as shipping pilots, carpenters, nurses, hotel keepers, sea captains, express agents, merchants, bakers, tailors, teamsters, engineers, wheel rights, blacksmiths, storeowners, store clerks and coopers. A few professionals persisted but opportunities were rare. There were two doctors and several church ministers. Minnie McKay was a teacher and William Bunch was a postmaster, but there were far fewer non-agricultural occupations available after the war than before, requiring most Euro-Americans to eke out a living on the increasingly smaller farms.

Photograph 4.2 This photograph shows a farm near Charleston at the end of the nineteenth century. The house features a waddle and clay chimney. *Courtesy Library of Congress.*

By 1870, illiterate black farmers occupied most of the farms in Goose Creek, but because of the large numbers of black Goose Creekers the small farms could not employ all of them.[257] Consequently, black males sought work as phosphate miners, railroad workers or turpentine laborers. Phosphate miners in groups up to a hundred or more lived in each of the five mining camps in Goose Creek.[258] There were few black craftsmen or professionals. One African American Goose Creeker was a factor (merchant) and some, like Nelson Richardson, were church ministers who titled themselves "divinity" and some black women found work as housekeepers in the few white homes where there were some expendable coins.

The post–Civil War phosphate "boom" helped immensely. Phosphate was an inexpensive local source of fertilizer that was needed for the exhausted South Carolina soils. It became an important export and a profitable substitute for the failed plantation system. Most of the expanding phosphate mines and fertilizer- manufacturing companies were locally owned during the decades following the war and all found a ready supply of plant managers among the newly idle planters and brick manufacturers. Hundreds of Goose Creek blacks also found reliable employment as laborers.

This new industry could trace its beginning to Goose Creeker, Francis S. Holmes, who resided at the Hayes Plantation. Professor Holmes long explored the marl sub layer that contained huge deposits of calcified bones of prehistoric creatures. This thirty-mile wide stratum reached from Port

Royal, South Carolina to Charleston. The "stinking stones," as the rocks were sometimes called, is the mineral deposit that transfers foul odors to well water but it also contains nutrients conducive to plant growth. Professor Holmes knew of the deposit, and believed that there was economic potential. Consequently, he and a business partner, Dr. N.A. Pratt, established the South Carolina Mining and Manufacturing Company in 1867.[259] The processing plant was located on the Ashley River, but the mines were widely scattered including several in Goose Creek. Fortunately, hundreds of Goose Creekers found employment at the mines and nearby plants during the last decades of the nineteenth century.[260]

Some Goose Creekers found work at the E. Boddington and Company phosphate plant. The mine, located near the Cooper River, used barges to float the fertilizer to markets and trams to carry rock to Boddington property at the railroad lines near Mt. Holly Station.[261] The company used machines to extract, haul, crush, wash and package the crude rock before loading the conveyors and shipping the fertilizer to markets. In the days prior to commuting transportation, Goose Creek men and boys who worked the local mines usually resided in barracks at the site for weeks or months at a time.

An economic recovery of sorts slowly stirred in the years following the hostilities so that by 1870 many new, small local businesses began to emerge to support the increasing number of small farms.[262] The small farms, numbering more than 800, could not provide the level of self-sufficiency customary during earlier eras. Thus a wider community of support consisting of small mills of various types, blacksmith shops, cart and wagon works and stores developed to meet the demands of the hundreds of new homesteads that were cleared out of scrub forests and plowed up in fields by hungry whites and emancipated blacks in every part of the Parish. By 1870, there were ten gristmills of which two used steam engines.

There were three turpentine stills, four blacksmith shops and three phosphate mines. Two phosphate mines used steam engines to crush the rock, but all employed large numbers of workers. Together the three phosphate mines employed a total of 240 men. Nine industries used wood and iron along with both skilled and non-skilled hand labor to make coaches, buggies, wagons and carts. Two cotton gins worked four horses each to supply power but they also relied on manual labor. Most mills employed one or two men milling corn, rice or sawing wood, but although all of the larger sawmills used steam power in 1870 each relied upon seven to nine laborers. Within five years after the war, 323 Goose Creekers were employed in non-agricultural occupations in thirty-eight industries.[263]

In 1880, Lincolnville and Summerville were excluded from the census count reducing the number of Goose Creekers to 9,070 residents of which almost all were African American. The Africans continued farming or laboring on the railroads and mines while the few Euro-Americans, who did not work a farm, owned and operated all of the industries, mills, grocery and dry good stores and held all positions as merchants, blacksmiths and carpenters.

The ground-up economic recovery that began slowly after the war continued toward the end of the century.[264] In 1880, one sawmill employed and boarded 24 single black men. Three gristmills employed 7 workers for six to ten hours a day, grinding corn for hominy grits and feed. The mills were valued from $22,400.00 to $28,000.00 and operated for four, six and twelve months a year. One lumber mill employed 10 men at a $.65 daily wage, but a day laborer typically made $1.00 and

Photograph 4.3 The photograph shows a phosphate processing plant in Goose Creek. ***Courtesy South Carolina Historical Society, Charleston, South Carolina.***

a skilled worker earned $2.00, which amounted to $600.00 to $800.00 annually. Two phosphate mines employed and boarded 225 men with the workers laboring ten-hour days. Remarkably, 20 percent of the miners were children but nevertheless these were attractive jobs with some phosphate workers earning $2.00 a day when most unskilled workers made half or less. One reason these higher wages were paid during this period was because returns on investments in the phosphate business were lucrative. One phosphate mine owner invested $1,000.00 and produced $5,000.00 in business. Another mine owner invested $6,000.00 and returned $18,000.00. These mines and processing plants were some of the economic successes in the 1870s and 1880s partly because they used the most advanced technology of the day. The mines near Back River and Goose Creek used steam power to crush the rock and trams to carry the products to rail lines or floated the finished fertilizer on barges down the Cooper River to market.[265]

Some Goose Creekers supported themselves outside of the mine and farm. A few African Americans in Groomsville worked on the nearby railroad line and traveled to their work area on tramcars. Others such as Littie Taylor and Zain Blisbon were nurses, Tony Peanut was a teamster, and Alfred Johnson worked at a distillery owned by a white man named Lazarus Parker. Some of the whites in Groomsville distilled turpentine, while others such as William Bailey was a Doctor of

Divinity, Ryan Thornley was an engineer and Joseph Cannon was the grocer. Thomas Ledbetter was a clergyman who served the European Americans at Groomsville Baptist Church. In 1888, the Baptist Church was relocated from its site next to the chapel of ease at Strawberry to land donated by the Grumes (Grooms) family and renamed "Groomsville Baptist Church." The old Groomsville church remains today on Groomsville Road 0.3 miles from its intersection with Cypress Garden Road. The old church and its cemetery continue to serve the community. The oldest cemetery stone marks the demise of Mary McCants who died in 1867.

In the southeastern section of the enumeration district where the City of Goose Creek incorporated seventy years later, blacks worked on small subsistence farms, phosphate mines and railroads. Some black craftsmen worked as brick masons while the whites owned the rice farms, mines, mills and stores and occupied the few skilled professions. The whites retained control of the rail stops and general stores and no blacks were employed at any of these places. Whites, such as Margaret Dickey, Charles Lice, Magnus Shiver and William Bun were grocers, while Emil Withers was a store clerk. Jonathan Brogdon was an engineer, and J. Douglas Bun was a trial justice, but the great majority of the white and black population in 1879 continued to plow and plant the fields.

Farms and Farmers

In 1879, there were 844 farms in the parish, which was almost four times greater than the 215 farms counted twenty years earlier.[266] With 56 percent of the farms in private ownership, and less than half of the farmers paying a fixed rent or a share of their crops, the Goose Creek landholdings compared similarly to the state average.[267] Table 4.2 shows the number and the proportion of farm ownership and tenancy in Goose Creek.

Table 4.2: The table shows farm ownership and tenancy in St. James, Goose Creek Parish in 1879 according to the 1880 *Census of Agriculture.*

	Number of Farmers	Percent of Farmers
Owned Land	473	56
Paid Fixed Rent	287	34
Paid Share of the Crop	84	10
Total Number of Farmers in 1880	844	100

Goose Creek farmers owned, rather than rented the majority of the farms in 1880, but ownership was typically tenuous with 180 Goose Creek farms seized by the state government that year (many in the Carnes Crossroads area) for non-payment of taxes[268] and the sizes of farms were considerably smaller than the 650-acre average twenty years earlier. Half of the farms were smaller than ten acres and 27 percent ranged from merely 11 to 30 acres. Nine percent of the farms ranged from 31 to 49 acres, and only 14 percent of farmers worked larger tracts. Throughout South Carolina, farms were small and continued to decrease in size. In 1880, the average farm size in South Carolina was 143 acres; in 1890 it was 115 acres; by 1900, it shrank to 90 acres.[269] Table 4.3 shows the number and percentage of farms of various sizes in Goose Creek in 1872.

Table 4.3: The table shows farm sizes in acres in St. James, Goose Creek Parish in 1879 according to the Agricultural Census of 1880.

Number of Acres per Farm	Number of Farms	Percentage of Farms
1–10	422	50
11–30	228	27
31–49	76	9
50 plus	118	14
Total	844	100

Emancipated Africans worked more than 80 percent of the Goose Creek farms in 1879 and owned many of them, but white farmers owned the largest farms. These white farmers typically kept five horses and mules to power the equipment and to till approximately 250 acres. The average annual return for a white owned farm was little more than $1200, which equated to the production of $3 to $8 per tilled acres. Black farms with a mean size of 127 acres and the production per acre ranging from $2 to $6 were typically smaller and less productive than the white farms, but both black and white farm units usually supported large, extended families and the members worked the fields and shared the harvests. Appendix XIV gives a listing of the largest white owned farms and the production and values of each and appendix XV gives the methodology used to identify the characteristics of African American owned farms used in this study.

Richard Myers was an African American farmer in Goose Creek who owned an average size farm during the unstable years of Reconstruction and two decades after. He was emancipated when he was forty years old and became a successful farmer who supported his wife Margaret, a nephew, "Washington," a young girl named "Rhail" and, "Comida," his granddaughter. Myers was a self-made and self-taught man. He appears as forty-four-year-old "Dick Myers" with his forty-year-old wife, "Peggy," in the 1870 census, but they were more formally named, "Richard" and "Margaret" Myers on subsequent public records. He claimed $100 value of personal estate, but owned no property nor could he read or write in 1870, but five years later he was a landowner and twenty years later he was literate.[270]

When Richard Myers was forty-nine years old he purchased two hundred acres of farm and forest for $750 from Mary A.R. Austin, a widow of Robert Austin.[271] This tract was located on the headwaters of Foster Creek, west of Back River Upper Road and north of Henry Middleton's 17-Mile House tract. Today Lindy Creek Road and West Greenview residential subdivision border the farm site. The area was generally referred to as Mt. Holly in the nineteenth century but it is now regarded as part of the Liberty Hall neighborhood.

Plat 4.3 was drawn in 1872 to show Henry Smith's large tract. Robert Austin's farm was located near the right margin. The plat describes the property two years before Richard Myers purchased 200 acres of the 390-acre Austin tract.[272] Myers raised chickens, produced eggs and planted or rotated 26 acres.[273] He worked two horses to plow his corn and cotton fields and annually gathered approximately 125 bushels of potatoes, along with 38 bags of rice.[274] After holding the entire 200-acre tract for only two years, he sold 50 acres to Josiah Green for $200 in 1877 and 25 acres to Jonas Stephens the following year. The unimproved lands remained in woodland and scrub forest but his property was appraised at $605, and it produced $450 of agricultural goods in 1872. Plat

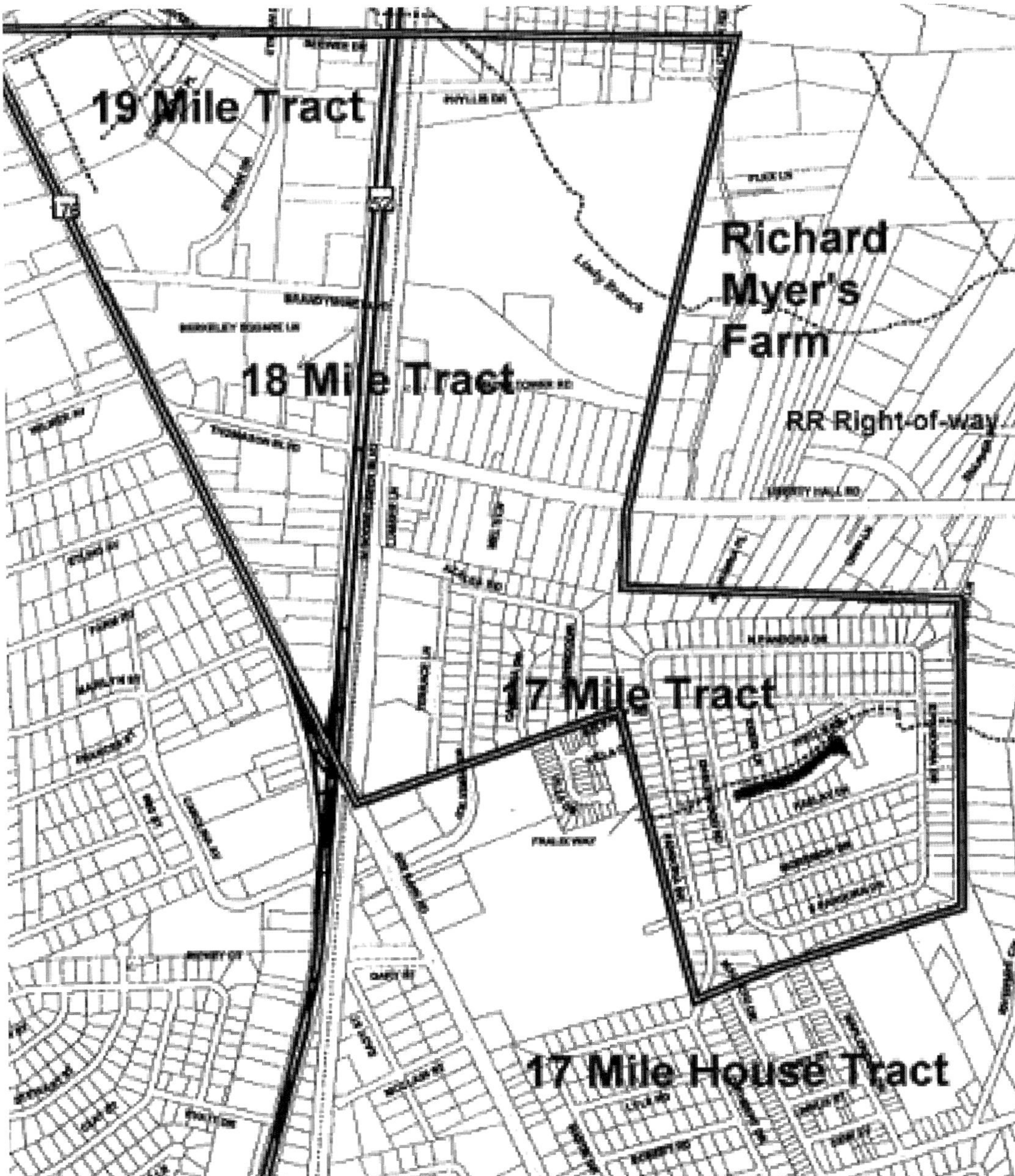

Plat 4.1 The plat was drawn by Langdon Cheves in 1918 from an 1872 survey and is shown as an overlay on a section of the City of Goose Creek as it was in 2003. The plat shows lands comprising part of the 17-, 18- and 19-mile tracts. The words "17 Mile Tract," "18-mile Tract," "19-mile Tract," "Richard Myers' Farm" and "RR Right-of-way" were added for this publication. The "RR Right-of-way" on Myers' farm labels a curved section of Railroad right-of-way that is platted on contemporary maps. This right-of-way may be the remains of the right-of-way sold by Myers to Edward J. Hanahan in 1895.

4.1 shows Myers' farm in relationship to surrounding tracts, as well as contemporary Goose Creek streets and subdivisions.

Later Myers sold more parcels of land and a right-of-way for additional cash to support himself during his senior years. In 1890 he sold ten acres to Henry Marone and five years later he transferred a fifteen-foot right-of-way through his property to Edward J. Hanahan for a railroad spur from Hanahan's Liberty Hall Property. Hanahan paid Myers seventy-five dollars for the right-of-way and used it to lay a tram line that carried phosphate rock from the Liberty Hall mines to train cars on the main rail line.[275] Three years before his death Myers sold twenty-three acres to Annie Bennett for five dollars and two years hence he accepted merely three dollars for a forty-acre tract he transferred to Richard Bryant.[276] Thus, through many small sales, Richard Myers allowed more African Americans to gain a foothold in the Carolina farmlands.

The means by which Richard Myers accumulated enough money to purchase a large amount of property remains a mystery. The kingly amount of $750 he paid in 1874 was equal to the annual salary of a skilled worker, and was unattainable by all but a few. He and the majority of black farmers in Goose Creek were property owners but his large farm was considerably bigger than most. Before Richard Myers died in 1899, he sold most of his property in small parcels, which explains how some minority farmers of the post Reconstruction era acquired farms in Goose Creek. Also the transfer of his remaining property after his demise explains how some lands fell into questionable ownership. All six children of Richard Myers' deceased brother, claimed the Myers tract, but Washington Myers, who was raised by Richard and Margaret, moved onto the land after Richard's death and continued to reside there. Thus, the dubious transfer of Myers land to the next generation offers partial explanation of how some Goose Creek properties entered into competing and questionable ownerships that persists today as "heir properties."[277]

The means by which most black Goose Creekers acquired ownership of their farms remains unknown. Some land was passed from parents to children without filing proper surveys or plats, and some lands were devised in wills that were not probated, but in some cases land transfers were government sponsored and properly recorded. The South Carolina Land Commission and the Freedmen's Bureau were both government agencies, which assisted newly emancipated blacks in acquiring land and livelihoods. Neither agency accomplished much in Goose Creek although both enjoyed some success elsewhere in South Carolina. The South Carolina Land Commission, a state agency, was created in 1869 to purchase tracts of land for resale in small parcels to farmers in exchange for modest amounts of interests. By 1877, the year that reconstruction ended in South Carolina, two thousand small farmers, the majority of whom were emancipated blacks, had acquired parcels of land through the agency. Unfortunately, no Goose Creekers acquired property through this agency and thus no Federal land transfer records explain the origin of minority farms in Goose Creek.

Without formal or government assistance, some African Americans used their own innovative funding methods to acquire property. Some pooled their dollars and bought shares in joint ventures called, "Societies." Such was the scheme of two black farmers, Cato Jefferson and Frederick Mitchell, who formed a society and purchased land in its name. Several more Goose Creekers were later included. Each member worked or rented part of the tract and each kept a copy of the deed to prove ownership.[278] In another instance, Frank Ladson, a twenty-six-year-old black farmer from

Charleston, teamed with James Rivers and bought a large two-hundred-acre section of Howe Hall from James Vidal. This purchase was the beginning of another society. The societies were pyramid investment schemes with dubious outcomes, but nonetheless they were the only means for some Goose Creek freedmen to claim real estate. Many of these society arrangements were conducted through mutual understandings and secured by mere handshakes. Thus, the arrangements were not properly recorded and later resulted in questionable titles and ownerships.

The society schemes were one of many ways through which African Americans acquired property, but other programs encouraged the recently emancipated workers to invest and save. The Freedman's Bureau, a Federal program, was created to provide relief to the destitute white and black citizens after the Civil War. In 1865, twenty thousand people received rations in the Charleston District.[279] The Freedman's Bank was established in Charleston, as well as other southern cities, as part of the reconstruction initiative, to provide opportunities for the destitute to begin the long financial journey to self-sufficiency and independence. Unfortunately, some recently emancipated Goose Creekers dutifully participated in the initiative and lost their meager savings. Cuffy Campbell grew up as a slave on William Tennent's plantation at Red Bank. In 1868, at the age of sixteen, he opened an account at the Freedmen's Bank. Although his parents resided in Goose Creek, the Superintendent of Shaw's Orphan Asylum in Ladson accompanied him, which indicates that he was probably residing at the orphanage.[280]

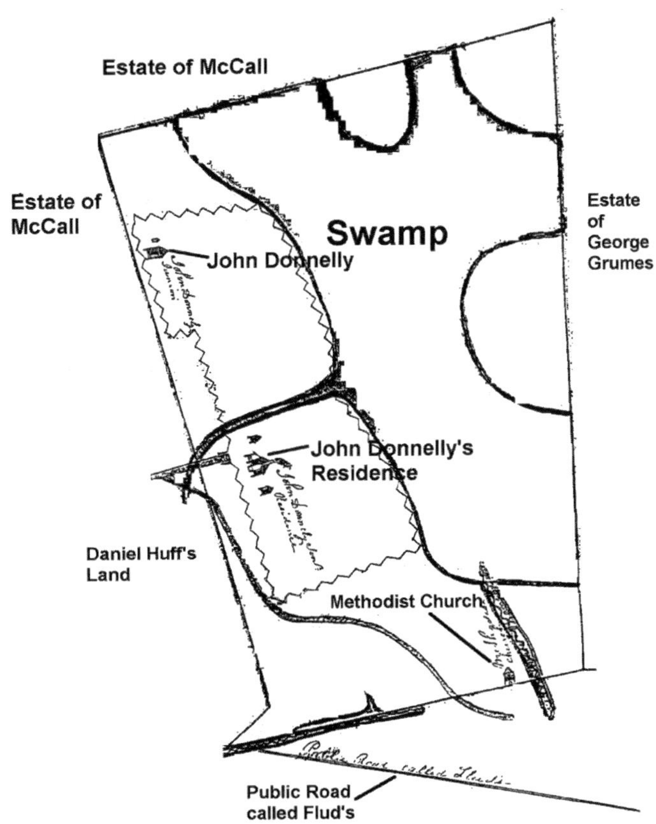

Plat 4.2 The plat shows 228 acres owned by John Donnelly Sr. and John Donnelly Jr. in 1831. Some of this property was bequeathed to African American farmers in 1870. The plat is in the private collection of the Donald Johnson Family, Goose Creek, South Carolina.

Henry Drayton was another emancipated slave who was born in Goose Creek, and at the age of thirty-eight opened a savings account. Also, forty-eight-year-old Sampson Grant and twenty-seven-year-old Jack Young, who according to their application were "brought up" in Goose Creek, opened accounts to save some of their money at the Freedmen's Bank.[281] This record of soberness by these four Goose Creek African Americans was dashed by a national depression in 1873–74. Charleston lost over a hundred firms to bankruptcy, including the National Freedmen's Savings Bank. Fifty-three hundred black and two hundred white citizens lost all of their savings.[282]

In addition to government programs and society schemes, some black Goose Creekers where assisted by white neighbors and friends. Benjamin Donnelly was the third generation of a Euro-American family that settled in the parish in the early 1800s. He bequeathed lands that were once part of his Mt. Holly farm to five people, some of who were black. These small farms became part of today's Strawberry Community on "old Highway 52" near the northern boundary of the modern City of Goose Creek. Donnelly bequeathed 400 acres to his widow, 65 acres to Thomas Pinckney (black), 25acres to Pompey (probably black), 15 acres to Paul (?) and 23.5 acres to Peter Christian (black).[283] "Pompey" was a popular name given to slaves and he likely was an early black landowner as the result of Donnelly's will, and Paul, with no last name cited in the transaction, could have been an early minority landowner.[284] Plat 4.2 shows the land owned by John Donnelly Sr. and John Donnelly Jr.

Additionally, oral history claims that the Innis rail stop near Poppenheim's Crossing, which appeared on maps of the post war era, was actually pronounced and spelled "Inn Nest." Peter Porcher, one time owner of Otranto gave this hundred-acre parcel of land that was situated on the north side of Goose Creek to a small number of freed slaves.[285] Later, this gift, located on land once owned by colonial planter, John Bowen was named "Bowen's Corner." Clearly, land was seldom bequeathed or otherwise given to African Americans from Euro-Americans, but these rare examples explain how a few emancipated African Americans acquired Goose Creek farms after the Civil War.

More Mt. Holly land transferred to black ownership during this period. P.J. Pinckney was an African American who owned twenty-five acres in Mt. Holly, as well as Thomas Pinckney, a forty-five-year-old black farmer who owned sixty-five acres there two years after the war ended. In the 1870s and later, two black farmers, Sampson Bryant, and Frank Brown, owned twelve- and thirty-seven-acre farms in Mt. Holly respectively. Both of their families kept land well into the twentieth century and some Bryant family members continue to own Goose Creek property today.[286]

James Vidal, owner of Howe Hall Plantation and other lands before and after the Civil War, sold a large section consisting of more than a thousand acres to two white farmers, Edwin J. Wright and William Tennent. He also sold a two-hundred-acre section to African Americans Frank Ladson and James Rivers for their society enterprise and eleven small parcels to minority farmers from 1869 to 1872 including twenty acres to William Gaillard "Trustee," twenty acres to Iden Butler, twenty acres to Daniel Wood, twenty-two acres to William Durant, twenty acres to Samuel Middleton and John Denny, twenty acres to Caroline Dawson, twenty acres to Richard Yeardon and two sales of sixty and twenty acres to John Gaillard "Trustee." These were rare opportunities for black farmers to purchase farmlands and it is likely that the Reconstruction Government programs assisted some buyers. Trustees were sometimes assigned by the Reconstruction Government to supervise the purchase of lands by emancipated slaves. Both William and John Gaillard were African Americans who were designated as trustees in the land transaction records. Both men bought parcels of Howe Hall Plantation but never resided there nor anywhere else in the parish.

Howe Hall is an example of an old and historic Goose Creek plantation that was subdivided during the depressed economy that followed the Civil War, and some described the division of the old plantations and the emergence of small farms in post war Goose Creek as a sign of poverty and despair. Perhaps such a gloomy description was accurate when perceived from the perspective of the white planter families, but to the liberated African American, the recently devised farm was both a home and castle. One writer related that Howe Hall was frequently derided as "Hog Hall" because the grand estate had been replaced by small homesteads with hogs.[287] Nevertheless, those hogs were the private property of liberated black families. Hams, shanks and bacon from "Hog Hall" were not signs of desperation to the black farmer and family members, but instead they represented a significant slice of freedom and self-determination.

Hogs were raised on every farm and sheep were raised on some. Rye and oats were grown occasionally for animal feed, and almost all farms throughout the parish grew some rice. Parish-wide, the average rice production per acre was a little over 1,000 pounds but some farmers, such as Dr. John Poppenheim, produced an average of 1,333 pounds per acre on his seventy-five acres. One rice farmer, Greccian Murray, produced 6,600 pounds on ten acres or 660 pounds per acre, but smaller farms produced as little as 300–400 pounds per acre. Farms in the eastern section of the parish consistently produced more rice per acre due to the availability of water reserves, dikes and drains surviving from the colonial period. The largest and most productive rice farms were situated on the Back and Cooper Rivers.[288]

Photograph 4.4 The photograph shows the Dallas Van Buren Carnes House located at Carnes Crossroads where Highways 176 and Alternate 17 intersect. The one-and-a-half-story house with a metal roof was built near 1880. The house is an example of the plantation cottage type. The photograph was taken in February 2003. *Author's collection.*

Some farms grew no rice, but all Goose Creek farms raised the three basics of corn, cotton and cattle. Corn is a versatile crop that can be preserved and used in various forms and cotton, although susceptible to disease and a volatile marketplace, was the only cash crop available for most. Cattle supplied meat and dairy products, which fed the family and brought in a few dollars when sold at market. Livestock was branded or the ears were notched and the brand or notch design was registered at the courthouse. Farmers delivered cows to market as needed for cash after individual cows were "rope trained" and led by men on foot or horse to market. Larger herds were driven. A favorite corral for cattle drives was located on a rise overlooking Daisey Swamp at the site of today's Devon Forest Subdivision. Herds from the western sections of the parish often watered there and remained overnight to arrive in Charleston the following day. A corral near the Oaks Plantation was another popular stop for herders from the northern or eastern directions, but all drives were different after emancipation because the white farmer could no longer rely upon slave labor. The drives required coordinated efforts with many white farmers working together to efficiently deliver the cattle to the markets in Charleston.[289]

Teamwork and versatility was the key to a productive farm because the challenges varied widely from neighborhood to neighborhood and within each section so that some farms reported as few as seven bushels of corn and ⅓ bale of cotton per acre while the most productive farms reported more than twenty bushels of corn and ½ or more bales of cotton per acre. One of the larger and more successful farms of the era was at Carnes Crossroads where the Dallas Van Buren House, built circa 1880, remains today.

The western section of the parish reported the lowest yields per acre, indicating the uncertainties of relying on rainfall in the absence of water reserves. Almost every farm kept some cows, but a few farms specialized in cattle production and grazed as many as forty-two head.[290] One of the most successful farms in the western section of the parish was the Whaley farm that was located at the 37-mile marker. This large versatile farm raised sizeable quantities of cattle, corn and cotton and is shown in photograph 4.5. The old Whaley farmhouse was constructed near the end of the nineteenth century.

No two of the more than eight hundred farms in the parish were identical, but most shared common characteristics. Typically, the one, two or three room farmhouses were built of wood and featured a kitchen with a dry sink. A brick chimney or stovepipe vented smoke from a wood burning cast iron stove through the wall or roof. Sometimes bricks were salvaged (stolen?) from old estates to build foundations for the house or to build a more permanent chimney. The records contain many complaints of landowners bemoaning bricks lost from old houses and gardens to rural robbers. These many petty thefts explain somewhat, why so few remains of colonial structures are recognizable today. Remnants of the main settlement of the Howe Hall Plantation are located contiguous to Liberty Hall Road near its intersection with Henry Brown Boulevard. The minuscule remains, however, are not discernable by casual observers and barely recognizable by experienced archaeologist. Howe Hall is similar to the division of large land tracts into small and less significant parcels, the grand homes and garden walls were separated into the many thousands of bricks to build foundations and chimneys for hundreds of small houses common in Goose Creek until the 1960s.

A well for water in the front yard and an outhouse for sewerage in the back yard provided all of the typical conveniences. The working farm relied upon a nearby mill to sell and grind the corn and

Photograph 4.5 The photograph shows the 37-Mile House. The photograph features handwritten notes that state "The Old 37 Mile House 'Whaley Place' Mr. F.O. Grooms owns it now 12 Sept. 1930." The photograph is in *Johnson's Scrapbook, Volume I*, among the collections of the South Carolina Historical Society, Charleston, South Carolina.

other grains, and a gin to remove the black cottonseeds and to purchase the cotton bag or bale. Other than selling the products directly to the mills and gins, railroads were the only cost efficient way to send products to market, unless boat travel was available on nearby deep water.

Well-accommodated farms used a number of outbuildings such as smoke houses, where salted meats were kept until cured and consumed. The meat was hung and sliced as needed. Coops sheltered chickens. The chickens provided eggs and the bird was consumed when it no longer produced a sufficient number. Corn was harvested and dried in a barn but always kept separate from the prized horses or cattle that were sheltered there. When dried, the corn was "broken" and "shelled" to collect the hard kernels. Some well-provided farms used hand mills to grind the corn kernels into varieties of meal, but large quantities were brought to the gristmill. Potatoes were preserved for the winter by "banking" in straw covered with earth. Banking also kept well-dried onions and fruits from spoiling for months. Farms with low wet areas grew rice and some made wine from grapes that grew easily in the subtropical Lowcountry.[291]

One favorite occasion of the farmers was the annual "grinding day" held each autumn. Stalks of sugar cane were pulled through large steel rollers powered by mules. The family gathered and enticed the mule to turn in a circle to squeeze out sugary slurry. The slurry was boiled in kettles to evaporate the water and leave the syrup for sugar, candy and other sweets. There was dancing to fiddle music, games for the younger people, and gossiping for the older generations. Many farmers planted sugar cane and many successful farms were as self-sufficient as possible. Farmers made all needed repairs, constructed outbuildings and fashioned their own furniture. Many also managed metal repair such as repairing wheel rims and replaced the broken wooden spokes on wagons and carts without assistance. The farmers generally divided their land among the children and most kept the unwritten law and never sold land outside the race.

Until the late nineteenth century, it was customary to erect fences around gardens to keep livestock out because the cattle and swine ranged freely except at night when they were brought into small corrals due to the threat of cattle and pig rustling.

After emancipation, the increased number of small farms made free ranging cattle impractical. Consequently, despite much debate, a stock law was passed by the General Assembly in 1881 that required all cattle to be fenced. In response, a mass meeting of citizens from Goose Creek and

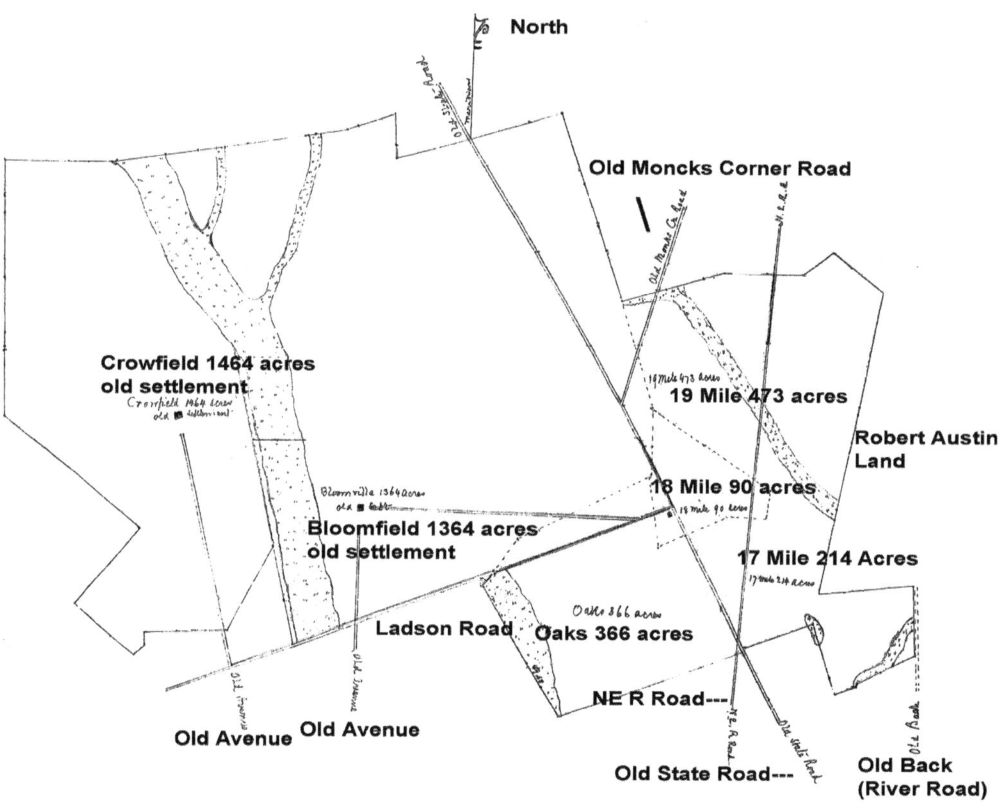

Plat 4.3 The partial plat was drawn from a survey made by T.J. Mellard in 1872 showing the lands owned by Henry A. Middleton. Henry A.M. Smith traced the plat. The tracing is in the possession of the South Carolina Historical Society, Charleston, South Carolina. The manuscript labels were added to this publication for clarity.

Colleton County convened in Summerville.[292] State Senator Fishbourne denounced the "stock law" and called for a petition to the governor against its enforcement. The stock law and political debates concerning it were some of the issues that reflected the social, political and economic changes occurring during this trying time. Many citizens contested that the poor man would surely lose everything if he had to purchase enough fencing for his acreage, and large landowners also found little merit in the requirement.

Henry A. Middleton was one of the largest Goose Creek landowners who rented small plots to tenant farmers and sharecroppers. As early as 1840, speculators acting on his behalf purchased Crowfield, his family estate that consisted of 1,464 acres. To this land he added the contiguous Bloomfield (Bloomville) tract in 1855. This 1,364-acre Bloomfield tract was purchased from Dr. Arthur Gibbes and others. He added 366 acres of the old Oaks tract and 1,143 acres of the 17-, 18- and 19-mile tracts that he purchased from Carlton Vose and others. According to a survey by T.J. Mellard in 1873, and shown as plat 4.3, the State Road, Moncks Corner Road, Back River Road, the railroad and Deas Swamp bordered this Middleton tract of 4,337 acres.[293]

The large Middleton tract was subdivided into small farms and rented for approximately two dollars annually per acre. The Goose Creek lands at Crowfield, Bloomfield, Springfield, Greenfield, 17-, 18- and 19-mile tracts, as well as the Oaks remained in the possession of the extended Middleton family, and were leased in this fashion well into the 1930s and 1940s. These properties represented the bulk of what is the commercial center of the City of Goose Creek today, as well as Crowfield residential, commercial and industrial areas.

The landowners were often absent and usually employed managers as overseers to care for the properties and collect rents. Some renters were enticed with free rent for the first year and others cleared additional land for the owner, or did varying work in lieu of rent payments, but an overseer was needed to manage the lease arrangements and to enforce the standard rental agreements, which included provisions that guaranteed timely payment by placing "holds" on the crops in lieu of rent. Thus, the overseer was charged with forcing every tenant farmer to plant every year and thus provide a collateral crop. Farmers who did not plant were evicted.

The End of the Century

In 1882, Charleston County was divided, and the name "Berkeley" was restored to a section of it. The little town of Mt. Pleasant was designated as the new county seat, and the Berkeley County Democratic Party convened there for the first time. Goose Creek delegates to the Mt. Pleasant convention in the summer of 1882 were G.W. Shingler, T.T. Connor, Dr. J.B. Wiggins, Dr. O.C. Rhame, L.S. Browning, George Connor, Charles Boyle, R.S. Pringle and T.H. Smith.[294] Charles Boyle was elected chairman of the temporary convention and a committee composed of one member from each parish assigned representatives to the state convention. Of the twelve state delegates, Goose Creek sent three: T. Henry Smith, George W. Shingler and Charles Boyle. In the county election of that year, T.H. Smith was elected County Chairman and Dr. T. Wiggins was elected coroner. Both men were from Goose Creek.[295] Four years later, T.S. Browning, R.S. Pringle and Charles Boyle of Goose Creek were elected to the State House of Representatives.[296] County officials from Goose Creek in 1888 were Representatives Robert S. Pringle and T.W. Wiggins.[297]

Again, this was a time of political unrest in South Carolina with the political division in Goose Creek drawn along more than the typical racial lines. In 1890, both the Republican and the Democratic parties disagreed amongst themselves on many issues and each party split into two groups. Almost all of the whites were Democrats, but remained split over the stock law debate and the predominantly black Republicans divided over the same issue. These breaks gave the parish four parties in addition to the independents, but the majority of the residents of Goose Creek supported one of the two factions of the Democratic Party when they voted at Hilton's Cross roads, Cooper's Store and Ten Mile Hill, the three polling places that year. The Stock Law requiring fenced–in cattle was eventually passed.

The later 1890s were good years for many Goose Creekers because the political situation calmed and by mid-decade the cotton crop rose to the best prices since the Civil War, but it was a troubling period for others. As the nineteenth century closed, the phosphate industry was no longer profitable and ground to a halt. Abundant phosphate deposits in Florida along with high state taxes made South Carolina phosphate no longer competitive beyond local use. The final blow came in 1893 when a hurricane destroyed the remaining factories and ruined the last working mines.[298]

Photograph 4.6 The photograph shows a person walking alongside a horse, rider and buggy on the shaded avenue approaching the Oaks Plantation entrance gate near the end of the nineteenth century. The photograph is in the *Johnson Scrapbook, Volume 1*, among the collections of the South Carolina Historical Society, Charleston, South Carolina.

Problems troubling to most occurred when the state constitution returned African American residents to a status of non-franchised second-class citizens. Article 2, section 6 of South Carolina's Constitution of 1895 specified in part that: "The General Assembly may require each person to demonstrate a reasonable ability, except for physical disability, to read and write the English Language as a condition to becoming entitled to vote. The legislature enacted regulations that appeared neutral, but were used to deny rights to black citizens. Those registered prior to January 1, 1898, had to be able to read any section of the Constitution submitted to them by the registration officer, or be able to understand and explain the provision when the official read it to them. Those registering after that date had to be able to read and write any section of the constitution submitted to them or show that they owned and paid taxes on property in the state valued at $300 or more during the previous year. These provisions allowed registration officials to openly discriminate against black registrants by providing difficult sections to them, and then by being hypercritical of the registrant's explanations. Whites were provided with easier sections and their explanations were graded more indulgently. In defending this approach, Senator Ben Tillman remarked that election officers were responsible to their own God and consciences and that there is no evidence of fraud if the official merely shows partiality or "discriminates."[299] Discriminate they did! Consequently, during those years, the black electorate that made up 80 percent of the population in Goose Creek was disenfranchised. When this occurred, Goose Creek disappeared from the political landscape of South Carolina.

The political frailty of the old parish resulted in a large portion of it, including white dominated Summerville, being assigned to the newly established Dorchester County in 1896. Three years later the assignment of magistrates further illustrated the shrinking stature of Goose Creek when by an act of the Assembly, the parish received three magistrates.[300] One magistrate was assigned to the sparsely populated upper part of the parish, one was assigned to the rural central portion and in the eastern section, where one hundred years earlier the wealthy planters commanded the attention of all of South Carolina, only one magistrate was assigned.

Table 4.4: The table shows the Goose Creek Rail Stops according to the 1895 Mills Atlas.

Name of Place	Population	Post Office	Railroad Stop	Express Office
Ten Mile Hill	0	Yes	No	No
Woodstock	0	No	Yes	Yes
Strawberry	12	No	Yes	Yes
Otranto	0	No	Yes	Yes
Mount Holly	0	Yes	Yes	Yes
Ladson	388	No	Yes	Yes
Oakley	96	Yes	Yes	Yes

During the closing years of the nineteenth century, Goose Creek lost most of its identity and because by that time almost all of the old plantation buildings and pleasure grounds were razed and reclaimed by the natural forests and wetlands, many physical characteristics of Goose Creek vanished forever. Furthermore, at that time, the old parish boundaries were no longer used for civil or legal administration except every ten years when census takers counted the residents. Outside attention occasionally came by way of visitors to a few remaining country estates, such as those shown in photograph 4.6. The photograph shows a person walking alongside a horse drawn carriage and rider on the Oaks Avenue near the turn of the twentieth century. By this time Goose Creek was an isolated and neglected corner of the South Carolina Lowcountry, but the Oaks retained some of its previous grandeur because of the infusion of money from a northern investor.

Goose Creek as a place vanished, and slowly new settlements with new identities appeared in its place. Rail lines increased in economic importance during the second half of the nineteenth century and rail stations such as Mt. Holly became predominant community centers. It featured a rail station, a post office and a general store so that newspapers of this era referred to much of the eastern parish as Mt. Holly. Thus, to the outside world, Mt. Holly as a name and place supplanted Goose Creek, but within the neighborhoods, black residents residing in clusters of small farm communities centered close to white washed country churches found new identities that were meaningful to them.

Little settlements such as Casey, on the Moncks Corner Road, emerged as a viable community in that section. Ministers of small churches such as: St. Paul's near today's Boulder Bluff Elementary School; Providence, organized in 1878 near the 23-mile house tract, and the Greater Mount Zion AME established on Howe Hall Road in 1885 provided much needed local cohesiveness.[301] The Greater Mount Zion AME Church began as a congregation prior to the Civil War when slaves gathered under shade trees to worship.[302] By 1861, the group was meeting regularly in a small wooden structure. The Greater Mount Zion AME first ministerial hierarchy established officially in 1885 included: Reverend T. Smalls, Pastor, Reverend Weatherspoon, Presiding Elder and Right

Photograph 4.7 The photograph shows St. Paul's Church located at the intersection of Stephanie and Amy Drives near Boulder Bluff Elementary School. The church burned and the few headstones were removed from its cemetery in the early 1980s. *Author's collection.*

Reverend James A. Shorter, Bishop. Grove Hall Church was situated a few miles west of Mount Zion. Grove Hall Church stood on the State Road east of Carnes Crossroads and in the central and western sections of the parish African American groups broke off from white institutions and built independent houses of worship at Wassamasaw, Longridge and Sandridge. After emancipation the African American members of Spring Hill Methodist at Sandridge separated and established their own church. Joseph Welch (white farmer) donated the land, and Springhill Church members (white and black) constructed a church building and parsonage for Ebenezer Christian Methodist Church on the State Road that is now South Carolina Highway 176.[303] The first church at the Ebenezer site was constructed in 1887. Families represented in the church cemetery are the Husser, Gaillard, Braddely, Harris, Brown, Butler, Miller, Myers and many more.

Small rural communities emerged during the turbulent political years following the Civil War and persisted as the only places of any significance for nearly one hundred years. These clusters of farmhouses near small churches were all that remained of a once proud and prosperous parish that virtually vanished from the maps of South Carolina. But, these little places were important because they were the homes of the men, women and children who singularly and collectively safeguarded the core values of rural South Carolina as they eked meager livings from the land that had sustained them for more than two hundred years.

Chapter V
Little Places
1900–1950

It is doubtful that the people living in Goose Creek during the first half of the twentieth century could foresee the dynamic potential of their rural countryside. From 1900 to 1950, the countryside was home to dozens of black families clustered on small farms near white-washed churches, and a few mixed race or white families nearby. Black families resided in little places named Grove Hall, Casey, Bowen's Corner, Back River, Strawberry, Howe Hall and Liberty Hall. White families owned and rented farms in places near rail stops, such as Mt. Holly and Groomsville and the mixed-race families clustered near places named Driggerstown and Varnertown. These families seldom ventured from their isolated homes, but nevertheless, they were connected to Charleston by way of the unpaved State Road, a small wooden bridge over Goose Creek and three rail lines. Photographs 5.1 and 5.2 show the condition of the Goose Creek Bridge and State Road during this period.

The rail lines were essential because the depots served as windows to the world where information and people flowed in and out, and the three railroad tracks that radiated from Charleston, connected the farmlands in the eastern parish to markets. The tracks provided inexpensive transportation of people and products from the fields and forests and returned fertilizer for the depleted soils, all of which kept the farms productive enough to sustain small groups of families. The countryside remained dormant during most of this era, but toward mid-century, the deep creeks and river waters made many of the properties attractive for industrial and military uses. Thus it was here, near mid-century where these little places with clusters of farms became the destination of new working families arriving from across the nation.

The People and the Property

The 1900 census enumeration area, entitled *St. James, Goose Creek Parish Township* included five districts with a total population of more than ten thousand. The population decreased markedly during the next twenty years, because the parish lines were adjusted and some densely populated sections were reassigned to Charleston County. In 1920, the smaller St. James, Goose Creek Parish was divided into two townships. The *First St. James, Goose Creek Parish Township* encompassed the central (Wassamasaw) and the western sections of the old parish and was composed almost entirely of modest homes on small farms with a few churches and general stores. There were no rail lines in those parts so most stores and churches were situated along the State Road (Highway 176). Some structures, including

Photograph 5.1 The photograph shows the Goose Creek Bridge, ca. 1904. The bridge is located near the St. James, Goose Creek Church. *Courtesy South Carolina Historical Society, Charleston, South Carolina.*

Photograph 5.2 The photograph shows an automobile on the State Road in Goose Creek, ca. 1925. The automobile is photographed near today's intersection of St. James and Westview Boulevards. The photograph is in the *Johnson Scrapbook, Volume 1*, among the collections of the South Carolina Historical Society, Charleston, South Carolina.

Photograph 5.3 The photograph shows four unidentified children on the front porch of the Stephen Williams House in 1930. The home is located on State Road (State Highway 176). The photograph is noted, "About 40 miles up Old State Road. Solid red cedar." The photograph is from the *Johnson Scrapbook, Volume I*, among the collections of The South Carolina Historical Society, Charleston, South Carolina.

a few stately homes, survived well into the twentieth century, and one, the *Stephen Williams House*, remains a residence today in the rural Sandridge Community in the upper section of the parish. Photograph 5.3 shows the House in 1930, prior to renovations.

The *Second St. James, Goose Creek Parish Township* encompassed the entire eastern third of the parish where sections would incorporate during the second half of the century as the City of Goose Creek, the Town of Hanahan and parts of the City of North Charleston. Separate first and second township population counts are not available in 1900 and 1910, but they are available for each census year from 1920 to 1950. Table 5.1 shows that the total number of residents in the first township (central and western parish) increased by only three hundred people during the thirty-year period, while the population in the second township (eastern parish) declined in 1930, and then increased significantly toward mid-century due to sub-urbanization. The reduction of the population for 1930 was caused by the reassignment of some sections from the second township to Charleston County after the 1920 census. The significant population increase in the 1940s resulted from the military build-up for World War II, which stimulated the expansion of the military facilities in Charleston and Goose Creek. Some of the workers at the new and expanded facilities sought homes in the eastern parish.

Table 5.1: The table shows the enumerations of the first and second St. James, Goose Creek Parish Townships for each decennial census year from 1900 to 1950.

Census Year	1900	1910	1920	1930	1940	1950
First Parish Township	N/A	N/A	1,372	1,450	1,607	1,672
Second Parish Township	N/A	N/A	4,639	3,209	3,401	5,043
Total Parish	10,300	5,620	6,100*	4,659	5,008	6,715

*Lincolnville was counted separately but included in the total. Thus the total is shown with a population that is 89 more than the sum of both parish townships.

The second township in the eastern sector included enumeration districts six, seven, eight and nine in 1930. These districts included the land that suburbanized during the second half of the century and incorporated into the several municipalities. Table 5.2 shows the number of people in each district and reveals that amount prior to the population expansion resulting from World War II. The districts contained an African American population that was as high as 90 percent in district eight/nine. These districts comprise sections of the greater Goose Creek area today. The average black population comprised 75 percent of the people residing in the eastern section, as well as the parish as a whole.

Table 5.2: The table shows the Second St. James, Goose Creek Parish Township Districts 6,7, 8 and 9 population counts and racial ratios according to the 1920 Census.

District	Number White	Number Black	Percent White	Percent Black	Total
First Township	467	868	35	65	1,335
Districts 6 and 7	451	674	40	60	1,125
Districts 8 and 9	193	1,738	10	90	1,931
Total	1,111	3,280	25	75	4,391*

* 268 mulatto and Euro/Native American residents increase the total of all residents to 4,652.

Mostly because of the high percentage of disenfranchised African Americans in the Goose Creek vicinity, the area continued to receive little attention during this time. In fact, Goose Creek, as a place, hardly existed at all during the first half of the twentieth century. Charleston and Berkeley newspapers at this time never referred to the wide area as "Goose Creek," but used the name only in reference to the creek itself, the reservoir that provided drinking water to Charleston County, and to a small section near the bridge. Only one hundred people who resided in the vicinity of the Goose Creek Bridge, the old St. James Church and the Oaks Plantation were considered residing in Goose Creek as late as 1940.[304] The locations of most white families were identified with the name of nearby rail stops and black and mixed-race families were not mentioned in the print media of that era.

The Otranto railroad station situated near the intersection of State Road and the road to Dorchester was one such rail stop. Plat 5.1 shows the location of the Otranto Railroad station near the beginning of the twentieth century. It was contiguous to the Atlantic Coastline Railroad and was near the State

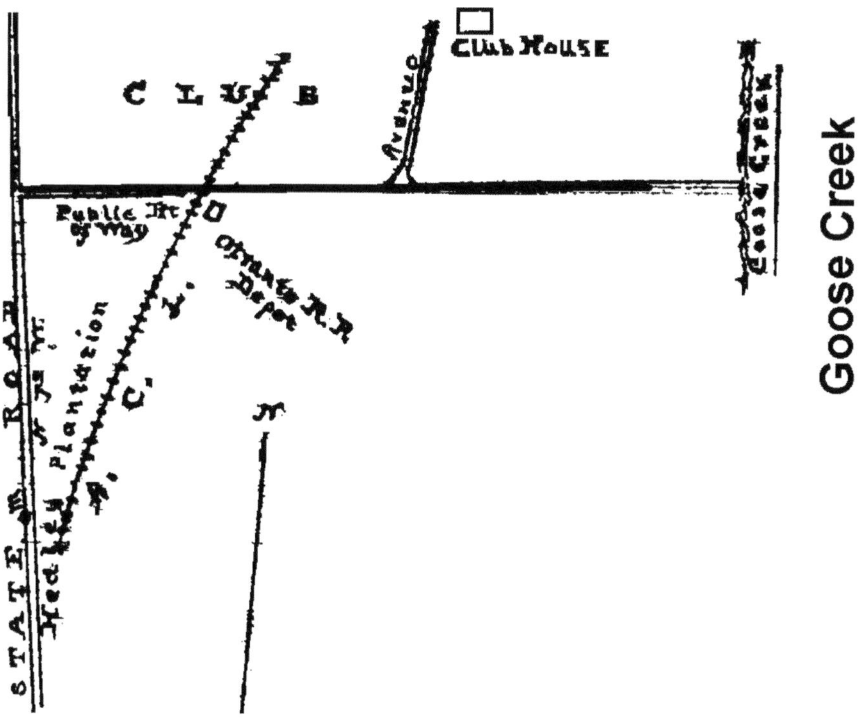

Plat 5.1 The plat shows the Otranto Railroad Depot at the intersection of the Atlantic Coastline Railroad and Otranto Road. Also shown are the State Road and the Otranto Club House as they were situated in 1934. In the collections of the South Carolina Archives.

Road and the Otranto Club House. The Hedley Plantation home was nearby and an inn operated for many years on the west side of State Road, but mostly it was a few scattered farmhouses clustered in a small place called "Deer Town" (Deer Park) that characterized the neighborhood.

Much of the land in the eastern section of the parish eventually comprised the municipalities of Goose Creek, Hanahan and the northern section of the City of North Charleston. Most of these tracts remained undivided with single owners or partnerships during this era and the remaining parcels were divided and sold as private farms. Some old Charleston families managed to keep large undivided tracts of land during the bleak economies after the Civil War and well into the twentieth century. The land of Crowfield, Bloomfield, the Oaks, 17-, 18- and 19-mile-house tracts, and Springfield were parceled into small tenant farms, but a single family and later a partnership retained ownership. Other large tracts, such as Otranto, Liberty Hall and Red Bank remained undivided and were held as hunting clubs. In rare cases, farmers like John Poppenheim successfully worked large tracts well into the twentieth century. Poppenheim, who successfully grew rice, may be the Goose Creek rice farmer at the floodgate shown in photograph 5.4.

Thus, some large undivided tracts remained in southern hands during the first several decades of the era, but non-local interests eventually purchased most of the properties early in the century. Lumber and paper companies, such as Westvaco, bought much of the St. James, Goose Creek Parish lands including Crowfield, Bloomfield, and large swaths of the central and western parish. Westvaco later sold Crowfield and Bloomfield for residential, commercial and industrial uses. The federal government purchased old plantations such as Red Bank, Brick Hope, Cedar Hill, White House, Parnassus and Marrington for military uses that required deep Cooper River water for ammunition ships and submarines. Lumber companies purchased Grove Hall, Mt. Holly and Thorogood Plantations and harvested timber until much of the lands were transformed into industrial parks. Much of Liberty Hall Plantation was worked by lumber companies, but remained intact and wooded until it was sold for residential, commercial and industrial uses early in the twenty-first century. Medway Plantation was purchased for private use in the 1930s, and unlike most of its neighboring tracts, it is protected by conservation easements.

At the advent of the twentieth century and until the lands evolved to other uses, most of the tracts remained characterized by large estates subdivided into tenant farms with small privately owned farms nearby. Part or all of some large estates, such as Mt. Holly, Button Hall and Howe Hall,

Photograph 5.4 The blurred photograph shows a man at a trunk gate in a Goose Creek rice field between 1901 and 1905. The photograph is a stereoscopic view from the Keystone View Company entitled "Flooding the Rice Fields." The location is latitude 33 degrees north and longitude 80 degrees west, which indicates the rice field is situated in Goose Creek. The photograph was taken from the cover of Michael Trinkley's *Liberty Hall: A Small Eighteenth Century Rice Plantation in Goose Creek.*

were subdivided after the Civil War and sold in parcels to dozens of African American farmers. These land holdings often passed to subsequent generations with unrecorded deeds and were divided among descendants. These generous acts unknowingly entangled the land in a legal labyrinth of heir rights, and without clear titles these lands were not marketable during the first half of the century when much of Goose Creek was purchased by outside interests. Consequently, many small, black-owned farms remained nestled side by side with large estates such as the farmers identified as "various owners Negroes" noted along the borders of the Liberty Hall tract on a 1944 plat.[305] By that time, outsiders like Henry G. Roosevelt owned the large Montague estate to the northwest of Liberty Hall, Sidney L. Legendre owned the Medway/Pinegrove tract to the north, and the Federal Government was buying the lands to the east.

Many African American families remained settled in tight-knit extended groups surrounded by largely unoccupied swaths of forestlands. In this isolated condition they retained much of their rural culture as long as ten decades after emancipation. Because the unclear titles kept the land unsuitable for purchase by the lumber, residential, commercial and defense industries, many of these mixed-use properties remain today in neighborhoods such as Howe Hall, Liberty Hall and Back River, all named after the colonial era plantations. Many of these anachronistic homesteads seem increasingly out of place, but they remain important aspects of the rural countryside that supported the hopes and dreams of dozens of Goose Creek families for a century after emancipation.

Racial Segregation

Slavery bound the white, black and racially mixed groups together in close working communities for almost two hundred years. During the years of slavery, there was no semblance of racial equity nor could racial harmony be supposed, but people of different races lived and worked in close proximity everyday, be it in the field, forest or main house. The race situation after emancipation required difficult realignment by all, but the adjustment was especially difficult for those who denied the reality of the Emancipation Proclamation. Alex was a slave owned by John Vose. Vose and Alex grew up together and trusted and loved each other. When emancipation was announced, Vose ruefully recounted that Alex, "remained with me for quite a while just as if he did not know he was free."[306] Alex finally walked away and never returned, as did most black Goose Creekers, but other emancipated African Americans, like many whites were bound to the land, and after a brief period of freedom in Charleston or elsewhere, returned to the Goose Creek lands that they knew.

Some of these African Americans selected new names and some Goose Creek freedmen such as Abraham Free, chose names that celebrated their newfound liberty. Some, such as (George) Washington Myers and Abraham (Lincoln) Born chose names of respected presidents. Others simply borrowed the name of a previous owner as did black Goose Creekers Thomas Drayton, Robert Ladson, Pompy Legare, Aren Waring, Sarah Capers, Samuel Mazyck and Daniel Moultrie.[307] All of their last names are identical to those of prominent white Goose Creek slave owners.

With new freedoms and new names many black Goose Creekers, out of economic necessity and familiarity, entered into new working relationships with old masters on or nearby the same plantation upon which they had long been enslaved. Thus, in many instances, the people and places looked remarkably the same before and after emancipation, but the relationship was just as remarkably different. The new relationships pitted old masters against new freedmen and visa versa, and neither master nor freedman possessed the necessary experiences or wisdom to transcend this incredible juxtaposition. Thus, great anxieties wrought from the need to adjust to the new relationship brought by emancipation caused emotional ills and adjustment pangs that lingered far into the twentieth century.

The adjustment angst began at the close of the Civil War. The white South Carolinians lived in fear of liberated blacks during 1865, and most whites were absolutely convinced that a bloody race war would ensue on July 4, 1865.[308] One Goose Creek landowner, who took refuge among the Union forces in Charleston, wrote on the morning of July 4, 1865 that the presence of retired confederate companies still wearing their uniforms appeared to frighten the Negroes, and he credited these deactivated units with keeping order because as he reasoned they, "kept the Negroes down."[309] Whatever the reason, no race riots occurred that day, but the fear of reprisals persisted among most whites and only dissipated slowly during subsequent years.

Racial segregation was entrenched as the dominant philosophy of all races partly because segregation was politically rooted as a result of the compromise of 1877. The compromise ended Reconstruction but it also gave Republican Rutherford B. Hayes the contested presidential election in exchange for white southern control of race relations. Because of this political arrangement and because of strong racial suspicion, segregation emerged as the prevailing position of both races that saw it as the safest and wisest choice at that time. Unfortunately, the price of segregation was high. Segregation led to rigid racial resentment, disenfranchisement of non-white citizens, and the egregious delay of economic and social rehabilitation.

Segregation caused both races to draw formidable barriers that forbade racial interaction that had previously been permitted. White children were no longer allowed to play with black children, and casual contact was greatly scorned. In response, non-white South Carolinians separated themselves from whites as much as possible as a reaction to white hostility and fear, or as another step toward true freedom and self-determination. For the most part, the races separated as a way of avoiding violence, but sadly, as the races moved farther apart, the suspicions understandably grew until the unequal, but mutual dependence and familiarity of the pre–Civil War era, gave way to unequal, separate and intensely suspicious and competing worlds.

As a consequence of distrust, the races steadily shifted into separate sections of the parish during the decades following Reconstruction. Little or no demographic movement occurred immediately after the war, but when the gradual shift began it was unrelenting for fifty years. By the twentieth century, racial sections of the parish were clearly discernable. At first, after the Civil War, the overwhelming black majority dominated the complexion of every part of the parish as before. Every section remained racially integrated.[310] Numerous African American families resided side-by-side with a few white families and even fewer mulatto families for ten to twenty years, but this integrated situation slowly polarized as the years passed and the races moved farther apart. By 1920, almost all Goose Creek whites resided in racial clusters, separate and distinct from all non-white neighborhoods.[311] Euro-American families named Saulisbury, Rudd, Mims, Hill, Hilton, Blanton, Grooms, Hutto, Smith, Singletary, Weatherford, Eadie, Myers, Ballentine, Mitchum and others, farmed lands contiguous to each other. African American families named Galliard, Husser,

Johnson, Polite, Watson, Dantzler, Green, Nash, Banks, Presley, Ray, Boyd, Washington, Brown, Pringle, Wiggins and more, also settled near each other. Husser Town, in the upper parish, and Pringle Town, remain recognizable black communities today. Also, by 1920, almost all of the so-called "mixed race" families including Native and European American genetically mixed families and African and European mixed families lived in district two. More specifically they resided in enumeration areas six or seven of that district, and most resided in proximity to each other within a few miles of Carnes Crossroads.[312]

Because the mixed race families gravitated to the same vicinity in the parish, the federal census classified almost all of the mixed race families as "mulatto" meaning the offspring of African and European parents, and mistakenly included in this classification some families with mixed Native American and European ancestry. These mulatto families assembled in neighborhoods with names such as "Driggerstown" and "Varnertown." These families named Bones, Moore, Droze, Hughs, Varner, Simms, Clark, Knight, Bread (Broad), Driggers and Dangerfield mostly resided on contiguous farms in a community that originated from early Native American families. Many of these mixed Euro/Native American family members were mistakenly recorded as mulatto on the census reports and because of their genetic connection with Native American ancestors some referred to all residents of this section as "Summerville Indians," or "brass ankles," whether they were African/European Americans or Native/European Americans.[313]

Some of these so-called Summerville Indians were mixed Native American and European heritage families who owned the lands near Carnes Crossroads since the late eighteenth century. William Clark farmed near Carnes Crossroads and an 1807 affidavit states that his two grandmothers were Native American. One grandmother was described as "a native Indian women'" and the other as "a Catawba Indian women."[314] His descendent, Mary Varner, married Henry Tann of Carnes Crossroads in the 1830s. Her sister, Geneva married Hampton Clark, who descended from William Clark. Thereafter, these families prospered and "Clark" and "Tann" became common names in the area throughout the nineteenth and into the twentieth century.[315]

The connection of these mixed families to the lands near Carnes Crossroads during the early nineteenth century attracted mulatto families to relocate there after emancipation. The Native and European American Tann family is listed on the census as "mixed race," as were the African and European mixed race Sweat, Russell, Weldon and Martin families living nearby. As the years passed, more mulatto families gravitated to small farms in the same vicinity and eventually lived in even closer proximity through intermarriage. By 1880, dozens of Native American and mulatto families named Tann, Pratt, Sweat, Bunch and Russell owned farms contiguous to each other.[316]

Native American families such as Varner, Dangerfield and Driggers are also associated with the Carnes Crossroads area. The households of William and Mary Varner appear in 1900, as does their granddaughter Geneva (Neva) Varner Clark. Mary Varner's parents, William W. Williams and Rebecca Roche were Native Americans and the Varners are related to the Native American families of the Clarks, and Tanns, who appeared in the area 100 years earlier. "Indian Mary" of Edisto had a daughter by William Elliot Edings. This daughter married John R. Dangerfield, who was born in Goose Creek in 1792. Their son fathered many children, one of whom was Caroline, who married into the Driggers family.[317] Caroline Dangerfield and Ruphus Driggers reared three children, Richard, Orin and Lillian. Their families grew, branched and expanded until dozens of Driggers

Photograph 5.5 The photograph shows Geneva Varner Clark and her three sons in 1938 standing near their home in Varnertown. The house was located approximately half a mile north of Carnes Cross Roads. The photograph was taken by Marion Post Wolcott. *Courtesy Library of Congress.*

Photograph 5.6 The photograph shows people fishing on a bridge at Ancrum Creek, ca. 1904. Today, College Park Road crosses Ancrum Creek at this location. Many "mixed race" families once populated this locale but the races of the fisherman and woman is not discernable in this photograph. The photograph was taken by William Henry Johnson and is in the *Johnson Scrapbook, Volume I*, among the collections of the South Carolina Historical Society, Charleston, South Carolina.

and Dangerfield families farmed near Carnes Crossroads in the first half of the twentieth century. Many of the Driggers family members clustered on small farms in the same vicinity, which became known as "Driggerstown." And by 1910 most of the 464 people residing there were "Driggers."[318] Driggerstown and Varnertown were the homes of the majority of Goose Creek racially combined families. Clearly, Goose Creekers of mixed heritage were consciously selecting their neighbors, as were the African and European American families in other sections of the parish.

Interestingly, Varnertown became a popular destination for Filipinos who came to Goose Creek by way of the Charleston Naval Shipyard in the 1930s. These Southeast Asian people did not easily fit into the race conscious parish, but they found it possible to settle near or within the mulatto and Native American areas. Thus, some Filipinos married into the Varnertown families and by 1932 introduced the surnames of Alfaro, Garcia, Ricafrenti, Bugaisan, Villanova, Rameres, Surrell and Soreano. The name Blas, a Guamanian name, was also introduced.[319]

Map 5.1 shows a section of the South Carolina State Highway Map published in 1951. It shows a part of the eastern parish near Carnes Crossroads where Driggerstown and Varnertown were

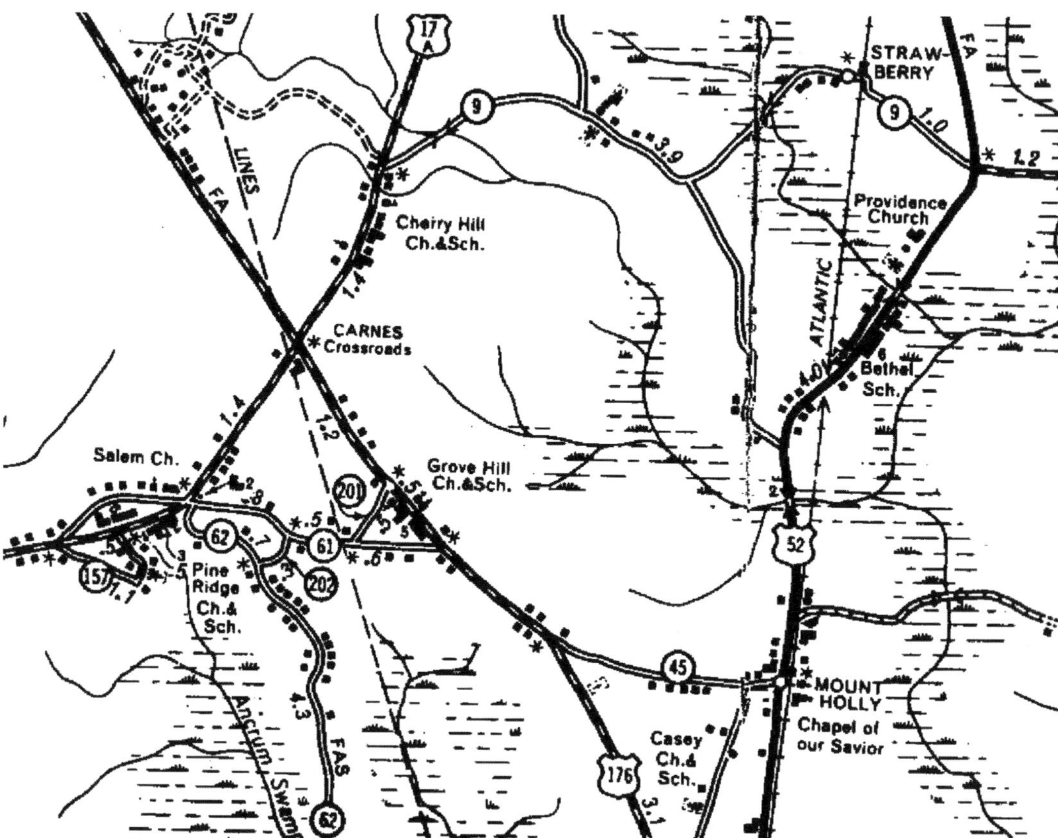

Map 5.1 The map shows a section of the eastern St. James, Goose Creek Parish. The section was taken from the South Carolina State Highway Map published in 1951 by the South Carolina Department of Highways and Transportation.

Photograph 5.7 The photograph shows four members of the Wassamasaw Tribe of Varnertown (Varner Town) Indians. *Left to right*: Heidi Varner, secretary and financial officer of the tribe; council members, Martha Dangerfield Varner, Idel Dangerfield Ruth and Mary Dangerfield Barrineau.

located. Today College Park Subdivision, Wide Awake and Sangaree dominate the Driggerstown vicinity and Varnertown is situated in a rapidly developing section north of Carnes Crossroads. These little places comprised the farms of mixed families of which today fifteen hundred are associated with the Wassamasaw Tribe of Varnertown Indian Council.[320] When a photographer arrived at Varnertown during the era of strict segregation in 1938, Geneva Varner Clark was the only resident who identified herself as an American Indian (Native American) and her photograph is among the Marion Post Wolcott collection at the Library of Congress. Today, proud mixed race residents, such as Richard Black, Richmond Clark and Lisa Leach, and many others including the ladies featured in photograph 5.7, work within the recently recognized Wassamasaw Tribe of Varnertown Indians Council to safeguard their precious Native American heritage.[321]

By 1930, the words "mulatto" or "mixed" were no longer used for census purposes. Instead the census reported that there were "White," "Negro" and two Japanese families residing in the St. James, Goose Creek Parish that year. Thus, in 1930 those with mixed genetics simply chose a major race they preferred. Understandably, some mixed citizens, such as Archibald Harmonfree and Daniel Sweat selected a preferred race prior to 1930. Both men appear as "non white" on the 1840 census, but as "white" on the 1850 record. Archibald Harmon married a white lady and fathered and reared six white children with her. His neighbor, Daniel Sweat, married a white lady also and fathered and reared six white children with her. As far as the federal census was concerned, the racial transition for these two Goose Creekers from non-white to white occurred over a brief ten-year period. Regardless of his race or racial percentage, some of Harmon's descendents remained near Carnes Crossroads into the twentieth century. John Harmon was a successful farmer who by 1915 owned and worked a large 1,044.5-acre tract near the 27-mile marker on the State Road west of Carnes Crossroads.[322] By mid-century, this part of the eastern parish was a genetic melting pot with African, Asian, European and Native American families and all three races were frequently represented within single households.

Making a Living

Regardless of race, making a living in Goose Creek was a matter of hard work for all. As one Goose Creeker explained while thinking back fifty years to her grandfather, "he hustled, he just hustled, he did what he could to make money, and he hustled everyday!"[323] He was not unlike other Goose Creekers whose predominate work was laboring on the farm. Agriculture remained the dominant economy during this period for white and black Goose Creekers, but the rural African Americans depended on the white-owned businesses for products, services and employment not available on the farms. The Goose Creek black often owned his small farm, which provided a large measure of independence, but he usually relied upon part-time employment to supplement his agricultural income. The *Woodstock Hardwood and Spool Manufacturing Company* employed unskilled laborers. This company operated at the old Woodstock Plantation and rail stop near Ladson, producing wooden spools for the textile industry. The *Ingleside Mining and Manufacture Company* owned a 1,639-acre tract on the old Hayes Estate, where the last of the dying phosphate mining continued a few more years.[324] Unskilled labor was in demand at the new Naval Ship Yard and sawmills, lumber companies and the railroads offered employment opportunities to hundreds.

The lack of transportation to and from work limited employment choice and made boarding at the company necessary for many. By the turn of the twentieth century, twenty or more Goose Creek men boarded at sawmills. Additionally, three phosphate mines boarded up to one hundred men and boys each.[325] The Stokes Camp owned by the Burton Lumber Company, erected barracks to house dozens of workers at the juncture of the CSX rail line and the company tramway on the Liberty Hall Plantation.[326]

A phosphate mining operation existed for about twelve years at Liberty Hall near the turn of the century. By this time South Carolina phosphate mining was a dying industry, but operations continued at Liberty Hall because there was an abundance of unskilled labor, and a "large and valuable deposit of phosphate rock"[327] that was needed on nearby farms. In Goose Creek mining continued to be second only to agriculture as a source of employment. Hundreds of Goose Creekers reported to the Liberty Hall Mine to dig with picks and shovels, haul rock on carts to steam powered crushers, carry the crushed rocks by wagon to the tramway and finally pull the loaded tramcar to the rail line.[328]

"J.F. Prettyman's old tram line," was one of several small gage rail systems used in Goose Creek to carry phosphate from the mines to the rail transport point.[329] Liberty Hall Road was later constructed on parts of the tramline right-of-way and that road intersects Goose Creek Avenue (Highway 52) today near the rail point. By 1930, the tramlines were inoperable, but some Goose Creekers continued to mine phosphate as the last of the industry died and the returns on their labor diminished.[330]

Plat 5.2 describes the *Ingleside Mining Company* located on the old Hayes Plantation conveniently near the Woodstock train depot. The Liberty Hall mine and the *Ingleside Mining Company* were the last employers in the Goose Creek phosphate business, and as a result of the closures, more Goose Creekers were forced to seek work elsewhere such as at the Mt. Holly Clay Products Company where

Photograph 5.8 Marion Post Wolcott took this photograph in 1938. It shows a clay-lined well and oven, with a crane hoist nearby. The farm also featured a cane press. Hampton and Geneva Varner Clark owned this well-equipped farm located half a mile north of Carnes Cross Roads. *Courtesy Library of Congress.*

Photograph 5.9 Marion Post Wolcott took this photograph in 1938. It shows Melvin, the youngest boy sitting on the front porch. Standing left to right are his brothers, Joe, Robbie and Hampton Varner Jr., near their clay-lined chimney. Hampton and Geneva Varner Clark owned the house located north of Carnes Cross Roads near South Carolina Highway 17A. *Courtesy Library of Congress.*

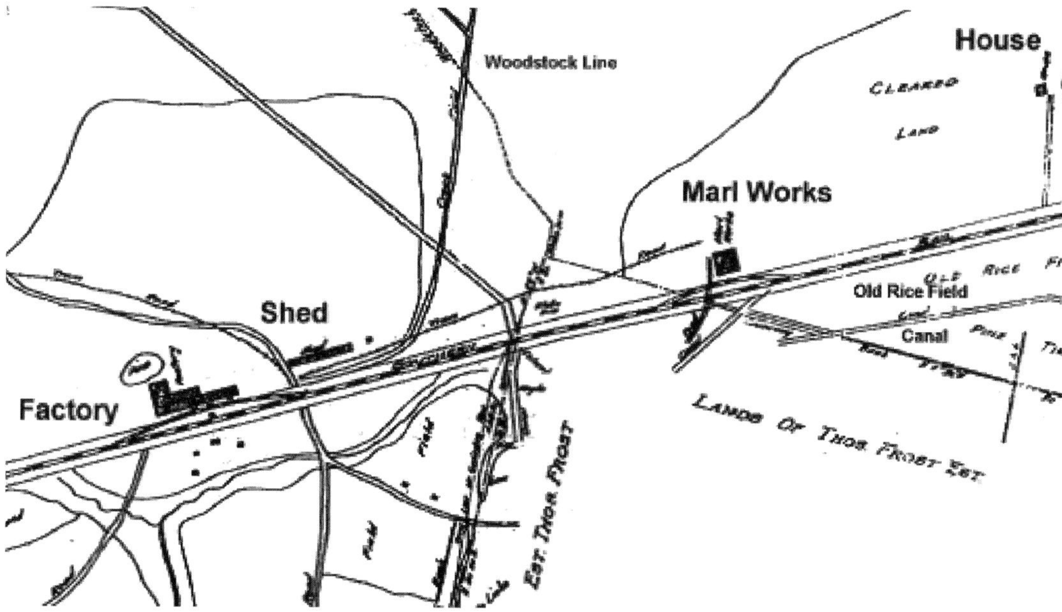

Plat 5.2 The plat shows the Ingleside Mining Co. consisting of 1,639 acres contiguous to the Southern Railroad. The factory, shed and marl works were located close to the rail line. The old Hayes main house, as well as the old rice field and canal are shown. The words "Factory," "Shed," "Marl Works," "Old Rice Field," "Canal" and "Woodstock Line" were added for this publication. *Courtesy South Carolina Department of Archives and History.*

brick and tile were produced, the Northeastern Railroad Company with a station in Mt. Holly or as part of the large labor team to dig a tunnel more than two miles long from Back River to Goose Creek to supply water to the Goose Creek water treatment plant at the reservoir. Some Mt. Holly men were employed by the Charleston Water Commissioners to dig, load carts, drive oxen and move tons of marl and clay from the tunnel. Others sought employment in Charleston.[331] As roads and transportation improved, longer commutes became possible, and by 1930, more workers were traveling daily to places of employment in the City of Charleston.[332] Photograph 5.10 shows some of the ladies who were employed by the *American Tobacco Company*.[333] Despite the increase of jobs in the city, farming persisted as the most common employment in Goose Creek in the 1930s and 1940s.

Some wealthy, white landowners rented small plots of land to tenant farmers during the first half of the twentieth century. Henry A.M. Smith and Langdon Cheves were two such men from Charleston families whose ancestors owned Goose Creek land since the earliest colonial times. They jointly owned and managed 1,209 contiguous acres of land during the first decades of the twentieth century.[334] Separately they owned more, and both rented parcels to tenant farmers for approximately two dollars an acre.[335] This annual rental was lucrative because Smith and Cheves owned many acres, expended little overhead and paid low taxes.

Landowners paid a seventeen-cent annual tax per acre in the 1920s, and even less in the earlier decades.[336] This meager real estate tax provided little support for the schools, roads and other public works, but residents were obligated to pay an annual one-dollar poll tax, three-dollar road tax and

Photograph 5.10 The photograph is entitled, "Ladies of American Tobacco Co." These six ladies, (from left to right) Cleo Bowers, Maggie Singletary, Florence Driggers, Lorean Thompson, "Lokey" Driggers and Celenia Harmon, are shown in the 1930s wearing white dresses with green trim and collars that were their work uniforms. The tobacco company was located on Meeting Street in Charleston. The "Smith" General Store is shown in the background on Myers Road called "Old Smith Road" at that time. Mrs. Eva Driggers Smith was owner of the general store. Courtesy Mrs. Lorean Thompson, daughter of Mrs. Eva Driggers Smith.

one-dollar tax for every dog they owned. Clearly the residents and not the absentee landlord were expected to carry the burden of public programs. Such tax laws were a boon to large landowners, but a burden to the residents. Additionally, tenant rights were few and the tenant-to-owner lease bond gave most advantages to the landowner.

James Nelson rented a house and eight acres from Langdon Cheves in 1913 on the Oaks Plantation lands that are a part of Pineview Subdivision today.[337] By the rental contract he promised to pay eight dollars a year for the right to live and farm on the land. He also granted a lien on all crops grown on the property and directed any factor, ginner or others who may receive his crops to deliver unto the landowner sufficient amounts to pay the rent.[338] In this fashion the rent was guaranteed, because the landowner, the storeowner, the mill owner and the local ginner, kept a close network that guaranteed the timely payment of rents in cash or crops. The system favored the absentee landowner, but although the fairness of such agreement is questionable, such tenant arrangements, as well as the wage and boarding arrangements at the phosphate mines and lumber camps, provided sufficient livelihood to prevent a human exodus from Goose Creek that was experienced in many other parts of South Carolina during these decades.

Photograph 5.11 The photograph shows a farm settlement in the 1940s. These types of farm buildings were typical in the St. James, Goose Creek Parish during the first half of the century. *Courtesy Library of Congress.*

Photograph 5.12 The photograph shows Mrs. Susie Jenkins serving coffee at the Liberty Hall Hunting Club. Susie Jenkins was born into slavery in Goose Creek in 1858 and remained to work her entire life in the vicinity. She died at the age of seventy-nine in 1937 and is buried at the neighboring Brick Hope Plantation. *Courtesy Mrs. Susie Simpson of Liberty Hall Road.*

A few families in Goose Creek continued to live in the ways of the by-gone plantation of past centuries. Some black families stayed on the plantation as caretakers to receive wages and other living benefits such as board or planting rights. Sidney and Gertrude Legendre purchased Medway Plantation and neighboring lands in 1930, and found the Gourdine family living there as they had for generations. The Legendres and Gourdines reached an understanding and continued in that relationship for many years. David Gourdine and his brother, Walter, served as hunting guides and land caretakers while their sisters, Lizzie and Rosa, cooked and cleaned.

Also during these years, the *Otranto Hunt Club*, the *Goose Creek Club for the Preservation of Game*, the *Liberty Hall Hunting Club* and the *Red Bank Hunting Club* used wide expanses of land for hunting deer, turkey and quail. The members usually resided in Charleston, and many were connected to the Goose Creek landowners through family or business. The memberships were small with ten or twelve men per club, but the clubs used large expanses of forests and fields because they paid the tenant farmers for the right to hunt over their lands. In 1909 the Goose Creek club paid thirty-one individuals with forty-two plots of land, a small fee to access their farms. The fee was customarily paid in produce, such as in 1909 the club leased hunting rights for one or 1½ bushels of peas per plot.[339] Tenant farmers on Crowfield, Bloomfield, Fredericks, Magnolias, 17-, 18- and 19-mile tracts, Bees, Howe Hall, Ararat, Gadsden and Blue House tracts also received produce in exchange for the hunting privileges. The tenants normally relinquished the hunting rights as part of their standard lease agreement with the landowner.[340] Nevertheless, farmers such as Maggie Johnson, Hampton Pringle, Dolly Leftenant, Alex Grant, R. Pinckney, Abbe Mazyck, R. Pringle, Ann Rivers, Sarah Rivers, July Myers, Jack Stevens, John Nelson, Ann Jerrydo, Lee Bennett, R. Robertson, Thomas Small, Renty Richardson, E. Palmer, H.E. Shepard, Tony Gaillard, Dennis Graham, Sandy Gourdin, D. Smith, Edward Pinckney, Hannah Brown, Alex Jones, Sol Milligan, Edmund Reece, H. Bennett, Sol Green, R. Moultrie and Cato Jefferson received payment in peas from the Goose Creek hunt club in 1902.[341]

The Goose Creek hunt club was situated on the eastern side of the water near the Goose Creek Church, but the *Otranto Hunt Club* occupied a house about 350 yards from the Otranto train station near the Atlantic Coast Line tracks on the west side of the Goose Creek Bridge.[342] The house was built and furnished by Edward L. Wells, and leased to the membership for $3 a year. The clubhouse shown in photograph 5.13 featured a front porch and scalloped siding. The Otranto Hunting Club paid John Watson $125 annually to serve as "game keeper" and deer driver.[343] He also served as sexton to the St. James, Goose Creek Church. Photograph 5.14 shows him in his official church capacity wearing a sexton robe. He resided in a small wooden house near the intersection of State Road and the church road and continued in his service to the church and hunt club until his death.[344] Many of his descendents continue to reside in Goose Creek today.

The *Liberty Hall Hunting Club* used thousands of acres, including much of the land that is the Department of Defense Property today as well as Medway Plantation. In 1912, a group of Charleston men built a hunting clubhouse on the site of the Liberty Hall Plantation main house and leased the rights to hunt the nearby land.[345]

The Marrington home of John Poppenheim was also a favorite meeting place for sportsmen. Poppenheim invited many guests, including "Billy" Sunday, a popular radio preacher, to his home to hunt at Red Bank, Marrington and Cedar Hill Plantations. Photographs 5.16, 5.17 and 5.18 show

Photograph 5.13 The photograph shows a house described as on the "Road to Goose Creek" in 1904. The house was built and used for the Otranto Hunt Club. *Courtesy South Carolina Historical Society, Charleston, South Carolina.*

Photograph 5.14 The photograph shows John Watson, the sexton of the St. James, Goose Creek Church. He was seventy years old when the photograph was taken near the turn of the twentieth century. The caption of the photo states "Well known character of a type that is passing...an old timer who was owned before the Civil War...not only a good sexton but an excellent deer driver and woodsman of the Goose Creek Country where he resides." The photograph is in the Johnson scrapbook among the collections of the South Carolina Historical Society, Charleston, South Carolina.

Photograph 5.15 The photograph shows the clubhouse at Liberty Hall when the plantation was used as a hunting preserve.

Photograph 5.16 The photograph shows riders with hunting dogs on the front yard of Marrington Plantation (ca. 1925). *Courtesy Terrance Larimer.*

Photograph 5.17 The photograph shows Billy Sunday and other hunters at the Marrington and Redbank Plantations owned by John Poppenheim during the early years of the twentieth century. *Courtesy Terrance Larimer.*

Photograph 5.18 The photograph shows Mr. and Mrs. Sam Seels at Red Bank Plantation, ca. 1930. He wore Jodhpur trousers and high boots when he served as a horse-mounted deer driver for the Red Bank Hunt Club. *Courtesy Terrence Larimer.*

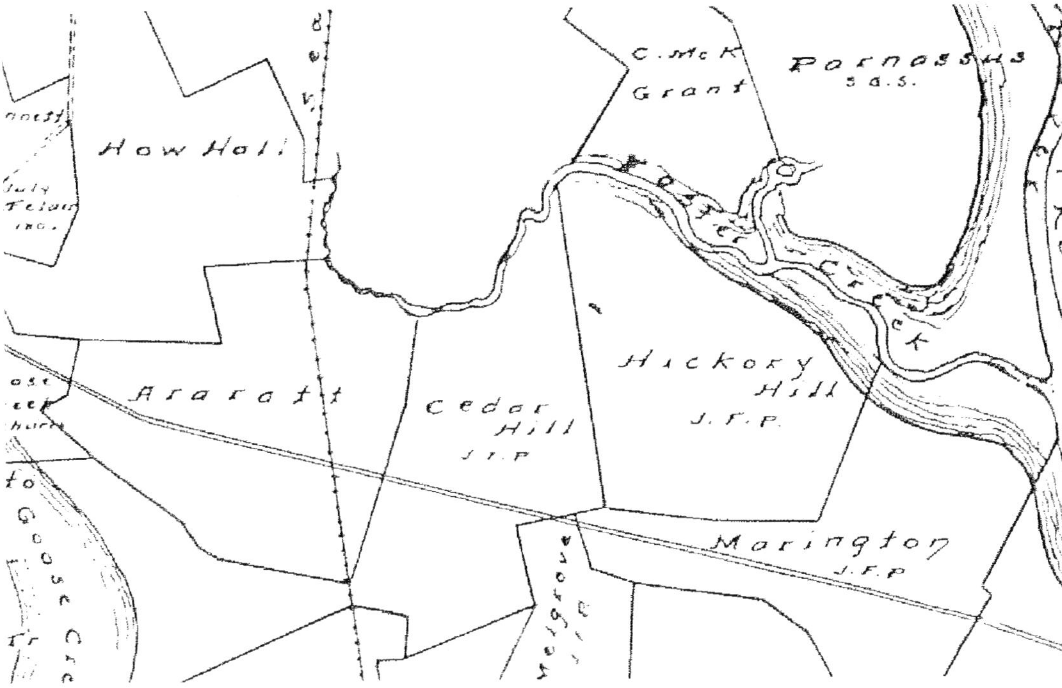

Map 5.2 The map shows lands bordering Foster Creek in the 1930s. This map is part of the John Palmer Gaillard Map, ca. 1936.

hunters at Marrington and map 5.2 shows some of the large tracts, which were used for hunting in the first half of the twentieth century.

The Black Neighborhoods

The African American church was the most important and dynamic institution in Goose Creek during this era. The church provided religious guidance, performed many important civic functions and was an agency through which the community organized. The church leaders were decision makers, social workers and community administrators. Every black Goose Creek subsection supported a church because there were no other local institutions to provide political or civil services. Some communities were very small with barely a dozen families in the congregation. Bowen's Corner was such a settlement. Other communities like Casey, Grove Hall and Howe Hall contained several dozen black families who made up large church congregations. However each church leader ministered only to the local neighborhood, so there was no community-wide cohesiveness in the greater Goose Creek area. Consequently, there were no opportunities for blacks to organize political, social or economic initiatives, as did their white counterparts. Whereas the whites attended political rallies at Wassamasaw, voted in the Democratic primaries at Carnes Crossroads and played grass root roles in county, state and national movements, the blacks created no organizations beyond their immediate neighborhood. It was the lack of opportunities for African American participation in wider initiatives that thrust the ministers of the black churches into important leadership roles in the lives of virtually every black citizen in Goose Creek.

Clearly the black clergyman was the most important leader in the African American communities. According to the 1906 census of religious bodies, almost all black Carolinians were affiliated with a church, and Goose Creek was no exception.[346] Most Goose Creek churches were United Methodist, African Methodist Episcopal, Episcopal or Methodist Episcopal denominations. The churches offered black Carolinians their most meaningful opportunities for independence, and aside from serving as a training center for community leaders, the church influenced education by exercising considerable control over the schools, the curriculum, the teachers and the students.

Casey was an African American settlement located on land that was once part of the old Mt. Holly Plantation. Oral history tells that this little place was first settled during the Reconstruction era. Some Casey residents tell of a freed slave, with the same name, who pitched a tent from which he preached to the local people.[347] This story is plausible because the name "Thomas Casey" appeared on a land record in the eastern Goose Creek Parish in 1733 and a "Casey" farm family resided west of Wassamasaw near the State Road prior to the Civil War.[348] The oral history is supported by a plat made from a survey conducted in 1850, eleven years prior to the Civil War, that shows "Casey's Dam" in Daisey Swamp on the boundary between Old Barn and Thorogood Plantations. The Casey Dam was situated approximately one mile north of the 20-Mile post on the State Road.[349] Thus, the Casey name appears on land records as early as 1733 and as late as 1850, and supports the oral historical account that Casey may have been an emancipated slave who borrowed the family name of his owner and simply walked to the Mount Holly vicinity.

The source of the name may never be satisfactorily determined, but enough consistent worshippers gave permanence to the settlement shortly after the Civil War. The oral history purports that Casey eventually built a log and clay cabin that was the first permanent community church. It was around that small cabin that a strong community spirit developed, and because the neighborhood was isolated to a large extent, it became almost entirely self-sufficient.

Three roads intersected at Casey, one of which was the State Road (South Carolina State Highway 176). It was a poorly maintained dirt road that was impassable during some times of the year. Occasionally, floodwaters required the mailman to use a small boat to access some homes along the road.[350] The Moncks Corner Road intersected the State Road and was Casey's main thoroughfare. Thorogood Avenue branched from the Moncks Corner Road and was busy with houses and farm activity until it entered forests on the approach to the main house at Thorogood Plantation. Near Casey was South Carolina Highway 52, which was laid out in the 1920s, but remained single lane and rock surfaced well into the 1930s. The community gristmill was located near the intersection of Highway 52 with State Road (Highway 176).

Casey featured a church, a school and an assembly hall, which in many ways symbolized the values of the black settlement. T.W Lewis represented the trustees of the church when this twenty-five-acre tract was purchased upon which the church was later constructed. The property began at the southeastern corner of Thorogood Plantation lands on Moncks Corner Road and followed the road to a point where it turned west until it intersected with lands owned by H.A. Middleton. The Middleton lands bounded the church property on the south and west.[351] Plat 5.3 shows the church

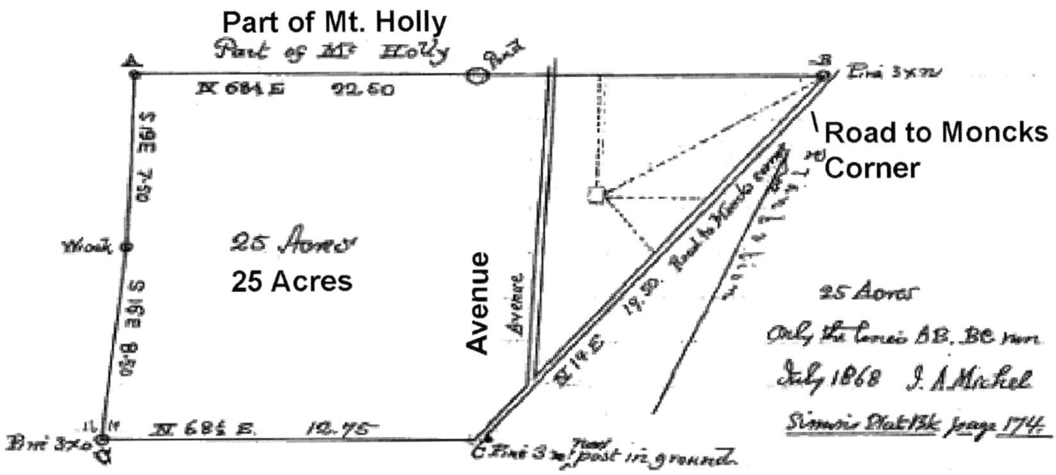

Plat 5.3 The partial plat shows the twenty-five-acre tract purchased by the Methodist Church at Casey [Caice]. The location of the church on the tract is shown as a square with four radiating lines between Thorogood Avenue and the Road to Moncks Corner. J.A. Mitchel drew the plat from a survey in July 1868. The plat is deposited with the Cheves papers at the South Carolina Historical Society, Charleston, South Carolina.

in relationship to the "Road to Moncks Corner" and the "Avenue" (Thorogood Plantation Avenue) within the twenty-five-acre tract purchased by the congregation.

The Casey Church was a beautiful white, wooden building that replaced the earlier log cabin. It was a large structure with stained glass windows, a chorus loft and an elegant ministry platform.[352] It was not unusual to find more than a hundred worshippers in the congregation on Sunday mornings. Some of the most frequent worshippers at Casey were Elizabeth Salley, C.J. Bryant, Pauline Gourdine, Wilford Johnson, Frank and Willie Mae Cohens, Frank Sass Sr., Janie Mae Bryan Jefferson and their families. The church was destroyed by arson in 1977 and today a thick copse of trees between the Casey cemetery and the Goose Creek Branch of the Berkeley County Library mark the location.

The Casey Cemetery contains dozens of silent stone reminders of the people of bygone days, one of which is a stone monument to Reverend William Evans who founded the Casey United Methodist Church. The monument states:

> *In Loving Remembrance / Our Dearly Beloved Pastor / Reverend Wm. Evans / The Founder of Caice Church / Born in 1822. / Died in 1887 / Aged 65 years. / Servant of God well Done / Thy Glorious Warfare is Past / The Battle Fought, The Race is Won / And Thou Art Crowned at Last.*

Photograph 5.19 The photograph shows the stone marker for the burial site of Reverend William Evans. The marker notes "Caice Church" as the preferred spelling of his congregation. The photograph was taken on March 8, 2002. *Author's collection.*

Photographs 5.20 and 5.21 The photographs show Casey [Caice] United Methodist Church as it appeared in 1977. This photograph shows a section of the interior. The photograph on the top of the opposite page shows the eastern elevation and front door. The church was no longer used for worship at the time the photographs were taken. *Author's collection.*

Photograph 5.21.

Reverend Hayward from Sumter was an early, full-time minister to the Methodist Church at Casey. He arrived by train at Mt. Holly and served the church for approximately twelve years during the 1930s and 1940s. Reverend C.J. Mack followed Reverend Hayward and was in turn succeeded by Reverend Pyatt. Reverend Pyatt's ministry was tainted by a fund-raising scandal which may have been little more than a bookkeeping error, but some contended that all of the money raised for the rehabilitation of the church was not spent in the proper manner. Regardless, the church was renovated during the tenure of Reverend Pyatt.

The Casey schoolhouse stood next to the church. This wooden structure was built in the 1930s, and was the sole source of local education for black scholars in grades one through seven in this neighborhood during the many decades of segregation. Casey school burned in 1966, though a chimney remained where the three-room school once stood until it was demolished for the construction of the Goose Creek branch of the Berkeley County Library. The Casey School was an important local institution of formal education and was open two months before and two months after Christmas. So many children walked to the Casey School from the Mt. Holly, St. Paul and Liberty Hall areas to attend the four month term that overcrowding sometimes required extra classes to be conducted in a nearby meeting hall. Mrs. Sadie Franklin, Mrs. Nathalie Chisolm and Mrs. Earlene Jefferson were among the black women who taught the African American children from the community. These educators remained well-respected teachers in the Goose Creek public schools for many years. Mrs. Earlene Jefferson, now retired, remains an active member of her church congregation today.

The schools in these communities were the product of cooperative efforts, and the teachers were expected to deliver many social services from the schoolhouse door. Men like Reverend James Harris, supervisory principal at Casey, directed the entire social service program for the isolated community, and the teachers were second in community importance only to the church minister. Educators worked to improve citizen health, road conditions and joined with churchmen to organize the local ministry and its programs.[353]

Across the Moncks Corner Road from the church stood the Casey Fellowship Hall. Many of the community decisions were made here following lively debates and from time to time "Sanctified people" held revivals here upon payment of an appropriate fee.[354] Not far from it stood a second smaller assembly hall where large groups would crowd inside to make community decisions and plan projects. Scattered within a short walking distance of the church were several dozen homes where the people of Casey reared their families. Henry A.M. Smith and Langdon Cheves owned and

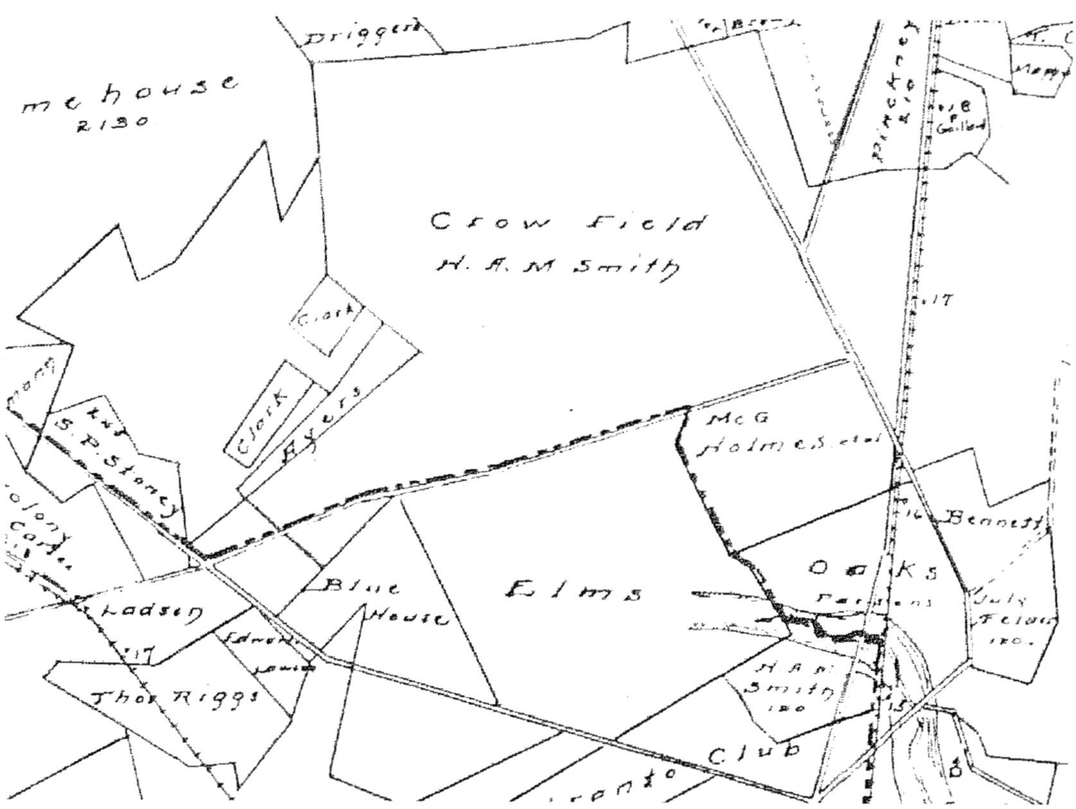

Map 5.3 The map is part of the 1936 Gaillard Map. It shows the names of landowners and the shape and location of farms and tracts.

managed lands where the residents of Casey and nearby Mt. Holly resided. Most of their tenants were African Americans who attended the church at Casey, some of whom were important leaders in that community.

Two of the farmers, John Jenkins and John Knight rented farm land and served as agents for the landlord by collecting rents and reporting on conditions to the owners, but most tenants were merely farmers such as Robert Barnwell, Lee Bennett, Morris Boden, Adam Bonaparte, Henry Brown, Abraham Sr., Abraham Jr., Richard, Bill and Ben Bryant, Albert Daniel, Phillip Driggers (white farmer), Abraham and Mary Fraser, Mac Jamison, Julius and Washington Myers, James and John Henry Nelson, Jack Stevens, Henry Amos Pinckney and H.E. Shepherd. These farmers typically rented five acres for three dollars annually, and supported medium to large extended family including nephews, nieces, parents and grandchildren. Nine of the 34 farmers renting land from Henry Smith in the early 1900s were black women. Remarkably, these women: Celia Clinton, Emma Drayton, Martha McGill, Alice Sumpter, Catherine and Carolina Whaley and Martha McKelvey represented more than 30 percent of the tenant farmers in this section.[355] These women supported extended families including grandchildren. For example, Martha McKelvey, supported five sons and one daughter on five acres of plowed ground (see appendix XVI for a listing of tenant farmers at Casey and the vicinity in 1910–14).

Families remained in Goose Creek and leased the same properties for generations. Prior to the twentieth century, the Myers, Stephens, Bryant, Sumpter, Pinckney and Green families farmed in the Casey and Mt. Holly neighborhoods. Beginning in 1886, Washington Myers rented land from Langdon Cheves at the 18-mile tract where the Shannon Park Shopping Center is situated today. Washington was the adopted son of Richard Myers who was chronicled in the previous chapter of this work. During this period Washington's niece Alice, and her husband John Knight, lived on the Oaks Tract, which is Pineview Subdivision today. Julius Myers moved into Alice Sumpter's house at the 17-mile tract when she married. Their farm stood near the Robert Road intersection with Red Bank Road. Nearby were the farms of William Myers, Jack Stephens and Florence Green who lived on a tract once owned by July Myers.

The Bryans (sometimes Bryants and by 1930 consistently Bryant) made up a longtime and extended Casey family. Alice Sumpter married Abraham Bryant and lived at Mt. Holly. By 1920, this seventy-two- and sixty-six-year-old couple were living next to their oldest son, forty-two-year-old Abraham Bryant, and his thirty-five-year-old wife and their five children.[356] Foxborough Road intersects Old Moncks Corner Road today about 150 yards from the site of Abraham Bryant's farmhouse. Nearby was Ben and Daisey Bryant's house where they raised their son, Herman and their daughter, Jennie Mae.

The next generation of Bryants remained at Casey. Simpson Bryant Sr. made caskets and tombstones in the 1930s and 1940s. He was also a blacksmith who shod horses, made wagon wheels and fashioned metal into hinges and hardware.[357] Like most farmers, he worked a few acres of land to put corn, potatoes and vegetables on the table. His brother, Joseph Bryant was the "week-end butcher" who traveled from home to home weekly to deliver meat.[358]

Also in the vicinity by 1920, was the family home of thirty-year-old Cornelius Gourdine and his twenty-seven-year-old wife, Ida, who reared their children, Ethel, Ernestine, James, Florence, Albertha, Lawrence and John. Today, the City of Goose Creek's public works building and elevated

Photograph 5.22 The photograph shows a house with African American children and a lady at the front porch. Homes such as this were typical in Goose Creek during the first half of the twentieth century. *Courtesy Library of Congress.*

water tank is situated near the corner of the property farmed by Rachel and Henry Pinckney, who took over the old Myers farm and house. Nearby was the residence of Lee Bennett who resided in a small house east of Old State Road. Today, Red Bank Road intersects the rail line near the site of the Bennett farm, and Bushy Park Terrace subdivision occupies the plowed fields. Map 5.3 shows a section of Goose Creek during the 1930s in the vicinity of Highway 52, the Atlantic Coastline Railroad and Old Moncks Corner Road. Some of the lands in the vicinity of Casey and Mt. Holly are labeled Bryan, Brown, Fowler, Chisolm and Pinckney. Other lands in the Mt. Holly area are labeled C. Mappus, Cunningham, Black, Gaillard, White and Bryan. The Bennett property is shown as well as July Felder's contiguous farm.

One woman who spent almost all of her life on these small black farms was Mrs. Loretta Parsons who came to Casey in 1930 at the age of nine and spent her life in the rural environs of Casey and Mt. Holly. Her favorite memories are of the Old Moncks Corner Road, the cool spring and the places where she played as a child. From these memories, it seems that Old Moncks Corner Road has since lost most of its splendor. It was once a country avenue with a natural green median between the carriage ruts. A green tunnel of foliage unfolded overhead and kept the road cool and breezy in the summer. Approximately one hundred yards from the western side of the road near its intersection with the Mt. Holly Road was a natural spring, which fed a land-locked pond. The pond was a favorite fishing spot, and the spring water was brought to the church and homes daily. The pond is now owned by the City of Goose Creek and graces the west grounds of the municipal center. The spring is located west of the intersection of Old Moncks Corner and Old Mt. Holly Roads. Today that location is west of the church that is situated on that corner and near a small bridge on Old Mt. Holly Road.[359] A low wet area with dense forest and under-brush characterizes the spring location today.

Sunday church services were eagerly anticipated. Often, Sunday service was a daylong event with morning and evening meetings attended by dozens of worshippers who, prior to the late 1940s, arrived by horse and buggy or on foot. The residents wore their best clothes and behavior for this favorite day of the week. The second Sunday in June was Children's Day in Casey. On this day, children came from as far as Summerville and Moncks Corner, many on wagons lined with boards for bench seats. The typical Sunday picnic was made special that day with plenty of lemonade, cookies, cakes and covered dishes. Meals were cooked over a wood burning stove in the Friendship Hall near the church.

Near Casey was Liberty Hall. This area was an important African American community since Reconstruction, and by the turn of the century, African Americans owned much of the property with some of it controlled by real estate societies. Most of the societies' farms ranged from 10 to 25 acres, but in one instance, a 46-acre tract surveyed in 1906 was owned by two societies and was divided into twenty-eight lots of approximately 1.6 acres each.[360] These small farm parcels often featured wooden clapboard houses with cedar roof shingles and shuttered windows. Such a home is shown in photograph 5.22. These small homes sheltered the families, and formed communities of interests in little places, such as Liberty Hall.

By 1930, Liberty Hall Road remained an unpaved wagon trail but it ran the length of the Liberty Hall Community. One of the larger farms near the intersection of Liberty Hall and Back River Road was owned by Cato Jefferson and his family. He shared this vicinity with more than a dozen families including: Peter Way, Peter Bennett, Christmas Leftenant, Peter Leftenant, Aaron Rivers, Ella Smalls, Gabriella Rivers, Mary Richards, Dinah and Frederick Mitchell, William Jefferson, Timothy and Mattie Leftenant, Mary Simpson, Lucinda Brown and Tillie Grant.[361] Also nearby were the families of Richard Roberson, Dolly Leftenant, Alexander Grant, Richard Mitchell, Edmund Reese, Prince Jones and W.M. Thomas.[362] In addition, the Alstons, Holmes, Smalls, Thompsons, Rollins, Baylocks, Jeffersons, Myers and other families lived on Liberty Hall Road.[363]

During the 1930s, other African American neighborhoods with churches and schools supported families similar to the people of Casey and Liberty Hall. On the "Church Road," (Foster Creek Road), were the Smalls, Read, McKelvey, Warren, Brown, Wade, Fields, Gibbes, Adkins, Reace, Watson, Delahony, Myers and McClary families.[364] Grave markers at the Bee Cemetery near Mallard Road mark the final resting places of Solomon Bennett, James and Fannie McClary, Hattie D. Loney, Henry and Julia Watson, Jack Atkins, Olivia McKelvey and Herbert Palmer, all of which resided nearby during this period. Residing on Howe Hall Road was a lone white family named Cunningham whose neighbors were the African American families of the Roundtrees, Williams, Jeffersons, Parkers, Barnetts, Jenkins, McCoys, Richardsons and others. The Rivers, Wilsons and Baylocks lived on Innis Road, near Poppenheim's Crossing. Along the new "Coastal Highway"

Photograph 5.23 The photograph shows a section of Back River Lower Road as it approaches Back River. The road has changed little for more than three hundred years and it is typical of the wagon paths that remained in the first half of the twentieth century. The photograph was taken on March 7, 2005. *Author's collection.*

(State Highway 52), were the Geathers and Saulisburys, as well as the Bradleys, Dingles, Gourdines, Mitchels, Polites, Millers, Johnsons, Rivers and Grahams. Similar neighborhoods were situated on the "Meeting Street Road" to Goose Creek, now the Otranto and Hanahan areas, Dean Hall Road near Strawberry and the white neighborhood at Mt. Holly. A lone black sharecropper, Jeff Johnson lived in a house where the old nature trail branches off the gravel on Marrington Road at the Naval Weapons Station.

All of the Goose Creek subsections were nearly self-supporting because most of the necessities of life were produced locally. Wheat, cotton, peanuts, hay, rice, sugar cane, tobacco, corn and nearly every variety of garden vegetables were grown. Work was available cutting pulpwood and firewood, sawing timber, digging phosphate and repairing or replacing the railroad tracks. The new highway construction project needed laborers for several years, and making corn whiskey, albeit risky, continued as a lucrative Goose Creek business.[365]

Most enjoyed access to a cornfield, which could be profitable since the easiest way to increase the value of corn was by distilling it into corn whiskey known as moonshine. During the 1930s and 1940s,

Hampton Varner made moonshine at his farm near Carnes Crossroads. He grew sugar cane as well as corn and his farm featured a deep well, cane press and a clay-lined oven for boiling molasses. Thus, every ingredient in a moonshine recipe: water, corn and sugar, was available on his well-equipped farm. The unlawful practice was common.[366] The *Charleston News and Courier* complained, "Prohibition had ruined Charlestonians' tastes...they willingly guzzled 'Hell Hole Swamp' corn."[367] The Berkeley County Sheriff occasionally brought charges before the magistrate in an effort to enforce the laws. On one occasion, a magistrate recorded the lyrics to a song sung by a "moonshiner" in Goose Creek. The lyrics celebrated:

> *Hurray for Charleston/ The Place where I been down/ Da tell me don't cry nigger Mr. Roosevelt coming round. /Da fed me Goose Creek Taters and a slice o de Maybank pie/ I'm going back to Charleston and stay till I die.*[368]

After writing the lyrics to the song, the magistrate arrested "Washington" (no first name was given) for making illegal whiskey and brought his case to court.

The lyrics of the moonshiners' song tell much about the political mood of the state and nation. It is likely that the song was not an original composition by Mr. Washington, as reported by the magistrate, but was a political news report passed by word of mouth through the rural countryside. Interestingly, much like the nursery rhymes of old England, news reports were sometimes encoded in songs, which ordinary citizens passed from place to place when they sang the memorized lyrics. Similarly, enslaved Negroes communicated from field to field in this fashion for centuries, but these were the years when President Franklin Delano Roosevelt kept "fireside chats" with America via radio and explained the New Deal plan to create jobs for all and to lighten the burden of the economic depression. These were the years when many unemployed and desperate men left the cities and returned to the farms to grow enough food to keep their families alive. Without radios, the promises of President Roosevelt and Charleston's Mayor Bernard R. Maybank were most effectively broadcasted via word of mouth. "Goose Creek taters" and a "slice o de Maybank pie" were news reports, as well as words of hope for Washington and anyone within hearing range.

The White Neighborhoods

White families were generally associated with rail stops. Rail stops were the places people assembled, and thus were usually the site of post offices and general stores, all of which were owned and operated by white Goose Creekers.[369] Poppenheim's Crossing was located at Innis rail stop, where Red Bank Road enters the Department of Defense property at the Naval Weapons Station today. Here, a few white families worked the nearby Marrington/Redbank lands. William Wilson was the caretaker for P.O. Mead Sr. and lived in a house that Mead provided. He reared a family there and his son, William Wilson Jr., grew up on that land and was later employed at the Naval Weapons Station. Strawberry, Mt. Holly, Otranto and Woodstock were rail stops, with white operated businesses and a few white households nearby.

Mount Holly was the most significant white Goose Creek neighborhood of the era and appeared on early maps as a station on the Atlantic Coastline Railroad. As late as 1940, it featured a railroad station, a post office, a sawmill, grits mill, sugar cane mill, a fertilizer merchant, casket maker, two stores and five houses. The surrounding community was composed of two large plantations and dozens of small farms owned, rented and worked by white families.

James A Hargroves Sr., resided for many years at the Mt. Holly Plantation house owned by Smith Richardson.[370] The Wade family lived at the Montague Plantation house. That house burned in 1977 but its remains can be found under large oaks east of the Boulder Bluff subdivision. The white population resided on small farms nearby. Although the white community was well entrenched, their numbers were too few and scattered to consistently support churches or schools. By the twentieth century the old St. James, Goose Creek Church held service only once a year, and although some white churches assembled from time to time, only one persisted more than a few years. The Chapel of Our Savior was open for worship for a short time in the 1930s near the Mt. Holly Station, but no reference to this church can be found after 1940.[371] The Smryna Methodist Church in Groomsville appears to have been the most popular house of worship for whites in Mt. Holly. It survives as a viable institution with many white Goose Creekers buried in the church grounds. Some European American families traveled to Summerville, Moncks Corner, Deer Town (now Deer Park) or the north area of Charleston for religious services, and most white children attended schools in Moncks Corner. Photographs 5.27 and 5.28 show the William Irvin Etling chicken farm and home on the Oaks Plantation land. This farm supported the only white family in the vicinity of today's Pineview Subdivision approximately two miles south of the Mount Holly train depot.

Photograph 5.26 The photograph shows the Symrna Baptist Church in Groomsville, which is located on South Carolina Highway 2. *Author's collection.*

Photograph 5.27 The photograph shows William Irvin Etling at his chicken farm in 1934. This property was part of the Oaks Plantation. The two girls in the center of the photograph are Laura and Wilma, Mr. Etling's daughters. Today the address of this location is 204 Etling Drive in Pineview Subdivision. *Courtesy Frances Etling Roberson.*

Photograph 5.28 The photograph shows the first house in Pineview. The chicken house shown in photograph 5.27 was demolished and the lumber was used to expand this house in the early 1940s. The oak trees in this photograph are now fully grown and provide shade to the front yard of a modern home at 204 Etling Drive. *Courtesy of Frances Etling Roberson.*

The white families of Mt. Holly were few in number, but represented the most significant Euro-American community in Goose Creek. Family names recorded toward the end of the 1930s were: C.B. Linder, J.R. Cannon, J.A. Hoyle, J.H. Dangerfield, G.W. Dangerfield, W.E. McKenzie, Waring Bunch, G.B. Cannon, Ed Lee and Alton Cannon, son of J.R. Cannon. Other whites residing in the vicinity of Mt. Holly were the Horton, Nix, Campbell, Brown, Droze, Lambright, Varner, Lawrence, Smith, Bell and B.W. Mixon families.[372]

Some quasi-institutions emerged in the isolated countryside. The ladies of Mt. Holly organized the Mt. Holly Home Demonstration Club that was well attended for many years. The club members participated in arts and crafts, chair caning and rug making, exchanging recipes and preserving techniques. Elizabeth Boykin coordinated the Home Demonstration Club for many years and was supported by active members such as Mrs. C.B. Linder, Mrs. D.T. Rhoad, Mrs. W.B. Nix, Mrs. G.W. Dangerfield, Mrs. Scarborough and Mrs. Alma Brown.[373] Their clubhouse remained standing until it was demolished for its lumber in 1972.

Map 5.4 The 1951 South Carolina Highway Map shows a section of the St. James, Goose Creek Parish. The words, "Rozier General Store" were added for this publication.

Photograph 5.24 The photograph shows James H. Rozier Sr. in the center with his wife, Agnes Jaudon Rozier and their sons Robert H. Rozier on the left and James H. Rozier Jr. on the right. Rozier operated the store for forty-two years and was instrumental in underwriting small loans to establish minority owned farms nearby. He also donated two acres of land for Bethel School, the first public school in Strawberry for African American children. The photograph was taken in 1954. *Courtesy James H. Rozier Jr.*

Photograph 5.25 The photograph, taken May 22, 2005, shows the Rozier General Store in Strawberry. *Author's collection.*

A few white owned homes and small businesses were located near the Strawberry rail stop about two miles north of Mt. Holly. The general store owned by James H. Rozier Sr. operated at Strawberry for many years. He and his bride, Agnes Jaudon arrived in 1935 to reside on 128 acres and operate the only store in the small community. He stocked the shelves with necessities for nearby farm families and then expanded his customer base by selling tracts of his land for $100 an acre, payable in small weekly increments along with grocery purchases at the store. Some African American families were able to purchase their little farms in this vicinity by using Rozier's general store payment plan.

Professor C.M. Furman owned four hundred acres in Strawberry during this time where he grew some cotton and employed field hands to pick it.[374] John Donnelly's descendents also continued to own some property in Strawberry next to Sam Huff's farm and A.S. Winter's land.[375] The Poppenheims and Kodamas became prominent citizens of Strawberry and Mt. Holly, after they retired from rice farming at their Marrington and Redbank Plantations. Members of both families joined the Smyrna Methodist Church in nearby Groomsville and some are buried on the church grounds.[376]

West of the Strawberry and Mt. Holly Stations was land owned by descendents of the Droze and other families that was contiguous to the State Road. The Droze Cemetery located on St. James Avenue (Highway 176) almost contiguous to Foxborough subdivision is a remnant of this small white neighborhood.

White, non-local investors such as P.O. Mead, H. Smith Richardson and Henry G. Roosevelt purchased large tracts of land and harvested timber for many years. Other investors were more transient. The Burton and The Midland Timber Companies purchased tracts, harvested the timber and sold the land piecemeal to interested farmers. James S. Simmons purchased several parcels of this property near Mt. Holly Station for $3,400 in 1905. The lands bounded the rail line and amounted to about two hundred acres. He sold the acres to small landowners.[377] These and the similar land transactions were instrumental in partitioning the large tracts, and allowed small farmers to establish a foothold of ownership in the twentieth century.

One effort to make money from the worn Goose Creek lands was merely speculative. An advertisement appeared in the *Charleston Evening News* on March 20, 1921, accompanied by a large drawing of an oil well and a plat of subdivided properties available for purchase. The advertisement was intended to use the potential wealth from underground oil fields to sell parcels of land. The 2,197 acres of oil speculation land owned by Coastal Land Corporation was located about one and one-half mile west of Carnes Crossroads and less than three miles from the unproven Mabeleanor oil well near Summerville. That land has yet to yield oil, but in recent decades the tract has become sprawling residential streets and commercial strips. Interestingly, Texas oil interests held four parcels of Liberty Hall property as speculative oil locations until 2003.

A reliable livelihood for some Goose Creekers was found in the ownership and operation of general stores. Cannon's store operated in Goose Creek proper near the entrance of the main avenue to the Oaks Plantation.[378] The Morning Star Grocery and Kodoma's Store operated at Mt. Holly near the railroad depot. George and Eloise Gowder purchased the Morning Star Grocery from Tom Addison in 1946 and managed the store for ten years.[379] Tokio Kodama and his family lived on the second floor over their store that was located near the Morning Star Grocery. This same Japanese family lived on Marrington Plantation for many years before it became part of the Naval Weapons

Photograph 5.29 The photograph taken in 1938 by Marion Post Wolcott is entitled, "White family's home near Summerville, South Carolina." This farmhouse was located in the St. James, Goose Creek Parish near today's Highway 17A. *Courtesy Library of Congress.*

Photograph 5.30 The photograph shows the Thorogood Plantation house. The gentleman walking across the front yard is probably Henry S. Richardson, owner. This photograph is part of the Johnson scrapbook, among the collections of the South Carolina Historical Society, Charleston, South Carolina.

Station.[380] Another store was located for a while at the Mt. Holly Post Office under the management of Mrs. Hilma Watkins. Also, Mrs. C.B. Linder managed the post office, as well as the store for many years. Orven and Anne Thomason operated Thomason's Store from 1946 to 1971 at the corner of St. James (Highway 176) and Thomason Boulevards and the Smith General Store operated south of Carnes Crossroads for decades.

The general stores of Goose Creek were multi-purpose establishments. Besides providing various groceries and hardware, the stores marketed much of the locally grown produce. The general stores were also loan offices for local farmers and the owners were sought to provide legal and medical advice, as well as family counseling.[381] Often the storeowners had the only means of motorized transportation that served as ambulances in case of emergencies, and carried many mothers to the hospital when childbirth was too difficult for the "grannies" or midwives. James H. Rozier Sr. drove many sick and injured to the hospital and according to Eugene Bryan, who grew up in Strawberry next to *Rozier's Store*, "it didn't matter what time of night or day, you could count on Mr. Rozier." Remains of the *Smith General Store* built in approximately 1920, and *The Singletary and Son General Store* built in 1930–31, stand today in the western section of the parish and the old building that was once *Rozier's* store remains in Strawberry.

In 1930, no Goose Creek home possessed a radio.[382] Consequently, the dearth of news and entertainment was broadcast by whatever gossip could be shared at the general store. Understandably, when the first radio arrived, as when the first televisions appeared twenty years later, the common place for its debut was the neighborhood store, where all gathered to witness the newest phenomenon.[383]

Photograph 5.31 The photograph shows the Smith General Store on South Carolina Highway 59 in a western corner of the parish, today no longer in use. The store was constructed about 1920. The store was operated by two generations of the Smith family who also managed a nearby sawmill.

No black Goose Creeker owned or worked in a general store in Goose Creek during this period, but it seems that the black farmer used the services regularly.[384] The general store was the only semblance of a bank where a black man could do business. One example of a loan arrangement is found in the records for July Myers. July Myers owed $633 to the Mt. Holly Mercantile Co. in 1914. He secured the loan with the mortgage of his farm and 8 percent interest. He paid off the loan when due, and secured the furtherance of the loan with the attachment of his two mules, one mower, one broken wagon, and twenty-five acres of land. A year later, Myers was able to pay $481 toward the debt, but was obligated in 1920 to pay off the remaining portion by giving the company two bales of cotton and all the cotton seed on account.[385]

Despite the lack of medical facilities and claims that health was considerably better during those days, people did get sick and were forced to rely on natural medicines. The result was a considerable repertoire of homemade cures. For sore throats, the swamp Spanish oak was a sure remedy. "My grandmother would chop it off, steep it with alum. It was a good gargle for sore throats," recalls one Goose Creeker. "It was good for you, but I hated the stuff because it would tie up your mouth."[386] For stomachaches, pains and bad colds, the plant called "rabbit tobacco" or "black root" was a common cure. It was dug up, washed and boiled and the boiled mash was allowed to steep and settle. A tea from the juice was sipped until it brought relief.

One of the most common trees in Goose Creek was the swamp willow or coastal plain willow. Most Goose Creek homes kept one planted at the chimney corner of the home. It was steeped to make a "stump drink" and used as a common remedy from fever and dysentery. Willow tree tea was the most common cure and it was said that, "It cures the dysentery nine times out of ten."[387] Sipping blackberry juice, a tea made of strawberry leaves or a tea made from the bark of persimmon trees relieved dysentery. For babies with hives or colic, catnip tea was prescribed. Catnip grew in small bunches in many yards, and a tea was made from it by boiling the leaves to induce sleep. The heartleaf or snakeroot grew with a long, winding root, which was coiled and placed into a jar with whiskey. After sitting for a time, the brew could be sipped for backache, or aches and pain from cold or rheumatism. For vomiting, high blood pressure or gas pains, garlic, commonly called "wild leek," was helpful. The bulb was cut up and placed in a jar with red vinegar, lemon juice and Epsom salts. It was also used for cooking. Medicinal treatment was a seasonal practice and every change of season the children (and consenting adults) received a fair amount of homemade medicine to prepare them for the new season. Home remedies provided for "clean stomachs, clean bowels and clean blood."[388]

Goose Creekers relied on each other and the products of the land for sustenance. Neighbors and family were the most important ingredients in community life and midwives, such as Lucille Jefferson-Gourdine brought most of the babies into the world.[389] Three gunshots in the air signaled "emergency," and all residents would do their part in fighting a fire or assisting an injured neighbor, but when absolutely necessary, they traveled twenty miles to Charleston or fifteen miles to Moncks Corner for medical assistance. The most reliable and familiar doctor after 1930 was Dr. William Henry Lacey. His home and office were in Moncks Corner, but he made house calls to Goose Creek and was summoned at all hours and sometimes by mistake. Once a young Goose Creek girl summoned him at three in the morning. She pleaded, "come quick, daddy got the gun after us again!" The doctor told her to call the sheriff. The doctor later recalled that, "Her father was a good fellow, just got these aberrations once in a while."[390]

In addition to the medicinal qualities of the natural products of the woods and marsh, herbs, roots and leaves of the Goose Creek countryside added spice to the local dinner table. Sassafras tea was kept handy in a bag in most kitchens and no stew or soup was complete without a bit of "pot magic." This small brown root was cooked with other foods to enhance the flavor. Poke weed or poke salad was an herb with palatable leaves, which were cooked while tender and young. Wild asparagus or smilax can still be found along the sides of the old Moncks Corner Road. This climbing vine was eaten raw or cooked as a vegetable in a soup or stew.

Public Schools and Education

By 1900, almost all Goose Creek children attended school some months each year, but the number of months of attendance depended upon the location of the children's home in proximity to the schoolhouse. The children of some neighborhoods attended two or three times more than those in other sections.[391] Both white and black children attended school, but white children usually attended twice as much. When black children attended school for three months in specific sections of the parish, white children of the same neighborhood attended six months. Where black children attended two months a year, white children attended four months. There were rare exceptions to this two to one attendance ratio based on race, but a few black children attended as many as eight or nine months.

The State Constitution prohibited children of one race from attending school with children of another race, thus separate faculties were required. Black Goose Creek teachers in 1900 were Anthony Lambert, Chinnis Droze, Carrie Washington and Gertrude Robinson. Lawrence Rhode

Photograph 5.32 The photograph shows Pineridge School. The school was built in the early 1920s on land donated by the Harmon family. *Courtesy Mrs. Lorean Thompson.*

was the only white teacher. All worked only 6 months that year.[392] Little change is notable during the next decades except that, Carrie L. Smith, Marvin Russel and Millie Mims were "tending school" in 1920. Interestingly, Carrie Smith was only sixteen years old.

The 1935–36 Berkeley School district budget funded 4 one- or two-room schools in the eastern third of the parish for white children. These schools named: Red Bank Plantation, Barrows (sometimes Varner), Medway Plantation and Pine Forest (sometimes Pineridge) employed only one teacher each at a seventy-five-dollar monthly salary. A teacher was employed at Pine Forest only two months that year. Photograph 5.32 shows Pine Forest (Pineridge) School in 1943. During those years, the Kodama family resided at Red Bank. This Japanese family did not easily fit into the racial segregation plan for school attendance, but the Kodama children attended the Red Bank Elementary School for white children and then commuted to Berkeley High School in Moncks Corner. The Red Bank School was a one-room schoolhouse located at the place of today's Storm Point Club at the Naval Weapons Station.[393]

The schools for black children in 1935–36 are listed in table 5.3. A small school on Howe Hall Road served the children of that section, and at one time there was a one-room school at Bowen's Corner, as well as a three-room school at Casey. There was also a school for black children at Grove Hall, about three miles from Casey, and a school for "mixed blood" children at Varner School situated .20 mile north of Carnes Crossroads on Highway 17A.[394] Additional nearby schools for African American boys and girls were named: Oakley Negro, Pineridge and Ladson Negro. Also, in 1930, Jenkins Reformatory was the home for seven black boys ages six to ten. It was located in Ladson on the old farm owned by Lamb Stevens. The lead counselor was a black man named Darcer McBeard and an unnamed mulatto guardian assisted him. This property is still owned by the *South Carolina Negro Aid Society*, and today is the site of the Huguenot granite cross that marks the location of the old French Huguenot Church of the frontier era.

The Berkeley School District budget for 1941–42 provided funding for five "Negro" schools in Goose Creek. Varner School was previously for "mixed race" children, where a long time educator, Ms. Annie Tupper taught youngsters such as Martha and Idel Dangerfield for many years, [395] but the school was reclassified as a "Negro" school in 1941–42. Howe Hall, Bowen's Corner, Casey and Grove Hall were also one, two or three room school buildings for elementary boys and girls. Students wishing to attend secondary schools boarded at the institution or with friends or relatives in Moncks Corner or Charleston because the fifteen-mile bus ride to either locale cost twenty cents and that was too expensive for daily trips. The Berkeley Training High School in Moncks Corner was open for African American youngsters in 1921. The building was enlarged from time to time as admission applications increased and under the supervision of Principal R.E. Ready, the school became an important Berkeley County educational institution.[396]

Table 5.3: The table shows Negro and "mixed" school attendance records for public schools in The Second St. James, Goose Creek Parish Township in 1935–36.

School	Enrollment	Number of School Days
Cayce	33	160
Grove Hall	15	160
Howe Hall	100	160
Bowen Corner	23	160
Varner School	20	160

Public Works Projects

Several important public works projects were completed during the first half of the century that impacted the Goose Creek and Charleston areas for many decades. At the turn of the century Charleston's water supply was provided by the privately owned Charleston Waterworks Company established in 1872. Goose Creek water was sought by the City of Charleston for many years because of its abundance and purity. Mrs. Poyas of Yeamans Hall noted in 1855 that the stream was about a mile from the house and was, "of such sparkling aspect, and so clear, as to have acquired the appellation of 'the silver spring,'" and the Charleston Water Company offered to purchase the spring early in the nineteenth century.[397]

The spring was inadequate to supply the needs of Charleston but the "silver spring" mentioned by Mrs. Poyas flowed into Goose Creek near The *Steam Pumping Station and Filter Plant* built by the water company in 1904 to pump water from Goose Creek. The water was first pumped to settling beds then to filters and finally into Charleston's distribution lines. The Charleston Light and Power Company purchased 1,882 acres of property spanning both banks of Goose Creek, built a dike across the lower end, and flooded it to hold and reserve the slow moving water.[398] This large reservoir and pumping station worked well at first, but in 1918 and 1927 the supply of water available at the reservoir was inadequate, due to severe drought and low water levels. These water shortages prompted the creation of the Charleston Water Commission that acquired the private water company and put it under public scrutiny and control.

To mitigate the chances of future water shortages, the commission tapped into the more abundant waters of the Edisto River. The first step required a 4½-mile tunnel aqueduct from the Edisto River to the Ashley River. This "first leg" was completed in 1928 and satisfied the demands of Charleston until 1935. It was then that the West Virginia Pulp and Paper Company approached the Charleston Water Commission for a five million gallon a day supply for their new industrial plant. To meet this demand, an additional 18½ miles of tunnel were burrowed to carry the Edisto water from the outfall shaft on the upper Ashley River to the Goose Creek pumping station. The project commenced in 1936. It required seventeen shafts sunk approximately 6,000 feet apart, connected by a seven-foot high tunnel. The tunnel was excavated completely below sea level at depths that varied from 40 to 80 feet. The entire tunnel was dug well within the impervious layer of marl, with a minimum cover of 20 feet of marl in a few sections but with as much as 40 feet of marl cover for the majority of the distance. The water tunnel is in use today providing the Goose Creek plant with a daily capacity of eighty million gallons. The marl layer and good engineering combined to provide an abundant source of potable water to more than one hundred thousand homes and businesses in the year 2000.

Another important public works project improved the public road thoroughfare. Since earliest times, the only land route through Goose Creek traversed the old Goose Creek Bridge. A more direct, north-south route was affected when the Berkeley County Board of Commissioners condemned sufficient property through Goose Creek, roughly parallel with the Atlantic Coastline Railroad, for a state highway. Today that route is known as Goose Creek Boulevard, James H. Rozier Boulevard and State Highway 52. The condemnation, acquired in 1927, required a seventy-five-foot swath of land through the entire breadth of the eastern parish.[399] The new route, at first known as the "Coastal Highway," opened many of the inaccessible tracts to traffic and trade, but it brought few immediate returns and it was the last public works project until the Federal Government purchased lands along the deep Cooper River waters to support its defense efforts during World War II.

On November 5, 1941, just more than a month prior to the Japanese attack on Pearl Harbor, the United States Ammunition Depot was established and throughout World War II, the depot was engaged in receiving ammunition from assembly plants, storing it, performing maintenance, and issuing it as needed for defense. Thousands of people moved to Charleston for employment at the naval facilities in North Charleston. By 1943, the Charleston Naval Base employed 26,500 people and the civilian community near the bases began to expand and with it came demands for homes and associated commerce in the sleepy Goose Creek countryside.

Goose Creek in the first half of the twentieth century was a simple place, with a few lumber and gristmills, general stores and white washed churches among the many small farms.[400] Although the little places in Goose Creek where people lived, worked and worshipped were isolated, both black and white Goose Creekers who recalled the era spoke of it favorably. Some black Goose Creekers fondly recalled the white landowners, such as Smith Richardson of Mt. Holly. White control was unquestionable with much of the land and all of the mills, stores and businesses owned by the whites, but there was a strong sense of black independence, pride and joy in the rural lifestyle. Thus the period from 1900 to 1950 appears to have been good times for those plowing the rural fields, but they were generally non-eventful for speculators investing in lands that changed little in value. Nevertheless, the first half of the twentieth century were defining years for the City of Goose Creek that incorporated soon after, and the rural landscape was the stage upon which one of the most technologically advanced communities emerged in the second half of the twentieth century. The Federal Military Complex recognized the deep waters and undervalued forests as an opportunity to develop and safeguard the world's most advanced weaponry. It was because of these foresights in the early 1950s that federal defense dollars flowed into the area, and started a juggernaut of residential and commercial development that forever transformed the countryside.

Chapter VI
Boom Town
1950–1980

The history of Goose Creek in the twentieth century is one of striking contrasts. During the first 50 years of the century, it was a poorly defined collection of small, rural settlements, but by the end of the century Goose Creek was a leading South Carolina city. The drastic alteration of the land during the last five decades of the century resulted from the installation of military bases on the worn plantation grounds and the economic boom that followed. These developments brought residents, investments, and new businesses to a section of South Carolina that had changed little since the Reconstruction Era. During and after World War II, defense related businesses in the Greater Charleston area employed 72,000 workers. The City of Charleston experienced only modest growth during these years, but the greater Charleston area, including Goose Creek, exploded to 225,000 people.[401] To accommodate the defense industry workers, the U.S. Housing Administration subsidized the construction of 5,000 rent-controlled housing units located north of the City of Charleston, near the naval facilities on the Cooper River. The jobs and houses brought an influx of families to the north area of Charleston County, as well as to Hanahan and Goose Creek in the southern-most part of Berkeley County.

The influx of families to south Berkeley County placed overwhelming demands on a county government that lacked experience in managing growth and providing infrastructure needed to accommodate a burgeoning population. Consequently, the people in a small section of the greater Goose Creek area incorporated into a municipality in 1961 in an effort to find solutions to the problems that came with rapid population growth. This defining event marked the beginning of the City of Goose Creek and thrust the little town hall into the midst of rousing political debates that raged for decades, but which laid the foundation and charted the direction of a dynamic community. Especially during the two decades from 1960 to 1980, the problems caused by the expanding population caused political battles that rallied the townspeople to the polls. Goose Creek City Hall became a forum in which residents dealt with local issues and eventually found the means to provide water, sewer, sanitation, public safety and other vital municipal services. But population numbers alone did not complicate politics. Population diversity added to the fray because almost all of the residents of Goose Creek during the period of 1950 to 1980 were from outside of the community and possessed few common visions of what their new city should become. The population was composed of residents with varied backgrounds, cultures, educations levels and ethnic origins. Diverse backgrounds made it difficult for the electorate to reach consensus on many of the issues, but it also brought diversity in thought that, when finally channeled, was a dominant force in the South Carolina Lowcountry. Goose Creek withstood the problems of rapid change on repeated occasions, and by 1980, the city settled into a predictable pattern of managed growth and municipal expansion.

1950s

The transformation of Goose Creek was evident in the 1950s as the influx of homebuyers with automobiles, radios, televisions and telephones threw down the barriers that had kept the small neighborhoods isolated for so long. For many whose ancestors lived in Goose Creek for many decades, even centuries, this transformation set in motion events that gave them a much wider sense of community. The transformation was obvious in the 1950s as the increase in pass-through auto traffic, along with events both large and small, clearly portended the irreversible changes stirring in the sleepy countryside.

The increased volume of traffic on Highway 52 was obvious as more and more workers in North Charleston commuted to rural homes. The highway opened as an unpaved gravel byway that put

Photograph 6.1 The photograph shows the Williams House located in Mt. Holly. This was one of the largest and finest homes built in Goose Creek in the 1950s. The building materials and construction style were typical of the era for new construction. The photograph was taken on March 20, 2002. *Author's collection.*

more Goose Creekers within commuting distance to jobs in the greater Charleston area. By 1950, the paved highway created a busy triangle intersection with State Highway 176 that greatly increased the commercial value of the contiguous lands. During the 1950s, Goose Creek farmer Jack Aichele, sought ways to diversify production and take advantage of the improving markets. In 1954, he dug irrigation ponds for tobacco fields and operated a successful plant nursery to supply the landscaping needs of new construction in Charleston County.[402] His nursery was situated on the triangle of land formed by the intersection of State Highways 52 and 176. The property encompassed all of the "downtown" section of today's modern city and spanned to today's Colonial Heights, Braemore

Photograph 6.2 The photograph shows an African American woman and children near their front porch in the Goose Creek vicinity. Some African American families were constructing new homes at that time, but many remained in much older abodes. The bicycle on the porch dates the photo after 1950. The oldest child may have been the inventor of the twin, two-wheel goat carts on the ground near him.

and Woodland Lakes Subdivisions and the Marguerite H. Brown Municipal Center. In 1950, John White, a well-known developer, loaned James Preacher Sr. $10,000, which he used to purchase land from Aichele in the triangle and build a gas station at the intersection of State Highways 52 and 176.[403] Mr. Preacher's gas station and Mr. Orvin Thomason's general store were the first businesses in the "triangle" that eventually became the commercial center of modern Goose Creek.

As automobile traffic increased on the rural highways, improved transportation and communication dissolved the rigid neighborhood boundaries in the black communities. Five Johnson brothers grew up as part of a sharecropping family on P.O. Mead's property. Military service in World War II carried the brothers to far reaches of the world. When Johnnie Johnson returned from the military in 1946, he arrived with leadership experiences from the military that would stay with him throughout his life. He did not return to full time farming but instead began a small worship group on Howe Hall Road. Later he moved his small assemblage of followers to a permanent church structure and established the *Calvary Church of God in Christ* on Liberty Hall Road in 1950. He was among a vanguard of new African American Goose Creekers who imported a progressive brand of leadership acquired from beyond the small church settlements. Other Goose Creekers also accepted new and wider responsibilities. The Reverend C.J. Bryant accepted chairmanship for area black churches to coordinate social programs throughout Goose Creek, as did Reverend Frank Sass on other occasions. For example he agreed to head the March of Dimes Drive as coordinator for all of South Berkeley in 1955.[404] These roles appear insignificant relative to today's civic standards, but these men were the first black Goose Creekers to boldly accept leadership roles beyond the confines of their small church. These little steps were the first of many taken by the black community that eventually led them to their rightful place among the vanguards of modern Goose Creek.

The highway also appeared to subtly change the attitudes of white Goose Creekers about their expanding world. After the road was built, the Mt. Holly 4H Club placed tables along the road to invite motorists to stop and rest. James Rozier (later elected Berkeley County Supervisor) erected a sign on the 4H clubhouse inviting passing motorists to join their group meeting the second Monday of each month.[405] Along with Rozier, Bonnie Bounds, Jimmy Lane, Franklin Thomas, Shirley Hopkins, Zona Thomas, Marcia Blaising and Rodney Thomas comprised the membership. The Mt. Holly Home Demonstration Club also met weekly to share advice among the membership. Members were Mrs. G.W. Dangerfied, Mrs. G.W. Bunch, Mrs. Tina Jordan, Mrs. Gordan Welch, Mrs. R.B. Myers, Mrs. Joe Metts, Mrs J.O. Cowart, Mrs. J.H. Rozier and Mrs. Annie Henderson.[406] The Mt. Holly Clubs sent their news of local events to the *Berkeley Democrat* weekly newspaper in Moncks Corner, the county seat.

The Cannon and Duncan families, residing within a quarter of a mile of the old Goose Creek Church, and the Poppenheims near Red Bank landing, were three white families in the vicinity during this period, but the families in Mt. Holly and Strawberry comprised the largest white community in the eastern section of the parish. The Morning Star Grocery Store at Mt. Holly was a favorite place for white and black Goose Creekers to meet during the 1950s. There a television stayed tuned for shoppers to get a glimpse of the wider world while purchasing groceries for the week or a treat such as a "Nehi grape soda and a sweet roll."[407] By 1950, the highway ended the white and black Goose Creeker's dependence on the railway station and general store to communicate beyond Goose Creek. Auto traffic increased, and the commercial interests at the triangle intersection supplanted Mt. Holly as the commercial center of the community. The days of isolation passed.

Photograph 6.3 The photograph shows Cannon's Store and the U.S. Post Office in 1961. The Goose Creek Post Office was located near the intersection of State Road and Oaks Avenue. *Courtesy Berkeley County Library, Moncks Corner, South Carolina.*

In addition to the highway, the radio and television mediums introduced these little places to the world. The media brought news that was unfiltered by the white owned rail stops. Word of the Supreme Court decision calling for integration of public schools stirred some black Goose Creek communities to action. A petition from black parents asking for the integration of the Berkeley public schools was circulated.[408] David Gadson, a teacher at Burke High School in Charleston County and his wife, Flora attended Grove Hall Baptist Church on the State Road and resided nearby. They were instrumental in securing the names on the petition and keeping the issue active. The petition was eventually presented to William M. Bonner, Superintendent of the twenty-two schools in Berkeley County. Seventy-three parents from Ladson and Sangaree signed the petition.

Photograph 6.4 The faded photograph, ca. 1950, shows a southbound school bus receiving passengers on unpaved Pineview Drive. The bus is near the intersection of Farm Road. *Courtesy Frances Etling Roberson.*

Governor James F. Byrnes prepared the state for the impending Supreme Court *Brown vs. Board of Education* decision that would force school integration. Shortly after his inauguration in 1952, he charged the General Assembly with their responsibility to meet the segregation challenge when he warned, "It is our duty to provide for the races substantial equality in school facilities." He justified the bold initiative by explaining, "We should do it because it is right. For me that is sufficient reason. If any person wants an additional reason, I say it is wise."[409]

The legislature passed the state's first sales tax of three cents on every dollar, which generated $124 million in five years to improve school facilities. Approximately two-thirds of the money was spent to renovate or build new black schools. The money, allocated in anticipation of the effects of the Supreme Court *Brown vs. Board of Education* decision, was intended to equalize the school facilities, to keep them separate and forego school integration. The Berkeley District responded to the legal threat of forced school integration by introducing a bond referendum. The bond referendum passed by a four to one margin county-wide, but the vote was very close in the Goose Creek area with the Carnes Crossroads precinct approving the measure by a twenty-six to twenty-five vote, and the Hanahan precinct approving the measure with a wider, but still close sixty-nine to fifty-one margin.[410]

As a result of the passage of the bond referendum, a new school was built to consolidate the one, two and three room "Negro schools" in Goose Creek.[411] The schools at Casey, Grove Hall, Howe Hall and Bowen's Corner were combined when the new Howe Hall Elementary School was built on Howe Hall Road to serve all of the minority students in the Goose Creek area. Reverend J.L.

Aiken served as its first principal and some of the first faculty members were Elnora Bradley, Sadie Franklin, Ethel Hines, Eula Mae R. Mood, Cleola R. Roper, Nathalee Chisholm, Willie Gamble, Jennie Mae Jefferson, Phyllis T. Myers and Maggie Sass. Following Aiken, L.C. Molony was a well-loved and respected school principal at Howe Hall for many years. However, his tenure was marred by the tragic death of a small boy, who was fatally injured when the top piece of the school flagpole fell and struck him on his head.[412]

The 1956–57 Berkeley School District budget required a forty-mill tax, dog and poll taxes, National Forests payments, Federal Assistance and state aid to support all of the district schools, including the new Howe Hall Elementary. Besides attending Howe Hall, the nearby African American children attended Oakley Negro School and Ladson Negro School. "Mixed" children attended Varner School at Carnes Crossroads. The few white children in Goose Creek were served by one-teacher schools at Red Bank Plantation, Barrows School near Carnes Crossroads, Medway Plantation and Pineridge near the intersection of Myer's Road and State Highway Alternate 17. Goose Creek students of high school age traveled to Moncks Corner and attended Berkeley High School or Berkeley Training School, depending on their race.

The Hanahan District, which managed its own public schools soon felt compelled by an increasing school age population to expand the classroom facilities. Principal Wade Marlette and PTA President Carl Meynardie of Fishbourne Elementary in Hanahan called for district-wide assistance.[413] The school was overcrowded and Hanahan's local resources were insufficient, but a special grand jury report stipulated that elementary classrooms be built at Fishbourne School in Hanahan. Secondary school age students continued to attend North Charleston High School on a tuition fee basis. The 1956–57 School District budget was significantly increased with a 40-mill property tax levy. The new building program and the annual teacher salaries (increased to $3,000), consumed the bulk of the revenues. It was apparent that the flood of new white residents to south Berkeley were demanding better schools and thus altering the politics of the formerly predominant black school district.[414]

During the 1950s, the face of rural South Carolina changed forever. The agricultural industry was modernized and thereafter required investments in mechanized farm equipment to operate cost effectively. No longer could a Goose Creeker with a mule, plow and credit from the general store make ends meet. The situation forced most sharecroppers, wage laborers and tenants to move out of South Carolina to jobs in Northern industries. Today, there remains a strong Goose Creek-New York connection, with many black families divided between Goose Creek and relatives "up north." In response to the exodus, the State Development Board was created in 1954 to recruit industry as one part of an ambitious economic stimulus plan. The States Port Authority in Charleston was brought up-to-date with modern facilities by a statewide initiative that was mirrored at the county level. Delegates from Berkeley and Charleston Counties passed legislation, which created the Bushy Park Development Area in the far eastern edge of the St. James, Goose Creek Parish. The Berkeley County Water Commissioners and the Charleston Commission of Public Works collaborated to bring that plan to action with Mayor William Morrison of Charleston heading the delegation from Charleston County and Senator Rembert Dennis representing Berkeley County.[415] The Bushy Park Project required the construction of a dike across Back River west of its point of confluence with the lower Cooper and a diversion canal to carry water through Durham Creek from the upper Cooper

River at Bluff Plantation to Back River. The canal and dike converted Back River from a tidal influenced, brackish waterway into a large fresh water reservoir for industry and municipal use. The project resulted in a fresh water reservoir that could supply 2.5 billion gallons daily. In addition, four thousand acres of industrial land was created, situated on land with fresh water access from the Back River Reservoir and tidal influenced Cooper River waters into which used water could be disposed.

The Bushy Park Development Board was assigned to issue revenue bonds for three million dollars to develop the project when the commission determined that enough industries were committed to locate at that Industrial site. The entire project in Berkeley County was completed in 1956. Verona Chemical Company, a subsidiary of German-based Bayer Corporation, was the first industry to locate in Bushy Park followed by Dupont polyester Fiber Plant. Berkeley County benefited by the creation of new jobs as well as industrial investments that increased the tax base. Charleston County in turn received a reliable source of water for industry and its expanding population. The impact of this project is immeasurable in terms of jobs and economic stimulus, and it continues to positively impact the Lowcountry today.

Near the Bushy Park dike and Reservoir was the Naval Weapons Station. The Army first used the Goose Creek Weapons Station Properties in World War I. After the war, the Navy acquired all of the Army property and expanded its holdings, using the area during World War II to supply ordinance to Atlantic Fleet vessels. After World War II, the federal military land served the Charleston Army Depot and was used occasionally as a storage area for munitions and other reserves. The storage function expanded during the Korean War until 1952, when that mission was ended. The base served as an embarkation, storage and vehicle transportation area and, in 1959, the Naval Weapons Annex was established in support of the Polaris Fleet Ballistic Missile Weapons System. This 5,219-acre area on the northern side of the facility was formerly part of Liberty Hall Plantation. Expanded military use of the old plantation lands was another catalyst for population growth in Goose Creek during the 1950s.

As new families arrived looking for homes, Jack Etling began building the much-needed houses on his family farm. "I laid out the first lots in October 1953," he remembered in a newspaper interview with the *Goose Creek Gazette* thirty years later.[416] He built the first subdivision (Pineview), thus initiating the construction of modern Goose Creek. A builder by trade, Jack Etling came to Goose Creek with his father in 1934 at the age of thirty. He recalled that there was nothing in Goose Creek at that time except, " a store at Mt. Holly and a dirt road that connected a few houses together." The dirt road was the State Road that later became St. James Avenue (State Highway 176). Mr. Etling was injured in an automobile accident and collected an insurance payment, which he used to purchase part of the old Oaks Plantation. He amassed 150 acres, which he combined with 116 acres from his father who died in 1943. The first houses he built sold for $9,660. Later the prices rose to near $14,000 and the last houses he sold in the mid-1970s brought nearly $25,000 each. The first streets in Goose Creek were named for Etling and his family. The Pineview subdivision streets of Marilyn, Frances, Jenny and Iris are names of family members. Virginia and Ellen Streets were names of friends. "I knew Goose Creek would grow, but I didn't think it would grow like this," Etling recalled in 1983.[417]

In spite of both the subtle and dynamic changes of the 1950s, Goose Creek remained a white controlled agricultural community throughout the decade. There was only one active political party.

Consequently, Goose Creekers voted at Carnes Crossroads and Wide Awake Precincts to elect the Democrat of choice. M.C. Cannon Jr. was elected as Magistrate for the South Berkeley Goose Creek area when he defeated Rufus Antley in 1956, and Theodore H. Stoney was elected to the solicitor's office instead of William Morrison.[418] By the end of the decade, schools remained segregated and a few new homes stood in Pineview and Forest Lawn subdivisions.

1960s

The transitions that occurred in the 1950s portended significant changes in Goose Creek, but certainly no one could foresee that by the end of the 1960s, Goose Creek would be one of the fastest-growing municipalities in the United States. Population growth was impressive each year during the 1960s, but in 1969 Goose Creek experienced an unprecedented 58 percent population increase, resulting from additional military and industrial investments in Charleston and Berkeley Counties.[419] During the 1960s, millions of investment dollars flowed to the military bases in both counties, and new industries at Bushy Park brought secondary commercial and residential demands. In 1960, the Navy's first missile assembly plant, known as the Polaris Missile Facility U.S. Atlantic Fleet Area or POMFLANT, was completed at the Naval Ammunition Depot in Goose Creek. Facilities were added at this time to assemble Terrier, Tartar, Hawk, Standard and Red Eye missiles.

The establishment of a town government in 1961 and its authorization of a water and sewer system were essential to support new housing for ballooning numbers of working families. During the 1960s transition, Goose Creek needed skilled community leadership, but the new Goose Creek residents were hardly in position to take charge of decision-making for the community to which they so recently arrived and knew so little about. The state and county officials were situated in the county seat in Moncks Corner, fifteen miles north of Goose Creek, and displayed little kinship with outsiders arriving in large numbers to the southern corner of their rural county. Consequently, Berkeley leaders gave scant attention to the haphazard development occurring in Goose Creek. The residents of Goose Creek were clearly overwhelmed by the magnitude of it all. There was no recent history of public cohesiveness or coordination in their area, and there were no power brokers to garner resources and address emerging issues. Conditions worsened resulting in foul tasting well water, sewage spilling from unreliable septic tanks, roadside clutter, traffic snarled roads, and no sign of relief. The arriving populace was surprised to find that there were no police, fire, emergency or sanitation services.

Seven men stepped forward to offer stewardship. One man, Waring Bunch, was employed as the superintendent of Medway Plantation. His family had lived in the parish for decades. Jack Etling was building and selling homes in Pineview subdivision. J.B. Brown Jr., Lonnie B. Holland, Edgar Neis, Edgar Anderson and Edgar Binnar arrived in Goose Creek from Charleston County to buy family homes in the country. These men pooled their talents to explore solutions to the increasingly foreboding circumstances. They shared mixed feelings and none of them wanted a town at first, but they concluded that they alone could improve the situation, and that the establishment of a town was the only way to garner resources needed to build essential infrastructures. Possibly all of those early leaders shared the feelings of Jack Etling when he recalled that he did not want a town but the situation was worsening. He lamented, " people kept sitting on my door step. They wanted a town but didn't know what to do!"[420] Finally, Jack Etling and a few interested neighbors received legal advice from a North Charleston attorney and set out to hold an incorporation election. Etling concluded that "Starting a town is a little bit complicated," but he persevered and, with some others, solicited seed money to advertise the incorporation referendum that would pose the question to the voters. He recalled, "Nobody had any money; somebody had to pay for the ad."[421]

The Goose Creek municipal incorporation election was set for Tuesday, March 14, 1961. The election committee appointed by the Secretary of State consisted of Clancy Walker, J.B. Brown and Lonnie B. Holland. Poll managers for the first election were Mrs. Lucile Nies and Sam F. Jernigan. As a result, a small section of the greater Goose Creek area incorporated on March 22, 1961. The vote for incorporation was fifty-four to nineteen in favor, with the name of "Goose Creek" winning the poll.

Mrs. Marion Hatchell was, in her words, "against a town at first because I wanted to live in the country, but I voted for the town because I wanted it better for the children." Her husband traveled with his job occasionally, and she wanted police protection for her three boys, daughter and herself.[422] Offering for mayor was Hilton Waring Bunch, Edgar Neis, Roger Anderson, and Edgar Binnar. E.W. Etling offered for council.[423] The residents of Pineview, Pineview Terrace, Greenview and West Greenview Acres subdivisions were eligible to vote in the incorporation election because their subdivisions, if successful, would make up the newest South Carolina municipality. The estimated population of five hundred citizens sent sixty registered voters to the polls that day in 1961. They elected Hilton W. Bunch as Goose Creek's first mayor, with fifty-three of the sixty votes.[424] Photograph 6.5 shows some of the first citizens of the City of Goose Creek including Mayor and Mrs. Waring Bunch.

This is a list of the City of Goose Creek's first elected and appointed officials. They served during the period of April 6, 1961–April 5, 1962:

H.W. Bunch, Mayor
Edgar Binnar, Council
E.W. Etling, Council
E.Q. Neis Jr., Council
Roger Anderson, Council
Clancy Walker, Clerk Treasurer
L.C. Turner, City Recorder
J.B. Brown, Town Marshall

On April 6, 1961, Mayor H.W. Bunch called the first meeting of town council for the City of Goose Creek to order. There appears to have been some confusion as to whether the newly incorporated place was a city or town. For the first decade, the matter was resolved by referring to the place as a "city" and the assembly as "town council." Considering some of the first initiatives opined by the people who were present at the first meeting, this landmark assembly of the new city was especially interesting. The council wanted the rules of order to require a two-thirds majority to pass a motion, a maximum of forty mills property tax, a twenty-five-mile-per-hour residential speed limit, effective yet fair and unobtrusive zoning, and a law making it illegal to dump trash on someone else's property.

Also of interest was the lone citizen in the audience who addressed town council that evening. Mr. St. Elmo "Speedy" Felkle asked if the council had zoning plans for a ten acre plot of land in which he was interested. Some of the matters brought before council for discussion during that first meeting would remain relevant issues for the next forty years, and Speedy Felkel would remain a controversial personality in Goose Creek's history even longer.

The first mayor and council accomplished much during the initial two-year term of office. In the beginning, they met every week in a building at the western corner of the intersection of Farm Road and St. James Avenue (Highway 176). This clapboard structure known as, "Turner's Barbershop," was owned and operated by C.L Turner. It eventually served many community purposes, with town and church members, Girl Scouts and others vying for the space. When Turner was appointed the first Town Recorder (municipal judge), part of the barbershop was converted to a courtroom. Thus, in this multi-purpose structure, inexperienced but caring men and women made important decisions for their infant city. It was here that four town officials each loaned five dollars to pay the annual dues to the South Carolina Municipal Association. They traveled to the association's office in Columbia, South Carolina, seeking advice on preparing budgets, passing ordinances and empowering officials for police service. The first town leaders did not know what to do, but they were enlightened and mature enough to seek the advice of those who did. Their wisdom put the town on good footing from the first meeting onward.

Photograph 6.5: The photograph shows the charter members of the Pineview Baptist Church in July 1961. *Right to left*: Albert Etling, (Little girl?), Rinda Etling, Leanne Smith, William and Winnie Smith with children Mark and Billy, Leonard Turner, Clinton Turner, Hattie Turner, Mrs. Duncan. *Center*: Waring and Mrs. Bunch, Anita and Debra McManus, Mr. and Mrs. Collien Bradham, Ronnie Altman, Reverend and Mrs. Doyle First Goose Creek Pastor, Frances Etling Roberson, Billy and Clara Yates and children, Buster and Lois Altman, Lee, Anne, Becky, Pattie, and hidden boy Robin Yates. *Courtesy of Francis Etling Roberson.*

During that first two-year term, the council adopted rules of order, received numerous legal opinions, set water lines and subdivision standards, borrowed $7,700 to operate the town for the first year, and appointed the first police chief. The first council also contracted for twice-a-week trash pickup and charged $18 a home annually for the service. They also set special fees (later known as franchise fees) for the telephone company, and established a 40-mill property tax and a $10 annual business license fee.

The lack of public services and facilities presented formidable obstacles to the young city, and the lack of operating revenue compounded matters. During the early years, town council members divided their attention between managing the fledgling police and fire departments, providing for drainage and finding money to pay for all of it. The first city revenue came from fines collected for charges of disturbing the peace. An automobile accident at the intersection of Goose Creek Boulevard and St. James Avenue (Highways 52 and 176) resulted in one injured party, and responding ambulances from two different private companies. The Goose Creek police officer fined both ambulance drivers for arguing and fighting over the right to transport the injured motorist.[425]

The city employed only one policeman during the early years who was not equipped with a radio and relied on his wife to relay messages. After taking a police call at her home, she would tie a white cloth on the front door knob to signal the passing cruiser that a message was waiting.[426] Frequent communication problems resulted in some alarming events, such as the accident on New Year's Eve, 1964 at the intersection of Highways 52 and 176, which resulted in a number of dead and injured motorists being thrown onto the highway. The unlit road and unusually dark night made it difficult for oncoming traffic to avoid hitting the victims. This incredible problem persisted until the South Carolina State Highway Patrolmen were summoned from a private phone.[427]

Town council discovered that some people were helpful citizens and others were obstructionists. Those who placed their household trash at their neighbor's curb to avoid the $18.00 a year sanitation fee made it necessary for the early council to tie penalties to the sanitation ordinance, and eventually require all to pay whether they wanted the service or not. Other citizens greatly helped the fledgling council. Mr. and Mrs. Charles Greene loaned the city $500.00, interest free, to pay for a special census.[428] With such help, slow but steady progress continued during the first term. At the end of the first month of operations, the treasurer reported that the city collected $100.00 in police fines and owed $176.00 in outstanding bills, but the end of the first fiscal year corrected the deficit with a treasury surplus of $1,085.37. By the end of the second year there was $2,652.80 on hand and in the bank.

Progress was steady during the second year of the first term (1962). Money was sufficient to re-appoint Weyman Turner as the lone police officer at a $375 monthly salary. The property at the south corner of Farm Road and St. James Boulevard (State Highway 176) was purchased from L.B. Grooms as the second town hall for $500 down and a total price of $4,500. A used tank truck was purchased for $250 and soon outfitted with a pump to serve as a fire truck.[429] Resources were stretched far enough to acquire meager firefighting and police equipment, but because salaries were not available volunteers filled important positions. Dellie Truelove served as the first volunteer fire chief beginning in the summer of 1963, and a few months later he submitted to council the first plans for a fire department garage to house two trucks.[430] His organization also coordinated with local Jaycees to augment the volunteers. He obtained two masks from Civil Defense to supplement the firefighting equipment, and required that a list of all firefighters' phone numbers be kept at each of the firefighter's homes. When a firefighter volunteer was called to duty, his wife was expected to continue the phone tree.[431] Chief Truelove rallied volunteers who provided the only fire suppression service available in the 1960s. He continued in service for four decades, first as a volunteer and later as an honorary chief.

The young city leaders sometimes acted above and beyond the call of duty. City leaders personally co-signed a loan to purchase the first police cruiser and fire truck. They signed again to bond some city employees. With few financial resources progress was slow, but the city endured and eventually found money to advance small projects. A citizen petition for streetlights resulted in an advisory referendum that led to the installation of hundred-watt mercury vapor lights. A fifty-cent monthly fee was added to every resident's Berkeley Electric Cooperative bill.[432]

Mr. Bobby Fesler requested assistance in establishing a ball team and playground.[433] Mayor Bunch favored the use of city money to support youth sports, and he insisted that all "Negro children" living within the town limits be allowed to use the playground and participate on all ball teams along with white children.[434] A year later, Harry Calvert from Greenview subdivision asked council for twenty-five dollars to help support the town's youth ball teams.[435] These men were two of the first of an increasing number of moms and dads who stepped forward to lay the foundation for an area-wide recreation program that continues today. William Crosby, President of the Greenview Acres Civic Club, regularly attended the early council meetings.[436] He too worked to establish and expand recreational services and led as the first Chairman of the Goose Creek Recreation Commission. Decades later he ably represented Goose Creek as a Berkeley County Councilman.

After two years, the council successfully conducted its first election to place a mayor and four council members into duly contested seats. Margarit Buell, Rita Meredith and A.J. Witcher served as election commissioners for the second city election on April 5, 1962. R.D. Winningham opposed incumbent Bunch but Mayor Bunch was returned to office and Mrs. Marion Hatchell was appointed the second clerk treasurer.[437] Mrs. Hatchell worked as town clerk two or three hours most mornings, some afternoons and evenings, and kept a typewriter in her home to produce city documents, such as minutes of meetings and correspondence. As a proud member of the mayor's team, she recalled, "Bunch did a lot for this place." Her words have never been challenged nor does anyone doubt the value of the essential contributions made by Mrs. Hatchell.

Town council used a committee management system that required each member of council to lead one of the committees: ways and means, budget, street and drainage, zoning and ad hoc committees. The committees studied issues and brought recommendations to the full board. The committee system was used for twenty-seven years primarily because there were few people available to do the work, and with no City Administrator it was costly for council to frequently depend upon the city attorney, Norman West. He offered advice and collected information for fees that quickly mounted beyond the means of the young city.

This is a list of the City of Goose Creek elected and appointed officials who served during the period of April 5, 1962–May 21, 1964:

H.W. Bunch, Mayor
E.W. Etling, Council

E.M. Griffin, Council
E.B. Binnar, Council
Gary Elsey (Resigned February 12, 1963), Council
Smith E. Hinnant (Sworn July 9, 1963 for unexpired term), Council
Marion W. Hatchell, Clerk Treasurer
Weyman Turner, Police Chief

The council also took steps to authorize volunteer deputies to assist the police chief in the battle with nighttime thieves.[438] Donnie H. Bradham, Earl Bounds and Lonnie B. Holland took an oath as special police officers and immediately began night patrols but in spite of this extra help the police department soon experienced difficulties. During Mayor Bunch's second term, Councilman Smith Hinnant asked council to remove the police chief for improper use of equipment, such as the practice of giving rides to minors in the cruiser and driving the car out of town on chases and patrols. This was the first of many conflicts between city council and their police department.

Candidates for council in the election of 1964 included Charles C. Caldwell, Edgar B. Binnar and Jack Etling. Jack Etling stated that he had seen "this place grow from woods to a town and I want it to continue to grow."[439] Mayor Bunch did not offer for reelection and incumbent councilman Smith E. Hinnant was elected as mayor in his stead. He defeated Freddie Gause with sixty-three of the seventy-four votes cast.[440] The following week Mrs. Hannah Mae Barrs was appointed City Clerk Treasurer by a narrow three to two council decision.[441]

Photograph 6.6: The photograph shows Turner's Barber Shop at the north corner of Farm Road and St. James Avenue (State Highway 176) as it was in 1951. It was a fifteen- by twenty-foot building that served as the first town hall, as well as the first municipal court house. The old structure also housed the original First Goose Creek Baptist Church and was the first community center where the Boy and Girl Scouts met regularly. *Courtesy of Francis Etling Roberson.*

This is a list of the City of Goose Creek elected and appointed officials who served during the period of May 21, 1964–May 17, 1966:

Mayor Smith E. Hinnant
Oliver Sona, Council
Charles E. Caldwell, Council
Oliver Yon, Council
Kelly Curtis (Resigned because of health reasons), Council
Hattie V. Turner (Elected to replace Kelley Curtis), Council
Hattie Mae Barrs, Clerk Treasurer
Sheldon E. Hopson, Chief of Police
Jetter Cain, Recorder

This is a list of the City of Goose Creek elected and appointed officials who served during the period of May 17, 1966–May 14, 1968

Mayor Smith E. Hinnant
Oliver Yon, Council
Oliver Sona, Council
Charles Caldwell, Council
W.R. Wren, Council
Nora Gonda, Clerk Treasurer
Faye McKinley, Clerk Treasurer (March 25, 1968 to June 10, 1968)

Mayor Smith E. Hinnant opened the ninety-third session of town council by confronting a myriad of problems that stirred the community to heated action during his two-term administration. The intersection of St. James Avenue and Goose Creek Boulevard (Highways 176 and 52) was becoming a busy focal point with the only gas station in town, which was owned and operated by James Preacher Sr. The station was a popular place for local citizens to gather, but a slight stir occurred when civic-minded citizens tried to improve the appearance of the intersection with a "litter campaign." Councilman Caldwell complained about trash and debris at Preacher's service station, and requested that Police Chief Hopson contact Joseph Owens of the Berkeley County Health Department to solicit his help with the trash problem.[442] This request resulted in heated encounters that pitted the rights of individual property owners against the powers of local government. The debates persisted, as did the litter problem, with no satisfactory solution. The same type of debate raged in regard to traffic law enforcement. The city received negative publicity when the *Charleston News and Courier* reported on February 20, 1964, that Goose Creek was singled out by the American Automobile Association as one of the thirty-eight places in the United States where members were warned to "exercise extreme caution" because motorists had a likely chance of getting a traffic ticket. Even though a heated verbal battle ensued between Goose Creek and the American Automobile Association representative with no resolution in sight, a more serious problem loomed.

The most controversial issue in twentieth century Goose Creek surfaced in the early 1960s when poor water and wastewater services emerged as a major political issue. The beginning of these problems can be traced to the construction of Forest Lawn subdivision. Saint Elmo "Speedy" Felkel embarked upon his Goose Creek development ventures in 1956 when he purchased 126 acres of land and took the lead in the water and wastewater business in Goose Creek.[443] He went into lot promotion and sales, with Forest Lawn as his first project. In 1959, he designed a water system with help from the Farmers Home Administration and named his water system the "Coastal Water Company." In the same year, the South Carolina General Assembly passed legislation permitting the operation of private wastewater companies. Speedy Felkel built the first private water system in South Carolina.

At that time, Forest Lawn, Maple Ridge and Pineview were the only residential subdivision in Goose Creek, but the problems experienced by the first Forest Lawn residents reappeared in other subdivisions as new homes sprawled across the countryside. The crux of the problem is found approximately twenty feet below the soil surface in a heavy stratum of marl. The Goose Creek marl is a firm, yellow substance containing a high percentage of carbonate of lime.[444] This marl strata contains the same phosphate beds, which provided livelihood for many Goose Creekers in the phosphate mines of an earlier era, but the new residents found it extremely difficult to dig good wells because the phosphate emitted a strong, sulfur odor that permeated the water and fouled its taste. Also, the clay and marl soils were impervious, often causing the septic disposal of wastewater impossible or at best, difficult to drain and filter through the soils. From the onset, there was a need for a water and wastewater disposal system that was independent of wells and septic tanks.

As available housing and business increased, the need for a solution to the water supply and sewer treatment problem became greater. At first, wells of varying depths and septic tanks were sufficient. In 1960, Ready Mix Concrete products, owned and operated by John T. Heyward, established a plant "near the beginning of Dual Lane" at today's main intersection of St. James Avenue and Goose Creek Boulevard (Highways 52 and 176).[445] A 380-foot deep well was drilled to supply 2,200 gallons of water a day to the concrete plant. This supply met the needs of that industry, but demands increased for other types of uses such as schools and churches that served hundreds of people and required reliable wells and septic systems with greater capacity.

The new Goose Creek Elementary School was funded in the 1961–62 school district's budget to accommodate 500 students.[446] Charles Gibson, and later Charles Bianchi served as the first and second principals, respectively. Two years later, Boulder Bluff Elementary opened with 560 students and Harry Calvert as the first principal. Karen Humphries rode a small school van from Dogwood Avenue in Pineview Subdivision to attend second grade at Boulder Bluff Elementary School.[447] She remembers the new school with the smell of fresh paint that was less than four miles from her home. Karen Humphries and all three of the school principals enjoyed long and distinguished careers with the Berkeley School District. They were all part of the wave of migration resulting from the expansion of nearby military bases that needed civilian workers, schools to support their families and a water and sewer system to support the new residential subdivisions.

In addition to the schools, new churches needed reliable water and sewer systems for increasingly larger congregations. In 1961, regular Sunday school and worship services began at the Goose Creek Presbyterian Church near the entrance to Greenview Acres at Old Back River

Road. Reverend Warren Wardlaw, of Yeamans Park in Hanahan led worship services for a rapidly expanding congregation. The church remained under the direction of Yeamans Park Presbyterian Church until the first minister, Reverend Raymond Wickersham, arrived and completed its organization.[448] The church was officially founded in 1962 and remained at its original location for twenty-four years. Finally it was moved to the Crowfield section of Goose Creek and renamed, "Peace Presbyterian Church."[449]

Demand for public service was high. Felkel extended his services to accommodate the new Boulder Bluff Subdivision and he requested and received a franchise from the town to operate a water and sewer company.[450] Requests from homeowners to connect to the Coastal Water and Sewer system were common at the town meetings in the summer of 1963. Residents of the new Camelot subdivision relied on Felkel's company for service, and expanding demands resulted in Felkel's system extending into other parts of the city. Other builders, in addition to Felkel, offered deals to the town. Mr. Jack Etling requested a permit to install a well and pump on Ellen Drive that he would give to the town when it was prepared to provide water service.[451] Water, now available on a limited basis, was sufficient for the housing demands, but the waste water system was soon overwhelmed and problems mounted. Frequent malfunctioning of septic systems prompted the Veteran Administration and Farmers Home Administration to stop issuing loans for new home purchases in Goose Creek.[452] Joseph Owens, director of the Berkeley County Health Department, stopped issuing permits for septic tanks because the sewage overflow threatened to contaminate the soil and spread disease.

The city explored the possibilities of establishing a publicly owned water system, but lacked sufficient assessed valuation (property value) to borrow the needed money. The City also considered replacing the shallow water wells by tapping onto Charleston water lines for a reliable source but neither plan would succeed without a reliable sewer system.[453] Council concurred that the town would not grow with more water customers until a sewer system was in place, and because the town could not afford a sewer system of their own, Felkel's plan appeared to be the best option.[454] Negotiations with Felkel over purchase and rates of both his water and sewer system continued for months. As a result of complaints about open manholes and spilling sewage, Brad Hicks and David Gilliam organized a health department for the town.[455] Problems persisted and a number of local meetings of disgruntled water customers applied pressure on City Hall for effective action. In support of the fledgling health board, and in response to the outcry, Mayor Hinnant denied sewer taps to seven newly constructed homes.[456] Nevertheless, throughout 1964 and 1965 houses were frequently connected to sewer in Greenview and Pineview subdivisions, and in 1968 the city granted a five-year exclusive franchise to Felkel to operate his water and sewer system.[457] There were few options. Speedy Felkel owned the only sewer service in town.[458]

The first of a number of serious problems for Mr. Felkel began when a Small Business Administration loan was disapproved. The extended lines were already in the ground, short-term notes were due and new construction was already dependent on Felkel's water and sewer lines.[459] The problems were compounded when city residents were not required to tap on to the private system, and continued to rely on numerous substandard wells and septic tanks. Consequently, Felkel was not able to garner enough customers to amortize the loans on schedule and the shortage of revenue resulted in a system that could not afford to expand or maintain itself in good working order.[460]

It was during these difficult years that the leadership of Malvin Mann emerged. Malvin Mann arrived in Goose Creek in 1963 and served as mayor of the City for four two-year terms. He came to be known by some as Goose Creek's "controversial mayor." Born in Independence, Missouri, in 1927, he served in the Air Force before settling in South Carolina to sell office furniture and supplies. He became interested in Goose Creek politics shortly after his arrival. In his words, "I was alarmed over some political figures I believed were harmful to Goose Creek."

Mann worked as campaign manager for Goose Creek's second mayor, Smith Hinnant. He was an active participant in the Goose Creek American Legion and presented a petition for more law enforcement. He was president of the Goose Creek Civic Club when that club bought the first police radio system.[461] Mann's initial bid for political office was unsuccessful when Hattie Turner defeated him in the race to fill the council seat vacated by the resignation of Kelly Curtis. This was the last time Mann was defeated until his bid for his fifth mayoral term in 1978.[462] Malvin Mann entered the mayoral race in 1968 against Smith Hinnant and Oliver Yon, and won by a large margin.[463]

This is a list of the City of Goose Creek elected and appointed officials who served during the period of May 14, 1968–May 20, 1970:

Mayor Malvin Mann
Carl V. Barrs Sr., Council
Charles Caldwell, Council
Adam R. Hernandez (Resigned Feb. 20, 1969), Council
Earl H. Bounds, Council
Michael H. Bowick (Appears July 8, 1969), Council
Vivian A. Woods, Clerk Treasurer

Mann rose to political leadership during years of turmoil. He recalled that the council meetings were quite disruptive or, in his words, "rousing." He also recalled that the city officials would have "fist fights and would slap each other around pretty good." The minutes of the meetings record none of these disruptions, but time and again controversy clouded business at hand during his tenure. Mann remembered his first term as mayor as being a difficult one. Goose Creek was badly in debt, had made little progress toward solving the water and sewer problems, and was regularly receiving bad publicity. In 1968, the police department consisted of two men, two badly worn cruisers and a police headquarters that was little more than a shanty. Complaints concerning water and sewer service continually dominated town meetings, including concerns from Jack Pittman and other citizens who worried about water with odor, low pressure, overflowing sewage, broken manhole covers and "black" water.[464] In spite of the persisting problems, the city boundaries expanded when Foxborough, Shannon Park and Colonial Heights' subdivisions annexed in the summer of 1971.[465]

Water and sewer problems, with "Speedy" Felkel as the central character, dominated council discussions [466] and they were the critical issues in the 1968 general election.[467] Republican Lloyd E. Sineath, Democrat Rembert C. Dennis and Independent W.A. Barnette were all state senatorial candidates that year. The Republicans controlled the majority of the Lowcountry delegation seats and feared that they would lose their dominance in the Charleston area if Rembert Dennis was re-elected. Goose Creek was "ready-made" for the Republican purpose, and Lloyd Sineath entered the race with great vigor. The water and wastewater issue became volatile and Sineath used the grassroots angst to mobilize local residents. Senator Rembert Dennis gave Goose Creek its first statewide coverage when he called for an investigation of the water and sewer system by the South Carolina Public Service Commission (PSC), but Sineath did not retreat.[468] Lloyd Sineath appeared before all of the civic clubs in Goose Creek and criticized Senator Dennis for the belated call to the PSC for assistance. Sineath also verbally attacked Senator Ernest F. Hollings for his inattentive service for troubled Goose Creek. In spite of the heavy opposition, Senator Dennis was re-elected amidst the controversy and with no solution in sight.

Goose Creek citizenry remained vocal following the 1968 election. Ed Caffrey aptly expressed the frustrations of many local residents when he complained that the "cost of water in our area…isn't all the water you can use for three dollars per month. It is really, all the water you can get for three dollars, and in our area that isn't much!"[469]

Community groups assembled to seek solutions and to voice complaints, many of which were aimed at "Speedy" Felkel. Mayor Malvin Mann used the community forums to unify the citizenry. He reported the presence of raw sewage in ditches, low water pressure and the lack of response from either the county or state government. In retaliation, Felkel blamed Malvin Mann's political motivations for the perpetuation of the inflamed controversy. He stated "if it weren't for Coastal Water Company, Goose Creek would still be a country cross roads."[470] Felkel repeatedly stated that he was "primarily interested in the betterment of Goose Creek and the further development of the area." He contended that opposition to him was due to his refusal to support Malvin Mann and that as a result Mann inflamed the citizenry against him.

Dr. Cecil Jacobs, the district health director, declared four subdivisions in Goose Creek "a public health hazard and a public health nuisance."[471] He said, "I saw homes with yards four to six inches deep in sewage, children's tricycles, trucks and other toys were floating in or covered by raw sewage." He continued, "The potential for transmission of disease to children and adults is as great as any situation I have witnessed in this country." Speedy Felkel stated, "With all the publicity, you get a lot of hot-heads and it's hard to control them." Felkel cited system sabotage as a cause for some of the problems. He continued, "another problem we have is a bunch of publicity-crazed town councilmen. I think we just supported the wrong man for mayor."

In January 1969, the PSC imposed a $100 a day fine on Felkel's company for failing to comply with the commission's orders, and in August it imposed a $1,000 fine for being late with a promised engineering study. The problems persisted and on October 17, 1969, the *Charleston News and Courier* reported that many Goose Creekers were enraged at the "inactivity and partiality" of the South Carolina Public Service Commission in its handling of the water company. They wanted firmer action. Representatives from four housing subdivisions in Goose Creek mailed letters to Governor Robert E. McNair requesting an audience to discuss the acute shortage of potable water. One letter stated that they had "lost faith in the South Carolina Public Service Commission." The same letter also stated, "During the past year, the residents have sought help from state and local health authorities, local politicians and the South Carolina Public Service Commission" but received no assistance.[472] Subdivision representatives were concerned that the Veterans Administration (VA) and Farmers Home Administration (FHA) might resume granting loans for new construction and thus place additional water service demands on an already failed system. In response, Governor

McNair met with Goose Creek residents and promised to take action. In the summer of 1969, a report from the Federal Housing Authority cited "certain deficiencies" in the Coastal Water Company's water and sewer system, and ordered that no FHA or VA loans for new construction be allowed in the Goose Creek area until health authorities certified the presence of adequate water and wastewater service.

The leadership bemoaned this halt of new construction, but the halt provided some benefits. It allowed time for the cash strapped government to make some important purchases. A new police cruiser was ordered, but the city had no money or credit to pay for it until Mayor Mann and Councilman Earl Bounds co-signed a bank loan. Soon after, Mayor Mann ordered a special 1968 census, which recorded a larger population and increased the city revenue from the state's wine and liquor rebates. The extra revenue allowed the police force to increase to four officers.[473]

It was also during this difficult time that Goose Creek received one of its sons home from Asia. On March 3, 1968, Larry Ronald Gourdine lost his life to hostile action thousands of miles away in the Vietnam Conflict.[474] Private First Class Gourdine, whose name harkens back to the earliest French Huguenot settlers, was the only Goose Creeker killed in that conflict. His remains were interred in the old Casey Cemetery at a site that is marked with an inscribed stone.

Mayor Mann provided firm leadership for the troubled city, but his methods were often questioned, and time and time again controversy arose. Many rebuked the mayor's leadership, and on more than one occasion, the city council called for Mann's resignation. Despite differing opinions of the "controversial mayor," the City of Goose Creek continued to improve municipal services. Few can deny the sincerity of Malvin Mann's good intentions for improving living conditions in Goose Creek. He admitted his personal attraction to adversity, but claimed that, "trouble rolls off my back like water off a drake."[475] His confrontations with "Speedy" Felkel resulted in the mayor exploring ways to purchase Felkel's private water company, as well as water from Charleston, instead of relying on Goose Creek wells. The deadlock between the two men led to a decisive meeting on January 14, 1969. Mayor Mann spoke for the record when he warned, "He (Felkel) has had a chance to do right and we expect him to do so."[476]

Although the water and sewer problems persisted through the end of the decade, this meeting in 1969 seemed to set the course for the development of the future City water system. Developer John White of Sanape Reality offered to give his Shannon Park sewer system to the Town and a week later, developer Max Hill offered the Foxborough water system to Goose Creek.[477] Nobody wanted to keep small, unprofitable water or sewer systems, and city leaders concurred that theirs was the only agency that could conceivably consolidate the several small systems into a congruent and cost effective whole.

Despite the controversy associated with Felkel, there were many Goose Creekers who respected him and admired his acts of generosity. He donated six acres of his property to the Greater Goose Creek Parks and Playground Commission and two acres to the Beverly Hills Civic Club for recreational purposes. "Felkel Field," an expansive playground named for him, is still a popular gathering place for hundreds of families and sports enthusiasts. Before it failed, Felkel's water and sewer system supported the phenomenal growth that characterized Goose Creek during the 1960s, and despite the increasing inadequacy of the private system, Mr. Felkel received considerable praise from Goose Creek city officials and residents during most of the 1960s.

By the end of the decade, the City of Goose Creek was clearly the political nexus of south Berkeley with its myriad of problems. The South Carolina General Highway and Transportation Map for 1963, two years after incorporation, showed Goose Creek with a population of 3,656. Within ten years after its incorporation, the population numbered more than 6,000. During that time an average of ten families a week moved into the city and a special census in 1968 revealed that the city's population had tripled since it incorporated in 1961.[478]

The problems confronting the young city in the 1960s were monumental to the city fathers, but some important steps were taken that impacted the community for many decades. One important agreement occurred when the city entered into a partnership with the Goose Creek Recreation Commission in 1966. That year the commission was established as a South Carolina special purpose district with a vague service area that included the City of Goose Creek. This early partnership for recreation helped greater Goose Creek emerge as one of the foremost communities for growing families. William Crosby served as the first chairman, with Joseph Byron, Wayne Eckert, John Cercopoly, and Oscar Crosby as commissioners. James R. Smith, Ray Heatley, Elton J. Wright, John Bryant, Ed Eubanks, Gilbert Lewis, Clayton Camp, Thomas Polk and John Stansfield were the recreation vanguards of the era. From the onset of its municipal experience, the city suffered a disproportionate share of problems and a considerable amount of bad publicity, but from that modest and troubled beginning a municipality emerged, and during the next decade it became the most populated corner of Berkeley County.

1970s

The municipal minutes referred to the "Town of Goose Creek" as the "City of Goose Creek" for the first time at the 260th meeting of council on September 14, 1971. Mayor Mann announced the name change and reported that new city limit signs would read "City," instead of "Town."[479] South Carolina law does not differentiate between the powers or responsibilities of city or town officials and identical charters are issued for all South Carolina municipalities regardless of the size. Thus the incorporation title of a South Carolina municipality reflects the state of mind of its citizenry more than any other factor. Some nearby municipalities of the same size as Goose Creek, and some that are much larger, retain "Town" in their title as a matter of choice rather than convention. Two such places are the Town of Summerville and the Town of Mt. Pleasant. The Goose Creek records do not evidence any justification for the change of name. It may merely be assumed that those living within the municipal boundaries in 1971 believed the dynamics of their place related more closely to a city than a town.

The same dynamics that probably motivated the municipal title change also caused years of instability. During this period of rapid population growth, appropriate management systems were sought that could effectively operate the growing municipality that depended upon a meager budget. Daunting problems surfaced during the early months of the new decade when controversies erupted in the police department. Goose Creek Police Chief William Bert Hopkins divided the department into two twenty-four-hour shifts with two police officers on each. Chief Hopkins and Patrolman Joseph Yusko manned one shift, while the other was headed by Patrolman James Hood and assisted by Marion Wilson. The police chief reported directly to Councilman Earl Bounds.[480] Hopkins resigned when city council demoted him to the rank of lieutenant and required that he serve as one of two Lieutenants reporting directly to Bounds. Shortly after the resignation, the city returned to the previous reporting configuration with James L. Hood serving as chief of police. This was the beginning of several years of police problems.

A series of issues lead to controversy and publicity in 1971 when the mayor terminated Police Captain Marion Wilson. Mann accused Wilson of misconduct, including threatening to shoot prisoners, but council balked and remained divided on the removal of Wilson while the Charleston newspapers publicized the debate. Controversy involving Mann's oversight of the police department continued prompting Charleston attorney J. Lawrence Duffy to request an investigation by the South Carolina Law Enforcement Division (SLED).[481] In his letter to Governor John West, Duffy cited a "grave and serious problem in the Goose Creek area" involving the "mayor and the law enforcement of that city." SLED investigated, but found no evidence of wrongdoing and Governor West terminated the operation after a short time.

Shortly after the SLED investigation, Police Chief James L. Hood resigned. He served from 1970 to 1972. Chief Hood blamed the mayor for a dispute that resulted in his resignation and accused the mayor of ordering him to cease issuing citations to intoxicated motorists.[482] The embarrassing dispute continued that year when Margaret Herring, City Clerk-Treasurer, requested another SLED investigation citing improprieties in City Hall. Mayor Mann dismissed her, whereupon she accused the mayor of favoritism in levying sanitation charges, mismanagement of the city's police retirement fund and unethical land transactions between the city and private citizens.[483] In response to the television and newspaper publicity, Mayor Mann explained to the council, "If and when I decide to do anything that might be illegal concerning the City of Goose Creek…I will make certain that no one employed by the City of Goose Creek knows about it." The mayor further pointed out that he might be "a little stupid but not entirely stupid."[484] In response to the controversy, 250 citizens signed a petition calling for Mayor Mann to be removed from office for "conduct generally unbecoming to a mayor," but the tenacious mayor endured. City recorder, Carl Barrs defended him and denied the validity of the impeachment petition.[485]

In an effort to streamline operations and prevent reoccurrences of the police unrest, the city continued its committee system, which divided the responsibilities of oversight and decision-making among the elected officials. The committees reported persistent problems in 1972, such as leaking sewage, livestock (including horses) in back yards and zoning issues that remained troublesome for many years. Nevertheless, progress was made during Mann's 1970–72 term. Table 6.1 lists the committees and chairpersons in 1972.[486]

Malvin Mann worked to expand the municipal boundaries. In 1970, Foxborough subdivision was annexed to the city and Boulder Bluff was annexed in June of 1971. Boulder Bluff temporarily added two thousand people to the municipality, but citizens, such as Loring E. Van Kleek opposed the Boulder Bluff annexation from the onset and worked to establish a Public Service District in lieu of joining the municipality.[487] Another citizen, Harold L. Elrod brought a successful suit against the annexation, in which he claimed that the annexed territory was greater than 25 percent of the municipal territory, and thus was in violation of state annexation laws.[488] A second election successfully added Boulder Bluff to the city.

Table 6.1: The table lists the city council committees and chairpersons.

Committee	Chairperson
Budget	Loius C. Hatchell
Business License	Michael H. Bowick
Parks and Playgrounds	William E. Infinger
Planning and Grants	Thomas G. Poor
Sanitation Department	Earl H. Bounds
Streets and Drainage	Thomas G. Poor
Vehicle Maintenance	Carl V. Barrs
Ways and Means	Carl V. Barrs

This is a list of the City of Goose Creek elected officials who served during the period of May 20, 1970–May 25, 1972:

Malvin Mann, Mayor
Carl V. Barrs Sr., Council
E.G. Wright, Council
Michael H. Bowick, Council
Earl H. Bounds, Council
Charles C. Caldwell, Council
Orris F. Caldwell, Council

Other advances followed. A citywide audible horn alarm system was installed to notify firefighters of emergencies. Mayor Mann signed a tax anticipation loan in 1972 from the South Carolina National Bank for $50,000 for the "proper operations of the fiscal affairs of the City." The loan was followed by an ordinance that taxed all homeowners a $5 a month ($60 a year) fee for the proper disposal of refuge. Joseph Daning appeared before council on behalf of the new Goose Creek Rescue Squad to request municipal space to keep the emergency vehicle and other equipment out of the weather. Progress was evident, but controversies continued due to rapid expansion of the city and increased responsibilities. Consequently, it was at this time that the first request for a city manager was brought to council. Councilman Carl Barrs requested that the city employ a manager and pay the municipal judge a salary commensurate with the duties.[489] The attention to the court raised looming questions about judicial duties, compensation, favoritism and division of powers, which prompted the municipal judge, Charles Caldwell, to resign amid controversy. Councilman Barrs replaced him the following year.

Charleston lawmakers became involved in solving a serious Goose Creek problem to the chagrin of many Berkeley lawmakers who failed to act. Their action was prompted by the fact that the Charleston water supply relied upon the purity of the water in the Goose Creek reservoir. However, the PSC failed to prevent the flow of wastewater into the Goose Creek water reservoir. In response, the Charleston delegation successfully used their legislative influences to place the Coastal Water Company into receivership that took over control of the company and immediately halted the pollution of the watershed. Bartley J. Riddock became the receiver for the company and immediately surveyed the conditions of the system. He reported that he could "not overemphasize the emergency of the situation that exists here." A report written for the water company by an engineering firm reported to Riddock in part that, "The health hazard is so acute that I cannot understand why there is not an epidemic."[490] Improvements were made with the company while it was in receivership and before it was returned to the private stockholders. The water and wastewater company was reorganized. It severed its ties with Felkel, complied with a strict reporting process to the Public Service Commission and was renamed the *Southeastern Water Corporation.*[491] Soon after Mayor Mann filed a petition with Berkeley County that called for a special referendum that would grant city authorities permission to own a water and sewer system. Toward that end, city council passed a resolution nullifying the proceeding of the prior administrations, which gave Coastal Water Company an exclusive five-year city contract. By this action, the company's franchise was disaffirmed. This action also prompted Foxborough Subdivision to withdraw the lawsuit it had entered into as a protest when the city annexed its seventy-four acres. The city agreed to allow the subdivision to provide its own sewer system and purchase water from the Charleston Commission of Public Works. This arrangement did not last very long but it did quiet the discourse temporarily.

Mann suffered bad luck prior to the 1972 election, which was reported by the Charleston daily paper. The news media reported:

> *Mann's inordinate ability to land on his feet in the wake of ominous controversy didn't work so well last year during an incident at the American Legion Post in Goose Creek! The city's mayor said or did something that caused the Air Force sergeant to strike the mayor with considerable force…A lot of people say I was involved in a barroom brawl, the mayor said, it was over in less than five seconds and brawls usually last much longer.*[492]

The incident resulted in the mayor being injured and losing one eye.

This is a list of the City of Goose Creek elected officials who served during the period of May 25, 1972–May 22, 1974:

Malvin Mann, Mayor
Carl V. Barrs Sr., Council
Michael Bowick, Council
Louis Hatchell, Council
William Infinger, Council
Thomas Poor, Council
Earl Bounds, Council

Table 6.2: The table shows the candidates for city council in 1972 and the number of votes received by each.

Council Candidate	Number of Votes
Carl V. Barrs	377
Michael H. Bowick	327
Thomas G. Poor	327
William E. Infinger	322
Louis C. Hatchell	322
James M. Richards	309
Uldis Jaunzemus	293
Edward D. Caffrey	268
Ray L. Grant	266
John W. Coates	247
Lewis M. Miller	246
Robert J. Bailey	229
Sidney A. Eadie	206
William M. Hill, Jr.	205
Robert J. Waldrop	204
E.J. Wright	188

These controversies stirred the electorate and brought three mayoral candidates along with 18 council candidates to the polls for the May 16, 1972 election. Again Mayor Malvin Mann won with 359 votes but Orris Caldwell received 301 votes and William E. Crosby received 209 for mayor, revealing that the majority of voters did not opt for the incumbent mayor. No run-off election was required in accordance with the law for plurality elections and Mann returned to the helm for two more years.

The six candidates with the most votes served a two-year term on council. The council candidates and the number of votes garnered are given in table 6.2. Interestingly, the controversial and heated election of 1972 generated a great amount of interest. Two non-elected council candidates, James Richards and Edward Caffrey, sought the mayor's post in subsequent elections. Richards served one two-year term as mayor in 1974–76, but Caffrey failed in his bid for that office in 1990.

City Hall and citywide controversies continued throughout the 1970s. Once again the problems were caused by the rapid increase in population and the demands placed on the fledgling government. To compound the growth problems, the new south confronted the old south in manners that approximated violence and hatred. As if to exemplify these changing and troubled times, three Ku Klux Klan (KKK) rallies stirred the citizenry with angst that spilled violence into the schools. Advertisement for a typical rally is shown as figure 6.1. That rally featuring speaker R.E. Scoggin, the KKK Grand Dragon for South Carolina, was attended by dozens of hooded members of the invisible empire. From 1972 to 1975 this group lit crosses on three occasions—on a vacant lot near the entrance to Boulder Bluff Subdivision, on land near the entrance to today's Braemore Subdivision and on a vacant lot at the entrance to Forest Lawn. In each instance, the rallies were conducted on property owned by S.E. (Speedy) Felkel.

Such rallies were not new to Goose Creek. KKK cross lightings and rallies occurred in Goose Creek during the 1950s, but these events were uncommon and presented images that were unwelcome by the great majority of the residents of the young city.[493] Black and white Goose Creekers refused to succumb to the violent and inflexible positions preached by the Klan. Indeed, whites and blacks showed more tolerance and flexibility in the Charleston Lowcountry than historians expected.[494] The majority of the members of both races grew up together, worked side-by-side and respected law and order. Neither race was inclined to damage the local community they both claimed and loved, nor were the newcomers inclined to embrace the message brought by hooded orators preaching hate. Whites and blacks had coexisted in Goose Creek since the 1680s resulting in a long history of separate co-existence and producing a tradition of civility that both sides drew upon during these difficult years. Nevertheless, there was violence throughout the state after 1968, when the courts ruled that "freedom-of-choice" plans for school attendance were unacceptable.

When schools opened statewide in the fall of 1970, all school districts operated unitary districts and a school year of racial unrest followed. A fight between a white boy and black boy at Goose Creek High School in 1973 instigated tussles and loud arguments that nearly closed the school. The fight, which would have merely resulted in school disciplinary action if it had occurred at other times, became an appeal for racial justice that reached the Governor's office. Various law enforcement offices sent manpower to the high school to restore order and student safety. More than seventy law enforcement officers patrolled the halls and grounds, but no school days were lost and the learning environment returned to normal within a week.

Shortly after the unnerving events at Goose Creek High School, issues unrelated to the racial discord resulted in more problems at City Hall. Councilmen William E. Infinger and Thomas G. Poor asked the mayor to resign during an executive session of council. Infinger alleged that the mayor had reneged on an unwritten agreement with council to refrain from interfering with police and court activities.[495] When Mann refused to resign, council acted no further on that matter and redirected its attention to moving into a new municipal facility.

The new City Hall was an understandable source of pride for the people of Goose Creek. City staff relocated from a small twelve-by-twenty-four-foot structure on Farm Road to a more spacious commercial structure on the corner of Farm Road and St. James Avenue (Highway 176). During the dedication of the new City Hall, Mayor Mann stated, "This is the finest office building in Berkeley County and would compare with any other office building in South Carolina." The building was once used as a laundry, ideally located and sufficiently large to house a growing municipal staff. The site was spacious enough for small outbuildings, which housed police and fire stations and a sanitation garage.

Under the leadership of Mayor Mann and city council, Goose Creek continued to work towards a municipally owned water and sewer system. The mayor proposed issuing $800,000 in municipal general obligation bonds to purchase the private system. The bond issue was approved by a referendum, but it was contested in court. Consequently, Mayor Mann's 1972–74 term ended without a city owned water system, and he did not seek the mayor's office in the spring of 1974. In his farewell comments to city council he stated, "I feel that the next administration should take immediate steps to get a city manager because this City is growing more every day and needs a full time manager."[496]

Figure 6.1 The figure shows a flier circulated and posted in April of 1973. The flier advertised a Ku Klux Klan rally with R.E. Scroggin as featured speaker. *Courtesy Mrs. Helen Connor.*

Photograph 6.7: The photograph shows the principals at the dedication of the third City Hall at the corner of Farm Road and State Highway 176. Appearing in the photograph from left to right are: Congressman Mendel Davis; City Councilmen Jack Etling and William Infinger; Mayor Malvin Mann; and Mr. Waring Bunch, first mayor of Goose Creek. City Hall was dedicated in February 1974. *Courtesy Francis Etling Roberson.*

Photograph 6.8: The photograph shows the third Goose Creek City Hall at 125 St. James Avenue. The building was razed in 2000. ***Courtesy City of Goose Creek.***

His farewell was not the political end of Malvin Mann. He returned two years later with an overwhelming victory. He continued as a colorful personality who was elected four times to the mayor's office during some of the most troubled years of Goose Creek municipal development.

This is a list of the City of Goose Creek elected and appointed officials who served during the period of May 22, 1974–June 15, 1976:

James M. Richards, Mayor
Thomas G. Poor Sr., Council
Orris E. Caldwell, Council
Uldis Jaunzemiz (Resigned Aug. 31, 1974) Council
Sidney A. Eadie, Council
Otis Crawford (Resigned Sept. 9, 1975) Council
Shirley Johnson (Sworn Oct. 31, 1974 for unexpired term) Council
Marguerite Brown (Sworn Dec. 9, 1975 for unexpired term) Council
Phil Hurt, Police Chief; Solon Lewis, Police Chief
Steven Best, Recorder
Janice Hulbert, City Administrator

The 1974 election was hotly contested and involved four mayoral and 19 council candidates. James M. Richards received 361 votes and topped the three other candidates, Louis C. Hatchell, Oliver Yon and Edgar Binnarr. During the first meeting of his administration, Mayor Richards introduced the seven police department employees and authorized a loan of $20,000 from The South Carolina National Bank to make payroll at the next meeting.[497] He asked city council to appoint Stephen Best, a professor at nearby Baptist College (now Charleston Southern University), as municipal judge, and Janice D. Hulbert as City Clerk/Treasurer (She would soon be appointed Goose Creek's first city manager.) James M. Richards served only one two-year term as mayor, but he brought a considerable amount of personal energy and farsightedness to the office. His greatest focus remained on keeping pace with the fast building program in new subdivisions such as Foxborough, and rectifying serious drainage problems in Colonial Heights and Boulder Bluff subdivisions, but disputes over sanitation fees persisted. Citizens complained that the fees were too high even though the sanitation department reported "$28,000 in the red" in 1974.[498] Unfortunately, Mayor Richard's contributions were overshadowed by a heated controversy concerning the city's purchase of the troubled water system.

The *Charleston Evening Post* reported on February 7, 1975, that Mayor Richards stated that the "time had come to inject some method into the madness." His methods involved immediate effort to purchase the beleaguered water system. Debate raged in city council meetings on both sides of the question. Jack Ray claimed he would pay $15.00 a month if he could "get water to make a good cup of coffee."[499] The City resolved to purchase the water and sewer system from Southeastern Water Corporation for $1,400,000.00 in 1975. Residential rates were set at $3.50 per month, plus a monthly charge of $.74 per thousand-gallon water usage above two thousand gallons. Commercial, multi-family and out-of-city rates were greater. The sewer fee was equal to the monthly water rate paid by the customer.

The new city-owned system was eligible for federal assistance through various environmental and community development grants, but even with the extra financial assistance Mayor Richards received mixed support from the general public. The city was ill prepared to expertly manage or finance an area-wide water and wastewater system, and although municipal bonds were sold for the purchase, few resources were available for day-to-day operations or improvements. Consequently, the city-owned system required higher user rates, but the quality of service remained poor and the long-awaited improvements were not soon realized. Water shutoffs and sewer overflows continued to occur and the impatient customers shifted their complaints from the private to the public officials in charge.

Customer frustration grew as the 1976 election approached. The divisive political nature of the City became a daunting challenge for Richards and his challenger, Malvin Mann defeated Richards by riding the wave of public frustration back into office. Richard's administration ended badly and Mann's last term began amidst his greatest challenges. Mayor Mann and his newly elected council members conducted their first meeting in the City Hall parking lot because outgoing Mayor Richards locked the doors to City Hall and refused to relinquish the keys, challenging the residency of newly elected Mann. A series of quick court injunctions corrected the matter, and Mann entered City Hall a few days later. During the first meeting in the parking lot, notary public Carl V. Barrs Sr. read the oath of office to Mann and the new council. Among the council members were Marguerite Brown, an incumbent who ran on Richards' slate; Michael J. Heitzler, a newcomer on Richard's slate; Mrs. Shirley Johnson, an independent; and three members of Mann's slate: Mrs. Nancy Lawson, John Barnette Jr. and William S. Gibson. After council recited their oaths, Mann convened a meeting and asked city council to appoint Barrs as city recorder (municipal judge) of Goose Creek. Heitzler objected that the council was acting in "haste and ignorance," but the motion passed. Later Gibson admitted that he did not know what a recorder was supposed to do. "I thought it was someone to record things," he quipped.[500]

The veteran mayor began his fourth term of office in the City Hall parking lot with what he said was "an inexperienced city council" and a multitude of persisting problems.[501] In October 1976, the South Carolina Department of Health and Environmental Control (DHEC) declared Goose Creek a "severe and urgent health hazard" due to its substandard and inadequate water and sewage systems. As a result, the DHEC imposed a moratorium on new water and sewer taps onto the city-owned system. The 1976 moratorium was the result of the accumulation of more than a dozen years of problems. The DHEC declared Goose Creek the number one priority statewide for the Environmental Protection Agency (EPA) 201 Phase I wastewater facilities construction grants. The city borrowed its 25 percent share of the $1.3 million total Phase I construction package, and rehabilitation commenced. At that time, Goose Creek was the only city in South Carolina that required prior approval from DHEC before accepting new water customers.

This is a list of the City of Goose Creek elected and appointed officials who served during the period of June 15, 1976–May 15, 1978:

Mayor Malvin Mann
Shirley Johnson, Council
Marguerite Brown, Council
Michael J. Heitzler, Council
Nancy Lawson, Council
John Barnette, Council
William S. Gibson, Council
Lois Hodges, Clerk Treasurer
Carl Barrs Sr., Recorder
Solon Lewis, Police Chief

This was another controversial term of office for Mann. In 1977, the mayor was released on a $2,000 bond after being served a warrant charging him with harassment. The charges were later dropped when a jury of the General Sessions Court could not reach a verdict.[502] The next year, the mayor threatened to resign due to a police department dispute. Later, his efforts to terminate the police chief were rebuked by council.[503] In another city council meeting convened in the City Hall parking lot, the Goose Creek Police Liaison Committee issued a report that cleared Police Chief Solon Lewis of accusations of theft. Councilman Heitzler, chairman of the committee, stated that Mann agreed to hold a special council meeting to receive the committee report, but cancelled at the last minute. Heitzler announced the meeting and with a majority of council present, called the body to order and read the report in the parking lot amidst thirty-five spectators.[504] The report, prepared by Heitzler and council members William Gibson and Marguerite Brown, reprimanded Lewis for "negligent" record keeping, but cleared him of any crime or malfeasance. The committee could find no "instances where Chief Solon B. Lewis violated any laws or ordinances," but found reason to fault other city officials for negligence. The committee also reported that there was a "poor and sometimes nonexistent system of receipts and receipt records." The report cleared Lewis, eight days after Mann called for Lewis' resignation for mishandling $225 of bond money. Mann was furious.

Shortly after the parking lot meeting, council member Michael Heitzler announced that he would challenge Malvin Mann in the 1978 election for the first four-year term in the City's history. Heitzler was one of only two council candidates elected from Richards' 1976 slate. He and Marguerite Brown garnered support from Shirley Johnson, who was elected as an independent, and William Gibson, who was elected from Mann's slate. These four council members constituted a majority on city council, but did not unify until the last months of the 1976–78 term thereby remaining ineffective until the next election.

As was the custom in Goose Creek, candidates for city council either aligned with a mayoral candidate or ran as an independent. Thus, both Mann and Heitzler teamed with six council running mates on their slates. Three candidates ran as independents. In all, fifteen council candidates vied for six available seats. Two incumbent candidates ran with Mann and two incumbents ran with Heitzler. The central issue of the campaign appears to have centered on the need for a full time city administrator. Mann contended that he was entirely capable of managing City Hall. Heitzler countered that current and future demands of the city required a full time, professionally trained administrator. Mann touted his success in managing the multi-million dollar sewer rehabilitation grant, and Heitzler asked for an opportunity to lend his untried leadership skills to the ever-expanding task.

Table 6.3: The table lists the mayoral candidates, the council candidates on mayoral slates and the independent council candidates.

Mann's Slate	Heitzler's Slate	Independents
John G. Barnette, Jr.	Marguerite Brown	Orris F. Caldwell
Edward D. Caffrey	Jospeh H. Daning	Albert Christopher
Albert B. Crosby	William S. Gibson	C. Larry Filyaw
Nancy J. Lawson	Phillip E. Hurt	
James A. Breacher	Shirley L. Johnson	
Joseph Spalviero	E. Calvin Woods	

The Evening Post, Friday, May 5, 1971.

The exciting contest in 1978 brought a record number of voters to the polls in an election that many believed would forge the direction of the city for many years. Flyers, posters, billboards, yard signs and radio advertisements stirred the citizenry as the campaign received wide media coverage. Foxborough citizens pooled their dollars and hired a pilot to fly a banner over the city that read: "Get out of the Mann Hole." Reporter Reba Griffin with the *Charleston News and Courier*, observed that the race for Goose Creek mayor was a contest of "striking contrasts."[505] The incumbent mayor had a track record, many contacts among the "Goose Creek Old Guard" and earned political experience. He had never lost a mayoral election. The challenger was a thirty-year-old school principal with little political experience and less knowledge of the workings of City Hall. Heitzler expected residents of recently constructed subdivisions to arrive at the poll in sufficient numbers to place him in office, and indeed most Goose Creekers were surprised when the newcomer and his entire slate were elected with record voter turnout.[506]

The six elected council members included incumbents Shirley Johnson, Marguerite Brown, William S. Gibson and newcomers Joseph S. Daning, Calvin Woods and Philip E. Hurt. The new

Photograph 6.9 The photographs shows the two candidates for mayor. The photos appeared side by side in a story appearing May 7, 1978, five days before the election, in the *News and Courier* and the *Evening Post*. The incumbent mayor, Malvin Mann, was twenty years older than the challenger, Michael Heitzler, and previously served eight years in the city's lead position

mayor and council appointed Gail McNaughton as City Clerk Treasurer, Solon B. Lewis, as Police Chief, Barfield Holland as Fire Chief and Carl V. Barrs as Municipal Judge.

The election of Mayor Michael J. Heitzler and his six city council running mates in May of 1978 brought stability to the turbulent political arena. Seven city officials, who professed a unity of philosophy and purpose, represented the city government that had been for many years divided on varied issues. In addition, the new mayor was elected for a four-year term for the first time in the city's history, and the six council members were elected for two and four-year terms, depending on the number of votes received. The longer terms of office contributed to the stability of the rapidly changing city.

This is a list of the City of Goose Creek elected officials who served during the period of May 15, 1978–May 1980:

Mayor Michael J. Heitzler
Shirley Johnson, Council
Marguerite Brown, Council
Joseph S. Daning, Council
E. Calvin Woods, Council
William E. Gibson (to May 1980), Council
Philip E. Hurt (Resigned September 11, 1979), Council
John G. Barnette Jr. (January 1980 to May 1980), Council
Doreen C. Davis (Elected May 1980), Council
Lagette Shiver (Elected May 1980), Council

The new leaders of the city soon attempted consolidation of the greater Goose Creek area through annexation of the unincorporated sections. However the new mayor wrongly believed that the enthusiasm that elected him inside the city limits could be mustered in the areas outside the city for successful annexations. He also wrongly believed that the need for public services in the unincorporated areas was obvious to most, and that the citizenry would rush to City Hall seeking services and regulations. Although he was wrong on both accounts, he was right to predict that sprawling sub-urbanization outside city limits easily overwhelms public services and infrastructure when it occurs in a planning vacuum. With the absence of county planning initiatives, the results of excessive multi-family dwellings, mobile homes and substandard construction, drainage and public services could be catastrophic to the city's efforts to properly guide the impending developments within the corporate limits. Consolidation offered a solution, and "consolidation through annexation" remained the central theme of the early Heitzler administration. He explained, "Consolidation is one way to improve the cost effectiveness of the municipal service and a method to counteract the efforts of inflation on municipal budgets." He also explained that all citizens would benefit from successful consolidation. He continued, "If consolidation is accomplished, Goose Creek may emerge as one of the larger and more prosperous municipalities in the state."[507]

The Naval Weapons Station, the Polaris Missile Facility and the Woodlawn Heights subdivision were annexed in 1978, making Goose Creek the largest city in Berkeley County with nearly seventeen thousand residents. Flushed with that success, the city officials enthusiastically sought the annexation of the Bushy Park Industrial peninsula and Crowfield. That enthusiasm darkened when the Bushy Park industrialists slowed the consolidation movement in the fall of 1979 by seeking an injunction. The city attempted to annex the Holly Court subdivision and the Bushy Park Industrial Park together through an annexation election. An injunction stopping the election was issued in response to a suit brought by five large industries located at Bushy Park. Mayor Heitzler, City Council and the Berkeley County Election Commission, who authorized the election, were named as defendants. The state leadership was appalled at the city's attempt to invade an industrial haven through annexation. South Carolina Governor Richard Riley paid a visit at Westview Elementary School to discuss the city's annexation efforts, as well as pending litigation with school principal and Mayor Michael Heitzler. Graciously, Governor Riley never chastised the young mayor for his unthinkable challenge to the powers of the state legislature and court, and simply wished him well.

During that year of ups and downs, one of the surest signs of Goose Creek maturity appeared in the form of a city newspaper. The first edition of the *Goose Creek Gazette*, Goose Creek's first newspaper, was published. The publisher and editor, Joyce Odum promised to "intentionally do nothing that will in any way be detrimental to Goose Creek, its people or its environment."

Joyce Odum did much more than keep her promise. She wrote about Goose Creek, the people, places and events both big and small. Through the newspaper, she helped define the place and its people when the City of Goose Creek was searching for its identity. A selection from her earliest editorials tells much about Joyce Odum and the community she quickly learned to love.

Photo 6.10 The photograph shows Joyce Pitman Odum, first editor and publisher of the *Goose Creek Gazette*. The first edition of the weekly paper appeared August 29, 1978.

Mr. John Coates brought me a banana the other day.

Now that doesn't seem to be a whole lot to write about but this is a special banana. Mr. Coates grew it, in Goose Creek! In his yard! On a regular banana tree!...and delicious I might add; taste a lot better than the ones you buy in the store.[508]

The wonder of Goose Creek for me lies not only in its vitality and location, but in its people. We come from everywhere. We have chosen this place as ours. We are from every state and many foreign countries. Our accents and drawls and clipped brogues blend together and we quickly learn to appreciate the differences in each other...Somebody said that since she'd gotten to Goose Creek she received the only obscene phone call in which she had to ask the fellow three times what he said...[509]

Just listen to the sounds: wisteria, mimosa, daffodils, azalea, tulips,...the colors of spring and summer in the south...are a yearly surprise and delight.[510]

Goose Creek was without water for several hours Monday afternoon...Charleston cut us off. Again. Something about repairing a main. When will it all end...Maybe we should just start making announcements when we are going to have water. At least we would all know when we can run in and take a bath, have a drink, wash some clothes so as not to be totally unprepared for the next inevitable, 'no water' day! [511]

The 1970s ended with two important acts that impacted the City for many years. The City enacted a comprehensive zoning ordinance and agreed to merge its small and dilapidated sewer system with the new and up-coming Berkeley County system. Berkeley County paid the City residents $1,200,000 for a sewer system that was a costly liability, and one that needed millions of dollars to upgrade to meet the new EPA Standards. The purchase of the Goose Creek sewer system enabled Berkeley County to pledge more users toward retiring loans for matching EPA grants. The grant money extended much needed lines and built a state of the art treatment plant. Consequently, residential and commercial construction commenced with seasoned businessmen such as John White developing 150 acres of land he bought in 1966 for $1,450 per acre. That same land sold for $55,000 an acre less than twenty years later. With the improved system he developed Berkeley Square Shopping Center, Shannon Park Shopping Center, Brandywine Shopping Center, Brandywine Townhouses, and Shannon Park Apartments. In concert with the explosion of new construction, the zoning ordinance established the foundation for planned development and carefully steered all subsequent residential and commercial projects toward a balanced and integrated whole. The payoff from both the sale of the sewer system and the enactment of the zoning ordinance was enormous in terms of saved dollars and improved lifestyles for the people of Goose Creek.

Chapter VII
The City of Goose Creek
1980–2003

What we have loved, others will love, and we will show them how.

—William Wordsworth.

During the last two decades of the twentieth century, the City of Goose Creek matured from a single-dimension, bedroom community to a diversified home and work place for more than thirty thousand residents. A strategic planning process that began in 1981 and continues to this day, guided the metamorphosis. The 2003 Strategic Plan, shown in appendix XVII, involved annual planning retreats where city officials, staff and sometimes citizen groups and other stakeholders, met for open discussions and systematic decision making steps that resulted in mutually agreed upon, municipal strategies. The process was driven by political input from each elected official and reaped many benefits, but most importantly the planning effectively unified the varied skills of the elected leaders, fused their commitment toward mutually held goals and formulated the strategic steps required to achieve them. These concerted planning efforts ended the controversies and negative publicity and quieted the political discord that divided the community during the 1960s and 1970s. The process also lifted the expectations of the residents to levels that were hardly imaginable in 1980. Senior council member Marguerite Brown, who served on council the entire period, believed that the most important achievement during that last twenty-five years of the twentieth century was the development of concerted teamwork within a governing culture that allowed for constructive dissent. She aptly stated that, "City council became better understanding of each other and felt free to express their ideas without being condemned."[512] The coordinated efforts of the city leaders reaped many rewards but were not without failures.

The 1980s began with the city leadership working toward annexing the greater Goose Creek area. Annexation efforts received strong opposition and produced mixed results, but as the decade progressed, city council identified more attainable goals that provided steady outcomes of measurable success and transformed the little city into a progressive and multidimensional place to live and work. Underpinning this process was a strategic plan that identified one, five and twenty-year goals that can be generalized into four categories: management of growth, improved service delivery, increased self-sufficiency and the nurturance of a unique identity.

Management of Growth

By the 1980s, community leaders were barely keeping pace with the influx of new residents. Goose Creek was sometimes referred to as "South Carolina's boomtown" because the city's population increased by 365 percent between 1970 and 1980 and the pace showed signs of quickening.[513] In 1980, Berkeley County boasted a population of 89,100, with 20 percent of that number residing within the Goose Creek city limits.[514] Annexations and a 3 percent annual population increase during the 1990s lifted the total count from 24,692 to 29,208 and the population was estimated at near 31,000 in 2003. Providing quality services to those numbers was a difficult task for city departments, and the sprawling subdivisions outside the city limits presented additional challenges during the last two decades of the century.

Table 7.1: The table shows population changes in municipalities within the Charleston Metropolitan Area, 1980–1990.

City	1980 Population	1990 Population	Percent Change
Charleston	73,757	80,414	9
Goose Creek	17,899	24,692	38
Hanahan	13,224	13,176	0
North Charleston	65,681	70,218	7
Summerville	11,985	22,519	88

The South Carolina State laws discourage annexation. However, sprawling new subdivisions near city boundaries worried Goose Creekers and stirred their efforts to annex the homes and businesses that were encroaching into planning vacuums. City leaders reasoned that annexation would place the unincorporated neighborhoods under the overall municipal planning and zoning schemes and bring essential services and regulations to the rapidly sprawling developments. Mayor Michael Heitzler stressed the need for the local government to "control the development rather than it control us," and to provide the essential planning and regulations that no other level of government was willing to extend.[515]

In April 1980, Ninth Circuit Judge Clarence Singletary prohibited the city from holding an annexation election in Holly Court Subdivision that could have brought Holly Court and the Bushy Park industries into the city limits. The judge chastised the city leadership when he stated that, "Never before has a municipality in South Carolina attempted to…reach out 6.5 miles along a 'shoe string' corridor to bring into the City a wholly restricted industrial area of tremendous value."[516] The embarrassing rebuke by the South Carolina Supreme Court did not deter the city leaders from attempting other aggressive annexations, nor did it slow new residents from rushing to its new surrounding subdivisions, such as Crowfield Plantation.

Crowfield, a three-thousand-acre planned community, was a development contiguous to the western boundaries of the city and within the city's natural growth corridor. It was planned by the Westvaco Development Corporation and designed to transform Westvaco timberlands into residential, commercial and industrial zones including ten thousand new homes for thirty thousand residents, over a twenty-year period. The development plan included many recreational amenities, such as hiking trails, parks and a lake. The city's aggressive annexation policy thrust City Hall into direct conflict with Westvaco Development Corporation. The city leadership sought the annexation of Crowfield as a prime example of developable properties that needed municipal planning and zoning, as well as fire, emergency medical and police services to augment the strict covenants written by the developer. The mayor insisted that the development plans could continue unimpeded and that the preferred lifestyles of the new Crowfield residents would be protected, but that "through annexation the community could get police and fire protection as well as other municipal services."[517]

Donald L. Jackman, Westvaco Vice President for Marketing, announced that Westvaco intended to leave the decision to annex three thousand acres to the residents as they purchased individual homes. The city recognized that Jackman's annexation plan would be haphazard at best, take at least twenty years to realize, and would clearly hamper municipal efforts to proactively plan for the expanding area. Thus, without the cooperation of Westvaco, the city tied sections of Crowfield to other new contiguous subdivisions and initiated annexation elections. This strategy successfully brought Fairfax residential subdivision into the city along with four hundred undeveloped Crowfield acres. Later, Westvaco and the City found common ground when Westvaco reversed its anti-annexation position and began a two-decade long record of cooperative work with the City of Goose Creek. Consequently, in 1984, Westvaco, Alumax Industries (later Alcoa) and the City jointly agreed to the boundaries of another annexation that would add Foxborough IV and twelve hundred acres of undeveloped Crowfield lands to the city. This unified effort was thwarted when actions to enjoin the annexation election were brought by a number of landowners near Foxborough. Billy and Patricia Stuckey owned land upon which they planned to build a trailer park contiguous to Foxborough subdivision and within the limits of the proposed annexation. The city was opposed to the Stuckeys' plan for a trailer park but other business owners nearby joined with the Stuckeys' resistance. The controversial annexation election failed by 4 votes and a modified second effort was required before Foxborough IV joined the city a year later without the trailer park.[518]

Westvaco Development Corporation continued close cooperation with Goose Creek, and eventually joined all of their remaining undeveloped lands to the city, but the few opposing businesses remained outside the corporate limits. The trailer park controversy was resolved when the city purchased the property from the Stuckeys. Today the Goose Creek branches of the Berkeley County Library and senior citizen center are located on a portion of the proposed trailer park site.

Successful annexation of the majority of upscale Crowfield Plantation development cast the die for many subsequent annexations in the years that followed. The owners of more than four thousand acres joined the City of Goose Creek from 1980 to 2003, but the matter of the developing residential and commercial properties on the outskirts of the city perplexes municipal leaders to this day. Municipal officials dread a well-planned city that is surrounded by poorly planned perimeters that detract from the potential lifestyles of all. A list and description of the tracts annexed to the City from 1980 to 2003 is given in appendix XVIII.

Annexation brought properties into the planning sphere of influence, but additional initiatives were needed to lessen the impact caused by the increasing population. One way to mitigate the negative effects of dense populations was by purchasing green space for passive uses and conservation. The reason most people moved to Goose Creek was the ideal setting between the open spaces of rural Berkeley County, and the employment opportunities and cultural amenities in nearby Charleston.

Toward the end of the century, Goose Creek leadership was concerned that new residential and commercial interests might leapfrog Goose Creek to the open places north and west of the city. Thus, by acquiring open spaces and greenswards for peaceful rural living with the convenience of jobs, schools and commerce, the city offered incentives to discriminating citizens to remain in the City. The City of Goose Creek purchased nearly two hundred acres of undeveloped open space for future passive uses. City-owned open spaces benefit Goose Creekers because the land will not be developed, will not place demands on infrastructure, will not crowd the roads and parkways and will not add to the population. These spaces characterize rural living in an increasingly urbanized sector and buffer an attractive hometown in which many may live and work.

Access from residential areas to green spaces and the commercial district is planned by way of a hiker/biker trail system. A thirty-mile trail system accessible by cyclists and walkers will tie residential areas throughout the city to planned central parks. The trails, as well as traffic calming devices, pedestrian crossing tunnels and safe zones, will provide convenient citywide movement. These conveniences, along with easy access to green spaces, will encourage Goose Creekers to stay home instead of migrating farther into the countryside. The *Charleston Post and Courier*, in a complimentary editorial, recognized these innovative efforts as an example for other jurisdictions.[519]

During the early years of the twenty-first century, available land, few restrictions and low interest rates fueled a Berkeley County building boom that had not been seen in twenty years. Residential developers anticipate that four thousand acres will be available for new homes near Sheep Island Road and Highway 176. "This is the most homes that will go in Berkeley County since the 1970s," reported Berkeley County Planner, Harold LeaMond and "No fewer than 20 subdivisions representing 6,949 homes were planned between Moncks Corner and Goose Creek."[520] Growth within the City is also expected to continue. According to City Planner Debbie Lieu, Goose Creek managed 1,873 lots in the construction or design stage in 2003.

Table 7.2: The table shows the historical population data from the United States census and projections for each census year until 2050. The projections were based on an 18 percent average annual growth rate.

Year	Population	Increase	Percent Increase
1970	3,825	N/A	N/A
1980	17,811	13,986	366
1990	24,692	6,811	39
2000	29,208	4,516	18
2010	34,912	5,257	18
2020	41,196	6,284	18
2030	48,611	7,415	18

* The first decennial census count was taken in 1970 because the City was incorporated in 1961.

* The average annual growth rate between 1990 and 2000 was 18 percent. This 18 percent annual growth rate was used to project the potential population.

Future perspectives of growth management will likely involve political contests pitting the cost of purchasing adequate amounts of green space against the cost of road construction along with other expensive infrastructure projects. Unless hundreds of acres of open space are purchased by the city, little is likely to slow the population increase that is currently expected to reach 41,196 within the Goose Creek city limits by 2020 and almost 50,000 by 2030. Table 7.2 shows the anticipated population numbers. An 18 percent average decennial rate of growth was experienced from 1990 to 2000, and that conservative rate was used to project the numbers for each ten-year count until the year 2030.

City leaders of today and tomorrow must explore all available avenues to conserve and protect the remaining undeveloped acreage. Land conservation is flourishing in South Carolina as groups set records for total acreage protected from development.[521] Unless city leadership is able to prioritize the purchase of green and open spaces ahead of other projects, population increases may place unprecedented and unmanageable demands on the roadways and other infrastructures.

Roadway improvement plans must be devised now to be complete in time to service the expected traffic counts. Table 7.3 indicates that the number of motorists on three of the city's main thoroughfares will exceed the road capacity within twenty years, if traffic increases are unchecked and highway improvements are not completed on time. The table indicates that traffic will be at a gridlock on three of the major roadways by 2023. College Park Road and Crowfield Boulevard are projected to remain within acceptable volume capacity beyond 2023 because of improvements already underway.

The City of Goose Creek wields two votes on the Charleston Area Transportation System Committee (CHATS) that channels all available federal and state highway funds in the Charleston Metropolitan Statistical Area toward prioritized road projects. The city must compete successfully with other counties and municipalities to stay ahead or at least meet the growing traffic demands. Table 7.3 indicates the importance of the city successfully competing for limited highway dollars through the CHATS prioritization process.

Additional efforts to accommodate future traffic demands are needed along with actions that slow population growth. Plans are required that serve expected numbers of citizens with mass transit and to channel pass-through traffic around the city. Successful planning and completion of the Henry Brown extension and by-pass will greatly help to by-pass auto and truck traffic traversing the city along heavily traveled US Highway 52. Such an extension and by-pass will connect motorists on the Henry Brown Extension Road, through the Liberty Hall/Brick Hope Plantation tract, to James Rozier Highway (Highway 52) north of the Goose Creek City limits. Conversely, the by-pass will connect commuter traffic north and west of Goose Creek, as well as give city residents easy access to Interstate 526 and all points beyond.

Undoubtedly, mass transit will be a controversial and expensive proposition within the next twenty years. It is also clear that, unless the beleaguered Charleston Area Regional Transportation Authority (CARTA) is upstaged by the futuristic monorail system, which recently failed a demonstration, CARTA will be the only viable mass transit system potentially available to Goose Creekers. Clearly, this choice will surely come at a high cost to users and taxpayers alike but will be less expensive than alternatives. Bus services connecting Goose Creek with Charleston and Summerville will remove thousands of vehicles from streets and highways, as well as reduce the expense of further unnecessary highway and bridge expansions. The City of Goose Creek has opted not to be a partner with CARTA, but it is likely that after years of difficult decision-making, with debates that will likely pit road-use fees against general tax schemes, CARTA will emerge as the least expensive and most viable option for Goose Creekers who stay home and those who wish to connect to employment, commerce and entertainment beyond the city limits.

Table 7.3: The table shows traffic counts, rates of increase and projected volumes for the major thoroughfares in the City of Goose Creek. The design capacity was provided by the South Carolina Department of Transportation.

Roadway	1990	2003	Increase	Percent	2023*	Design Capacity	Over or (Under)
Goose Creek Blvd. (52)	32,026	39,500	7,474	23.3	60,051	49,200	22%
Redbank Road	12,203	18,800	6,597	54.1	44,644	35,700	25%
College Park Road	9,295	13,000	3,705	32.9	25,444	35,700	(29%)
St. James Ave. (176)	20,400	33,300	12,900	63.2	88,692	44,700	98%
Crowfield Blvd.	10,200	13,800	3,600	23.3	20,951	35,700	(41%)

In the past twenty years, the City of Goose Creek has managed the population growth by proactively and aggressively exercising control over developable lands. Notwithstanding, the initiatives that preserve the pleasant lifestyles by managing growth must be accompanied by consistently improved municipal service delivery.

Improved Service Delivery

Goose Creek strategic planners recognized the need to employ the most qualified workers, to train them and to reduce their attrition at all levels. One way to accomplish this goal was to stabilize the political environment so that key staff leaders could envision life-long careers through City employment. Throughout the last two decades, that stable political environment was maintained by Mayor Michael J. Heitzler and council member Marguerite Brown who served continuously throughout the twenty-three-year period, and by Councilman Daning and Phillips who also served for the greater part of that time. Additionally, Municipal Judge Shirley Johnson served three terms on council before assuming court responsibilities, and has skillfully served the city throughout the era. The majority of council members served several consecutive four-year terms and many municipal commissioners and executive staff served admirably across many years, gaining and reapplying valuable knowledge and skills earned from their experience. Appendix XIX lists the municipal officials and their years of service from 1980 to 2003.

Other participants in helping to maintain a stable political environment were principal players in the election of 1984. This city council election was hotly contested when two newcomers, Trudy Aull and Earl Clenner, along with a councilman from a previous era, Orris Caldwell, defeated three council incumbents: Doreen Davis, Lagette Shiver and Calvin Woods. The election remained cordial, the incumbent officials graciously bowed out and the newly elected council members quickly found their own pace and purpose on the city board. These six leaders, those leaving office and the newly elected, unselfishly rose to the higher expectations of the city. At a City Hall where locked doors and threats became too common during the previous decades, the smooth transition of authority validated the maturity of the rapidly changing electorate.

Photograph 7.1 The photograph shows incumbent City Council members Lagette Shiver, Doreen Davis and Calvin Woods when they picked up petitions to run for re-election in 1984.

Another significant turning point occurred two years later with the election of 1986. Since Michael Heitzler was first elected mayor, eight years earlier, much doubt remained in the minds of many Goose Creek citizens as to whether the city would continue with the same leadership or revert to the previous management style and culture. The 1986 election returned Heitzler and reinforced citizen expectations of the city and its leadership. Joyce Odum, editor of the *Goose Creek Gazette* wrote about a "magical change":

> *the people of Goose Creek issued a mandate in the City's election last week...the people spoke forcefully and without ambiguity. They told Mayor Michael Heitzler, about 9 to 2, that they like the direction in which he's leading the City...the City's metamorphosis seems to some as almost a magical change... Goose Creek has changed in form and structure, substance and direction. And the vast majority of its citizens like the way it's going.*

The "form and structure, substance and direction" cited by Joyce Odum in her column was obvious to many and the "metamorphosis" she claimed had indeed occurred. The city had taken a new and progressive course from which it would not be diverted for more than two decades. Mayor Heitzler was elected to his sixth four-year term in 2002. The consistency of his management style and the subsequent political stability during more than two decades of his leadership encouraged young professionals to envision lifelong careers with the city government. Key municipal staff members such as City Administrator Dennis Harmon and Police Chief Harvey Becker also remained to contribute decades of career experience and invaluable abilities that placed the city at great advantage.

Dennis Harmon was appointed City Administrator in 1978. He graduated from the University of South Carolina and brought management experience from Lexington County and the Town of Manning. In 1983, merely five years after arriving in Goose Creek, the Lowcountry Chapter of the American Society for Public Administration named Harmon "Administrator of the Year." This award and recognition of excellence early in his career was a source of pride for every Goose Creeker. It was only one of many honors he would receive during his distinguished career with the city. His skilled leadership was recognized statewide, and helped Goose Creek, which had enjoyed little name recognition before his arrival, become a prestigious place among the South Carolina municipalities. On July 31, 2003, he marked his twenty-fifth year as City Administrator of Goose Creek. "I knew Goose Creek had potential, but I didn't know it had this kind of potential," Harmon exclaimed,[522] an observation shared by all city leaders of that era.

Another long-term city employee who brought stability to Goose Creek is Police Chief Harvey Becker, who was employed as a patrolman in 1980 and rose through the ranks in nine years to be appointed Goose Creek Police Chief in 1989. His formal academic and police training include a diploma from the FBI Academy, but his greatest asset is his modest, open, and genuine approach to the officers and citizens he serves. His greatest challenges include maintaining adequate manpower,

Photograph 7.2 Goose Creek Police Chief Harvey Becker (center) was the city's newest police officer in 1980. He rose through the ranks to earn the position of chief of police and is shown here with some of his officers in 1989.

Photograph 7.3 The photograph shows a line of citizens outside the Goose Creek recreation center on Old Moncks Corner Road three days after Hurricane Hugo left coastal South Carolina without power. The city of Goose Creek returned to full power and municipal services within forty-eight hours. The recreation center served as a relief distribution center for a wide area.

planning and recruitment along with keeping the best available technology in service.[523] As a result of his stewardship, the *Commission on Accreditation for Law Enforcement Agencies Incorporated* (CALEA) awarded the 76-member police department the prestigious National Certification in 2003.

The 1980s ended with Hurricane Hugo, the most destructive hurricane in Goose Creek since the "extreme" storm of 1752.[524] After midnight, September 22, 1989 the eye of Hurricane Hugo struck Charleston but the upper segment of the storm struck the South Carolina coast at McClellanville with 135 mile-per-hour winds. The city awoke Friday morning to thousands of downed trees, fallen power lines, and damaged homes and businesses. Fortunately most of the relatively new housing developments in Goose Creek featured underground electrical wiring, which withstood damaging winds and rains, resulting in less destruction to the electrical distribution system that was suffered by other nearby communities. Amazingly, electrical power was returned to most of the city within 48 hours. Consequently, Goose Creek became a destination for thousands of people from surrounding communities seeking open businesses, grocery stores, banks and laundries. The National Guard assisted the Goose Creek police in directing the resulting bumper-to-bumper traffic.

The hurricane placed maximum demands on the city staff, facilities and equipment before, during and after the storm and reinforced the obvious obsolescence of city facilities. City Hall, the police department and fire station were clearly no longer adequate for the growing municipality. As a result, the public works facility, consisting of six thousand square feet of employee service space, was erected in 1992 to accommodate the divisions of water, streets, sanitation and garage departments. The Marguerite H. Brown Municipal Center was completed in 1999, and early in the new century, a second fire station and an expansive community recreation center were completed to continue a building program that spanned fourteen years and neared twenty million dollars in total capital costs. Appendix XX lists the capital projects and corresponding costs. Mark Phillips, who led as a councilman during most of the period, remained an advocate of facility expansion. He recognized the need to match facilities to the expected levels of service delivery, and touted the spin-off effect of higher morale that result when adequate facilities improve the efficiency of employees and lifts the expectations of the customers.[525]

Fortunately, demands of the expanding population during the last two decades were met without a property tax increase, but more revenues for expanded services and facilities were needed to accommodate the increasing volume of service. Revenues and expenditures for general operations increased fourteen-fold during this period due to the need for expanded city departments. Appendices XXI and XXII show comparisons in revenues and expenditures of departments during the twenty-three-year era. The lone fire station that was serviced by four full-time firefighters in 1980 increased to two stations serviced by thirty-two full-time employees in 2003. A similar multi-step increase in manpower in all departments was realized, in addition to new services such as municipal planning that were not previously offered. Expanded and additional services increased expenditures. However, city council, by diversifying revenue sources, avoided property tax increases during the entire period. Nine different types of grants, including Community Development Block Grants and Economic Development Grants infused almost eight million dollars into the municipal coffers, supplementing capital expenses. The gradual increase in license fees, augmented with the local option sales tax, helped keep revenue sources diversified and property tax rates unchanged. Property tax revenue accounted for more than half of the city revenues in 1980, but dropped to merely 5.5 percent in 2003.

Table 7.4: The table shows the household incomes of families in various increments in 1990 and 2000 and the change in dollars and percent.

Income	1990	2000	Change	Percent Change
Less than $10,000	596	479	(117)	(20)
$10,000–$24,999	2,259	1,437	(822)	(36)
$25,000–$49,999	3,678	3,025	(653)	(18)
$50,000–$74,999	917	2,338	1421	155
$75,000–$99,000	148	974	826	558
$100,000–$149,999	35	571	536	1,531
$150,000 or more	7	97	90	1,285
Total Households	7,640	8,921	1,281	17

Remarkably, not only have property taxes remained at a low level, but also the real cost to citizens in dollars has defied inflation. The mayor's *Report to the People* in 1984 claimed that the average Goose Creek family paid only $225.00 annually for city services. A special circular distributed by the mayor almost twenty years later, in 2003, pointed out that it cost him only $221.60 in city taxes and fees that year. Incredibly, even with cable television franchise fees added since 1984, the mayor's tax increase represented less than 1.6 percent increase over a nineteen-year period. General revenues have increased by nearly 1,500 percent and operating expenditures by nearly 1,300 percent from 1980 to 2003 but city residents have avoided increased municipal taxes that typically are associated with inflation and program expansions. Appendices XXI and XXII provide the amounts of revenues and expenditures in appropriate categories during the review period.

The desire to effect the same optimistic projection throughout the next twenty years remains challenging especially when federal and state mandates pass costs to local governments. One example of possible unfunded mandates is the management and treatment of non-point surface drainage and runoff. The costs of managing surface run-off may present formidable expenses to future city councils that may be forced to either increase tax rates or find new revenue sources through untried taxes or fees.

Table 7.5: The table shows the population of various racial groups in 1990 and 2000 and the percent of difference.

Racial Groups	1990	2000	Percent Change
White	20502	22,929	4.8
Black	3141	4153	32.2
Hispanic (of any race)	1020	1182	8.9
Asian or Pacific Islander	651	810	24.4
American Indian, Eskimo, or Aleut	116	171	47.4
Other	282	455	61.3

Table 7.6: The table shows the distribution of different age groups in 1990 and 2000 and the percent of difference.

Ages	1990	2000	Change	Percent Change
19 and Under	10,343	11,148	805	8
20–34	7,785	7,567	(218)	(3)
35–54	5,270	7,613	2,343	44
55 and Over	1,294	2,878	1,584	1.2

The citizens' demands in the twenty-first century will evolve according to real and perceived needs. Tables 7.4 through 7.6 show that Goose Creek citizens became richer, older and more diversified during the 1990s. There was a 144 percent increase of residents aged sixty-five years or over, and a total of more than twenty race and sub-race categories, such as Cuban, Guamanian and Chamoro. Older residents lift expectations on public services such as passive recreation and public safety, while a more diversified citizenry brings multiple talents and varied expectations. Indubitably, future Goose Creekers will be richer, more racially diverse and older. Consequently, one can reasonably expect future Goose Creekers to have more disposable dollars and leisure time. Ample opportunities for shopping, dining and entertainment should be available within the city limits, and expectations for recreational opportunities must evolve to accommodate the aging demographics.

The young community boasted growing families who coordinated volunteer youth sports programs soon after the city was incorporated. The volunteer efforts became a Special Purpose District when the voters authorized its development and established the Goose Creek Recreation Commission, which was a body of seven citizens appointed by the South Carolina Governor to oversee recreation in the greater Goose Creek area. The City of Goose Creek had been concerned with recreation since incorporation because young families always expected their local government to provide recreational services. Since recreational needs transcended corporate boundaries, the city at first deferred the responsibilities to the Goose Creek Recreation Commission. Consequently, the city and the commission enjoyed many years of mutual support and benefits, but near the end of the century, recreational demands clearly outstripped the ability of the recreation commission to keep pace. The limited taxing authority, rising costs and increased population in need of expanded facilities resulted in the recreation commission entering into a new contracted partnership with the city. The city withdrew from the district taxing boundaries but used its municipal taxing authority to pay the commission an annual fee to manage and operate all recreational programs for city residents. The terms of the agreement were multi-faceted and based on city recreational improvements in exchange for transfer of all the commission's real properties within the city limits to the City of Goose Creek. In exchange, the city promised to lease the old facilities, as well as the new and improved facilities, with five-year renewable terms for a nominal fee. This new arrangement worked well as the new century commenced, but at the same time the city steadily assumed more recreational responsibilities. It began co-sponsoring concerts and symphonies that the recreation commission could not afford on its own, and in 2003, purchased the Crowfield Golf and Country Club. It is likely that the management and operational governance of recreational services will shift from the commission to the city, as the steadily increasing demands for active and passive recreation require taxing and police authority that South Carolina cities can offer, but tax districts such as the recreation commission are not empowered to provide. This shift of recreational responsibilities to the city will realize another advance toward municipal self-sufficiency.

Self Sufficiency

Business confidence plummeted when the United States Navy announced the closure of the Charleston Naval Base and Shipyard in 1993. The closure threatened to drastically change the economy and growth patterns of Goose Creek and all of greater Charleston. The economic engine that was primed and fueled by the infusion of defense related investment dollars and the resulting paychecks was the primary reason Goose Creek emerged during the recent decades, and was one of a few important aspects of the city's local economy. For example, one year before the closure was announced, Lockheed Missiles and Space Company received a contract for $1.2 billion to develop the Navy Trident II D-5 missiles.[526] However, this was the last significant military contract, and after 1995, nuclear powered submarines no longer made the Charleston Naval Base their homeport. The Polaris missile facility in Goose Creek that serviced those submarines and their nuclear tipped missiles also departed and took with them three hundred Marine guards and the surface ships that restocked the ammunition at the station's piers. Appendix XXIII gives the text of the sign at the former entrance to the Polaris Facility. A total of twenty-two hundred Charleston area jobs were lost, and many Goose Creekers were forced to relocate in search of reemployment. But remarkably, although the population growth slowed and then stopped temporarily in the greater Charleston area, the count increased in Goose Creek. While the municipalities of Charleston, Hanahan and North Charleston lost population and Summerville experienced no change, the City of Goose Creek enjoyed an unexpected 11 percent increase during the uncertain and transient period from 1990 to 1994.

Across the board, Goose Creek experienced temporary slowdowns or halts in growth as measured by retail sales, retail occupant vacancies, housing starts, property tax revenues, business license revenues and building permit revenues. But employment opportunities quickly flowed back to fill the void left by lost federal jobs and paychecks. It appeared, in spite of the doomsayers, that base closure had a positive effect on the City of Goose Creek. The Naval Weapons Station within the city limits remained a tenant base for other Federal Programs such as the Border Patrol Training School and two Navy nuclear power schools that provides training for thousands of submariners each year. Navy engineers and technicians developed the Space and Naval Warfare Systems Center (SPAWAR) in contiguous Hanahan to devise improved military communication. At the end of the Desert Storm conflict, the Navy brought seventeen million pounds of ammunition back to Goose Creek from the Persian Gulf, and a private contractor that refurbished Army equipment relocated to the Army's Combat Equipment Group-Afloat at the former POMPLANT (Polaris Missile Facility) within the city limits of Goose Creek, after receiving a large contract from the Army.[527]

Although the employment impact was minor and quickly mitigated, the potential impact on the local economy alarmed the Goose Creek leadership and stirred them to rethink their strategic plan. The Goose Creek city council was previously content with a residential city that offered homes for workers who commuted to jobs in Charleston County, but they eventually recognized the dangers of remaining a single dimension "bedroom community." The new economic situation in the greater Charleston area required Goose Creek to compete with neighboring municipalities and communities for the limited investment dollars to assuage the outflow of jobs and families that previously provided their revenue base. Prior to the threat of base closure, it was not necessary for Goose Creek to compete with the neighboring municipalities of Hanahan, Summerville, Charleston, North Charleston or Mt. Pleasant. It was not necessary for Goose Creek to boast job opportunities, better schools, parks, or an attractive downtown in order to attract investors and new families. On the contrary, Goose Creek suffered from too many people coming too fast to its city limits, and city council never conceived of the possibility that the wave of immigrants that fueled its local economy for three decades could ebb. Its proximity to military connected jobs and the open spaces for development comprised Goose Creek's competitive edge during the last forty years. These advantages affirmed the wisdom that shaped the leadership's mission and controlled the inevitable growth. Without the influence of a major employer nearby, Goose Creek was forced to compete within the greater Charleston area, South Carolina and the world and to confront their longstanding strategic plan that was no longer applicable.

The leaders of Goose Creek decided to become better masters of destiny and formed an aggressive economic development effort centered upon attracting businesses and jobs. The shock of base closure forced a new, competitive and aggressive strategy that vied for limited jobs and investments and separated Goose Creek from the other competing Lowcountry municipalities. Consequently the city framed a new economic development initiative that accomplished the following:

- Employed an Assistant City Administrator for economic development and formed the Economic Development Advisory Commission.
- Created a reliable water- treatment and distribution system that was independent of Charleston.
- Created a redevelopment project based upon a tax increment-financing plan that captured tax revenues and increased the tax base for redevelopment of underused and blighted commercial areas.
- Created a downtown development plan to focus commercial interests and the subsequent investments that broaden the tax base and create jobs.

Water

As population increases, so does the demand for water. As increasing amounts of water is pumped from area wells, the water table drops due to the fact that aquifers do not quickly renew their water supply. The unreliable water wells in Goose Creek were deactivated when the city tapped on to a water main to the Charleston Commission of Public Works. This immediate remedy made Goose Creek dependent upon a political entity in a different county with no political accountability to their customers in Goose Creek. As a consequence, Goose Creek customers experienced fifteen years of water rate hikes that increased rates by 15 percent to 30 percent annually. During the 1980s, the demands for water tripled and the city was required to buy larger amounts from the Charleston Commission of Public Works at wholesale prices that were doubled, merely because the Goose Creek customers resided outside of Charleston County. To add to the problems, the city's distribution system was inadequately installed, required major upgrades and lacked system redundancies. Without system-wide line looping and backup supplies, the entire city or at least large sections of the city, were denied water service while repairs were affected. Water turn-offs were common during the 1980s that required frequent, and understandably unpopular, public notifications.[528]

The only solution to this untenable situation was to identify another source that could be made accountable to Goose Creek customers. The treatment of surface water was the feasible solution, so after unsuccessful investigations into building its own water intake and treatment facility, the City of Goose Creek joined with like-minded public bodies to create the Lake Moultrie Water Agency. This agency contracted with the South Carolina Public Service Authority to affect the first regional approach to water distribution in the Lowcountry. The system has the capacity to draw twenty-four million gallons per day from Lake Moultrie and distribute water through twenty-six miles of water lines. The Lake Moultrie Water Agency is a joint municipal water agency comprised of the Berkeley County Water and Sanitation Authority, the City of Goose Creek, Moncks Corner Public Works Commission and Summerville Commissioners of Public Works. These four agencies buy the capacity of the water system and sell the water to agency customers. The South Carolina Public Service Authority, commonly known as "Santee Cooper," owns the system's treatment plant, as well as the pump stations and offices near Lake Moultrie's Lions Beach. Santee Cooper also owns the twenty-six miles of transmission pipeline and a million-gallon centralized elevated tank. The water system has two forty-eight-inch pipelines that extend one-half mile into Lake Moultrie. The pipelines are submerged in water that is roughly forty feet deep to provide for optimum withdrawal. Screens at the end of the intake pipelines prevent large materials from entering the pipes. The water is pumped into the treatment plant where it is purified and filtered. This treatment insures water safety, but Lake Moultrie is known for extremely clean water even before it is treated because Santee Cooper has been managing Lakes Marion and Moultrie since their existence and continually monitor the water source and quality. Although the plant is presently rated at twenty-four million gallons a day, it can be inexpensively upgraded to thirty-six million gallons.

Redevelopment Project

South Carolina law allows cities to create redevelopment areas and issue tax increment bonds to fund improvements in those areas. Accordingly, City Council enacted the Goose Creek Redevelopment Project and in 1996 defined a redevelopment area consisting of 1,017 acres of commercial and industrial properties. Based upon the combined assessed value of those acres, the city was authorized to borrow up to $17,200,000 in tax increment bonds. The 1996 assessed value of that total acreage in the redevelopment area amounted to $2,969,142. As the value of those acres increases, so do the assessed values, and consequently the real property taxes. The city was authorized by state law to garner all additional property taxes for fifteen years, to use toward redevelopment of the defined district. The Goose Creek redevelopment plan has seven primary objectives:

1. Diversify and strengthen the economic base of Goose Creek and thus make it more resistant to external economic downturns.
2. Attract high quality jobs into the city limits.
3. Expand the revenue base to enable the city to provide basic services and high quality amenities at affordable costs.
4. Improve quality of public services through better public facilities.
5. Improve the appearance and image of the city through better design, landscaping, lighting and more.
6. Improve movement of people on major roadways, as well as hiker/biker trail ways.
7. Build stronger civic identity to keep those residents with the highest expectations for themselves, their neighbors and the city.

The plan required that all garnered revenues be reinvested to support the redevelopment of the defined area and also projected that more than seventeen million dollars could reasonably be expected. Table 7.7 lists the expected expenditure amounts and planned uses.

The Tax Increment Finance District quickly succeeded in generating reinvestment revenues. The city, as an active partner with Westvaco Development Corporation, marketed the industrial tracts at the Crowfield Corporate Center. By the late 1990s, four major investors located there: Quoizel

Incorporated with its 350 employees in the production of lighting equipment, Rapid Granulator, Corning and a speculative structure eventually occupied by Jamar Distributors. With the surge in assessed value of the properties on which these industries stand, the city issued the series 1997 bonds to borrow $6,585,000. The money was used to build the Marguerite H. Brown Municipal Center housing City Hall, Municipal Court and the Police Station.

Table 7.7: The table shows the projects and associated costs in the Goose Creek Redevelopment Area also known as the Tax Increment Financing (TIF) District.

Project	Cost
Roadway Improvements	$3,500,000
Utilities Improvements	$4,250,000
Municipal Center	$6,000,000
Landscaping/Signage	$2,000,000
Property Acquisition	$1,000,000
Associated Costs	$450,000
Total	$17,200,000

The tax increment bond financing did not decrease the revenues received by other taxing authorities, including the school district and the Berkeley County government. All taxing districts continued to receive all of the old revenues, as well as all of the new personal property revenues from automobiles, machinery and equipment. Consequently, the Goose Creek Redevelopment Project grew new personal property taxes for all taxing districts while foregoing new, real property tax revenues during the redevelopment period. At the end of the fifteen-year redevelopment period, all taxing districts, including the school district, will reap the benefits of a rejuvenated commercial zone and the accompanying increased revenues, as well as better facilities and higher expectations from the residential and commercial citizenry.

Downtown

The City of Goose Creek and its Economic Development Advisory Committee were determined to strengthen the community by creating a recognizable and vibrant commercial center. In 1999, during a three-day charette exercise, 150 citizens and staff members gathered ideas for the development of the commercial core. The charette process brought Goose Creekers together at Shannon Park Shopping Center, where a number of issues emerged. Those issues included:

- The need to improve the appearance of the commercial center with land and streetscaping, as well as more appealing building aesthetics.
- The need to connect the commercial center to the surrounding residential areas by way of pedestrian friendly access.
- The need to expand the quality and quantity of retail services, as well as accessibility to entertainment and cultural gathering places.
- The need to clearly identify the central commercial core of the city by marking its boundaries, as well as capturing the unique features of the community as a whole.

Photograph 7.4 The photograph, taken in 1991, shows the pavement, rooflines and overhead power and communication lines that characterized the commercial center of Goose Creek. *Courtesy City of Goose Creek.*

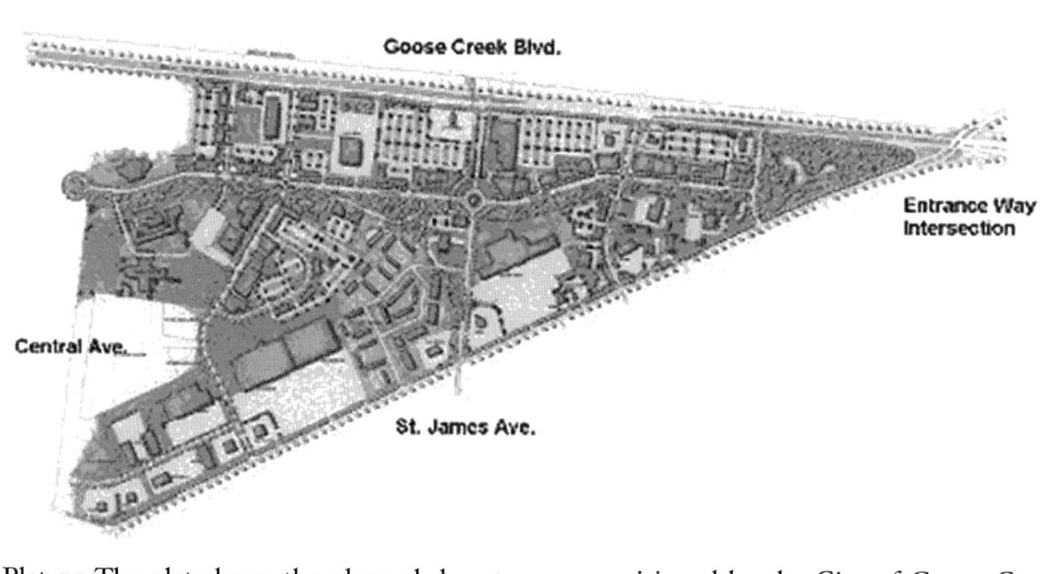

Plat 7.1 The plat shows the planned downtown as envisioned by the City of Goose Creek Economic Development Committee in 2002.

Following the charette exercise, thirty community leaders in government, business and industry formed a steering cadre that advised the Economic Development Advisory Committee. Nine months of work resulted in a downtown plan that incorporated streetscapes, entryways and overlay zoning. The resulting master plan redefined downtown Goose Creek with a "main street" and a central business district, residential areas and green space. Plat 7.1 shows a rendering of the planned downtown. The plan intends to re-orient the focus of motorists by reframing Highways 52 and 176 toward the center and into a main street. The downtown redevelopment program is currently a work in progress with little overt evidence of accomplishment. Eventually business and commercial development will be pulled inward toward a business center, instead of stretched along speedy and congested thoroughfares.

Nurturance of a Unique Identity

During the closing years of the twentieth century and the opening years of the twenty-first century, an independent water system, a self-sustaining redevelopment area and a well-planned commercial center did much to create the self-sufficient community the people of Goose Creek demanded. This progress is best attributed to a citizenry who set high standards and found ways to meet goals. This "can-do" attitude developed during the twenty-three-year period from 1980 to 2003 and resulted from a concerted effort to develop and nurture a positive citywide self-concept. From the beginning, the city needed a solid "sense of place" to gel people of varied origins into a citizenry with high expectations who were committed to a safe, well-planned and orderly community. Toward that end, the city leadership sought opportunities to define the people who lived and worked in Goose Creek.

Communities often measure themselves by what they read in the media. Negative publicity during the heady 1960s, '70s and '80s embarrassed Goose Creekers and lowered expectations. Shortly after the first election of Councilman Joseph Daning in 1978, he aptly urged the city leadership to "get the press on our side and shift the perspectives from negative to positive."[529] He and his council colleagues, along with dozens of citywide supporters, succeeded in altering the beliefs of an entire city through a series of planned events during the succeeding decades. The positive events began with speeches and parades during the early 1980s and evolved twenty years later into original architecture that told the city's story and celebrated its many accomplishments.

The city celebrated its twenty-year anniversary on Saturday April 11, 1981 with a parade, assemblies, speakers, booths, dances and the official unveiling of its two newest street signs. Highways 52 and 176 were renamed "Goose Creek Boulevard" and "St. James Avenue" to inform a recently arrived citizenry that they were part of a long association with the St. James, Goose Creek Parish. Sitting on council for the twentieth anniversary celebration were Lagette Shiver, Shirley Johnson, Marguerite Brown, Joseph Daning, Doreen Davis and Calvin Woods. From that event evolved an annual celebration called "Colonial Days," so named and designed to define Goose Creek as a place with a long and interesting past. Early efforts brought council member Doreen Davis to serve as coordinator of the festivities. She successfully brought television and movie actor Keenan Wynne to serve as parade marshal at the Colonial Days celebration and parade. The management of the annual "Colonial Day" parade and festivities eventually transferred to the Goose Creek Recreation

Commission, who later substituted the successful, annual Fourth of July celebration. City council still felt compelled to find ways to bring people together for recreation and entertainment. In recent years, city leadership undertook new municipal responsibilities of providing opportunities for citizens to assemble with their neighbors and celebrate life in Goose Creek. The Symphony Orchestra concert and the annual Jazz Festival attract hundreds each year to the great lawn at the municipal center.

Another series of events in the early 1980s set a long-term course that further defined the people of Goose Creek. The events centered upon a notorious collection of buildings at the entrance to Goose Creek. A group of Goose Creek citizens formed a task force to improve conditions at a collection of bars and adult- use establishments contiguous but outside of the city limits, commonly referred to as the " corner" or "strip." The 11 citizens who composed the task force elected Mayor Heitzler as the chairman. Reverend Robert Nix represented the Goose Creek Ministerial Association. Darrel Eidem, Jim Soapes, John Thompson, Hank Niles, Beth King, Julie Droze, Ruth Potts, Ben Hooper, Merrill Cox, and Mike Miller served as representatives of schools, businesses and county council. The group requested that the South Carolina Alcoholic Beverage Commission (ABC) not reissue a license to one establishment and to check the legitimacy of the other licenses in the area. The task force also accused the businesses of engaging in illegal activities, such as gambling and prostitution.[530] After visiting the establishments with Mayor Heitzler, solicitor Charles Condon publicly stated:

> *The strip is an outrage. I want it closed up! I'm going to make every effort to close that place. I was shocked!* [531]

He sent the South Carolina State Law Enforcement Division (SLED) officers to make two arrests. The adult bookstore closed that week.[532] As a result of an eight-month investigation resulting from the attention given to the establishments, Berkeley County Sheriff James W. Rogers was indicted along with Moncks Corner businessman, James Ray Scarboro. The indictment alleged that Rogers and Scarboro took bribes to allow illegal gambling by organized crime figures. Dean Powell was appointed Berkeley County Sheriff and immediately paid personal visits to the bars at the "strip." The new sheriff said his deputies were not picking on Goose Creek but noted that the "triangle" has historically been "a problem for the whole county."[533] Rogers was sentenced to fifteen years in prison for conspiring to participate in racketeering activities and Scarboro received a sentence of seven years.[534] The "Strip" is still operating today at the intersection and although it now complies with the law it is still perceived by most as a blight on the greater Goose Creek area. Nevertheless, in dealing firmly with these businesses the city established its moral and ethical standards as an important part of their defined identity.

Identity is not only affected by what one believes and acts upon, but also by appearance. The upscale Crowfield Plantation development became an architectural and landscaping model for the city. Councilman Joseph Daning patiently prodded the city leadership for years to lift the appearance of the city with an architectural review ordinance for commercial property, and Councilman John McCants fathered an ordinance to enforce appearance standards in residential areas. Each effort improved the physical appearance of the city and lifted the expectations of its people.

The construction of the Marguerite H. Brown Municipal Center in 1999 was a culmination of eight years of planning to provide essential operational space, and create a new architectural

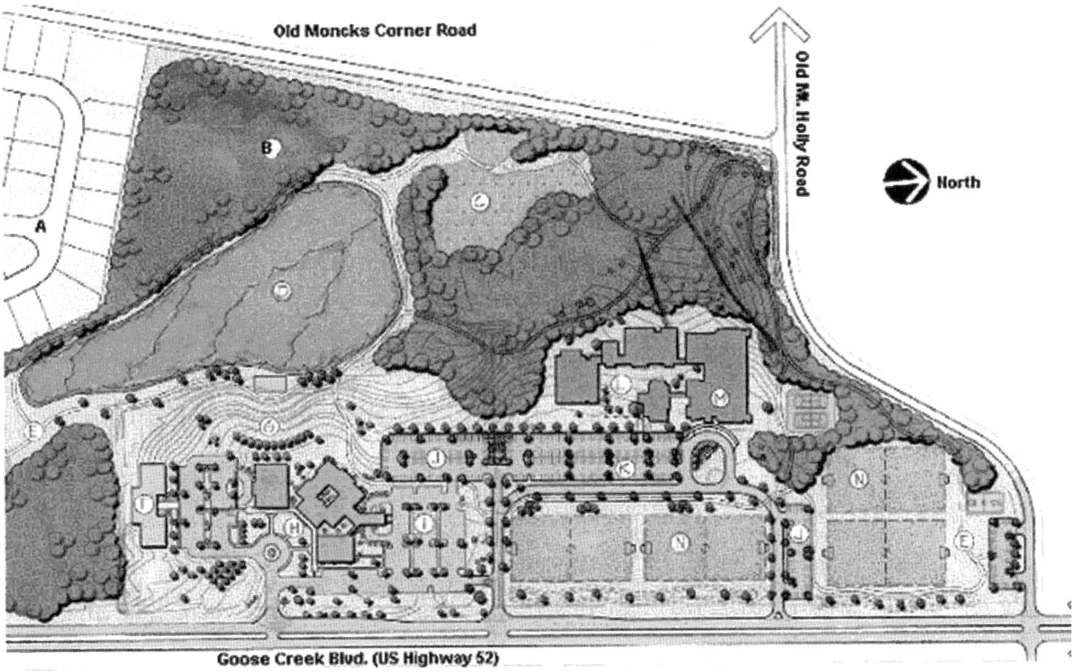

Plat 7.2 The plat shows a rendering of the master plan of the City of Goose Creek municipal center, community center and park. The plan was designed and drawn by Seamon, Whitesides and Associates Inc. Mount Pleasant, South Carolina.
Key: A–Residential Area; B–Wooded Area; C–Wetland; D–Lake; E–Hiker/Biker Trail System; F–Future Training Center; G–Great Lawn; H–Municipal Center; I–Parking; J–Future Parking; K—Future Parking; L–Future Community Center Phases II and III; M–Community Center Phase I; N–Recreation Space.

focus on the eastern section of Goose Creek that balanced the colonial brick and wrought iron architecture in Crowfield on the western side of town. The architecture and design that highlight brick, earth tones, porticos and columns call back to the colonial era and recalls the long history of the community. The municipal center is expected to become the centerpiece to passive and active municipal parks near the northern boundary of the municipal limits. This lovely center serves as a recreation, meeting and work place and speaks volumes about the government of Goose Creek and the expectations of the citizens and sets architectural standards for future commercial development throughout the municipality.

The strategic planning process has successfully guided the City of Goose Creek for more than two decades and offers the best template for success in the near future. The one, five and twenty-year goals that have channeled the city's resources toward the management of growth, improved service delivery, increased self-sufficiency and the nurturance of a unique identity, must address the identified needs of a changing population. Clearly, strategic planning has succeeded because its inception was grounded on the belief that the free exchange of ideas is essential to a fair political process. The most efficient path toward goals is a political system that supports the free exchange of ideas on which this planning process has found success. The bright future of Goose Creek stands upon this core and essential belief.

Future Perspectives

At the annual two-day strategic planning retreat in 2003, Goose Creek City Council met to answer one question: "If you left Goose Creek on March 13, 2003, and did not return until March 13, 2023, what would you like to see upon your return?" Interestingly, the exercise began with a historical description of the changes that occurred in the last twenty years, and then projected the trends from those twenty years into the next twenty. Some changes in the most recent decades are obvious: the city boundaries have expanded, the population has doubled, the commercial center has grown and new roads, neighborhoods, schools and recreational facilities have sprung up to the amazement of most. Although all of the city leadership agreed that the changes have generally been for the better, they also believe that the challenges confronting Goose Creekers in the next two decades are both promising and daunting.

Much promise is found in the success of the last two decades. Those decades witnessed markedly improved lifestyles that began promising historical trends of a manageable growth rate, an aging, better educated and more diversified population and an increase in expendable wealth and leisure time all of which bode well for the immediate future. There were also numerous personal and group successes such as that of Goose Creeker Nancy Mace. She was one of the first two women who graduated from The Citadel, the previously all male military college of South Carolina. Another source of pride were the students, faculty and staff of Stratford High School whose football team brought home the state title in 1992. But the last two decades also brought challenges that are as foreboding as the trends are encouraging.

A wave of people populated the City of Goose Creek during the last decades of the twentieth century. By the turn of the century, a steady influx of new families came close to building-out the last useable properties. Consequently, succeeding waves of potential families will find less available housing in the city and be tempted to leapfrog Goose Creek to the open rural lands north and west of the city. As lands north and west of the city are populated, Goose Creek will likely become a busy transit hub for people passing through on the way to work and home again. A central key to a bright Goose Creek future is to find ways to keep Goose Creek a destination for discriminating home buyers seeking livable and safe neighborhoods.

The Goose Creek community, although much more self-sufficient than in earlier years, remains susceptible to a single event that could alter the dynamics of the local economy. Three more rounds of base closures are planned by the United States Department of Defense during the next fifteen years, each of which may threaten to close or downsize the military properties that currently occupy approximately 50 percent of the incorporated Goose Creek lands. The U.S. military is charged with finding all means to save taxpayer dollars, as well as to increase the defense capacity of the nation. Toward this goal, the armed forces are evolving toward the concept of "jointness" on all military bases. Jointness implies that military units co-use the same facilities and avoid duplication of the same functions in a given area. An example of jointness would be unified personnel and payroll facility that manages records and payroll for all military employees connected to a base—Air Force, Army, Marine Corps, Navy or other.

Photograph 7.5 The photograph shows the mayor and city council at the dedication ceremony of the Marguerite Brown Municipal Center. *Left to right*: Council Members Salvatore Gondalfo, James "Kimo" Esarey, John McCants, Mark Phillips, Marguerite Hood Brown; Mayor Pro Tem Joseph Daning; Mayor Michael Heitzler.

The Naval Weapons Station in the City of Goose Creek enjoys a degree of jointness because it is the home of Army Material Command's Combat Equipment Group Afloat, as well as nearly fifty other tenant units, including the U.S. Border Patrol training facilities and the Naval Nuclear Power Training School that occupies more than fifty acres in the central part of the old Marrington Plantation. This jointness, as well as a huge expansion of intelligence and information technology developed at SPAWAR in the Naval Weapon's Station East Annex in the neighboring Town of Hanahan, is the home of 6,800 active-duty military, 3,400 civilian employees and 860 reservists.[535]

Regardless of the obvious benefits to the nation and the local economy, the City of Goose Creek would successfully endure the closure of Federal Defense related facilities. The thousands of acres of developable properties, including almost seventeen miles of frontage on fresh and tidal influenced water, make those lands some of the most desirable on the east coast for private development. Clearly, the decision to keep or close the facilities is a matter of concern for the city but it is considered by some to be a win-win situation for the local community. If the base remains operational, Goose Creek will continue its longtime joint venture with all the benefits and responsibilities that come with the partnership. Conversely, if the base closes and the land is privatized, the City of Goose Creek would be forced to endure a period of economic downturn and employment transitioning but would undoubtedly emerge as an expanded and prosperous "boom town" in South Carolina. The emerging boomtown would attract thousands of upwardly mobile families, as well as commercial and industrial investors seeking water front lots and unspoiled expanses of pristine coastal woodlands.

If the Naval Weapons Station closes, Goose Creek would quickly emerge as the fourth or fifth most populated municipality in South Carolina with the potential of becoming the richest per capita city in the state.

In addition to the prospects of base closure, the city must also remain vigilant in its political efforts to monitor and affect the means by which local governments are funded in South Carolina. According to the Institute for Public Policy and Research, College of Liberal Arts, University of South Carolina, an overhaul of the local government funding system is needed to allow local governments to address the needs of the twenty-first century while being fully accountable to the taxpayers. An important dimension of local government authority and autonomy is the ability to control its sources of revenue, including setting tax and fee rates, as well as choosing which revenue sources to use. The sources of revenue for the City of Goose Creek have changed over the last thirty years, the most significant being the reduction of reliance on property taxes. There is now more reliance on local sales taxes, charges and fees. City of Goose Creek property tax revenue declined from more than 50 percent of the city total revenue in 1970 to less than 10 percent today. Goose Creek receives 47 percent of its revenue from local sources, with the remaining from state and federal sources. Goose Creek business license fees are an important revenue source, and will be increasingly important in the future. User fees and charges are the fastest growing revenue source for the city. They represented 30 percent of the City revenue in 2003, resulting in a budget that is increasingly dependent on license fees, permits and charges to supplement property taxes. The local option sales tax has been one of the most successful innovations in South Carolina to benefit the people of the City of Goose Creek. Impact fees remain a steady, though not significant, revenue source.

The city leadership has intentionally diverted the tax burden away from property owners toward tax and fee payers who demand and require the service. Thus, the local sales tax collects operational revenues from those passing in and out of Goose Creek but who do not live in the city. Whatever may be the passed-through costs, taxes or fees, the Goose Creek leaders are rightfully held accountable for municipal tax or fee increases, and they are equally accountable for reduced or unsatisfactory services. Future flexibility is required in controlling the revenue streams. Appropriately, the State sets some parameters on local revenue streams, but local officials need greater flexibility to meet diverse needs, circumstances and preferences and to guard against the increasing inclination of the State to control the internal affairs of hometowns.

Goose Creek's sitting council is diverse by race, ethnicity, sex and age, but its members are remarkably similar in their commitment to the vision and mission they defined and have followed for many years. The vision and mission served the people of Goose Creek well in the past two decades and offer a clear and effective roadmap to the next, but as 2003 neared its close, new challenges tested the municipal roadmap. On November 5, 2003, Goose Creek police officers entered Stratford High School to confiscate drugs and other contraband. The video taped event caught the attention of the media and was aired nationally and internationally, as arguments swirled about racial profiling and fourth amendment protections. The year ended without resolution to the heated debate as the various prosecutors and defendants prepared cases for expensive litigation and as personalities seeking national exposure, such as Jesse Jackson, unsuccessfully attempted to rally Goose Creekers in opposition to their police department. Remarkably and most importantly, as the year ended amidst the storm of controversy the people of Goose Creek heaped support upon their council representatives and the city leadership remained united and committed to the core beliefs and convictions from which the vision and mission of their community has ascended across the decades.

Vision

Goose Creek is a city that has achieved a balance between growth, the environment and the preservation of the small town character. The city's primary concern is for the lifelong needs of all its citizens. Goose Creek is a partnership between its people, businesses, community institutions and its governments in the determination of the city's future.

Mission

The City of Goose Creek seeks to serve the needs of its people, businesses and community institutions for a safe, secure and healthy environment, and facilitates planned and managed growth and economic development. The city shall fulfill its mission by ensuring that the highest quality of essential services is provided and by serving as a forum for identifying and addressing the needs of the community. The city assumes a leadership role in determining the future direction of the community.

Chapter VIII
Ghosts and Legends

Ghosts, goblins and other forms of apparitions have always had their place in American history. Most of the spirits that delighted and frightened the American people for hundreds of years are poorly documented, but appeared during every historic era. Almost all of the stories, from the headless horseman of Sleepy Hollow to the more real witches and demons of Puritan New England, came down to us with some basis in fact. Goose Creek too, from its earliest period, had its share of unexplainable phenomena. Its long history produced some of the most interesting tales in South Carolina. Goose Creek has several ghosts, an unusual wedding and a premature burial story—tales that rival those conjured by Edgar Allen Poe. Remarkably, the Goose Creek legends are based on fact. The stories are about real people, real places and with an accurate fix on the time of occurrence. If fact gives way to fiction somewhere, it is for the reader to decide, and those who doubt the authenticity of the reports should visit the old St. James, Goose Creek Church or the Medway House. Even the most unimaginative visitor to either place will be moved by the eerie timelessness. Ghosts dwell in both places. At the church a moment of silence may be broken by the rustling memories of colonial planters. Listen for the voices of horsemen on the muddy road near the church and the clatter of their horse hooves on the bridge spanning the creek. Occasionally, visitors to the old Medway House peer from the front lawn up to the second story front window. Sometimes they catch a glimpse of a ghostly figure glaring through the small glass panes. In Goose Creek it is easy for visitors to hear the past, and feel realities and unrealities that have been forgotten by most during the last three centuries.

Mary Hyrne of Goose Creek Plantation

The main house at Yeamans Hall Plantation was once known as "Old Goose Creek," and is one of the most interesting South Carolina residences. The mansion near the creek was originally built as a defense against Indians and it featured surrounding breastwork and gun loopholes in the foundation. For the purpose of withstanding long sieges, a well was dug underneath the house and a tunnel was excavated from the residence to the creek to allow hidden escape or entry. The old house was a perfect abode for ghosts and spirits. It featured trap doors, secret chambers and all of the necessities of a good ghost story.

A small room with an entire double floor and trapdoor was built off the back porch. Here the family concealed valuables when threatened by Indians, "redcoats," "Yankees" or thieves. As the years passed, this secret place was forgotten by most, except for a boy named Paul. For some time, this slave boy hid there during the day and made mischief at night. Once, during a three-week period, the housemistress feared that the young boy drowned or was kidnapped. From that time on it was called Paul's hole.[536]

Paul's mischief is explained in terms of a childish prank and he was eventually discovered, but another mystery remains unexplained to this day. This quaint old plantation home possesses a haunting spirit, which has been reported time and again for almost two hundred years. The last sighting of the spirit was only a few years ago during a social event at the Yeamans Club House. The first sighting is told as "The Story of Mary Hyrne."

In colonial days, families of means hired private teachers to educate their children. Schools were rare and the occasional church-sponsored tutors were often inaccessible to many of the more remote plantations. Thus, Mrs. Latham (no first name appears in the records) left her native Ireland to seek employment as a governess in Charleston.[537] Widowed and without means of support, she endured the ordeals of the voyage with hopes of teaching in America. Upon arrival she immediately learned of the Goose Creek Plantation, where she could teach four little girls. Thus, she set out on the journey by coach over miles of rough dirt and clay roads from Charleston to the banks of a wide winding creek. Old Goose Creek Plantation rested at the gooseneck bend of the creek for which many believe it was named. The glassy creek and wide expanse of open marsh near which the plantation stands retain much of its timeless beauty today. For Mrs. Latham, the vista and the moss-laden oaks were very strange and beautiful. She had never seen such landscapes in her native Ireland. The travel into the rustic countryside was a pleasant change after the long ocean voyage, but the ordeal was also exhausting for the new governess so that soon after Mrs. Henry Smith and her small daughters welcomed the new governess she retired to her accommodations at Yeamans Hall.

Mr. Smith had died some years before and the family had settled on the first floor of the old estate. As Mrs. Latham climbed into the second floor, Mrs. Smith offered to have one of her servants sleep there so the governess would not be alone. To this Mrs. Latham replied, "Oh, really, Madam, I will not be afraid to stay up there. What could possibly happen to me? I beg you, don't give it a thought."[538] So Mrs. Latham moved into the second floor to rest alone in her room overlooking the marsh and creek.

The next morning was Sunday. The family gathered downstairs with the servants to read the Sunday service. Mrs. Latham remained upstairs to read *The Turkish Spy*, a novel by Giovanni Marana, that she brought with her to gratify her interest in romance.[539] After a short while the morning service was suddenly disrupted by the trembling and wide-eyed appearance of Mrs. Latham on the stairway. She cried out hysterically, "Who was that who just went out?" The family and servants were startled and amazed by the interruption. No one could pass without going through the hall and no one had, but Mrs. Latham was so visibly shaken and unconvinced by the family explanation that everyone searched for the mysterious visitor.

After some calming, the governess related her experience, which she retold for years thereafter. She had been sitting in her room, reading of romance, when she heard a disturbance in the outside hall. She listened intently as footsteps approached her door. The door opened slowly to reveal an old lady dressed in a black gown with a muslin neckerchief crossed on her breast. Her head was covered with a white cap.

Mrs. Latham was puzzled because she knew nothing of this elderly occupant of the house, but she remained polite and invited the lady in. Receiving no response she repeated, "Come in, won't you?" There was still no response, only a disapproving glare. Mrs. Latham moved toward her as the mysterious lady moved slowly off. A cold draft filled the room, recounted the governess. She was repelled, but at the same time incredibly attracted to the lady, and was drawn by a strange force to follow her as she glided several paces ahead to the next room and the one beyond, where she vanished! It was then that a panic filled the governess as she ran back through all of the rooms, searching and thinking that she had some how missed the visitor.

Although the entire family searched the home, and the mysterious elderly visitor was nowhere to be found, the alarmed governess could not to be pacified by assurances from the family that the home was safe. She insisted that she was not mistaken about the strange visitor and gratefully accepted the offer to have someone sleep upstairs so she would not be alone if revisited again.

Sunday was a gathering time for the family. The following Sabbath Mr. Benjamin Smith came to visit his brother's widow. The new governess was immediately upset by the appearance of Mr. Smith. She became hysterical, crying out, "You are like her. Heaven help me, you are the living image of the lady who glared at me!" Mr. Smith seemed to immediately understand the lady's alarm and talked gently for some time to calm her tears.

"My mother, Mary Hyrne, spent the last years of her life in the rooms upstairs," he told her. "She seldom came down, and it was customary for the family to take their work or books up to sit with her. She was a kind, dear old lady. In the closet of one room she had many little partitions built, in which she kept sugar dainties for her small grandchildren."[540] Mr. Smith reasoned that his deceased mother was probably concerned about the influence Mrs. Latham might have on the minds of her granddaughters. The governess was reading a romantic novel on the Sabbath instead of attending the family worship service. His very pious mother had returned to protest the behavior of the governess and express her concerns for the children's welfare.

The spirit of Mary Hyrne never appeared again to protest the presence of the Irish immigrant, and the young governess became a faithful and pious teacher who lived to instruct four generations of the Smiths, as well as children of other Charleston families. She also found romance and married. Throughout her long life she retold the story of Mary Hyrne's protest many times and delighted in having such an exciting tale to tell.

This delightful story of the ghost lady of "Old Goose Creek" is based on a considerable amount of historical fact. Mary Hyrne was the only daughter of Colonel Edward Hyrne and Elizabeth. Their daughter, Mary, married Thomas Smith, the second Landgrave, and she lived her entire life at the country mansion overlooking Goose Creek.[541] In her later years she was sickly, and spent most of her time confined on the second floor of the mansion. She entertained her grandchildren with doll parties and sugar dainties. Her son, Benjamin, strongly resembled his mother and thus was the reason he so alarmed Mrs. Latham, upon his visit on her second Sabbath in America.

Mary Hyrne Smith died in 1777 at the age of 80 years, and centuries have passed since her ghostly figure appeared before the young governess, but there are many who still sense her ghostly spirit at Yeamans Hall. During the early twentieth century, Yeamans Hall Country Club developed on the

Photograph 8.1 The postcard photograph shows the St. James, Goose Creek Church and graveyard near the time of the ghostly tale. ***Courtesy Library of Congress.***

spacious grounds, and in 1963 some ladies were decorating the central clubhouse for the enjoyment of the members when one of the party was separated from her friends and was puzzled to see a glaring old lady approach her. When the apparition vanished, the startled club member asked, "Who was that old lady in an old-fashioned black dress with a muslin neckerchief and a little white cap?" One older colleague answered in a voice full of respect, "It was Mary Hyrne – protesting again."

Not a word she deigned to say, But like a specter stalked away.[542]

The Morbid Tale of Miss Coleman

A rare, old book with no author's name was printed in New York City that contains a curious story of a premature burial at the St. James, Goose Creek Church. Only one hundred copies of this rare manuscript were printed when *The Goose Creek Church, A Morbid Tale* was published in 1901. According to this quaint old book, Charles Carrington survived a strange and frightening experience almost two hundred years ago.

While Charles Carrington was visiting a Goose Creek plantation he became weary at the house party and wandered away for a brisk walk. After a while he approached the old church, which at that time, was surrounded by a ruined wall and a rusting iron gate. A drizzling rain forced the weary wanderer through the graveyard toward the church side door. He opened the unlocked door and entered into the protection of the gloomy, damp and moldy church structure. The dimly lit shelter protected him from the chilly mist, but as he stood at the side of the chancel he remained chilled and felt an odd sense that he was not alone. As his eyes adjusted to the dim light, his heart quickened when he heard approaching footsteps. Eerily he watched as a solitary young woman approached along the central aisle and knelt in silence near the winding stairway to the raised pulpit. As he watched from a mere five paces away, she prayed a few moments, arose, turned to him and as she approached she introduced herself as Miss Edith Coleman.

As his anxiety lessened, her company became oddly endearing and their awkward introductions turned to pleasant conversation. He learned that she was a member of an ancient Goose Creek family and many of her ancestors were buried in the family vault outside the musty old sanctuary. The old graveyard, on such a gloomy day was unsettling to the young man and he became further uncomfortable as their conversation centered on the ancient cemetery. Miss Coleman attempted to assuage his uneasiness by explaining the folly of fearing death and of fearing the dead. "Surely," she said, "the dead can do no harm, and life is as great a mystery as death."[543]

The reasoning offered by Miss Coleman did not console Mr. Carrington. He feared the graves, the vaults, the markers of death and the heavy sense of ghostly presence pervading throughout. Miss Coleman showed her family vault to Carrington where her father insisted that all family members be entombed. In spite his uneasiness Charles Carrington departed with mixed feelings. He bid his farewell and hurriedly returned to the house party.

During the following week Charles Carrington made daily visits to the old church to meet with Edith Coleman. As could be expected when a young man meets an attractive woman, his conversation led to romance, but Edith remained aloof from Charles' earnest pleas of love. She sparred with him by challenging his concept of love and she spoke so earnestly of the serious aspects of love that it puzzled and frightened the young man.

"Would our love outlive the fires of youth when the finger of time had placed its seal of age and decay? No, no, a thousand times no! Man's love droops, then fades and dies."

The intensity of her words startled him, but he could not draw back.

"Put me to any test, Edith," he cried, taking her unresisting hand and looking longingly into her face, as she laughed her low, sweet laugh.

"You swear it?"

"I swear it!"

"Then follow me."

He followed her to her family vault. The young couple paused before the metal entrance door, but in the instance that Charles glanced beyond the tomb and back, Edith mysteriously disappeared. He became confused and alarmed and surmised that his companion had somehow entered the dreadful vault. With nervous strength and energy, he grabbed the iron vault handle and in a burst of force broke the rusting lock. The door fell outward and something that had evidently been leaning against it fell in a confused mass at his feet. Breathless from his burst of strength and his fearful state, he could only stand and stare at what lay at his feet. It was a human body. He put his hands up to his

Photograph 8.2 The photograph shows a small boy holding a large key at the side door of the Goose Creek Church. The photograph is included in *Johnson's Scrapbook, Volume 1*, among the collections of the South Carolina Historical Society, Charleston, South Carolina. The photograph is entitled, "Key Keeper, Goose Creek Church."

eyes and for a moment stood there swaying. Then with a moan he fell forward upon his face beside that awful heap.

For months following this dreadful experience, Charles Carrington lay near death with a raging fever. He remembered nothing at first, but as he regained his senses the ghastly details of his experience slowly returned to his memory. When he regained strength, he returned to his host's plantation to investigate the tormenting event. His rescuers recanted that they found him lying facedown in front of the Coleman vault by a broken vault door that had been forced open. Next to him was the crumpled body of Edith Coleman in a horrible state of decomposition. They explained that Edith Coleman was the eldest daughter of their neighbor, Mr. James Coleman. She had died a few months before and from the evidence found at the vault they conjectured that the young lady was still alive when she was placed in the coffin and vault. The coffin lid was pushed askew, the lining was ripped and torn, and many marks left by tearing fingernails marred the coffin inner walls. Edith had struggled valiantly for her freedom, but after forcing her way out of the coffin and dragging herself to the iron vault door she died from exhaustion and the sheer fear and panic of her condition.[544]

Charles Carrington never told his hosts of his meetings with Edith, nor offered explanation for his mysterious accident at the door of the vault. He departed from Goose Creek and returned to his home in another parish and never visited the old church again.

This tale, like so many Goose Creek stories, has its basis in historical fact. There was a premature burial at the Goose Creek Church. It seems that a young woman was buried in a vault near the front

Photograph 8.3 The photograph shows the tomb where Elizabeth Ann Smith is buried. This raised tomb with a protective brick wall is located opposite the front doors of the St. James, Goose Creek Church. The photograph was taken July 23, 2003. *Author's collection.*

door of the old church. Soon after the burial a servant woman claimed that she heard shrieks in the vault. Her hysteria was ignored as silly superstition, and when a small boy was sent to perform his duties at the church and returned with the same claim, both stories were ignored. A few months later the body of another member of the same family was taken to the vault for burial. When the vault was reopened, the startled family members found that the young woman had torn her way out of the wooden coffin and died imprisoned by the walls of the brick vault. For many years thereafter the vault was not sealed in fear of another premature burial.[545] Photograph 8.2 shows a small boy at the St. James Church. The photograph is undated and provides no evidence of the child's connection with the premature burial, but it does validate the practice of using a small boy to perform duties at the church and this boy may have been the one who heard the plaintive cries.

Brick vaults were typical features at southern churches. The cool brick enclosures were sometimes used to temporarily hold bodies until the family arranged a proper burial. Such a holding vault can be seen today at Strawberry Chapel in Berkeley County and photograph 8.3 shows a brick vault situated near the front door of the Goose Creek Church. Darker bricks in the face of the vault suggest that the bricks were installed later than the original construction and possibly replaced an iron door similar to the one forced open in the ghostly story of Miss Coleman. A marble slab on top of the vault bears the following inscription:

Here Lies the Body of
Elizabeth Ann Smith
The Amiable and Deservedly
Beloved Wife of Captain
Benjamin Smith
Who died the 26 March, 1769
Aged 27 years
also Their Daughter
Mary Smith Who Died
September 9th 1768 Aged 3 Years
5 Ms and 8 Days.

The name of the young woman on the Goose Creek vault is not the same as the woman met by Charles Carrington in the ghostly tale. There is no documentation of the authenticity of the reports of the premature burial, nor justification for the difference in names.

The Ghost of "Old Bandison"

During the colonial era, the American colonists were called upon often to assist in many of the British wars against the Spanish and French. In 1739, General Oglethorpe attacked the Spanish at St. Augustine. The Carolina Regiment was an auxiliary force supporting Oglethorpe under the command of Colonel Alexander Vanderdussen of Goose Creek and Lieutenant Colonel Francis LeJau, son of the Goose Creek minister.[546] Little is known of Colonel Vanderdussen before this time, but he lived in Carolina as early as 1731 and owned a plantation on Goose Creek across the water from Yeamans Hall. He also served as a member of the Commons House for St. James, Goose Creek. Like Oglethorpe, he had seen service in foreign wars and was esteemed as an experienced soldier.

Colonel Vanderdussen continued as a member of the Commons House for many years, and at one time, was one of the King's council. He was elected six times to the Royal Assembly, but was removed from council for being "disordered in his mind," and by 1756, trustees were named to his estate. He died three years later and left no heirs.[547] After his death, his lands were deserted for a time and the grounds became overgrown and the house fell into disrepair. It was at this time that the haunting story of ghosts at the house and on the grounds began to circulate. The ghost stories persisted for many years, but it is likely that the house and land probably became the resort of runaway slaves who used the land as their retreat and preferred to spread the rumors of ghosts to keep intruders away. Local African Americans would say, "If you go there, Old Bandison will catch you." They were referring to Colonel Vanderdussen, the former owner, who had lived in great style in the house that he had built overlooking the winding creek. He raised cattle, built a dairy and grew rows of mulberry trees, which he cultivated for the production of silk. He is reported to have been a severe master, and as he aged and his mind became more addled, bizarre stories of "Old Bandison" (Vanderdussen) perpetuated and spread throughout the neighborhood and many believed that after his death, he indeed would return to, "Revisit the glimpses of the moon, making night hideous."[548]

Vanderdussen's old house was eventually rebuilt and occupied by William Johnson who reared a large family on the site, undisturbed by ghosts. Among the family was the Honorable William Johnson, Associate Justice of the Supreme Court of the United States.[549]

"Mad Archie" Campbell

Captain Archibald Campbell was an officer in the King's army during the Revolutionary War. During the period of British occupation of Charleston, Goose Creek was within British lines and the St. James, Goose Creek Church was familiar to the British soldiers who used it as a place of worship. Thus, it was not unusual for British soldiers to be seen at the church, but in 1780, the church was the scene of the unusual wedding of Mad Archie Campbell and Paulina Philps.

Captain Campbell was a young officer reputed to be a proud and swanky soldier. He was a man of his word, but also a man who acted presumptuously. In 1780 he attended a Tory ball in Charleston where the British invited Whig ladies. Few Charleston ladies attended because of the occupation and their strong feelings of loyalty to the patriots but nevertheless, it was at this ball that British Captain Archibald Campbell met the daughter of a prominent South Carolina family, Miss Paulina Philps. The young and beautiful Paulina captivated him, but Miss Philps was not interested in the young captain and ignored him for another man at the ball. The young captain, chided by his army friends, challenged his comrades to a wager.

"I intend to marry the lady," he stated in a voice just short of a shout. He was rebutted by a burst of laughter. "I'll wager," said one of Archie's friends, but Archie took the initiative to make the bet. "Nay, gentlemen. It is I who will wager, my Arab filly to your fifty pounds, that within three days I will be married to the lady and with her consent." His wager was quickly accepted.[550] The following day Captain Campbell went to 43 East Battery in Charleston to offer a sunny ride to the lovely Miss Philps. She appeared eager to ride in the fine gig, which was a blatant show of respectability. They rode through the streets of town until they passed through the neck and entered the countryside. The road became more primitive until it was little more than a dusty wagon trail, but the young captain drove his steed faster and faster, over the fearful pleas of Miss Philps. They finally arrived at a wooden bridge, and after crossing, young Paulina first saw the ancient Goose Creek church.

During that time the Reverend Edward Ellington was the minister. He was called to the door of the rectory, whereupon the wild-eyed captain announced his intentions to be married to the lovely lady. The good Reverend, noticing that she was nearly faint, protested, "Not without the consent of the lady." Mad Archie immediately confirmed his impetuous reputation, drew his pistol and shouted, "Unless you comply, you shall be instantly shot, and the lady's virtue could only suffer in consequence. I say, sir, make haste!" When he pointed the pistol at Paulina Philps, she hurriedly consented.[551]

After the nervous wedding, the proud husband drove his new bride back to Charleston at a modest pace while the decorum of his new bride noticeably changed. The young girl lost her fear and apprehension as she told her family: "Until we arrived at Goose Creek, I had never thought seriously about marrying Captain Campbell. Indeed, I supposed his wild talk to be only a soldier's way of making love."[552] She told her friends that when Campbell was particular in his attentions at flattering her, she had considered it nothing more than what all British officers were in the habit of doing. That day at the church surely changed her mind.

Mad Archie won his wager of £50 and he and his beautiful bride, Paulina spent a year of marriage at Exeter Plantation on the western branch of the Cooper. They had one daughter but lived happily only for a short time. Sadly, at the battle of Videau's Bridge, the advanced companies of the British and American armies met near the clubhouse at the bridge. During the battle, Captain Campbell was forced to surrender when he was unhorsed, either by falling or by the death of his steed. He was seated on the root of a tree, guarded by a sentinel. A few moments later he tried to escape, and despite his guard's warning, he continued to run. He was shot in the back and killed.[553] The lovely Paulina reportedly died soon afterwards but the spirits of Mad Archie and Paulina never departed the Lowcountry. There are many reports of his return to both the old church and Exeter Plantation. When the night falls soundly on the pines near the Goose Creek Church or the quiet waters of the Cooper River, some say they can hear the stealthy rustling of the spirits of the two rebellious lovers.

The Ghost of Medway

Ghosts abound at the old Medway house on Back River. Of all the eerie spots in Goose Creek, Medway is without a rival. "It was just the place for ghosts to walk, for strange voices to be heard, for unusual things to happen," claimed John Bennett, author of *The Treasure of Peyre Gaillard.* In this book of treasure and intrigue, Bennett immortalized the atmosphere of Medway Plantation. He revived the eerie sense of desolation and haunting allurement found within the walls of the well-built old house. Of the countryside, he wrote, "we rode through a desolated country, from which the old plantations had almost vanished; even the brick foundations of the ancient houses had been carted away by the Negroes to build crooked chimneys to their cabins." The three mile long entrance road traversed several low swampy areas that required logs to be laid side by side to raise the horsemen or carriage above the water and soft earth as they trekked the "corduroy" road to the ancient main house near Back River. Bennett wrote, "It was certainly true that there was something ghostly and sad and strange about the whole demesne.[554]

Many ghosts are said to walk in the low-ceiling rooms of the old Medway house. Thick walls with large fireplaces and narrow windows protect them. The Medway main house is situated on expansive plantation grounds and is approached by a long entrance road, bordered by tall pines and moss-ladened live oaks. The old home stands on an expanse of well-kept lawn spreading down to Back River. The house is the oldest masonry home of record in the state and was constructed in 1686, just sixteen years after the colony at Charles Town was founded. Jan Van Arrsens built the structure for his wife, Sabina de Vignou. The high Dutch gables of the home were fashioned to induce evil spirits to walk down and leave the house in peace. Van Arrsens did not live long to enjoy his home on Back River and upon his death, his widow married Landgrave Thomas Smith, governor of Carolina. There is no trace of Van Arrsens' grave but Landgrave Smith died at the age of forty-six and was buried on the plantation grounds where a marble slab marks the final resting place.

For centuries it has been reported that the old Dutchman returns to the ancient house to assert his possession. One who has sufficient nerve to sleep in the upstairs bedroom on the south side, a

Photograph 8.4 Some have claimed to see a vision of a head, face and torso of a person dressed in white. The vision appears in the second-story window on the east side of the Medway House. The photograph was taken April 17, 2003. *Author's collection.*

part of the original structure, is likely to wake in the night to see old Van Arrsens seated before the fireplace. He sits there contently enjoying both his pipe and his home.[555] Downstairs there is another ghostly visitor, that of a beautiful young woman whose heart was broken by the death of her husband while he was hunting. The Medway Plantation grounds abound in deer, wild turkey and other game animals. Hunts have been held here for hundreds of years. At one such hunt, a gathering of deer hunters and their wives, including a young couple, met at the ancient home. The young girl begged her husband not to go because she had a foreboding fear of disaster as she watched him leave with his comrades. Near dusk the hunters returned, carrying an improvised stretcher upon which was the lifeless body of her husband.

She was heart broken and upon returning to Medway House she fell ill with fever and died shortly after. For many years she has haunted the spot where her heart died at the sight of her husband's stretcher. Night after night she comes back to the place of her anguish to wait for her young husband. Some have reported that the hunter's young bride stands by the north window of the Medway main house to peer through the small panes of glass. Others say that they have heard only the rustling of her gown as she waits.

Another story tells of a romantic young lady who is sometimes seen waiting for the spirit of her lover, who promised but failed to appear to her after his death. It seems that old Samuel Marion and young Miss Polly Seed, believed in the possibility of a dead friend reappearing to a loved one. They promised each other that whoever died first would return to meet the other in the upper north room. After the old gentleman died, Miss Polly waited patiently one day in the north room, but the promise was not kept.[556]

Many other ghosts and apparitions abound in the old plantations and gravesites in Goose Creek. Old "Pontoux," the ghost of Parnassus plantation on Back River, haunts the cool spring above the high bank of Back River. This ghost is reportedly the spirit of Zachariah Villeponteaux, the Goose Creek church vestryman.[557]

This and other spirits continue to haunt the ancient Goose Creek plantations, churches and graveyards. The swampy Goose Creek water, dense pine and oak forests stir the imagination and provide ideal settings for spirits. Visitors with sufficient nerve and desire can visit the old sites at dusk, and may sense the apparitions of old Goose Creekers who lived and loved in a unique corner of South Carolina.

Chapter IX
Conclusion

The Africans, Barbadians, English, French and Native Americans comprised an unusual demography in Goose Creek during the difficult frontier period, but in spite of many hardships, the frontiersmen and their descendents successfully established a plantation society that made fortunes from naval stores, rice and indigo, and greatly influenced colonial policies. The Native American population steadily declined to extinction, but the enslaved African American numbers increased to exceed 75 percent of the Goose Creek population. When the prosperous plantation society succumbed to malaria and soil exhaustion toward the end of the eighteenth century, most of the more than two hundred smaller farms that supplanted the grand estates continued to depend on slave labor. Subsequently, after the Civil War and the emancipation of the African Americans, the land was further divided among black and white landowners, as well as tenant and "share crop" farmers who worked more than eight hundred small farms and struggled in obscurity near churches and rail stops for a hundred years, until the U.S. Department of Defense realized the value of the worn lands. During World War II, national defense initiatives brought thousands of military personnel and civil servants to Charleston and Berkeley Counties spawning secondary commercial and industrial interests that resulted in the flow of investment capital. In the process, rural Goose Creek began a slow metamorphosis that consistently gained momentum until there was a steady influx of families near the middle of the twentieth century. The newcomers supplanted the scattered white settlements and the African American culture, and installed in its place a racially diverse and progressive citizenry with lofty expectations and the talents to achieve. Thus, during the last decades of the twentieth century, Goose Creek emerged as a progressive Sun-belt city and a destination for upwardly mobile, middle class families and retirees.

From this long and interesting past evolved the contemporary City of Goose Creek—a proud product of the American republic. But Goose Creek is more than one of the polyglots of hometowns that make up the nation. It is a special place with a unique history and future. It is in Goose Creek, South Carolina, where homeowner Cynthia Hudson, while preparing a backyard flowerbed, collected a shoebox of pottery and ceramic shards, which are relics of the wealth of Bloomfield Plantation.[558] Future gardeners will likely collect similar treasures from fresh flowerbeds at Liberty Hall and Brick Hope Plantations, the old rice estates once owned by French Huguenots, and now the newest residential neighborhoods in the city. Goose Creek is a place where frontiersmen and planters lie buried in ancient churchyards, colonial era tombstones with inscribed names of revolutionary patriots stand veiled in dense forests and remnants of indigo vats, brick kilns, tar pits and ancient walled gardens lie hidden on high ground that is the destination of new residents from far and near. Today, fishermen and recreational shrimp net casters test the same waters that schooners and sloops plied when they carried products from farms and forests to colonial Charleston market places. The same waterways that once carried rice and bricks now float nuclear training submarines at the Naval Weapons Station, where American sailors are instructed in the world's most advanced technology.

No other place is quite like Goose Creek. No municipality in the United States shares the city's title, nor do other places share the family names so prevalent in its phone directory. The Charleston Metropolitan Area telephone directory contains names of contemporaries such as Porcher, Manigault, Howe, Barker, Legare, Marion, Godin, Keating, Villeponteaux and many more, which are the same names as the first immigrants who ventured to the Goose Creek frontier. Many contemporary Goose Creek family names, such as Middleton, Singleton, Gourdine, Gadsden and Mazyck, share their nominal lineage with owners of grand estates of the colonial era. Other Goose Creek names such as Bunch, Brown, Cannon, Droze, Mallard and Sineath hearken to the families of farmers of the nineteenth century. Added to these old Goose Creek bloodlines are recent arrivals from every corner of the world.

Prior to incorporation in 1961, the story of Goose Creek was written in terms of two separate and segregated racial groups. The story was always written on separate pages—one page for white people or one page for black people and never both groups together. Today, according to the 2000 census, forty-two ethnic groups are represented among the residents of the City of Goose Creek. All bring their unique lineage and ensure that the future history will always be written on the same page. Today, the forty-two ethnic groups making up the whole are neatly bound by the reality of the city limits, but they are more firmly tied by the common incentive that brought them home to Goose Creek. Their stories are as varied as their numbers, but their unique Goose Creek history is written as a unified story in this work's last chapters, as it will in many chapters to come.

Unfortunately, the dualistic history of Goose Creek keeps secrets that require further research to divulge. What were the contributions of the black household to post–Civil War Goose Creek? How did black landowners acquire land? The black farmers in Goose Creek, as well as those in many other places in South Carolina, dominated the landscape for one hundred years after emancipation, but cultural contributions made by emancipated Goose Creekers were silenced and blurred by a white minority that enforced white racial dominance. White control reigned for a hundred years after emancipation, and black illiteracy along with the dearth of media and other communications kept African American families sequestered in little settlements near small, wooden churches. Much remains to be learned about the land, farmers and families and their schools and churches that provided a modicum of culture and local government during the ten decades after the Civil War. Hopefully, the research of future Goose Creek scholars will tell a more complete story of the residents of the "little places" in Goose Creek, better explain their contributions, carry this work forward and add to the historical lexicon of the South Carolina Lowcountry and the State. More research is also needed to uncover the mystery of heir properties in greater Goose Creek.

Heir property is primarily located where former slaves, through various means, acquired land after emancipation. Records indicate that in some cases dubious legal transfers of properties occurred, and in other instances tracts owned by real estate societies were often divided without legal title transfers.

Subsequently, during the first half of the twentieth century, when the land was inexpensive and the taxes were low, the Federal Government, lumber companies and prosperous northern speculators purchased the available remains of the Goose Creek estates and transformed them into expansive military, residential and commercial developments that eventually defined the City of Goose Creek. But most of the land with unclear titles stayed in minority holdings because valid titles were too difficult and expensive to obtain. Today, many tracts of land in greater Goose Creek remain in small, private holdings with unclear titles and rapidly increasing land values.

It is likely that large sections of greater Goose Creek will become legal labyrinths and litigant battlegrounds when heir property values increase to levels for family or other interests to invest time and money in sorting out the rights to ownership. This work will likely have profound effects on the lives of the landowners and their families, as well as impact the planned development of the community at large. The city should be proactive to secure planning and zoning authority in the areas where potential land transfer and development may occur.

Its unique history makes Goose Creek an inimitable part of Americana, but the potential rewards reaped from its story can only be realized in a community where residents are connected singularly to its history and exponentially to each other. "Interconnection" is a common characteristic of a wholesome small town, and the best thing about Goose Creek is the small town ambience that persists in spite of its mercurial growth. Most agree with Rhonda Knodel, a Goose Creek restaurant owner, when she exclaimed that the best thing about Goose Creek is that it "feels like a small town."[559] But the small town ambience in the City of Goose Creek has always been at risk. The modern city was born during an era of automobiles and interstate highways that ingrained a culture of sub-urbanization and resulted in some people living in one place, working in another and going to church or recreation in a third. Thus, the full sense of community in Goose Creek remained elusive resulting in the sense of displacement and unease. Uncomfortable feelings can arise from the social need for "tribal" connections beyond the family. Such connections give a sense of belonging, familiarity and safety, and are a highly valued aspect of healthy communities. In response, Richard Buckner, a successful Goose Creek businessman and the longtime chairman of the city's Economic Development Commission, prepared the city for a large financial investment in 2003 toward a connectivity project that creates and builds relationships beyond the family.

The central feature of the planned connectivity project is a distinctive "downtown" that is highlighted by an entrance feature and defined by street-scaping. An entrance feature with flowing water, roughcast bricks and five alighting bronzed geese is planned for the main highway intersection that is the front door of downtown. The intersection is heavily traveled and the volume of traffic frequently requires motorists to stop. Here, the Goose Creek entrance feature will mark a moment of arrival and begin to tell Goose Creek's story. Beyond it, distinctive streetlights and landscaped medians and intersections will create a definitive downtown that invites residents to visit, meet and learn about Goose Creek and each other.

These meeting places will be physically connected by an inner-core trail system running throughout the downtown zone. In this way, the pedestrians will be connected to a citywide system of passive and active parks. This physical network will provide many opportunities for people to slowly move in and out of each other's space and form social and emotional ties. As Goose Creek expands many more meeting places will be needed to provide similar moments of interpersonal connection.

Photograph 9.1 The photograph shows Canada geese feeding on the great lawn at the Marguerite H. Brown Municipal Center. The City hopes the architecture of the structures and the open space ambiance of the municipal center, as well as the management of the contiguous water and park, will influence architecture and landscape standards throughout the municipality. The photograph was taken June 9, 2003. *Author's collection.*

There will be many opportunities to enrich the common knowledge of Goose Creek's unique heritage and history. Historical markers will provide depth and meaning to the new downtown and to the parks and meeting places throughout the city. Here Goose Creekers will claim their common heritage and realize the joint ownership of their hometown's future. Remarkably, one of the newest arrivals to Goose Creek summed it up best when he explained, "My wife and I moved here because we liked the 'ghostness' of this place, not in a bad way but in a good way. We like all the history."[560] The South Carolina Downtown Development Association expanded on the benefits of this "ghostness" when it explained: "unquestionably, your history is important, it surfaced over and over again, people want to capture it in some way."[561]

Goose Creek's unique "ghostness" is found among thousands of spirits who live in the land records, census pages, plantation diaries and many other chronicles of past lives. Goose Creek is heaped with hundreds of years of recorded tales beginning with the storied lives of the earliest settlers and told as each related to the rivers, creeks, forests and fields that sustained them during every era. The creek from which the community derives its name, and the surrounding waters and lands have been the most important influences upon the people that came before and those arriving almost daily. The same waters and lands that led the earliest colonists to settle and prosper were, in the latter half of the twentieth century the primary attractions to modern residential, commercial and industrial development, and there is no doubt that these resources will be the essential elements that sustain future Goose Creekers. Thus both volumes of *Goose Creek: A Definitive History*, tells the story of thousands who came before and illuminates the heritage that all Goose Creekers may claim. Most concertedly, the volumes describe the common thread that is the creek itself and, with the last chapters, begins another journey for all who come home to Goose Creek and who love the people, the name and the place.

Appendix I
Petitions for Canals

Petitions to the South Carolina General Assembly for Canal Projects in the St. James, Goose Creek Parish.

- Asking in 1786 that the commission be empowered to make several cuts through the marsh on Goose Creek to facilitate navigation (S.C. Archives S165005 General Assembly Reports, 1786, Number 46).
- Asking to be allowed to cut a canal from the Chapel Bridge to Back River in 1796 (S.C. Archives S165015, Year 1796 Item 15). John Ball presented a counter petition to this request claiming that he would be damaged by such a waterway. The General Assembly organized a committee to ascertain the conflicting claims. The project was never undertaken (S.C. Archives S165005, 1796, Number 94);
- Asking that a "channel " be cut from Wassamasaw Ford to Bacon's Bridge in 1805 (S.C. Archives S 165005, 1805, Number 65);
- Asking that the waterway of the Cypress and Wassamasaw Swamps be opened (S.C. Archives S165015 Year 1812 Item 79);
- Asking for a lottery to fund a canal from Back River (S.C. Archives S165015 Year 1812 Item 79);
- Asking in 1819 that the waterway from Four Hole Creek and Mallard Lake to Bridge Lake be made navigable (S.C. Archives S165015, Year ND, Item 1060);
- Asking that the waters from Four Hole Swamp be opened to the Edisto River (S.C. Archives S165015 Year 1819 Item 161).

Appendix II
Petitions for Roads

Petitions from residents of St. James, Goose Creek Parish to the General Assembly for the establishment or repair of roads.

- A petition from Henry Izard, Chairman of the St. James, Goose Creek Road Commission asked in 1807 for an improved system of keeping roads in good repair. He complained that the current system of assessing contiguous landowners put increasingly more expense and responsibility on those living closer to Charleston. Those in the most distant neighborhoods kept the roads in repair only for their own use while the landowners closer to Charleston kept the roads in repair for themselves and all the users in every more distant neighborhood. He requested that a toll system be arranged so that those using the road paid in proportion to the amount of distance traveled (S.C. Archives S165029 Year 1807 Item 12);
- A petition asking for the opening of a Post Road was submitted by residents of St. James, Goose Creek, St. Johns and St. Matthews Parishes requesting that a 25 mile road be opened from Vance's Ferry on the Santee to Cannon's Ford at Wassamasaw (S.C. Archives S165015 Year 1813 Item 108);
- A petition asking that toll gates be located at equal distances on the State Road between Charleston and Columbia and that tolls for two horse wagons be reduced (S.C. Archives S165015 Year 1839 Item 26);
- A petition in 1848 signed by fifty-seven residents of the Goose Creek and St. Johns Parishes including ten highway commissioners asking the Legislature to assume ownership of a road between Nelson's Ferry in St. Johns Parish to George Whaley's residence on Gaillard Road in St. James, Goose Creek Parish (S.C. Archives S165015 Year 1848 Item 2745). This road was privately built to provide access to the 31-Mile Railroad Station but according to the petitioners it became widely used and a great convenience to all the farmers. The petitioners claimed that the road caused a reduction in transport costs for a bale of cotton from $1.30 a bale to $.50 per bale (S.C. Archives S165015 Year ND, Item 2745).
- A petition asking that a road is established between Gaillard Road and Wassamasaw Ford (S.C. Archives S165015 Year ND Item 1443).
- A petition of citizens in the upper parish protesting the closing of the road from Four Hole Swamp and from the State Road at William Harts to the State Road at Dean Swamp. The

petitioners explained that 22 families lived in that area and used the road to travel to church, deliver their farm goods to markets in Charleston and reported to "Battalion of Regimental Muster"(S.C. Archives S165015, General Assembly Petitions).

• A petition asking that John H. Isaacs be awarded a charter to operate the Cypress Causeway (S.C. Archives S165015 Year 1854 Item 2908).

• A petition asking that a road be constructed from John Baylor's residence on the east side of Wassamasaw Swamp to a road near Mr. Dehays' residence (S.C. Archives S165015 Year 1858 Item 2704). Thirty-eight residents of St. Johns and St. James Parishes signed this petition. The request was denied. The petition stated:

That for many years past, the entire body of land lying on the east side of Wassamasaw Swamp...was an uncultivated waste, and without a settlement. Within the past five years this body or tract of land has been purchased and is now partly in cultivation by a thriving and industrious class of farmers and they are fast bringing into use these lands, which were of little profit to the State.

• A petition from John Poppenheim, Chairman of the St. James, Goose Creek Road Commission asking in 1865 for the state to establish a toll gate at Ten Mile Hill and to collect a moderate fee for the construction and repair of bridges (S.C. Archives S165015 Year 1865 Item 29).

• A petition asking that a road be established between Dean Swamp and Wassamasaw Ford (S.C. Archives S165015 Year ND Item 1442).

Appendix III
Highway Commissioners
St. James, Goose Creek Parish

The table lists State Highway Commissioners for the years 1844, 1856 and 1863.

1844	1856	1863
Edward W. Norris	James Wiggins	James Wiggins
Thos. Ray	Gresgian Murray	John J. McCants
James Wiggins	John B. Earnest	John W. McCuller
Isaac Bradwell	Wm. Glezer	J. F. Poppenheim
Jas. S. Shingler	J. F. Poppenheim	John Murray
Greshian Murray	Christopher Fitzsimmons	L.C. Warnock
John J. McCants	John Murray	Aaron Shier
John B. Earnest	John Lawrence	Caswell Hart
Lewis Bradwell	Joseph Brownlee	Thos. J. Mallard
John Wilson	Hugh Winter	James E. Heape
Jos. T. Crawford	Thomas Mims	Wm. H. Smith
Wm. L. Glezer	E.G. Shuler	John T. Browing
John W. McCuller	John Shingler	J.J. Browning
C.L. Deazle	L.C. Warnock	John Keizer
J. F. Poppenheim	C. Graves	G.C. Owens
W.W. Ancrum	Aaron Shier	Wm. Whaley
		Chester T. Coe

Appendix IV Landowners

The table shows landowners in the central and western sections of the parish from 1792 to 1860 according to the South Carolina Department of Archives and Records. The table is augmented with information derived from the *Directory for the District of Charleston Comprising the Places of Residence and Occupation of the White Inhabitants of the Following Parishes to wit…St. James (Goose Creek)* in 1802. The directory provided the number of the nearby mile marker or verified the location in Four Hole Swamp.

Name	Date	# Acres	Place	Mile Marker/ Four Hole
Elisha Mellard	1792	400	Dean Swamp	Four Hole
Thomas Harry	1792	500	Dean Swamp	Four Hole
Robert Fulwood	1792	10,000	Dean Swamp	
William Dangerfield	1793	232	Wassamasaw	32
Joseph Mezell	1795	300	Wills Bay	
Robert Bowman	1796	200	Wassamasaw Swamp	
James Mims	1796	500	Sandy Run	
Thomas Ray	1797	230	Cain Branch	
James Mellard	1797	500	Dean Swamp	Four Hole
Michael Reavel	1797	76	Sandy Run Branch of Deans Swamp	
Josiah Furman	1797	400	Four Hole Swamp	
Josiah Furman	1797	71	Four Hole Swamp	
Penelope Wilson	1797	500	Edisto River	
Michael Ravelle	1797	500	Sandy Run and Bee Tree Run	
Matthew Ravelle	1797	500	Sandy Run and Bee Tree Run	
Archibald Revell	1797	500	Cat Fish Branch Four Hole Swamp	
Elisha Mellard	1797	500	Cain Run Branch	Four Hole
Thomas Ray	1797	500	Cain Run Branch	
William Owens	1798	500	Sandy Run and Allen Branches	28
William Cree	1798	500	Timothy Creek	
Benjamin Wiggins	1798	500	Four Hole Swamp	
Samuel Gaskins	1798	500	Four Hole Swamp	

Name	Date	# Acres	Place	Mile Marker/ Four Hole
Samuel Gaskins	1798	500	Dean Swamp	
William Ballentine	1799	200	Four Hole Swamp	
Edward Luten	1799	356	Four Hole Swamp	
Samuel Gaskins	1800	638	Wards Bay	
Zachariah Dehay	1801	345	Caton's Bay	
Rolen Winningham	1801	404	Near Sandy Run	
Elisha Mellard	1802	1,000	Dean Swamp	Four Hole
Peter Pye	1802	561	Sandy Run	
Henry Markley	1802	433	Fishroes Bay	
William Smith	1804	283	Will's Bay	Four Hole
Issac Lynes	1804/08/02	400/147/26	Lynes Creek/Wassamasaw	31
Hugh Winter	1804	51	Wassasmaw	
David Murray	1805	200	Four Hole	
Malachi Nettles	1806	1,000	Dean Swamp	40
Benjamin Blackman	1809	1,000	Miskeetor (Misquito) Bay	
Robert Law	1809	1,000	Tupelo Bay	40
Philip Kellar	1809	1,00	Four Hole Swamp	Four Hole
James Cree	1809/13	993/640	Wassamasaw	40
Joseph Rumph	1809	903	Dean Swamp	
Thomas Rumph	1811	1,000	Pigeon Bay	
James Nettles	1812	1,000	Black Tom Bay	31
Malachi Nettles	1812	925	Dean Swamp	
John Weatherford	1813	431	Four Hole Swamp	28
John Jackson	1812	468	Dawson's Mill Branch	
James Packer	1813	360	Black Tom Bay	
John Whaley	1813/14	1,000/994.5	Black Creek - Four Hole Swamp	
Edward Thomas	1815	553	Buzzard/Pigeon Bay	
Francis Curtis	1816	620	Black Tom Bay	
Dempsey Collins	1816	455	Blackton (Black Tom) Bay	
James Wilson	1817	320	Sandy Run	
Elias Rudd	1818	216	Four Hole Swamp	Four Hole
George Crawford	1819	152	Four Hole Swamp	
Joseph Pye	1820	400	Wilkinson's Bay	
George Ballentine	1820	353	Dean Swamp	
Elisha Ballard	1820	394	Dean Swamp	
John Donnely	1820	574	Long Branch	
Burlington Rudd	1822	352	Four Hole Swamp	Four Hole
James Harvey	1823	467.5	Hawkin's Bay	
James Blanton	1833	282	Wassamasaw	
Jacob Peagler	1833	228	Wassamasaw	

Name	Date	# Acres	Place	Mile Marker/ Four Hole
Robert Austin	1833	90	Flat Bay	
Isaac Peagler	1833	271	Jinkin's Bay	
Jacob Peagler	1834	228	Wassamasaw	
James Ballentine	1834	414	Tupelo Bay	
John Ray	1834	520/780	Dean Swamp/Sandy Run	
William Threaty	1834	1,000	Wassamasaw	
Sims White	1835/1840	990/1,752	Black Tom Bay	
William Caleb	1835	1,500	Vlack Creed/Wassamasaw	
John Taylor	1836	1,300	Wassamasaw	
John Fultz	1836	1,156	Wassamasaw	
Joseph Crawford	1837	500	Blakc Tom Bay	
John J. Browning	1841	213	Wassamasaw	
Benjamin Blackman	1845	1,600	Four Hole Swamp	
John McCants	1846	240	Wassamasaw Swamp	
William Whaley	1846	480	Wassamasaw	
John Keizer	1846	814	Long Branch	
Benjamin Johnston	1846/46	1,000/2,000	Wassamasaw/Black Tom Bay	
Martha Johnston	1846	1,000	Pigeon Bay	
Benjamin Godfrey	1846	800	Cat Fish Branch-Four Hole Swamp	
MAry Johnson	1846	1,500	Pigeon Bay	
William Maybin	1846	1,296/406/2,087	Wassamasaw/Caton's Bay/ Pigeon Bay	
Malachi Grooms	1846/46/46	542	Caton's Bay	
Samuel Dodd	1846	771	Timothy Creek - Four Hole Swamp	
Peter Bannister	1846	450	Sandy Run	
Alexander Clark	1846	453	Sandy Run	
Benjamin Johnston	1846	2.000	Black Tom Bay	
William Mellard	1846	900	Dean/Four Hole Swamps	
John Parker	1847	856	Black Tom Bay	
Thomas Bradwell	1849	40	Rum Neck	
Edwin Shuler	1849	5334	Rice Field Swamp	
Augustine Thrower	1850	234	Sandy Run	
Edwin Shuler	1851	242	Boney's Bay	
David Dehay	1851	78	Blue Water Gully Branch	
Hugh Winter	1852	1,424	Keating Creek/Wassamasaw	
Samuel Stall	1857	333	Pigeon Bay	
Jonas Driggers	1857	109	Black Tom Bay	
John Packer	1858	249	Sandy Run	
John Browning	1860	1,020	Black Tom Bay	
Total/Mean Acres 101/744		**75,180**		

Appendix V
Planters

The table lists the names and locations of planters in the Wassamasaw and Four Hole sections of the parish found in the *Directory for the District of Charleston Comprising the places of residence and occupation of the White Inhabitants of the Following Parishes to wit…St. James (Goose Creek) in 1802.*

Name	Location at Mile Marker/Four Hole	Name	Location at Mile Marker/ Four Hole
Thomas Blackman	29	Mary DeHay	31
John Brown	29	Elizabeth Fewaux	28
Thomas Bowman	31	Thomas Fallin	Four Hole
Gideon Browning	31	William Fallin	Four Hole
Sarah Bowman	40	Arnold Harvey	31
James Bradham	Four Hole	Thomas Harry	Four Hole
Benjamin Baron	Four Hole	John Jackson	28
Daniel Bowman	Four Hole	Jessie Joiner	Four Hole
Isaac Bradwell	Four Hole	William King	Four Hole
Mary Broadham	Four Hole	Philip Keller	Four Hole
William Chubb	Four Hole	Mathine	29
John Crawford	Four Hole	Gracey May	33
Patrick Crawford	Four Hole	James Manning	34
James DeHay	32	William/Joseph/James Nettles	31
George Nettles	40	George Staggers	33
James Packer	43	John Snell	Four Hole
George Poller	43	Allen Smith	Four Hole
William Riley	28	John Jink Singletary	Four Hole
Jane Rudd	Four Hole	Ezekiel Smith	Four Hole
Frederick Snell	28	Matthew Smith	Four Hole
Thomas Strother	32	Michael Singletary	Four Hole
John/Charles Smith	29	James Thornley	33
Jane Winters	33	john Thornley	28
John Winters	32	Samuel Ulmore	33

Name	Location at Mile Marker/Four Hole	Name	Location at Mile Marker/ Four Hole
Judy Wilson	40	Peter Varner Senior/Junior	32
George Whaley	Four Hole	John Wilson	30
Stephen Williams	Four Hole		

Appendix VI
Representatives and Senators

The list shows the names of State Representatives and Senators Representing St. James, Goose Creek Parish in 1791–1865.[562]

1791	Aaron Loocock. He declined to serve January 25, 1791.
1791–91	William Allen Deas Sr. Signed Treaty of Commerce with England.
1791–93	Gabriel Manigault. Resigned after 1793 session.
1791	Stephen St. John replaced Aaron Loocock.
1792–95	Robert Thornley. Captain in the Revolution under Francis Marion. Died while serving as a Senator.
1792–99	Thomas Rhett Smith served in House and Senate.
1794	Benjamin Gray replaced Gabriel Manigault.
1794–95	Henry Deas served in House and Senate and resigned when elected Solicitor of the Southern Judicial Circuit.
1795, 1800–07	David Deas was elected to replace Henry Deas.
1796–97	John Bowen
1796–99	William Allen Deas brother of David, Henry and John Deas.
1796–1801	Henry Izard son of Ralph Izard.
1800–01	Captain Elish Mellard.
1802–04	Moses Glover son of Joseph Glover
1802–05	John Dupont
1804	Archer Smith died before taking his seat.
1805	Dr. John Willson later became Senator.
1806–08	William Witherspoon also served as Senator.
1806–08	Archibald McDowell
1808–11	Charles Glover resigned upon election to the Senate.
1808–09	Benjamin Paul Williams
1811–15	Major George Keckley elected to replace Charles Glover.
1816–19	John Reardon
1820–21	Joseph Mims
1823–23	Nathaniel Lawrence
1824–25	Thomas John Smith

1826–29	William Mellard served in the Senate 1844–48 and 1856–60.
1830–31	Isaac Bradwell
1832–35	John L. Strohecker
1838–39	Dr. John Willson served as Senator 1840–44 and 1849–56.
1840–41	George Henry Smith
1842–43	William Washington Ancrum
1844–47	James Simon Shingler
1847–51, 1858–59	Josiah Cockfield McKewn was elected to replace Colonel James Simon Shingler. He also served as Senator.
1852–57	Dr. Joseph Murray.
1860–61	Morgan Calhoun Connor.
1862–63	J.B. Rhame
1864	Lewis E. Connor.

Serving in the Senate from St. James, Goose Creek were:[563]

1776	John Parker in the Legislative Council of the First Assembly
1776–78	John Parker in the Legislative Council of the Second Assembly
1778–80	John Parker
1781–82	William Logan.
1796–1800	Robert Thornley
1800–04	William Allen Deas
1804–05	Robert Thornley
1805–08	Henry Izard
1808–11	William Witherspoon
1811–12	Charles Glover
1812–16	Jacob Belzer
1816–36	John Norvelle Davis
1836–40	James Mims
1840–44	John Willson
1844–48	William Mellard
1848–49	vacant
1849–56	John Willson
1856–60	William Mellard
1860–64	Josiah Cockfield McKewn
1864–65	Joseph Murray, M.D.

Appendix VII
Slave Ownership

The table shows slave ownership in St. James, Goose Creek Parish according to the 1830 census.

Number of Slaves in 1830	Number/Percent of Owners
0	57/16
1-10	96/27
11-20	99/28
21-50	80/22
51-100	23/6
100+	4/1

The table shows slave ownership in St. James, Goose Creek Parish according to the 1860 census.

Number of Slaves in 1860	Number/Percent of Owners
0	142/40
1-10	11/31
11/20	48/13
21-50	38/11
51-100	13/4
100+	5/1

Appendix VIII
Randomly Selected Small Farms

Twelve of the smaller farms in the eastern sector of the parish recorded on the *Agricultural Census* in 1860 were randomly selected for this publication. The table shows *1860 Agricultural Census* information of farm production of those selected farms in the eastern section of St. James, Goose Creek Parish.

Name	Number of Improved Acres	Number of Unimproved Acres	Number of Total Acres	Value of Farm in dollars	Number of Heads of Cattle	Number of Bushels of Corn	Number of Ginned Cotton Bales	Number Pounds of Rive
John Cullers	100	650	750	3,000	100	700	12	0
B.A. Donnely	50	110	150	1,000	20	200	0	0
Elisha Driggers	60	120	180	700	55	400	0	0
Henry Huff	30	130	160	700	3	200	0	0
Wm. Drose	20	30	50	200	3	200	0	0
Rebecca Winters	100	400	500	500	0	200	0	0
Lewis Cannon	40	300	340	1,500	37	300	0	0
Wm. Hudson	50	440	490	1,200	62	500	0	0
Daniel Baxter	20	180	200	700	0	150	0	0
William Williams	20	30	50	150	3	150	0	0
John Donnely	30	230	260	500	100	400	0	0
John Donnely Jr.	20	85	105	200	25	100	0	0

Appendix IX
Magistrates
St. James, Goose Creek Parish

The table lists magistrates according to reports to the South Carolina General Assembly at the South Carolina Department of Archives and History.

1844	1848	1856	1863
Thos.Mullard	Adam Smith	A.P. Livingston	J.J. Browning
Alfred Shuler	H. McCall	William Whaley	William Whaley
Timothy Joyner	A.R. Danne	Charles D. Graves	Nelson Joyner
Isaac Bradwell Senr.		Thos. D. Ledbetter	
John Wilson		John B. Earnest	
J.J. Browning			
Geo. Grooms			
Thomas Gantt			
T.C. Tharin			

Appendix X
Gibbes Memorial

Memorials to Col. John Gibbes, Jane Gibbes, Ralph Izard and Peter Taylor on the interior walls of the St. James Church.

Underneath this lyes the late Col. John / Gibbes who deceased on the 17th August / 1711 Age 40.

Near this place / Lyes the body of Jane Gibbes / Late wife of Mr. Benjamin Gibbes / Who departed this life ye 19th of / August 1717 / Aged 35 years.

Under the window, on the outside of this / wall lies the remains of the Honourable / Ralph Izard of the Parish of St. James / Goose Creek. / He was born on the 23rd Jany 1742 and / departed this life on the 30th of May 1804. / He was eminently adorned by the virtues of / public and private life. / The good of his country / which his accurate judgement enabled him to / promptly discover. He pursued with the most / undeviating integrity and the most ardent zeal. / His private life was marked by a high / spirit of honour and justice / His dignified manners, his cultivated and / polished mind, his ready wit, / Commanded respect and admiration from all; / While the sincerity of his friendship, / his conjugal and parental virtues. / The melting tenderness of his manly and / noble heart secured their esteem, their / veneration, and their love / His whole life was a poetical lesson of active and useful virtues / and his death of resignation and fortitude. /Hoc Ago.

To the Memory of / Peter Taylor Esq. / Who lies interred near this Place / He adorned the several Relations / And Stations of Life he passed through / With a Conduct / Worthy the Christian and Gentleman. / He departed this life / Oct. 1st 1765. / Aged 67 years. / And by him lies his first wife / Mrs. Amerentia Taylor / and their son Joseph.

Appendix XI
Milliechamp Testimonial

Testimonial presented to Rev. Timothy Millechamp upon his departure from Goose Creek.

SOUTH CAROLINA

We, the Churchwardens and Vestry of the Parish of St. James, Goose Creek, do Certify whom it may concern, that the Rev. Timothy Millechamp, Missionary for the Venerable and Honorary Society for the Propagation of the Gospel in Foreign parts to this parish, has behaved as a worth Clergyman of the Church of England among us, nigh the space of fourteen years, and whom we believe well affected to the present Constitution, both in Church and State and in all things, whether respecting his Life or Doctrine, acquitted himself as a good Pastor, and Discharged the Duties of his Holy function with all Diligence and Fidelity, to the Advancement of the good work the Society are engaged in, and to our Benefit and Approbation, Given under Hands at the Parish Church in the Province aforesaid the 25th day of June 1746.

BENJ. MAZYCK
GIDEON DUPONT/ Churchwardens: WILLIAM MIDDLETON/PETER TAYLOR/ZACK./ VILLEPONTOUX/RICH. SINGLETON/HENRY IZARD/THOMAS MIDDLETON/Vestrymen.

Appendix XII
Bromley Memorial

Thomas Bromley's Memorial Inscription from St. James Church, Copied by Samuel G. Stoney and Translated by Norman A. Chamberlain.

Vere suo dum Vivens sub hoc Menore nunc mortuus / Requiescit / THOMAS BROMLEY generosus / Ex antiquo Stirpe in agro Castrensi oriundus / LONDINI natus / Banco regio apud Anglos rerum forensium / PROCURATOR / Curiae magnae Cancellariae ibidem / ADVOCATUS / Concionibusque Plebis in Provincia Carolinae Australia / AMANUENSIS / Et quod maximum / Viris bene potantibus quadquaversum / A CALVULIS / Et festivis undicumque omni genere Facetiae / EXPEDITISSUMUS / Morbo obiit Bilioso / Vigesimo Secumco die Augusti / ANNO SALUTIS / 1765 / Etatis / 35 / Where be your Gibes now? Your Gambols? / your Song? Your Flashes of Merriment / there were wont to set the Table / in a Roar?

Translation:

In the flower of his years, beneath this grave where in life he was wont to rest, now in death rests Thomas Bromley, Gentleman, of an old family in the county of Chester, and born in London. He was an attorney in the Court of King's Bench and barrister of the High Court of Chancery in England, and clerk to the Commons House of Assembly in the Province of South Carolina; but above all, wherever good fellows met and the cup went merrily round, foremost in quip and crank. He died of bilious fever in the year of Grace August 22nd 1765, at the age of 35.

Appendix XIII
St. James School Solicitation

A list of contributors to the St. James, Goose Creek School Construction Fund.[564]

Whereas nothing is more likely to promote the practice of Christianity and Virtue than the early and pious Education of Youth. We, whose names are here underwritten, do hereby agree and oblige ourselves, our Executors and Administrators, to pay yearly for three years successively, viz: On or before June 18, 1745, 1746, 1747, to the Rev. Mr. Millechamp, or to the churchwardens for the time being, the several and respective sums of money over against our names, respectively inscribed, for the setting up of a School House in the Parish of St. James, Goose Creek, on the land for that purpose purchased for instruction children in the knowledge and practice of the Christian Religion, and for teaching them such other things as are suitable to their capacity.

Name	Amount in Pounds	Name	Amount in Pounds
S. Middleton	100	W. Blake	100
Wm. Middleton	100	Cornelius Dupre	5
John Morton	60	Alexander Dingle	5
Zach. Villepontoux	50	Stephen Bull	5
Peter Taylor	25	G. Dupont	7
Thomas Middleton	50	Henry Izard	60
Richard Singleton	20	James Kinloch	40
William Allen	25	Gideon Foucheraud	10
Martha Izard	20	Maurice Keating	10
Susanna Lansac	10	James Bayley	15
Jane Mrris	20	Joseph Hasfort	5
Joseph Norman	20	James Marion	15
Richard Tookerman	5	Peter Pocher	15
Benjamin Mazyck	15	James Singleton	10
Paul Mazyck	50	Isaac Porcher	5
Robert Brown	15	Benj. Singleton	10
William Wood	100	Rachel Porcher	5
Robert Adams	5	Thomas Singleton	10

Name	Amount in Pounds	Name	Amount in Pounds
Peter Taylor	1000	Benj. Coachmen	100
John Channing	100	Thomas Smith	50
C. Faurcheraud	100	Henry Smith	50
Robert Hume	100	Sedgewick Lewis	25
John Parker	70	James Lynch	30
W. Withers	50	James Coachmen	40100
Benj. Smith	30	John Deas	25
John Mackenzie	100	Peter Tamplet	50
John Moultrie Jr.	100	Joseph Dobbins	25

Appendix XIV
Largest Landowners in 1879

The table shows the agricultural record of the largest Goose Creek landowners in 1879 according to the *1880 Agricultural Census*.

Name of Farm Owner	Number of Acres Tilled	Number of Total Acres Owned	Total Value of Farm, Equipment and Live Stock
Jacob E. Wiggins	200	3,363	$5,200
John W. Hulta	400	2,503	$3,310
Fletcher Mims	200	1,800	$2,850
James Wiggins	450	4,060	$7,550
David Shule	200	2,000	$2,400
William Thomas	200	619	$2,050
William Josephine	200	2,000	$4,325
Mary Mellard	200	350	$1,170
E.B. Whiting	336	4,010	$22,750
W. Walter	600	600	$5,650
Dr. Pankim	305	1,105	$5,000
J.J. Noisette	226	466	$5,000
J.Y. Meetze	452	652	$1,050

Appendix XV
Randomly Selected Black-Operated Farms

The table shows randomly selected black farmers in 1879 with information about their farm and family from the 1880 agricultural and enumeration census. These farmers were selected for this publication to approximate the typical wealth of black families during this period. Information from the 1880 *Agricultural Census* was augmented with family information from the 1880 *Enumeration Census* to provide the data for the randomly selected black farmers.

Name of Farmer	Own/Rent/Share	Number in Family	Number of Farm Acres	Total Value of Farm in Dollars
Joseph Zimmerman	Owned	8	585	1550
Dick Carson	Rented	2	130	540
Peter McKelvey	Owned	4	143	820
Simon Polight	Rented	10	35	50
Linus Hussel	Owned	5	60	245
Ben Hussel	Owned	7	110	385
Caesar Washington	Rented	7	20	110
Nero Washington	Rented	4	15	55
Richard Myers	Owned	4	121	605
Louis Duggins	Owned	3	46	620

Appendix XVI
Tenant Farmers

The table lists the names of tenant farmers at Casey and in the vicinity for the years 1910, 1911, 1912, 1913 and 1914. The information was taken from the Cheves Papers and the 1910 Census.

Name	1910 Rent	1911 Rent	1912 Rent	1913 Rent	1914 Rent	Notations Made by the Landlord	1910 Census Information	Number in Family as per 1910 Census
Barnwell, Robert	$10		$10	$10	$10		four children	6
Bennett, Lee	$10		$10	$10	$10		one child	3
Boden, Morris	$10		$10	$10	$10		one nephew, one neice residing with the family	5
Bonaparte, Adam	$10		$10	$10	$10		two grandsons residing with the family	5
Brown, Harry	$10		$10	$10	$10	he left in 1911		7
Bryant, Abraham	$10		$10	$10	$10		two children	4
Bryant, Richard	$10		$10	$10	$10	Richard Bryant died in 1913		7
Bryant, Abraham Jr.							two children	4
Bryant, Bill					$3		Not in census	
Bryant, Ben				$.50	$.50	for chicken yard on our side of the line		
Clinton, Celia	$10					she left in 1914	she was a female head of house hold with one son	2
Daniel, Albert				$10	$10		four children	6

Name	1910 Rent	1911 Rent	1912 Rent	1913 Rent	1914 Rent	Notations Made by the Landlord	1910 Census Information	Number in Family as per 1910 Census
Driggers, Philip(W)				$4	$4		while farmer not found in 1910 census	
Drayton, Emma	$10	$10	$10	$10	$10		not found in census	
Fraser, Abraham	$10					he died in 1914	his neice lived with the family	34
Fraser, Mary Ann			$10	$10		she married Richard Bryant		
Gourdin, Elmore	$10		$10	$10	$10		not found in1910 census	
Harley, Minda	$10		$10	$10	$10		A female head of house hold with six daughters and one nephew	8
Jamison, Mac	$10		$5.25			paid, moved away and died in 1917		2
Jenkins, John, agent						John Jenkins died in 1915, a great loss, a good man.		7
Knight, John	$10		$10	$10	$10		two children	4
McGill, Martha	$10					she left 1914		2
Myers, Julius			$10	$10		he died in 1917	not found in the 1910 census	
Myers, Washington					$5		not found in the 1910 census	
Nelson, James	$10		$10	$15	$15		four children	6
Nelson, John Henry	$10		$10	$10	$10		seven children	9
Stephens, Jack	$2.50		$2.50	$2	$2.50 remitted		five children	7
Sumpter, Alice	$10					she married Abraham Bryant. Julius Myers took her house in 1914	not found in 1910 census	
Sheperd, H.E.					$6		not found in 1910 census	

Name	1910 Rent	1911 Rent	1912 Rent	1913 Rent	1914 Rent	Notations Made by the Landlord	1910 Census Information	Number in Family as per 1910 Census
Pinckney, Henry Amos	$2.50				$6		son, granddaughter and daughter-in-law	6
Whaley, Carolina	$10		$10	$10	$10		first name not legible on the census. Reported on censis as male head of house hold with wife, nephew and mother	4
Whaley, Catherine	$10		$10			she did not pay. Died on 1914	female head of house hold with children and granddaughter	6
McKelvey, Martha							female head of house hold with five sons and one daughter	7

Appendix XVII
Vision and Mission Statements with Strategic Action Plans

Vision Statement

Goose Creek is a city that has achieved a balance between growth, the environment and the preservation of the small town character. The city's primary concern is for the lifelong needs of all its citizens. Goose Creek is a partnership between its people, businesses, community institutions and its governments in the determination of the city's future.

Mission Statement

The City of Goose Creek seeks to serve the needs of its people, businesses and community institutions for a safe, secure and healthy environment, and facilitates planned and managed growth and economic development. The city shall fulfill its mission by ensuring that the highest quality of essential services is provided and by serving as a forum for identifying and addressing the needs of the community. The city assumes a leadership role in determining the future direction of the community.

Goals and Objectives

One-Year Planning Cycle

(1) Beautification planning/environmental protection

(a) Implement Methods to Further Protect Trees For Areas

Action items

- City Council To Review Tree Protection Ordinance
- Adopt Tree Protection Ordinance

(b) Formalize Plan to Install Electrical and Communication Lines Underground with Berkeley Electric Cooperative and others

Action items

- Prepare GIS Maps For Areas Identified for Underground Utilities
- Determine Costs For Undergrounding Utilities
- Formalize Plan to Underground Utilities

(2) Adopt economic development strategy/plan

Improve the Identity of the City and Downtown Area

(1) Continue Planning Effort for Downtown Redevelopment

Action items

- Adopt Model Ordinances for Redevelopment District
- Design and approve entrance amenities and streetscaping
- Prepare Financing Plan

Attract Diverse Business

Action items

- Determine Types of Business to Recruit
- Determine Recruitment Methodologies
- Actively recruit restaurants
- Explore Sunday sale of alcohol

(3) Develop hiker/biker trail system

(a) Construct Phases IV and V of the West Greenview/Greenview Acres Trails

(b) Review the Hiker/Biker Trail Master Plan and Prioritize Future Projects

(c) Consider coordination of hiker/biker trails with development of stormwater system

(4) Develop agendas to interact with others

(a) Send Clear Messages to State/County Governments/School District

Action items

Develop Agendas

(5) Develop more efficient communication methods

(a) Explore Additional Methods to Communicate With/Involve citizens

Action items

Conduct City Council Workshop to Develop Initiatives

Make Use of Internet Communication More Thoroughly

Expand Citizen Advisors to 500

(6) Consolidate greater Goose Creek area

(a) Identify/Address Annexations

(1) Contact Owners of Undeveloped Property for Annexation

Action items

- Identify Goals and Objectives
- Develop Methodologies/Incentives
- Initiate Annexation Process

(7) Increase efforts to safeguard physical and environmental resources

(a) Acquire Vacant Properties/Open Space for Future Generations

(1) Identify/Prioritize Properties to be Acquired

(2) Explore Development Rights/Conservation Easement

Action items

- Conduct City Council Workshop(s) To Develop Initiatives

(8) Explore methods to assist the Goose Creek recreation commission in pursuing recreational/cultural opportunities for citizens of all age groups

Action items

- Meet with the Goose Creek Recreation Commission to Review the Community Center Project
- Develop An Action Plan
- Implement the Plan

(9) Review plan for improved sanitation collection system

Action items

- Determine Course of Action
- Prepare Financing Plan
- Implement the Plan

Five-Year Planning Cycle

(1) Expand water system

(a) Acquire Crowfield Water System

Action items

- Obtain System Map (CCPW)
- Cost System
- Determine Potential Financing Methodologies
- Negotiate Purchase of Systems (post 2006)

(2) Beautification Planning/Environmental Protection

(a) Continue US Highway 52/US Highway 176/Railraod Beautification Projects

Action items

- Review Plans for Potential Redesign
- Apply for Urban Forestry Grants for Additional Tree Planting
- Review Tree Planting Plan for US Highway 52 in Anticipation of Highway Construction

(3) Plan for curb and guttering

(a) Pineview Subdivision

(b) Greenview Acres

(c) West Greenview Acres

(d) Boulder Bluff

(e) Bushy Park Terrace

(f) Camelot Subdivision

(g) Commercial Areas

(h) Review feasibility of storm water utility

(i) Review feasibility of lake system

(4) Develop more efficient communication methods

(a) Develop Automated Business Directory

(5) Develop a transportation plan

(a) Develop Hiker/Biker Trail System

- Construct the Braemoor/Colonial Heights Trail
- Construct the MHB Municipal Center Trail

(b) Road Transportation Plan

(c) Mass Transportation Plan (Investigate CARTA)

(6) Increase efforts to safeguard physical and environmental resources

(7) Explore methods to assist the Goose Creek recreation commission in pursuing recreational/cultural opportunities for citizens of all age groups

(8) Consider a city conference center facility

(9) Implement boardwalk plan in nature preserve behind the MHB Municipal Center

(10) Develop master plan for central park & x.o. bunch properties

(11) Explore opportunities to redevelop housing

Twenty-Year Planning Cycle

(1) Improve drainage conditions in goose creek

(2) Accommodate a changing population

(3) Investigate access and use of Goose Creek, Foster Creek and the Cooper River

(4) Plan for citywide oversight of community amenities (crowfield)

Without a clear direction it is difficult, at best, to provide the essential public services and guidance for a growing, maturing community. To this end the Mayor, City Council and staff have actively engaged in a strategic planning process for the past several years. The strategic planning process is conducted over a two-day period where departmental briefings are presented, key community issues are identified and explored and goals and objectives are established. The preceding Vision Statement, Mission Statement and, Goals and Objectives are products of the strategic planning process, and provide a clear direction for the Goose Creek Community.

Appendix XVIII
Annexations

The table shows annexations to the City of Goose Creek from 1980 to 2003. More than four thousand acres were added to the city during that period.

Year	Property Description	Total Acres (rounded up)
1980	parcels (The records do not identify the parcels)	24
1981	single family lots/undeveloped tracts Fairfax/church/ playground	432
1982	no annexations during this year	0
1983	Persimmon Hill (undeveolped tracts)	407
1984	none	0
1985	Stratford Forest Pool/single family/Wallace Road/church/ single family lots (Foxborough IV)	149
1986	single family (Hunters Woods)/church/commercial	340
1987	sangle family.church.Crowfield undeveloped	1460
1988	none	0
1989	none	0
1990	single family/commercial/park	67
1991	single family/church	14
1992	church/recreation area	6
1993	single family lots	2
1994	single family lots	2
1995	single family lots	2
1996	single family lots/commercial	38
1997	single family lots (Cherry Hill and Stratforf Forest)	28
1998	single family lots (Cherry Hill)	26
1999	single family lots (The Commons/Hunters Woods)	11

Appendix XIX
Elected and Appointed Officals

The following table shows the elected and appointed officials, as well as executive staff officers and their tenures during the period of 1980–2003.

Official/Year	80	81	82	83	84	85	86	87	88	89	90	91	92	93	94	95	96	97	98	99	00	01	02	03
Mayor																								
Michael Heitzler	X	X	X	X	X	X	X	X	X	X	X	X	X	X	X	X	X	X	X	X	X	X	X	X
Council Members																								
William Gibson	X																							
John Barnette Jr.	X																							
Calvin E. Woods	X	X	X	X	X																			
Doreen Davis	X	X	X	X	X																			
Lagette Shriver	X	X	X	X	X																			
Shirley Johnson	X	X	X	X	X	X																		
Marguerite H. Brown	X	X	X	X	X	X	X	X	X	X	X	X	X	X	X	X	X	X	X	X	X	X	X	X
Joseph Daning	X	X	X	X	X	X	X						X	X	X	X	X	X	X	X	X	X	X	X
Earl Clenner					X	X	X	X	X	X														
Trudy Aull					X	X	X	X	X	X	X	X												
Oris Caldwell					X	X	X	X	X	X	X	X												
Wendell McRae							X	X	X	X	X	X	X	X	X	X	X							

Official/Year	80	81	82	83	84	85	86	87	88	89	90	91	92	93	94	95	96	97	98	99	00	01	02	03
Council Members																								
Mark Phillips							X	X	X	X	X	X	X	X	X	X	X	X	X	X	X	X	X	X
Dina Dukes											X	X	X	X	X	X	X							
John McCants													X	X	X	X	X	X	X	X	X	X	X	X
Salvatore Gandolfo																	X	X	X	X	X	X	X	X
Kimo Esarey																			X	X	X	X	X	X
City Clark																								
Gail McNaughton	X	X																						
Paula Nunimaker		X	X	X	X	X	X	X																
Barbara Nimocks								X	X	X	X	X												
Adele L. Wolfe												X	X											
Sherry Ferguson													X	X	X	X	X	X	X					
Kelly Lovette																			X	X	X	X	X	X
Municipal Judges																								
XCarl V. Barrs	X	X	X	X	X	X	X	X	X	X	X													

Official/Year	80	81	82	83	84	85	86	87	88	89	90	91	92	93	94	95	96	97	98	99	00	01	02	03
Munucipal Judges																								
Pete DeLuca		X																						
Thomas M. White			X	X																				
Janson Kauser				X	X	X	X	X	X	X	X	X	X	X	X	X	X	X	X	X	X	X	X	X
George F. Miley					X	X	X	X	X	X														
Shirley Johnson							X	X	X	X	X	X	X	X	X	X	X	X	X	X	X	X	X	X
Drake Donahue														X	X	X								
Gene Janikowski															X	X	X	X	X	X	X	X	X	X
Economic Development and Advisory committee																								
Eddie Tuttle	X	X	X																					
Mike Rose	X	X	X	X																				
Bobby Tuggle	X	X	X	X																				
Richard Buckner															X	X	X	X	X	X	X	X	X	X
Joe Daning															X	X	X	X	X	X	X	X	X	X
William Greene															X	X	X	X	X	X	X	X	X	X

Official/Year	80	81	82	83	84	85	86	87	88	89	90	91	92	93	94	95	96	97	98	99	00	01	02	03
Economic Development and Advisory COmmittee																								
Ron Henderson															X	X	X	X	X	X	X	X	X	X
Dean Infinger															X	X	X	X	X	X	X	X	X	X
Ron Anderson																		X	X	X	X	X	X	X
Joseph Bagwell																		X	X	X	X	X	X	X
Architectural Review Board																								
Sharon Clopton														X	X	X	X	X	X	X	X	X	X	X
Glenn LePine														X	X	X	X	X	X	X	X	X	X	X
Tom Risso														X	X	X	X	X	X	X	X	X	X	X
Gordon Vincent														X	X	X								
Gary Becker														X	X	X	X							
JoAnn Butler														X	X	X	X							
Chris Lane														X	X	X	X							
Dean Tokarsky															X	X	X							
Kristen Bowden																		X	X	X	X	X	X	X

Official/Year			82	83	84	85	86	87	88	89	90	91	92	93	94	95	96	97	98	99	00	01	02	03
Architectural Review Board																								
John Moody																		X	X	X	X	X	X	
Howard Rayburn																		X	X	X	X	X		
Karen Powell																		X	X					
Rick Drewel																				X	X			
Michael Collins																						X	X	X
Gray Berenyi																							X	X
Sarah Hanson																							X	X
Planning Comission																								
Jerry Class	X	X	X	X	X	X	X	X	X	X	X	X	X	X										
Walter Rice	X	X	X	X	X	X	X	X	X	X	X	X	X	X	X									
Gayle Hood	X	X	X	X	X																			
John Thompson	X	X	X	X	X																			
Dennis White	X	X	X																					
Bob Gilchrist	X	X	X																					

Official/Year	80	81	82	83	84	85	86	87	88	89	90	91	92	93	94	95	96	97	98	99	00	01	02	03
Planning Comission																								
Oliver Yon	X																							
Charles Martin	X																							
James Williams		X	X																					
Williard Hill		X	X	X	X	X	X	X																
Randy Suddeth		X	X	X	X	X	X	X	X															
Joe Saenz				X	X	X	X	X	X	X	X	X												
John Elam				X	X	X	X	X	X	X	X	X	X	X										
Evelyn Watts					X	X	X	X	X	X	X	X	X	X	X	X	X	X	X	X				
Barry Washington									X	X	X	X	X	X	X	X	X	X	X	X	X	X	X	X
Allen Wall											X	X	X	X	X	X	X	X	X	X	X	X	X	X
Fred Bricketto													X	X	X									
Ralph Calhoun														X	X	X	X	X	X	X	X	X		
Ronald Litzenerger															X	X	X	X	X	X	X	X	X	X
Furman Reynolds															X	X	X	X	X					

Official/Year	80	81	82	83	84	85	86	87	88	89	90	91	92	93	94	95	96	97	98	99	00	01	02	03
Planning Comission																								
Christine Turner															X	X	X	X						
Brian Ward															X									
Virginia Stevenson																		X	X	X	X	X	X	X
Alfred Jenkins																				X	X	X	X	X
Jerry Tekac																				X	X	X	X	X
Connie Myers																							X	X
Zoning Board od Appeals																								
Pauline Chambers	X	X	X	X	X	X	X	X	X	X	X	X	X	X	X	X	X	X	X					
Harvey Owens	X	X	X	X	X	X	X																	
Harold Moon	X	X	X	X	X	X																		
Joe Spalviero	X	X	X																					
Harold Dasinger	X	X																						
James Preacher	X	X																						
Willard Hill	X																							

Official/Year	80	81	82	83	84	85	86	87	88	89	90	91	92	93	94	95	96	97	98	99	00	01	02	03
Zoning Board od Appeals																								
Darrell Eiden	X	X	X	X	X	X	X	X	X	X	X	X	X	X		X	X							
Sal Gandolfo			X	X	X	X	X	X	X	X	X	X	X	X	X	X								
Priscilla Pierce			X	X	X	X	X	X	X	X	X	X	X	X	X									
Dan Nicholson			X	X	X	X	X	X	X	X														
John Sheppard				X	X	X	X	X	X	X	X	X												
Ron Sluder						X	X	X	X															
George Mathews									X	X	X	X	X	X	X	X								
Ray Brame											X	X	X	X	X	X	X	X						
Brad Kenney												X	X	X	X	X								
Reid Hartis															X									
Robert Morse															X	X	X	X						
Ronald Faretra																X	X	X						
Robert Williams																	X	X	X	X	X	X	X	X
Butch Cliff																		X	X	X	X	X	X	X

Official/Year	80	81	82	83	84	85	86	87	88	89	90	91	92	93	94	95	96	97	98	99	00	01	02	03
Zoning Board od Appeals																								
Gerald Payne																		X	X	X	X	X	X	X
Marlene Coleman																				X	X	X	X	X
Teri Ferrao																				X	X	X	X	X
Van Williams																				X	X	X	X	X
CITY ADMINISTRATOR																								
Dennis Harmon	X	X	X	X	X	X	X	X	X	X	X	X	X	X	X	X	X	X	X	X	X	X	X	X
Police Chief																								
Richard Ruonola	X	X	X	X	X	X	X	X	X	X														
Harvey Becker										X	X	X	X	X	X	X	X	X	X	X	X	X	X	X
Fire Chief																								
Barfield Holland		X	X	X	X	X	X	X	X	X	X	X	X	X	X	X	X	X	X					
Steve Chapman																			X	X	X	X	X	X
Director of Public Works																								
John Askins	X	X	X	X	X	X	X	X	X	X	X	X	X	X	X	X	X	X	X	X				
Steve Price																				X	X	X	X	X

Official/Year	80	81	82	83	84	85	86	87	88	89	90	91	92	93	94	95	96	97	98	99	00	01	02	03
Finance Director																								
Gail McHaughton	X	X																						
Paula Nunimaker		X	X	X	X	X	X	X																
Joe Bagwell								X	X	X	X	X												
Lee Moulder												X	X	X	X	X	X	X	X					
Ronald Faretra																			X	X	X	X	X	X
City Planner																								
Robert G. Boesch					X	X	X	X	X															
Timothy McAuliffe									X	X														
Hubert Harell										X	X													
Debbie Lieu												X	X	X	X	X	X	X	X	X	X	X	X	X

APPENDIX XX
CAPITAL PROJECTS

The table lists the municipal buildings constructed from 1980 to 2003.

Facility	Year Compleate	Cost
Public Works Center	1991	$2,300,000
Municipal Center	1999	$6,580,000
Fire Station II	2003	$1,200,000
Recreation Center	2005	$5,500,000
Total		$15,580,000

Appendix XXI
Revenues

The table shows the general revenues in dollars for the years 1980 and 2003.

Revenue Sources	Year 1980	Year 2003
Property Taxes	$258,453	$2,168,552
Licenses/Permits/Fees	$123,128	$3,494,869
Service Charges	$ NA	$1,011,132
Fines/Forfeitures	$ 67,892	$ 442,391
Miscellaneous	$ 43,949	$ 451,027
State.Federal	$212,364	$3,415,228
Total Revenues	$739,396	$10,983,199

Appendix XXII
Expenditures

The table shows the expenditures in dollars for the various city departments excluding the water division of the Department of Public-Works for the years 1980 and 2003.

Department Expenditures	Year 1980	Year 2003
Legislative	$ 20,426	$ 166,629
Administrative	$110,992	$ 684,753
Police	$376,905	$3,162,427
Fire	$ 86,346	$1,362,047
Sanitation	$176,166	$ 176,166
Recreation	$ NA	$ 675,021
Court	$ 10,319	$ 199,325
Planning	$ 813	$ 143,081
All Else (Note 1)	$ 1,873	$3,743,780
Total Expenditures (Note 2)	$840,108	$10,891,796

Note 1: The "All Else" total includes debt service, health board and library in 1980 and maintenance, garage, capital outlay and debt service in 2003.

Note 2: A Fund balance of $100,712 carried over from 1979 was used to balance the accounts at the end of 1980. Water and sewer in 1980 was $4,297,341. The Water Department without the sewer in 2002 was $8,428,884.

Appendix XXIII
Polaris Missile Facility Sign

Text of Freestanding Plaque Erected Near Former Entrance to Polaris Missile Facility Atlantic.

Polaris Missile Facility Atlantic [small caps]
(Pomflant)
Established March 29, 1960

Site of Navy's first Fleet Ballistic Missile (FMB) Facility, which for 35 years was a major contributor to this nation's deterrent force. First and only facility to process all five generations of Fleet Ballistic Missiles; Polaris A1, A2, A3; Poseidon C3; and Trident IC4. Out loaded each of the original 41 FBM Submarines and provided sole missile support to the Atlantic FBM Submarine Fleet. These vessels with their missiles were the primary U.S. strategic deterrent that ensured the security of the free world and ultimately resulted in the collapse of the Soviet Union and the demise of Communism. Assembled and tested 6,324 missiles, employed approximately 1,200 military, civil service and contractor personnel, and was the Navy's largest nuclear capable storage site. Security was provided by the largest U.S. Marine Security contingent in the United States.

Disestablished January 5, 1995

Notes

1. Maxwell Clayton Orvin, *Historic Berkeley County, South Carolina, 1670–1900* (Charleston, South Carolina: Comprint, 1973), 148.
2. Michael Trinkey, Debi Hacker and Natalie Adams. *Broom Hall Plantation: "A Pleasant One and in a Good Neighborhood"* (Columbia, South Carolina: Chicora Foundation Inc., 1995), 51.
3. Samuel David Dubose and Frederick A. Porcher, *A Contribution to the History of the Huguenots of South Carolina* (New York: The Knickerbocker Press, 1887; Reprinted Columbia, South Carolina: R.L. Bryan Company, 1972), 8.
4. S.C. Archives S165015, General Assembly Petition, Number 1501.
5. Richard Hrabowski, *Directory for the District of Charleston Comprising the places of residence and occupation of the White Inhabitants of the Following Parishes to wit…St. James (Goose Creek)* (Charleston, South Carolina: John Hobb, no.6 Broad Street, 1809).
6. 1810, United States Census and Slave Schedules.
7. 1830, United States Census.
8. Walter B. Edgar. *South Carolina: A History* (Columbia: University of South Carolina Press, 1999), 442; *Royal Gazette*, June 30, 1780.
9. S.C. Archives, Carmille, John and others, Petition asking for the emancipation of a slave and her children by him. Series 1650515, Item 01807, Year ND.
10. *Julia E. Carmille vs. The Administrator of John Carmille, Geo. Pringle et al.* Cases at Law determined in the Court of Appeals of South Carolina, from November 1840 to May 1842 Columbia, South Carolina: A.S. Johnson, 1841–1843, 454–72.
11. Thomas Jefferson Papers, Series 1. 1784 General Correspondence. 1651–1827. George Abbot Hall, December 31, 1784, *Table of Exports of 1782/ Produce from Charleston, South Carolina.* 492.
12. S.C. Archives S165015 Year 1810 Item 8.
13. M. Eugene Sirmans, *Colonial South Carolina, A Political History 1663–1763* (Chapel Hill: University of North Carolina Press, 1966), 48.
14. David Duncan Wallace, *South Carolina: A Short History* (Columbia: University of South Carolina Press, 1951), 190.
15. S.C. Archives S165015 Year ND Item 3360.
16. S.C. Archives S165029 Year 1807 Item 5.
17. Edgar, *South Carolina: A History*, 283.
18. S.C. Archives, S165015, 1822, Number 27.
19. *South Carolina Historical and Genealogical Magazine* (*SCHGM*), Vol. 68: 244.
20. S.C. Archives S165029, Year 1851, Item 6.
21. Ibid.
22. Ibid., Year 1807, Item 5.
23. S.C. Archives S165015, Petition to the General Assembly, Number 2697.
24. Ibid., Number 2703.
25. Russell J. Cross, *Historic Ramblin's Through Berkeley*, (Columbia, South Carolina: R.L. Bryan Company, 1985), 28.
26. Harold Hilton, Berkeley County landowner, interview at his home in Sandridge, South Carolina, April 26, 2003.
27. Ibid.; Nathaniel Hilton, *St. James, Goose Creek Planter, Charleston District Ordinary Letter of Testament, 1858.* The testament is among the private papers of Harold Hilton. Sandridge, South Carolina.

28. Cross, *Historic Ramblin's*, 174.
29. Hilton interview.
30. Cross, *Historic Ramblin's*, 176.
31. Albert Dean Betts, *History of South Carolina Methodism* (The Advocate Press, Columbia, South Carolina. 1952), 238.
32. Betts, *South Carolina Methodism*, 232.
33. W.J. Townsend, H.B. Workman and George Eayrs, eds., *A New History of Methodism*, 2 vols. 1st ed. (London: Hodder and Stoughton, 1909). 53
34. Ibid.
35. Ibid., 107.
36. S.C. Archives General Assembly Petition S165015, Year 1855, Item 5.
37. United States Census Bureau, Social Census for St. James, Goose Creek Parish, South Carolina, 1850.
38. Social Census, 1860.
39. Edgar, *South Carolina: A History*, 253.
40. Orvin, *Historic Berkeley County*, 156.
41. Louise N. Bailey, *Biographical Directory of the South Carolina House of Representatives: Volumes III, IV, 1775–1815* (Columbia: University of South Carolina Press, 1986), vol. 1: 262.
42. S.C. Archives S165015, Year 1832, Item 5.
43. *Charleston Mercury* December 10, 1841.
44. William A. Schaper, *Sectionalism and Representation in South Carolina* (New York: De Capo Press, 1968), 208.
45. *SCHGM* Vol.83: 128–33.
46. *Charleston Mercury*, December 12, 1841.
47. Wallace, *Short History*, 143, 144.
48. Bailey, *Biographical Directory*, 391.
49. Larry Koger, *Black Slave Owners, Free Black Masters in South Carolina, 1790–1860* (Columbia: University of South Carolina Press, 1995), 209–12, 218, 228.
50. *SCHGM* Vol.83: 135 and 1830 Slave Schedule.
51. *Charleston Mercury*, August 24, 1935.
52. S.C. Archives Series S165015, Year 1823 Item 54.
53. S.C. Archives Series S165005 Year 1823, Item 104.
54. United States Enumeration Census and Slave Schedule, 1840.
55. Ibid.
56. United States Census Enumeration Reports and Slave Schedules, 1820, 1830, 1840, 1850, 1860.
57. Alston Deas collection of property records, 1823–1895. The papers are deposited with the South Carolina Historical Society. Charleston, South Carolina. Alston Deas Papers, 11/516/68.
58. Ibid., 11/516/70.
59. United States Enumeration Census 1850 and 1860.
60. United States Census of Agriculture for St. James, Goose Creek Parish, South Carolina, 1860 and United States Census 1860 Slave Schedule.
61. 1860 Census and Slave Schedule.
62. 1860 Agricultural Census
63. 1860 Agricultural Census and United States Census, Products of Industry, 1860.
64. Samuel Gaillard Stoney, *Stoney Family Documents, 1775–1935 and Plantation Journal of Medway 1852–1853* (The documents and papers are among the collections of the South Carolina Historical Society, Charleston, South Carolina), 1202.01.
65. Stoney, *Plantation Journal*, 1202.01.
66. L.B. Wayne, "Burning Brick: A Study of a Lowcountry Industry" (PhD diss., University of Florida, Gainesville, 1991).
67. Charles W. Graves, ca. 1818–1870: *Papers and Plantation Journal 1846–1875.* Papers are among the collections of the South Carolina Historical Society, Charleston, South Carolina. 34/0183.
68. Ibid.
69. United States Census Bureau, Products of Industry for St. James, Goose Creek Parish, South Carolina, 1850.
70. Census of Products of Industry, 1850 and 1860.
71. Census of Products of Industry, 1860.
72. S.C. Archives S2113190, V.43: p.188, Item 1.
73. Edward L. Hutchinson, *Edward L. Hutchinson Papers, 1800–1855*: Papers are deposited with the South Carolina Historical Society, Charleston, South Carolina.

74. S.C. Archives S213190 V.43: p. 188, Item 2.
75. Orvin, *Historic Berkeley County*, 171.
76. *Charleston Courier*, September 10, 1851.
77. Michael Moltke-Hanson, and David Moltke-Hanson, *Intellectual Life in Antebellum Charleston*, (Knoxville: University of Tennessee Press, 1986), 154.
78. *Charleston Courier*, August 18, 1851.
79. Ibid., March 9, 1855.
80. Orvin, *Historic Berkeley County*, 173.
81. E. Milby Burton, *The Siege of Charleston, 1861–1865* (Columbia: University of South Carolina Press, 1970), 1.
82. Ibid., 4.
83. Chris W. Phelps, *Charlestonians in War, The Charleston Battalion* (Gretna, Louisiana: Pelican Publishing Company. 2004).
84. Dordal Family Papers. The papers are in the possession of the Dordal Family, Goose Creek, South Carolina.
85. Ibid.
86. Ibid.
87. Phelps, *Charlestonians in War*, 205–238.
88. John Beaufain Irving, *A Day on Cooper River*, enlarged and edited by Louisa Cheves Stoney (Columbia, South Carolina: R.L. Bryan Co., 1932), 62.
89. Phelps, *Charlestonians in War*, 172.
90. Cross, *Historic Ramblin's*, 267.
91. Robert P. Stockton, *Historic Resources of Berkeley County* (Moncks Corner, South Carolina: Berkeley County Historical Society, 1990), 26.
92. Burton, *Siege of Charleston*, 263.
93. Ibid.
94. *Charleston Courier*, July 14, 1863.
95. *Charleston Mercury*, May 6, 1863.
96. Records of the Board of Soldier's Relief. The records are among the collections of the South Carolina Historical Society, Charleston, South Carolina.
97. S.C. Archives General Assembly Miscellaneous Communications, 1863, Number 3.
98. S.C. Archives, General Assembly Petitions S165015, 1865, Number 22.
99. Burton, *Seige of Charleston*, 39.
100. Marcy, Henry Olando, *Diary of a Surgeon: U.S. Army, 1864–1892.* The South Carolina Historical Society, Charleston, South Carolina. 34/0496.
101. Ibid., March 1, 1865.
102. Ibid.
103. Ibid.
104. *Charleston News and Courier*, November 9, 1884.
105. *SCHGM* Vol. 60: 218.
106. *Charleston News and Courier*, August 17, 1877.
107. Ibid.
108. S.C. Archives S126099 Item 1582.
109. Burton, *Siege of Charleston*, 92.
110. Ibid., 35.
111. Joseph Ioor Waring, *St. James' Church, Goose Creek, South Carolina: A Sketch of the Parish from 1706–1896* (Charleston: Lucas & Richardson Co. Printers and Engravers, 1897), 1.
112. Historic American Building Survey, Library of Congress, Washington, D.C. HABS SC-72.
113. E.A. Poyas, *The Olden Times of South Carolina* (Charleston: S.G. Courtenay & Co., 1855), 177.
114. Waring, *St. James' Church*, 24.
115. Minutes of the Vestry of the St. James, Goose Creek Church, Goose Creek, South Carolina, 1872–1925. The minutes are among the collections of the South Carolina Historical Society, Charleston, South Carolina. Hereinafter cited as Vestry Minutes.
116. Vestry Minutes.
117. Ibid.
118. Frederick Dalcho, *A Historic Account of the Protestant Episcopal Church in South Carolina* (Charleston: A.E. Miller, 1802; Reprinted 1969), 51.

119. *Letters of the Society for the Propagation of the Gospel in Foreign Parts to the Ministers of St. James Church, Goose Creek, 1702–1765.* The letters are among the collections of the South Carolina Historical Society, Charleston, South Carolina. Letter 1704. Hereinafter cited as SPG letter.
120. SPG letter.
121. Ibid.
122. Waring, *St. James' Church*, 6.
123. Arthur Henry Hirsch, *The Huguenots of Colonial South Carolina* (London: Archon Books, 1962), 68.
124. Transactions of the French Huguenot Society, among the collections of the South Carolina Historical Society, Vol. 11: 11, 5.
125. Ibid., Vol.16: 42.
126. Ibid., Vol.16: 40.
127. Ibid.
128. Ibid., Vol. 20: 21.
129. Waring, *St. James' Church*, 7.
130. Hirsch, *Huguenots*, 68.
131. Poyas, *Olden Times*, 187.
132. Waring, *St. James' Church*, 7.
133. Poyas, *Olden Times*, 188.
134. Waring, *St. James' Church*, 2.
135. Dalcho, *Protestant Episcopal Church*, 248.
136. Waring, *St. James' Church*, 2.
137. Dalcho, *Protestant Episcopal Church*, 71; Edward McCrady, *History of South Carolina* 4 vols. (New York: McMillan, 1897–1901) vol. 1719–1776: 435.
138. Register of St. Andrew's Parish, 1728–1897. The register is among the collections of the South Carolina Historical Society, Charleston, South Carolina.
139. Frank J. Klingberg, *The Carolina Chronicle of Dr. Francis LeJau, 1706–1717* (Berkeley and Los Angeles: University of California Press, 1956), 50.
140. Waring, *St. James' Church*, 4.
141. Klingberg, *Dr. Francis LeJau*, 92.
142. Journal of the House of Commons, December 15, 1732.
143. Ibid., February 27, 1742.
144. Ibid., June 6, 1746.
145. Dalcho, *Protestant Episcopal Church*, 258.
146. Klingberg, *Dr. Francis LeJau*, 93–94.
147. Ibid., 96.
148. Hirsch, *Huguenots*, 87.
149. *SCHGM* Vol.51: 165.
150. Waring, *St. James Church*, p. 9.
151. Johnson, *Traditions and Reminiscences*, 382.
152. Ibid., 383.
153. Ibid., 384.
154. Waring, *St. James' Church*, 17.
155. Henriette Kershaw Leiding, *Historic Houses of South Carolina* (Philadelphia: J.B. Lippincott, 1921), 26.
156. Charles Fraser, *A Charleston Sketchbook, 1796–1806* (Rutland, Vermont: Charles E. Tuttle Co., 1940), 17.
157. Waring, *St. James' Church*, 17.
158. Vestry Minutes.
159. *Charleston News and Courier*, April 22, 1900.
160. Ibid., April 17, 1904.
161. *News and Courier*, April 23, 1906.
162. Waring, *St. James' Church*, 22.
163. Vestry Minutes.
164. Leilla Sellers, *Charleston Business on the Eve of the American Revolution* (Chapel Hill, North Carolina: University of North Carolina Press, 1932), 30.
165. *News and Courier*, April 20, 1925.
166. *South Carolina Gazette*, August 26, 1765.
167. Poyas, *Olden Times*, 144.

168. McCrady, *South Carolina*, vol. 2: 707n.
169. Waring, *St. James' Church*, 23.
170. Poyas, *Olden Times*, 192.
171. Alston Deas Papers, the South Carolina Historical Society.
172. Edgar W. Knight, *Public Education in the South* (Boston: Ginn and Company, 1922), 26.
173. George Smith McCowen, *The British Occupation of Charleston, 1780–1782* (Columbia: University of South Carolina Press, 1981), 121.
174. Dalcho, *Protestant Episcopal Church*, 244–63.
175. Newton Edwards and Herman G. Richey, *The Schools in the American Social Order* (Boston: Houghton-Mifflin Co., 1911), 3.
176. Frank J. Klingberg, *An Appraisal of the Negro in Colonial South Carolina* (Washington, D.C.: Associated Publishers, 1941), 4, 5.
177. Waring, *St. James' Church*, 6.
178. Klingberg, *Appraisal of the Negro*, 8.
179. Ibid., 8, 2.
180. Ibid., 18.
181. Ibid., 20.
182. Ibid.
183. Klingberg, *Dr. Francis LeJau*, 123.
184. Klingberg, *Appraisal of the Negro*, 26.
185. Frederick Patten Bowes, *The Culture of Early Charleston* (Greenwood, South Carolina: Greenwood Press, 1902), 35.
186. Poyas, *Olden Times*, 182.
187. *SCHGM* Vol. 32: 25.
188. Edwards and Richey, *Schools*, 134.
189. Statutes, Vol. 2: 342–46.
190. "Report of the Committee on Education," in *Acts, Reports and Regulations of the General Assembly of South Carolina*, (Columbia, South Carolina: R.W. Gibbes, 1858), Act no. 325.
191. Edwards and Richey, *Schools*, 136.
192. Henry A.M. Smith, *Henry A. M. Smith Papers, 1744–1922* (Among the collections of the South Carolina Historical Society), 11/404/9; Memorial Book, Vol. 5: 74.
193. Edgar, *South Carolina: A History*, 175.
194. Klingberg, *Dr. Francis LeJau*, 50.
195. Wallace, *Short History*, 82.
196. Ibid.
197. Ibid., 8.
198. Ibid., 9.
199. Smith Papers, 11/404/2.
200. Ibid., 1102.00.
201. Cheves Papers, 34/0320.
202. Smith Papers, 11/404/2.
203. Ibid.
204. Smith Papers, 1102, plat on microfilm.
205. S.C. Archives, S165015, Year 1812, Item 125.
206. S.C. Archives, S165005, Year 1826, Item 73.
207. Reports of the School Commissioners to the State Legislature, 1830–1860. S.C. Archives, S165015, Item 561.
208. 1860 Census.
209. S.C. Archives, Reports of the School Commissioners, 1830–1860.
210. S.C. Archives, Report of the School Commissioners, 1856.
211. S.C. Archives S165005, numbers 14 and 44.
212. 1840 Schedule 6-Social Census.
213. S.C. Archives S165018, Year 1828, Item 32.
214. S.C. Archives S165029, Item 2.
215. Poyas, *Olden Times*, 193.
216. *SCHGM* Vol. 16: 43.
217. S.C. Archives S165005, Report of Commission on Education to the General Assembly.

218. S.C. Archives S165005, Year 1848, Item 127, Page 5.
219. Bowes, *Culture of Early Charleston*, 41.
220. S.C. Archives S165015, Item 2696.
221. 1850 Schedule 6-Social Census.
222. Waring, *St. James' Church*, 5.
223. S.C. Archives S165029, Year 1854, Item 20.
224. Ibid.
225. 1860 Schedule 6-Social Census.
226. S.C. Archives, S165029, Year 1860, Item 6.
227. Ibid., Year 1854, Item 20.
228. Ibid., Year 1860, Item 15; Vestry Minutes.
229. Vestry Minutes.
230. Ibid.
231. *SCHGM* Vol. 57: 65.
232. Ibid., 67.
233. Ibid., 75.
234. Ibid., 76.
235. 1870 Enumeration Census.
236. Orvin, *Historic Berkeley County*, 195.
237. Edgar, *South Carolina: A History*, 463.
238. 1870, Census of the Products of Industry and Census of Agriculture.
239. S.C. Archives, Petition to the General Assembly, S165015, 1865, Number 22.
240. *Records of the Assistant Commissioner for the State of South Carolina, Bureau of Refugees, Freedmen and Abandoned Lands, 1865-1870*. National Archives microfilm publication M869 roll 34. Records are online at <http://freedmensbureau.com/scarolinaoutrages1.html>. April 30, 1866. Hereinafter referred to as Records of the Assistant Commissioner.
241. Irving, *Day on the Cooper River*, 20.
242. Ibid., 21.
243. Letter from Edward Keckley to his daughter, December 10, 1868. Keckley Family Papers #: 43/2073 at the South Carolina Historical Society, Charleston, South Carolina.
244. Freedmens Bureau Reports of murders and outrages, October 1865–1868 in South Carolina: Records of the Assistant Commissioner, for the State of South Carolina, Bureau of Refugees, Freedmen and Abandoned Lands, 1865–1870. National Archives Microfilm Publication M869, Roll 34, "Reports of Muders and Outrages, Oct. 1865–Nov. 1868." April 30, 1866.
245. Records of the Assistant Commissioner; Freedmen Bureau Reports, May 1867.
246. Records of the 18th Regiment.
247. William Henry Johnson, *William Henry Johnson Scrapbook, ca. 1920–1933*. Scrapbook I: 150. The book is among the collections of the South Carolina Historical Society (34/293).
248. *Charleston News and Courier*, September 1, 1876.
249. Ibid., August 28, 1876.
250. Orvin, *Historic Berkeley County*, 180.
251. *Charleston News and Courier*, June 11, 1877.
252. Orvin, *Historic Berkeley County*, 178.
253. Ibid.
254. *Charleston News and Courier*, October 4, 1872.
255. Edgar, *South Carolina: A History*, 411; Cheves Papers, 34/320, "Nelson Contract."
256. Census Reports, 1790 to 1930.
257. 1870, Enumeration Census.
258. 1870, Enumeration Census.
259. *Charleston News and Courier*, March 31, 1870.
260. 1870, 1880, 1890, 1900, Enumeration Census.
261. S.C. Archives Series L10005 Reel 3 Plat 1653 and E. Boddington and Company report, 1882.
262. 1870, Products of Industry Census.
263. Ibid.
264. 1880, Census of the Products of Industry.
265. Ibid.

266. 1860 and 1880, Census of Agriculture.
267. Census of Agriculture and Enumeration Census, 1880 and Edgar, 1998, p. 450.
268. Elias Ball Bull Papers, "Poor white farmers, St. James, Goose Creek Parish." 376.02 (H)01.01.01-17 and Forfeited Lands List, Sinking Fund Commission, Columbia, South Carolina, W.B. McDaniel, General Book and Job Printers, 69 Main Street. 376.02 (H)01.01.01.18. Boyh documents are among the collection of the South Carolina Historical Society, Charleston, South Carolina
269. Edgar, *South Carolina: A History*, 451.
270. 1870, 1880, 1890 Enumeration Censuses.
271. Langdon Cheves Papers, 34/320. Including 1848–1940: *Financial Papers, 1860–1925.* no.1167.01.02 and 1848–1940: *Miscellaneous land papers, 1735–1932,*1 no.1166.01.01. The papers are deposited with the South Carolina Historical Society, Charleston, South Carolina. Hereinafter referred to as Cheves Papers.
272. S.C. Archives Series L10005 Reel 2 Plat 1342.
273. 1880, Census of Agriculture.
274. Ibid.
275. Cheves Papers, 34/320.
276. Ibid.
277. Ibid.
278. Ibid.
279. Edgar, *South Carolina: A History*, 396.
280. Records of Deposit, Freedmen Bank 1868.
281. Ibid.
282. Edgar, *South Carolina: A History*, 397.
283. Smith Papers, 11/404/2.
284. Ibid.
285. Hilton Interview.
286. S.C. Archives Series L10005 Reel 3, plats 1597, 1685 and reel 8, plats 4265, 4270; 1880 Enumeration Census.
287. Stoney, *Plantations of the South Carolina Lowcountry*, 76.
288. 1880, Agricultural Census.
289. Hilton interview.
290. 1870, Agricultural Census.
291. Joan Mitchum Moore, interview with Pearlie Victoria Cales Mitchum, born 1913 in Cales Town, Berkeley County. Interviewed Saturday June 24, 2002, in Cross, South Carolina.
292. *Charleston News and Courier*, January 9, 1882.
293. Cheves Papers, 34/320; MCO Plat Book B: p. 40, 1873.
294. *Charleston News and Courier*, July 20, 1882.
295. Ibid., July 9, September 6, November 25, 1882.
296. Ibid., November 10 and November 14, 1886.
297. Orvin, *Historic Berkeley County*, 195.
298. *Charleston News and Courier*, April 24, 1881.
299. Michael Trinkley, director of the Chicora Foundation, Columbia, South Carolina. Literacy tests to eliminate black voters, online at <http://sciway.net>.
300. Orvin, *Historic Berkeley County*, 204.
301. *African Methodism in South Carolina, A Bicentennial Focus, Seventh Episcopal District* (Tappan, New York: Custombrook, Inc. Custombrook Inc, 1987).
302. The Greater Mt. Zion AME. Church, 142nd Anniversary Program Publication; interview with Vermell Watson at Westview Elementary School, Goose Creek, South Carolina, November 4, 2002.
303. Hilton interview; Cross, *Historic Ramblin's*, 176.
304. *South Carolina General Highway and Transportation Map, 1940* (Columbia; South Carolina Department of Transportation, 1940). Berkeley County.
305. Michael Trinkley, *Liberty Hall: A Small Eighteenth Century Rice Plantation in Goose Creek, Berkeley County, South Carolina* (Chicora Research Contribution Series 62. Chicora Foundation, Inc., Columbia, South Carolina. 2003), 25.
306. Dordal Papers.
307. 1870, Enumeration Census.
308. Edgar, *South Carolina: A History*, 381.
309. Letter from Edward Keckley to Aunt Lizzie, July 4, 1865, among the Keckley Family Papers.
310. 1870, 1880, Enumeration Censuses.

311. 1920, Enumeration Census.
312. Ibid.
313. Watson interview, November 4, 2002.
314. Theresa M. Hicks, ed., *South Carolina Indian Traders and Other Ethnic Connections Beginning in 1670* (Spartanburg, South Carolina: Peppercorn Publishers Inc., 1998), 261.
315. Ibid., 252.
316. Ibid., 353–55.
317. Ibid., .260.
318. 1910, Enumeration Census.
319. Hicks, *Ethnic Connections*, 353–55.
320. *Charleston Post and Courier*, April 17, 2005.
321. Ibid.
322. S.C. Archives, McCrady Plat number 3002.
323. Interview with Julia Garret, custodial supervisor at Westview Primary School, Goose Creek, South Carolina, September 14, 2002.
324. S.C. Archives L10005, Reel 5, Plat 3070.
325. 1890, 1900, 1910, Census of Enumeration.
326. Michael Trinkley, *Cultural Resources Survey of the Liberty Hall Tract, Berkeley County, South Carolina* (Chicora Research Contribution 354. Chicora Foundation, Inc., Columbia, South Carolina, 2002), 20.
327. Ibid., 23.
328. Ibid.
329. Cheves Papers, 34/0320.
330. 1930, Census.
331. 1930, Enumeration Census; Parson interview.
332. 1930, Enumeration Census.
333. Lorean Thompson interview, November 18, 2003.
334. Cheves Papers, 1166.01.01.
335. Ibid.
336. Ibid., Berkeley County tax receipt, #7841, dated December 27, 1928.
337. Cheves Papers, 1166.01.01.
338. Ibid.
339. Henry Workman Conner, *Henry W. Conner Papers, 1890–1948*. The papers are deposited with the South Carolina Historical Society, Charleston, South Carolina, no.1256.02.05 and 28-235-1.
340. Cheves Papers, 1166.01.01, Nelson Contract.
341. Conner Papers, 28-235-2.
342. Ibid., 28-235-3.
343. Ibid.
344. Watson interview, December 28, 2003.
345. Larimer Papers; Larimer/Lowndes interview.
346. Newby, *African Methodism in South Carolina*, 253.
347. Interview with Bertha Middleton, resident of Casey, South Carolina, at Westview Elementary School, Goose Creek, South Carolina, January 21, 1972.
348. S.C. Archives S111001, V.5, Page 34, Record 1.
349. Hutchinson. papers.
350. Photograph entitled *Mail Boat on State Road, Goose Creek, 1904*. The photograph is among the collections of the South Carolina Historical Society, Charleston, South Carolina.
351. Cheves Papers, 34/0320.
352. Parson Interview.
353. Interview with Gertrude Trescott, educator at Westview Elementary School, Goose Creek, South Carolina, April 15, 1972.
354. Parson interview.
355. Cheves Papers, Tenant Records, 1910–1914; 1910 Census.
356. 1920, Enumeration Census.
357. Interview with C.J. Bryant at his residence in Mount Holly, South Carolina, August 8, 1976.
358. Parsons interview.
359. Plat, 1902, Mount Holly, among the collections of the South Carolina Historical Society.

360. S.C. Archives L10005, Reel 3, Plat 1643.
361. Smith Papers, 1902 Plat.
362. Smith Papers, 1102, Plat of 1903 on microfilm.
363. 1930, Enumeration Census.
364. Ibid.
365. Interview with Fred Moseley, farmer, at his home on Liberty Hall Road, Goose Creek, South Carolina, October 15, 1978.
366. Interview with Heidi Varner et al. at Westview Elementary School, Goose Creek, South Carolina, April 25, 2005; Photograph LC-USF34-050595-D, courtesy of the Prints and Photograph Division, Library of Congress, Washington, D.C.
367. Edgar, *South Carolina: A History*, 483.
368. *Berkeley Democrat*, March 13, 1932.
369. Enumeration Censuses, 1870–1930.
370. Interview with Eloise Gowder, Berkeley County librarian at the Berkeley County Library, Moncks Corner, South Carolina, May 1, 1972.
371. *South Carolina General Highway and Transportation Map, 1940.*
372. 1930 Census; *Berkeley Democrat*, February 6, 1936, May 6, 1937 and September 7, 1932.
373. *Berkeley Democrat*, November 24, 1938.
374. Furman plat, 1907.
375. S.C. Archives Series L10005, Reel 3, Plat 1517.
376. *Berkeley Democrat*, September 14, 1932.
377. Berkeley County Deed Book C #13 p. 7.
378. Interview with M.C. Cannon, Berkeley County magistrate and sheriff, at the Philippine Hut Restaurant, Goose Creek, South Carolina, June 8, 1972.
379. Gowder interview.
380. Ibid.
381. Ibid.
382. 1930 Enumeration Census.
383. Interview with Mr. Eugene Bryan at his home in Strawberry on June 7, 2005.
384. Census Reports, 1900–1930.
385. Cheves Papers.
386. Interview with Loretta Parsons, resident of Casey, at Westview Elementary School, Goose Creek, South Carolina, April 4, 1978.
387. Parsons interview.
388. Ibid.
389. *Goose Creek Gazette*, May 12, 2004.
390. Ibid., December 12, 1984.
391. Census 1900, 193.
392. 1900 Enumeration Census.
393. Larimer/Wilson Interview.
394. Interview with Jennie Mae Jefferson, educator and former resident of Casey, South Carolina, at Boulder Bluff Elementary School, Goose Creek, South Carolina, March 17, 1978; interview with Heidi Varner, May 12, 2005.
395. Varner Interview, April 25, 2005.
396. Maxwell Clayton Orvin, *A History of Moncks Corner, Berkeley County, South Carolina* (Charleston, 19610, 64.
397. Poyas, *Olden Times*, 52.
398. S.C. Archives, L10005, Reel 2, Plat 1083.
399. Cheves Papers, 1166.01.01. Order of Board of Commissioners, June 1927.
400. Jack Etling, Private Papers of Jack Etling, Map of Small Farms, 199.
401. Edgar, *South Carolina: A History*, 57.
402. *Berkeley Democrat*, November 1954.
403. *Charleston News and Courier/Evening Post*, November 20, 1983.
404. *Berkeley Democrat*, December 28, 1955.
405. Ibid., February 22, 1956.
406. Ibid., August 15, 1956.
407. Gowder and Watson interviews.
408. *Berkeley Democrat*, August 17, 1956.

409. Edgar, *South Carolina: A History*, 522.
410. *Berkeley Democrat*, May 9, 1956.
411. Ibid., July 15, 1953.
412. Trescott interview.
413. *Berkeley Democrat*, February 25, 1953.
414. Berkeley School District Budget for 1956–57, Berkeley School District, Department of Education, Moncks Corner, South Carolina.
415. *Berkeley Democrat*, June 17, 1953.
416. *Goose Creek Gazette*, August 29, 1984.
417. Interview with Jack Etling, president of Pineview Development Company at Goose Creek City Hall, Goose Creek, South Carolina, February 4, 1972.
418. *Berkeley Democrat*, June 20, 1956.
419. Ibid., August 18, 1971.
420. *Goose Creek Gazette*, August 29, 1984.
421. Ibid.
422. Interview via telephone with Mrs. Marion Hatchell, city clerk treasurer, City of Goose Creek, South Carolina, April 18, 2002.
423. *Berkeley Democrat*, March 8, 1961.
424. Ibid., March 22, 1961.
425. Interview with Malvin Mann, mayor, city of Goose Creek, South Carolina at Goose Creek City Hall, January 20, 1977.
426. Ibid.
427. Ibid.
428. Town Council Minutes, July 5, 1961.
429. Iibd., November 6, 1962.
430. Ibid., October 3, 1963.
431. Ibid., November 19, 1963.
432. Ibid., August 14, 1962.
433. Ibid., October 22, 1963.
434. Ibid., November 5, 1963.
435. Ibid., May 10, 1964.
436. Ibid., August 14, 1962.
437. Ibid., March 5, 1962.
438. Ibid., July 14, 1964.
439. Ibid., May 5, 1964.
440. Ibid., July 9, 1964.
441. Ibid., July 16, 1964.
442. Ibid., October 1, 1964.
443. Interview with S.E. Felkel, developer and landowner, at Goose Creek City Hall, Goose Creek, South Carolina, May 14, 1972.
444. *Charleston News and Courier*, May 30, 1970.
445. *Berkeley Democrat*, January 6, 1960.
446. Ibid., February 7, 1962.
447. Karen Humphries Martin, teacher at Westview Elementary School, Goose Creek, South Carolina, March 22, 2001.
448. *Berkeley Democrat*, January 11, 1961.
449. *SCHGM* Vol. 90: 145.
450. Town Council Minutes, August 24, 1962.
451. Ibid., January 8, 1963.
452. Ibid., August 22, 1963.
453. Ibid., June 4, 1963.
454. Ibid., March 23, 1964.
455. Ibid., October 26, 1964.
456. Ibid., October 13, 1964; October 26, 1964; December 8, 1964.
457. Ibid., March 1, 1966.
458. Ibid., March 7, 1968.

459. *Charleston News and Courier*, August 6, 1968.
460. Ibid.; Mann interview.
461. Town Council Minutes, March 28, 1967.
462. Mann interview.
463. Town Council Minutes, June 4, 1968.
464. Ibid., June 11, 1968.
465. Ibid., July 23, 1968.
466. Ibid., May 28, 1968.
467. *Charleston News and Courier*, August 11, 1968.
468. Ibid., May 15, 1962.
469. Ibid., May 27, 1962.
470. Felkel Interview.
471. *Charleston News and Courier*, January 16, 1962.
472. Ibid., June 11, 1962.
473. Town Council Minutes, September 4, 1962.
474. National Records and Archives.
475. *Charleston News and Courier*, April 29, 1973.
476. Town Council Minutes, January 14, 1962.
477. Ibid., February 11, 1969; February 17, 1962.
478. *Berkeley Democrat*, March 15, 1973.
479. Town Council Minutes, September 14, 1971.
480. Letter to City Council, June 9, 1970.
481. *Berkeley Democrat*, February 9, 1972.
482. *Charleston News and Courier*, February 4, 1972.
483. Ibid.
484. City Council Minutes, November 21, 1972.
485. *Hanahan News*, April 4, 1973.
486. City Council Minutes, May 25, 1972.
487. *Charleston News and Courier*, March 27, 1971.
488. Ibid., May 10, 1973.
489. City Council Minutes, September 19, 1972.
490. *Charleston News and Courier*, July 6, 1970.
491. Ibid., August 30, 1973.
492. Ibid., April 29, 1973.
493. Ibid., November 30, 1955.
494. Edgar, *South Carolina: A History*, 540.
495. *Hanahan News*, 1973.
496. City Council Minutes, April 9, 1974.
497. Ibid., May 30, 1974.
498. Ibid., October 10, 1974.
499. Ibid., September 9, 1975.
500. *Charleston News and Courier*, May 12, 1976.
501. Mann interview.
502. *Charleston News and Courier*, May 18, 1977.
503. *Charleston Evening Post*, June 10, 1977.
504. *Charleston News and Courier*, June 9, 1977.
505. Ibid., May 7, 1978.
506. Ibid., May 10, 1978.
507. Michael J. Heitzler, *Historic Goose Creek, South Carolina, 1670–1980* (Easley, South Carolina: Southern Historical Press, 1983), 237.
508. *Goose Creek Gazette*, December 12, 1972.
509. Ibid., May 16, 1980.
510. Ibid., April 23, 1980.
511. Ibid., August 13, 1980.
512. Interview with Marguerite Brown at the Marguerite Brown Municipal Center, Goose Creek, South Carolina, September 3, 2003.

513. *Charleston News and Courier/Evening Post*, November 20, 1983.
514. *Goose Creek Gazette*, December 24, 1980.
515. *Charleston News and Courier/Evening Post*, November 20, 1983.
516. *Goose Creek Gazette*, April 16, 1980.
517. *Charleston News and Courier/Evening Post*, November 20, 1983.
518. *Goose Creek Gazette*, November 28, 1984.
519. *Charleston Post and Courier*, October 9, 2003.
520. Ibid., October 13, 2003.
521. Ibid., October 10, 2003.
522. *Charleston News and Courier*, July 23, 2003.
523. Interview with Harvey Becker, chief of police, city of Goose Creek, at the Marguerite H. Brown Municipal Center, September 23, 2003.
524. Jonathan Mercantini, "The Great Carolina Hurricane of 1752," *South Carolina Historical and Genealogical Magazine* 103, no. 4 (2002): 351–65.
525. Phillips interview, October 22, 2003.
526. *Charleston Post and Courier*, October 3, 1992.
527. *Charleston News and Courier*, January 13, 2003.
528. *Goose Creek Gazette*, October 13, 1981.
529. Joseph Daning, mayor pro tem/city council member, city of Goose Creek. Interview at Marguerite H. Brown Municipal Center, October 14, 2003.
530. *Goose Creek Gazette*, May 1, 1981.
531. Ibid., May 22, 1981.
532. Ibid.
533. Ibid., September 9, 1981.
534. Ibid., February 2, 1982.
535. *Charleston Post and Courier*, January 18, 2003.
536. Irving, *Day on the Cooper River*, 100.
537. Ibid., 104.
538. Poyas, *Olden Times*, 95; Martin, *Charleston Ghosts*, 67.
539. Poyas, *Olden Times*, 95.
540. Ibid., 96.
541. Ibid., 83.
542. Irving, *Day on the Cooper River*, 108.
543. *A Morbid Tale*, 2.
544. Ibid., 21.
545. Waring, *St. James' Church*, 28.
546. McCrady, *South Carolina*, vol. 2: 196, 197.
547. Walter B. Edgar and N. Louise Bailey, *Biographical Directory of the South Carolina House of Representatives* (Columbia: University of South Carolina Press, 1974), vol. 2: 686.
548. Irving, *Day on the Cooper River*, 73.
549. McCrady, *South Carolina*, vol. 2: 197.
550. Martin, *Charleston Ghosts*, 89.
551. Johnson, *Traditions and Reminiscences*, 67–62.
552. Martin, *Charleston Ghosts*, 90.
553. Johnson, *Traditions and Reminiscences*, 68.
554. John Bennett, *The Treasure of Peyre Gaillard* (Charleston: South Carolina Historical Society Microforms, 1981), 2, 3, 5.
555. Martin, *Charleston Ghosts*, 85.
556. Irving, *Day on the Cooper River*, 62.
557. Ibid., 21.
558. Interview with Cynthia Hudson at Westview Elementary School, Goose Creek, South Carolina, November 22, 2003.
559. *Goose Creek Gazette*, July 23, 2003.
560. Interview with Mark Sowers, director of security at the Naval Weapons Station, at the Goose Creek Police Department, Goose Creek, South Carolina, June 12, 2003.
561. Designing Goose Creek, *An Input Process and Design Charette for the City of Goose Creek*, (Columbia: The South

Carolina Downtown Development Association), The report is among the City of Goose Creek archives at the Marguerite H. Brown Municipal Center, Goose Creek, South Carolina, p.v-1.
562. Journals of the House of Representatives; Edgar and Bailey, *Biographical Directory*.
563. Emily Bellinger Reynolds and Joan Reynolds Faunt, *The Biographical Directory of the Senate of South Carolina, 1776–1964* (Columbia: The Senate Research Committee. South Carolina Department of Archives and History, 1964).
564. Wallace, *Short History*, 12.

BIBLIOGRAPHY

Primary Sources

Unpublished Interviews

Michael Heitzler interviews with:

Becker, Harvey, chief of police, September 23, 2003, at Goose Creek City Hall, Goose Creek, South Carolina.

Best, Stephen, professor of biology at Charleston Southern University, at The Oaks, March 12, 2004.

Brown, Marguerite, city councilperson, September 3, 2003, at Westview Elementary School, Goose Creek, South Carolina.

Bryan, Eugene, June 7, 2005, at his residence in Strawberry, South Carolina.

Bryant, C.J. Sr., August 8, 1976, at his residence at Mt. Holly, Goose Creek, South Carolina.

Calvert, Harry, deputy superintendent of Berkeley School District. May 22, 2003, at the Berkeley County Department of Education Board Room.

Cannon, M.C., Berkeley County magistrate and sheriff, June 8, 1979, at Philippine Hut Restaurant, Goose Creek, South Carolina.

Daning, Joseph, mayor pro tem/city council member, City of Goose Creek. Interview at Marguerite H. Brown Municipal Center, October 14, 2003.

Etling, Jack, president of the Pineview Development Co., February 4, 1979, at Goose Creek City Hall, Goose Creek, South Carolina.

Felkel, Saint Elmo "Speedy," developer and landowner, Goose Creek City Hall, April 14, 1979, Goose Creek, South Carolina.

Garret, Julia, custodian supervisor at Westview Primary School, September 14, 2002, at Westview Elementary School, Goose Creek, South Carolina.

Gowder, Eloise, Berkeley County librarian, May 1, 1979, at the Berkeley County Library, Moncks Corner, South Carolina.

Hatchell, Mrs. Marion, city clerk treasurer, City of Goose Creek, South Carolina. Interview via telephone, April 18 and June 6, 2001.

Hilton, Harold, Berkeley County landowner, April 26, 2003, at his home in Sandridge, South Carolina.

Hudson, Cynthia, November 22, 2003, at Westview Elementary School, Goose Creek, South Carolina.

Jefferson, Jennie Mae, educator and former resident of Casey, March 17, 1978, at Boulder Bluff Elementary School, Goose Creek, South Carolina.

Legendre, Gertrude, owner of Medway Plantation, at Medway, March 12, 1996.

Martin, Karen, teacher at Westview Elementary School. Interview March 22, 2001, at Westview Elementary School, Goose Creek, South Carolina.

Mann, Malvin, mayor, City of Goose Creek, January 20, 1977, at Goose Creek City Hall. Goose Creek, South Carolina.

McCants, John, city councilman at Marguerite Brown Municipal Center, October 22, 2003, Goose Creek, South Carolina.

Middleton, Bertha, resident of Casey, South Carolina. January 21, 1979, at Westview Elementary School, Goose Creek, South Carolina.

Moseley, Fred, Goose Creek farmer, October 15, 1978, at his residence on Liberty Hall Road, Goose Creek, South Carolina.

Parsons, Loretta, resident of Casey, South Carolina, April 4, 1978, at Westview Elementary School, Goose Creek.

Phillips, Mark, city councilman at Marguerite Brown Municipal Center, October 22, 2003, Goose Creek, South Carolina.

Sowers, Mark, director of security at the Naval Weapons Station, Goose Creek Police Department, June 12, 2003, Goose Creek, South Carolina.

Stubor, Gary, director of Goose Creek Parks and Playgrounds, October 9, 2003, Goose Creek, South Carolina.

Trescott, Gertrude, educator at Westview Elementary School, April 15, 1979, Goose Creek, South Carolina.

Varner, Heidi, and Martha Dangerfield Varner, Idel Dangerfield Ruth and Mary Dangerfield Barrineau on April 25, 2005, at Westview Elementary School, Goose Creek, South Carolina.

Watson, Vermell, custodial supervisor, Westview Elementary School, November 4, 2002, Goose Creek, South Carolina.

Private Papers

Alston Deas Papers. Alston Deas collection of property records, 1823–1895. Papers deposited with the South Carolina Historical Society. Charleston, South Carolina.

Ball Family Papers. *John Ball Plantation Records, 1831–1841*. Papers deposited with the South Carolina Historical Society. Charleston, South Carolina.

———. *Back River Plantation Records 1812–1834*. Papers deposited with the South Carolina Historical Society. Charleston, South Carolina.

Ball, Jane Hayward. *Scrapbook, 1900–1929*, Scrapbook deposited with the South Carolina Historical Society. Charleston, South Carolina. Call no. 34/0261 Cheves, Langdon 1848–1940.

Bull, Elias Ball. Elias Ball Bull Papers, "Poor white farmers, St. James, Goose Creek Parish." 376.02 (H)01.01.01-17 and Forfeited Lands List, Sinking Fund Commission, Columbia, South Carolina, W.B. McDaniel, General Book and Job Printers, 69 Main Street. 376.02 (H)01.01.01.18. Both documents are among the collection of the South Carolina Historical Society. Charleston, South Carolina.

Brewster and Burke Papers. *Abstract of title to Red Bank Plantation, 1880*. Papers deposited with the South Carolina Historical Society. Charleston, South Carolina.

Cheves, Langdon. 1848–1940: *Miscellaneous land papers, 1735–1932.* Papers deposited with the South Carolina Historical Society. Charleston, South Carolina.

———. 1848–1939: *Abstracts of Titles, 1694–1850.* Papers deposited with the South Carolina Historical Society. Charleston, South Carolina.

———. 1848–1940: *Financial Papers, 1860–1925.* Papers deposited with the South Carolina Historical Society. Charleston, South Carolina.

———. 1848–1939: *Abstracts of Titles, 1694–1850.* Papers deposited with the South Carolina Historical Society. Charleston, South Carolina.

Chicken, George d. 1727: *George Chicken Journal, 1715–1716.* Papers are deposited with the South Carolina Historical Society, Charleston, South Carolina.

Conner, Henry Workman: *Henry W. Conner Papers, 1890–1940.* Papers are deposited with the South Carolina Historical Society, Charleston, South Carolina.

Deas-Alston Collection: Papers deposited with the South Carolina Historical Society. Charleston, South Carolina.

DeSaussure Papers: DeSaussure family papers, 1716–1938. The papers are deposited with the South Carolina Historical Society. Charleston, South Carolina.

Donnelly Papers: Papers in the private collection of Thomas and Elizabeth Johnson, Charleston, South Carolina.

Dordal Papers: Papers in the private collection of the Dordal family. Goose Creek, South Carolina.

Fraser, Alexander. *Alexander Fraser correspondence, 1774–1791.* Papers deposited with the South Carolina Historical Society. Charleston, South Carolina.

Glover. *The Glover Family Papers 1731–1841*: Papers deposited with the South Carolina Historical Society. Charleston, South Carolina.

Graves, Charles W. Ca. 1818–1870: *Papers and Plantation Journal 1846–1875.* Papers are among the collections of the South Carolina Historical Society, Charleston, South Carolina.

Graves family. *Graves Family Papers, 1853–1854, 1854–1855.* Papers are among the collections of the South Carolina Historical Society. Charleston, South Carolina.

Hilton, Nathaniel. *St. James, Goose Creek Planter, Charleston District Ordinary Letter of Testament, 1858.* The testament is among the private papers of Harold Hilton. Sandridge, South Carolina.

Hutchinson Edward L. d. 1855, *Edward L. Hutchinson papers 1800–1855.* Papers are deposited with the South Carolina Historical Society, Charleston, South Carolina.

Izard family. *Izard family papers, 1801–1861.* The papers are deposited with the South Carolina Historical Society. Charleston, South Carolina.

Johnson, William Henry. 1871–1934.*William Henry Johnson Scrapbook, ca. 1920–1933.* The scrapbook is among the collections of the South Carolina Historical Society. Charleston, South Carolina.

Keckley family. *Keckley family papers, 1816–1977.* The papers are deposited with the South Carolina Historical Society. Charleston, South Carolina.

Larimer, Terrence: Private papers in his possession at the Naval Weapons Station Charleston, Goose Creek, South Carolina. The papers include notes from his interviews with:

Brower, Ida Kodama. Goose Creek, South Carolina. July and August 1998.

Ford II, Frank. C. Goose Creek, South Carolina. August and September 1998.

Herrin George. Goose Creek, South Carolina. June 1998

Kodama, Henry. Goose Creek, South Carolina. July 1998.

Lowndes II, E.F. Goose Creek, South Carolina. August and September 1998.

Manucy II, Orian A. Goose Creek, South Carolina.1988.

Norman Spell. Charleston, South Carolina. April 1996.

Wilson, William. Moncks Corner, South Carolina. March 1997.

Letters of the Society for the Propagation of the Gospel in Foreign Parts to the Ministers of St. James Church, Goose Creek, 1702-1765. The letters are among the collections of the South Carolina Historical Society, Charleston, South Carolina and on microfilm at the South Carolina Department of Archives and History, Columbia, South Carolina.

Liberty Hall Club. *Tales of the Liberty Hall Club* as told to E.F. Lowndes II.by Frank C. Ford in June 1985. The tales are among the private papers of Terrence Larimer, Naval Weapons Station Charleston, Goose Creek, South Carolina.

Liberty Hall Hunt Club Log, 1912. The log is among the private papers of Terrence Larimer, Naval Weapons Station, Charleston, Goose Creek, South Carolina.

Lieber, Oscar M. *Vocabulary of the Catawba Language, with some Remarks on its Grammar, Construction and Pronunciation,* among the collections of the South Carolina Historical Society. Charleston, South Carolina.

Loocock, Aaron. *Bond of Indemnity, 1792.* Deposited with the South Carolina Historical Society. Charleston, South Carolina.

———. Private papers including his will in 1793 are among the collections of the South Carolina Historical Society. Charleston, South Carolina.

Loyalist Claims. On microfilm among the collections of the South Carolina Department of Archives and History. Columbia, South Carolina.

Manigault, Gabriel. *Gabriel Manigault papers, 1775–1839.* Deposited with the South Carolina Historical Society. Charleston, South Carolina.

———. *Gabriel Manigault letters 1805–1808.* Deposited with the South Carolina Historical Society. Charleston, South Carolina.

———. *Gabriel Manigault papers with the Journal, 1774–1784.* Deposited with the South Carolina Historical Society. Charleston, South Carolina.

Mazyck Family Document, 1683–1807. Deposited with the South Carolina Historical Society. Charleston, South Carolina.

Mazyck, Stephen. *Stephen Mazyck Letter in 1776 at Spring Field Plantation in Goose Creek, to his brother Alexander,* Deposited with the South Carolina Historical Society. Charleston, South Carolina.

Marcy, Henry Orlando. *Diary of a Surgeon: U.S. Army, 1864–1892.* Deposited with the South Carolina Historical Society. Charleston, South Carolina. 34/0496.

Middleton, Henry Augustus. *Henry Augustus Middleton Business and plantation papers, 1828–1887.* Deposited with The South Carolina Historical Society. Charleston, South Carolina.

Middleton, Thomas. *Thomas Middleton papers, 1787–1849.* Deposited with the South Carolina Historical Society. Charleston, South Carolina.

Ravenel, William. 1806–1888. *William Ravenel Papers, 1746–1886.* Deposited with the South Carolina Historical Society. Charleston, South Carolina.

Records of the 18th Regiment of the South Carolina Militia, South Carolina, Adjutant and Inspector General's Office on deposit at the South Carolina Historical Society. Charleston, South Carolina.

Smith, Henry A.M. *Henry A.M. Smith papers 1744–1922.* The papers are among the collections of the South Carolina Historical Society. Charleston, South Carolina.

———. *Henry A.M. Smith papers 1883–1924.* The papers are among the collections of the South Carolina Historical Society. Charleston, South Carolina.

Smyth, Stoney Adger. *Stoney Adger Smyth Collection including the Medway Plantation Day Book, 1872 and the Medway Plantation Hunt Book 1875-1918.* The papers are among the collections of the South Carolina Historical Society. Charleston, South Carolina.

South Carolina Militia, 7th Brigade, 30th Regiment order book, 1793–1814 in Vanderhorst's Regiment Order Book. The book is among the collections of the South Carolina Historical Society, Charleston, South Carolina.

Stoney, Samuel Gaillard. *Samuel Gaillard Stoney Papers* and *Stoney Family Documents, 1775–1935 and the Plantation Journal of Medway 1852–1853.* The papers are among the collections of the South Carolina Historical Society. Charleston, South Carolina.

Wragg Family Papers, 1708–1860. Deposited with the South Carolina Historical Society. Charleston, South Carolina.

Plats deposited with the South Carolina Historical Society, and the Charleston County Library, Charleston, South Carolina.

Braker, Susannah. Plat drawn at the request of Susannah Braker, Administrator to the Estate of Jacob Braker, deceased. I have resurveyed the…land attached to the 19-mile House belonging to the estate of P. Jacob Braker containing 467 acres…1821.

Ficken, John. Plat for John Ficken, McCardy plat number 1712, C3184.

Furman, C.M. Plat of a piece of land containing 400 acres…C.M. Furman. McCrady Plat 1517, C3182.

Goose Creek Church. Plat of a tract of land situate in St. James, Goose Creek, contains 270 acres belonging to the Goose Cr. Church. Surveyed May 1888. Name not legible. Plat is on microfiche and among the Henry A.M. Smith Papers. The plat shows the location of the "Old School House" at a point N50 S 11.70 and N 14 ½ S 22.

Goose Creek Dam. Plat of Goose Creek Dam, McCrady plat 2992, C 3184.

Harmon. Plat of the Harmon tract of 1044.5 acres, 1915. McCrady plat 3002, C3184.

Ingleside Mining. Plat of Ingleside Mining, 1639 acres, McCrady plat number 3070, C3184.

Izard, Ralph. Plan of a body of land called the Elms Clubhouse and composed of Sundry Tracts, In the parish of St. James, Goose Creek and St. George Dorchester, Charleston District.(C.141). Series L10005 Reel 8, Plat 4229.

Johnson, William. William Johnson plat for 550 acres of marshland on Cooper River and Goose Creek, Charleston District, surveyed by J. Schreiber. Series 213190, Volume 20: Page 199.

Martindale Plantation Situate on Southern Railroad in St. James, Goose Creek Parish, Charleston District… survey made June 1840.

Onsitt, John. Plan of a body of land made at the request of the executors of John Onsitt and Margaret Riddle, formerly Margaret Onsitt to resurvey and divide the property containing 666 acres recorded in book H number 7, page 5. 1802. Resurvey and division made 1792.

Stoney, Samuel G. 1906 plat of Medway Plantation consisting of 5,492 acres combining 5 tracts. Survey and plat made by Simons-Mayrant Company.

Thornley, Robert. Plat for 460 acres on branch of Wassamasaw Swamp, Charleston District, surveyed by John Diamond. Series 2131190, Volume 9, page 87.

Von Kolnitz George. Plat of George Von Kolnitz, McCrady plat 1644, C3182.

Photographs and Prints

The Elms, Country Seat of Ralph Izard. Thomas Middleton painted the watercolor in 1817. The image is among the Thomas Middleton private papers in the collections of the South Carolina Historical Society, Charleston, South Carolina. Image 0177-1-Elm

The Elms Ruins, Charleston County, South Carolina. The photograph is among the collections of the Library of Congress.

Online Records of the State of South Carolina at the South Carolina Department of Archives and History, Columbia, South Carolina.

Criminal Journals, 1769–1776.

Index to Multiple Records Series 1675–1929.

Legislative Papers, 1782–1866.

Plats for State Land Grants, 1784–1868.

Will Transcripts, 1782–1855.

Acts, Reports, Laws, Ordinances, Records, Regulations and Statutes

Charleston County Court of Ordinary, Inventories, Appraisements and Sales Books, 1839–1870. Charleston County Office Building, Charleston, South Carolina.

Record of Wills, 1786–1868. Charleston County, South Carolina. Charleston County Office Building, Charleston, South Carolina.

Register of Mesne Conveyance Records for Charleston County, South Carolina (Records of Deeds between buyer and seller, 1719–2003). Charleston, South Carolina.

SCIWAY, South Carolina Information Highway. <http://sciway.net>.

St. Andrew's Parish. Parish Register of St. Andrew's Parish, 1728. The register is among the collections of the South Carolina Historical Society, Charleston, South Carolina.

St. James Church, Goose Creek. *Minutes of the Vestry, 1872–1925*. The minutes are among the collections of the South Carolina Historical Society, Charleston, South Carolina.

Transcripts of Charleston County wills, estate inventories and miscellaneous records prior to 1869. The records are on microfilm at the Charleston County Library, Charleston, South Carolina and at the South Carolina Department of Archives and History.

U.S. Census Bureau. Census of Agriculture for St. James, Goose Creek Parish, South Carolina 1850, 1860, 1870, 1880.

———. Census of Mortality for St. James, Goose Creek Parish, South Carolina 1850, 1860, 1870, 1880.

———. Federal Population Enumerations for St. James, Goose Creek Parish, South Carolina for the years 1790, 1800, 1810, 1820, 1830, 1840, 1850, 1860, 1870, 1880,1890, 1900, 1910, 1920, 1930. Washington: Government Printing Office.

———. Products of Industry for St. James, Goose Creek Parish, South Carolina 1850, 1860, 1870, 1880.

———. Slave Schedules for St. James, Goose Creek Parish, South Carolina, 1840, 1850, 1860.

———. Special Enumeration Census for the City of Goose Creek, April 14, 1979. Available at the South Carolina Department of Archives and History, Columbia, South Carolina.

———. Social Census for St. James, Goose Creek Parish, South Carolina 1850, 1860, 1870, 1880.

U.S. Mapping Service. <http://www.mapping.usgs.gov/>.

Windsor Hill Nomination Form. National Register of Historic Places Nomination Form. United States Department of Interior February 4, 1976. Records are on deposit at The Institute of Archaeology and Anthropology, University of South Carolina, Columbia, South Carolina.

Plats on Microfilm at the South Carolina Historical Society.

Deans Swamp, 1819. 33-68-13.

Elms Plantation 1785, 32-29-6.

The Elms Plantation, 1801. 32-44-9.

Goose Creek Church, 1888. 32-77.

Howe Hall 1780, 33-82-6.

John Onsell Estate, 1792. 33-62-33.

Lands Adjoining Goose Creek Reservoir, 1917. 32-88-5.

Martindale Plantation. 33-72-23.

Medway, Back River, 1792. 33-62-12.

Oakgrove Plantation, 1784. 47-5-4.

Sociable Hill Plantation, 1788. 32-32-7.

Wassamasaw, 1786. 33-64-17.

William Bull Plat of Button Hall, 1778. 33-40.

William Parker Estate, Wassamasaw, 1790, 33-16-47.

Secondary Sources

Unpublished Sources

Papers and Reports

Freedmens Bureau Reports of murders and outrages, Oct. 1865-1868 in South Carolina: Records of the Assistant Commissioner, for the State of South Carolina, Bureau of Refugees, Freedmen and Abandoned Lands, 1865-1870. National Archives Microfilm Publication M869, Roll 34, "Reports of Muders and Outrages, Oct. 1865–Nov. 1868." April 30, 1866.

Gunn, Victoria Reeves. "Hofwyl Plantation." The manuscript is on file with the Georgia Department of Natural Resources, Atlanta, Georgia.

Sambits, Nancy. "The Economic Decline of an Agricultural Community: a case study." Unpublished and unbound manuscript at Caroliniana Library, 1989. Columbia, South Carolina.

Smith, M.T. "Depopulation and Culture Change in the Early Historic Period Interior Southeast." PhD diss., Department of Anthropology, University of Florida, Gainesville.

Wayne, L.B. "Burning Brick: A Study of a Lowcountry Industry." PhD diss., University of Florida, Gainesville, 1991.

Published Sources

Archaeological Studies and Reports

Adams, Natalie. Archaeological Reconnaissance of the Berkeley County Landfill Extension. Chicora Foundation, Inc., Columbia, South Carolina, 1993.

———. Archaeological Survey of the Goose Creek Water Main Extension, Berkeley County, South Carolina. Chicora Foundation Inc., Columbia, South Carolina, 1994.

———. Archaeological Survey of the Santee-Cooper Moncks Corner Eastside Carnes Crossroads Transmission Line, Berkeley County, South Carolina. Chicora Foundation Inc., Columbia, South Carolina, 1993.

Bailey, Ralph Jr. *Cultural Resources of the Ingleside Plantation Tract, Charleston County, South Carolina.* Prepared for the Albert Weber Manufacturing Company, Summerville, South Carolina, 1997.

———. Principal investigator of the *Cultural Resources Survey and Testing of the Persimmon Hill Tract, Berkeley County South Carolina*. Brockington and Associates, Inc., Atlanta, Charleston, Raleigh, 2002.

Bailey, Ralph Jr., and Bruce G. Harvey. *National Register of Historic Places Evaluation of 29 Sites at the Charleston Naval Weapon's Station, Berkeley and Charleston Counties, South Carolina.* The report is among the papers of the Natural Resources Office at the Naval Weapon's Station, Charleston, South Carolina, 2000.

Bridgeman, Kara. Cultural Resources Inventory of the Charleston Southern Athletic Field, Charleston County, South Carolina. Prepared for the Charleston Southern University, Charleston, South Carolina, 2000

Brockington, P.E. Jr., M.V. Markham, C.S. Butler, and D.C. Jones. *Cultural Resources Survey of the Charleston Naval Weapons Station, Berkeley and Charleston Counties, South Carolina.* Final Report Prepared for U. S. Army Corps of Engineers, Savannah District. Brockington and Associates, Inc., Atlanta, Georgia, 1998.

Caballero, O.M. *Archaeological Investigations of the Proposed U.S. Highway 176 Widening, Goose Creek to U.S. 17A, Berkeley County, South Carolina.* Prepared for the South Carolina Department of Public Safety and Transportation. New South Associates Inc., Stone Mountain, Georgia, 1987.

Charles, Tommy. *An archaeological reconnaissance of the St. James Church properties of the diocese of South Carolina in Goose Creek, Berkeley County, South Carolina.* University of South Carolina Institute of Archaeology and Anthropology, Columbia, South Carolina, 1988.

Drucker, Lesley M. *A cultural resources overview of the Bushy Park Auxiliary Canal study area.* Berkeley County, South Carolina. S.C. Archaeological Services, Columbia, South Carolina, 1981.

Elliot, Daniel T. *Crowfield Archaeological Survey*. Manuscript on file, Chicora Foundation, Inc., Columbia, South Carolina.

Garrow, Patrick H., and Daniel T. Elliot. *Crowfield Archaeological Survey.* Prepared for Westvaco Development Corporation, Summerville, South Carolina, 1987.

Grover, J.E. *Historic and Archaeological Resources Protection Plan for Naval Weapons Station, Charleston*: Final Draft Report Prepared for U.S. Army Corps of Engineers, Savannah District. Pan-American Consultants, Inc., Tuscaloosa, Alabama, 1997.

Poplin, Eric C. *Archaeological reconnaissance of the Mt. Holly Plantation, Berkeley County, South Carolina*, Institute of Archaeology and Anthropology, University of South Carolina, 1978.

Sipes, Eric D., and Pat Hendrix. *Cultural Resources Survey and Testing of the Persimmon Hill Tract, Berkeley County, South Carolina.* Prepared for Hussey, Gay, Bell and Deyoung, Inc., Mount Pleasant, South Carolina, 2002.

Tippet Lee, and Michael Trinkley. *Archaeological Survey of the Proposed Goose Creek-Ladson Connector*. Prepared for the South Carolina Department of Safety and Public Transportation, 1979

Trinkley, Michael. *Archaeological Survey of the Proposed Devon Forest, Berkeley County, South Carolina*, Chicora Foundation Inc., Columbia, South Carolina, August 7, 2000.

———. *Cultural Resources Survey of the Liberty Hall Tract, Berkeley County, South Carolina*. Chicora Research Contribution 354. Chicora Foundation, Inc., Columbia, South Carolina, 2002.

———. *Liberty Hall: A Small Eighteenth Century Rice Plantation in Goose Creek, Berkeley County, South*. Chicora Research Contribution Series 62. Chicora Foundation, Inc., Columbia, South Carolina, 2003.

———. *Management Summary of Archaeological Data Recovery at a Portion of Crowfield Plantation and its Slave Settlement, Berkeley County, South Carolina*. Chicora Foundation Inc., Columbia, South Carolina, 1996.

———. *Landscape and Garden Archaeology at Crowfield Plantation: a Preliminary Examination*. Chicora Foundation Inc., Columbia, South Carolina, 1992.

Trinkley, Michael, Debi Hacker, and Natalie Adams. *Broom Hall Plantation: "A Pleasant One and in a Good Neighborhood,"* Chicora Foundation Inc., Columbia, South Carolina, 1995.

Trinkley, Michael, Debi Hacker, and Nicole Southerland. Archaeology at an *Eighteenth Century Slave Settlement in Goose Creek, South Carolina, Berkeley County, South Carolina*. Chicora Foundation Inc. Research Series 57, Columbia, South Carolina, 2003.

Webb, Robert S., and Mary E. Gantt. *Evaluative Testing at Crowfield Main House Site (38BK102) and Slave Complex (38BK1011), Berkeley County, South Carolina*. Prepared for Westvaco Development Corporation, Summerville, South Carolina, 1997.

Articles Published by the South Carolina Historical and Genealogical Society

Ariel Abbot Journals. *South Carolina Historical and Genealogical Magazine* 68 (1967): 244.

"The Brief and Tragic Career of Charles Lowndes." *South Carolina Historical and Genealogical Magazine* 70: (1969): 220–23.

"The Diary of William Dillwyn in 1772." *South Carolina Historical and Genealogical Magazine* 36 (1935): 107–10.

Dunlop, J.G., ed. "Letters from John Stewart to William Dunlop." *South Carolina Historical and Genealogical Magazine* 32 (1931): 25.

"Extracts From Harriott Horry's Receipt Book." *South Carolina Historical and Genealogical Magazine* 60 (1959): 28.

Goodman, Richard. "Dr. Garden's Flower," *Carologue* 19, no. 3 (Fall 2003).

Jervey, Elizabeth Heyward. "Death Notices From the *State Gazette* of South Carolina of Charleston, S.C." *South Carolina Historical and Genealogical Magazine* 51 (1950): 165.

Mathews, Maurice. "A Contemporary View of Carolina in 1680." *South Carolina Historical and Genealogical Magazine* 55 (1954): 153–59.

Mercantini, Jonathan. "The Great Carolina Hurricane of 1752." *South Carolina Historical and Genealogical Magazine* 103, no. 4 (2002): 351–65.

Morgan, Philip D., ed. "A Profile of a Mid-Eighteenth Century South Carolina Parish: The Tax Returns of Saint James, Goose Creek." *South Carolina Historical and Genealogical Magazine* 81 (1980): 51–65.

"Papers of Gabriel Manigault, 1771–1784." *South Carolina Historical and Genealogical Magazine* 64 (1963): 11.

Salley, A.S. Jr. "Diary of William Dillwyn in 1722." *South Carolina Historical and Genealogical Magazine* 36 (1935): 107–10.

Smith, H.A.M. "Charleston and Charleston Neck. The Original Grantees and the Settlements Along the Ashley and Cooper Rivers." *South Carolina Historical and Genealogical Magazine* 19 (1918): 3–76.

———. The French Huguenot Church of the Parish of Goose Creek, South Carolina. Transactions of the Huguenot Society of South Carolina in *South Carolina Historical and Genealogical Magazine* 16 (1915): 43.

———. "Goose Creek." *South Carolina Historical and Genealogical Magazine* 29 (1928): 1–25, 71–96, 167–92, 265–79.

Thomas, J.P. Jr. "The Barbadians in Early South Carolina" *South Carolina Historical and Genealogical Magazine* 31: 75–80.

Waterhouse, Richard. "Economic and Changing Patterns of Wealth Distribution in Colonial Lowcountry South Carolina." *South Carolina Historical and Genealogical Magazine* 89 (1988): 203–17.

Webber, M.L. "Tombstone Inscriptions." *South Carolina Historical and Genealogical Magazine* 40 (1939): 33–40.

Maps

Burr, David H. Map of North and South Carolina, Exhibiting the Post Offices…1839 From his The American Atlas (London, J. Arrowsmith, 1839).

Charleston District, South Carolina. Surveyed by Charles Vignoles and Henry Ravenel 1820. Approved for Mill's Atlas 1825.

Gaillard, John Palme. *Map of Berkeley and parts of Charleston and Dorchester Counties S.C.* The map depicts the land holdings from 1850 to 1900. The original is among the collections of the McClellanville Museum.

Gascoyne, Joel. *A New Map of the Country of Carolina.* Library of Congress.

Map of Game Preserves and Forest Holdings of P.O. Mead and W.L. "PA" Stribling situated in Berkeley County, S.C. Surveyed, 1933–34 by J.T. Kullock Inc. Among the private papers of Terrence Larimer, Naval Weapons Station Charleston, Goose Creek, South Carolina.

Mills, Robert. *Mills' Atlas of South Carolina.* 1825 Easley, South Carolina, Southern Historical Press, 1980.

South Carolina 1839 (Color Counties) U.S. Coast Survey, A.D. Bache, Superintendent, 1865.

South Carolina. Relative Importance of Places shown by Size and Type. Rand McNally Indexed Atlas 1910–1915

Tanner, Henry Schenck, 1786–1858. *Tanner Map* 1833. Act of Congress, *A new map of South Carolina with its canals, roads & distances from place to place along the stage & steamboat routes.* From his *A New Universal Atlas* (Philadelphia, 1836). Library of Congress.

Periodicals

Charleston City Gazette, South Carolina Historical Society and on microfilm at the Charleston County Library, Charleston, South Carolina.

Charleston Courier, South Carolina Historical Society, Charleston, South Carolina.

Charleston Evening Post, Charleston, South Carolina.

Charleston Evening Post, North Metro Edition, Charleston, South Carolina.

Charleston Mercury, Charleston, South Carolina. On microfilm at the Charleston County Library, Charleston, South Carolina.

Charleston News and Courier, Charleston, South Carolina.

Rauschenberg, B.L. "Brick and Tile Manufacturing in the South Carolina Low Country, 1750–1800." *Journal of Southern Decorative Arts*, 1988.

Royal Gazette, on microfilm at the Charleston County Library, Charleston, South Carolina.

South Carolina Gazette, on microfilm at the Charleston County Library, Charleston, South Carolina.

State Gazette of South Carolina, on microfilm at the Charleston County Library, Charleston, South Carolina.

Waterhouse, Richard. *The Caribbean, and the Settlement of Carolina.* Journal of America Studies vol. 9: 259–281.

Wright, John K. "The Study of Place Names: Recent Work and Some Possibilities." *Geographical Review*, 1929.

Journals of the House of Representatives

Journals of the House of Representatives, 1783–1784. Theodora J. Thompson, Editor. Published for the South Carolina Department of Archives and History by The University of South Carolina Press, Columbia, South Carolina. 1977.

———, *1785–1786.* Lark Emerson Adams, Editor. Published for the South Carolina Department of Archives and History by the University of South Carolina Press, Columbia, South Carolina. 1979.

———, *1787–1788.* Michael E. Stevens, Editor. Published for the South Carolina Department of Archives and History, The University of South Carolina Press, Columbia, South Carolina. 1981.

———, *1789–1790.* Michael E. Stevens, Editor. Published for the South Carolina Department of Archives and History, The University of South Carolina Press, Columbia, South Carolina. 1984.

———, *1791.* Michael E. Stevens, Editor. Published for the South Carolina Department of Archives and History, The University of South Carolina Press, Columbia, South Carolina. 1985.

———, *1792–1794,* Michael E. Stevens, Editor. Published for the South Carolina Department of Archives and History, The University of South Carolina Press, Columbia, South Carolina. 1988.

Plats traced from the originals among the Henry A.M. Smith Collection at the South Carolina Historical Society, Charleston, South Carolina

Bee, Susannah. Plan of Mrs. Bee's land at Goose Creek, St. James. 1 plat: tracing; 46 x 61 cm. Request #: 32/120/A005 Property owner.

Beresford, John. This plat contains three thousand acres of land being formerly laid out unto Joseph Thorogood and Lyeth in Berkeley County on a branch of Swamp within land that empties itself into Medway River. Request #: 32/120/A250

Black Tom Bay. General plan of a piece of land about Black Tom Bay. 1 plat: tracing; 46 x 61 cm. Request #: 32/120/A099

Broughton, John. Robert Daniel, Esq. Landgrave 527 Acres land upon Midway River or Black River [S.C.]. 1 plat: tracing; 46 x 61 cm. Request #: 32/120/A284

Glen, John and Daniel Cannon. Plat of a 566-acre plantation. The plat may have been commissioned to settle a boundary dispute between John Glen and Daniel Cannon.

Matthews, M. Copy of a plan of a body of land in Goose Creek, part now forming part of the glebe of St. James Church and part now belonging to the estate of Benjamin Coachman, dec'd. 1 plat, 2 pages: tracing; 46 x 61 cm. Request #: 32/120/A027

Mt. Holly, St. James, Goose Creek. 1 plat : tracing ; 46 x 61 cm. Request #: 32/120/A235

Postell, John. Plan of a tract of land in Berkeley County, S.C. belonging to John Postell. 1 plat: tracing ; 46 x 61 cm. Request #: 32/120/A200(bottom)

Ravenel, Henry. The Goose Creek road from Ten Mile House to Vance's Tavern with the relative situations of the plantations, drawn to regulate the cutting of timber for the state road. 1 plat: tracing; 46 x 61 cm. Request #: 32/120/A007

Books

African Methodism in South Carolina, A Bicentennial Focus, Seventh Episcopal District. Tappan, New York: Custombrook, Inc., 1987.

Bailey, Louise N. *Biographical Directory of the South Carolina House of Representatives: Volumes III, IV, 1775–1815.* Columbia: University of South Carolina Press, 1986.

Ball, Edward. *Slaves in the Family.* New York: Farrar, Straus and Giroux Publishers, 1998.

Bauer, William Rudolph. *The Sineath Family,* Columbia: The R.L. Bryan Company, 1970.

Bennett, John. *The Treasure of Peyre Gaillard.* Charleston: South Carolina Historical Society Microforms, 1981.

Betts, Albert Dean. *History of South Carolina Methodism.* Columbia, South Carolina: The Advocate Press, 1952.

Bowes, Frederick Patten. *The Culture of Early Charleston.* Greenwood, South Carolina: Greenwood Press, 1902.

Brown, Douglas Summers. *The Catawba Indians: The People of the River.* Columbia: University of South Carolina Press, 1966.

Burton, E. Milby. *The Siege of Charleston, 1861–1865.* Columbia: University of South Carolina Press, 1970.

Calhoun, Jeanne. *The Scourging Wrath of God: Early Hurricanes in Charleston,* Leaflet No. 29. Charleston, South Carolina: The Charleston Museum.

Chaplin, Joyce E. *An Anxious Pursuit: Agricultural Innovations and Modernity in the Lower South, 1730–1815.* Chapel Hill: University of North Carolina Press, 1993.

Coclanis, Peter A. *The Shadow of a Dream: Economic Life and Death in the South Carolina Low Country 1670–1920.* New York: Oxford University Press, 1989.

Cooper, Thomas, and David J. McCord. *The Statutes at Large of South Carolina, (1682–1838),* 10 vols. Columbia: A.S. Johnson, 1838.

Correspondence of Ralph Izard of South Carolina for the Years 1774 to 1804, with a short memoir. Volume 2.New York: Charles Francis & Co., 1844.

Crane, Verner W. *The Southern Frontier, 1670–1752.* Durham, North Carolina: Duke University Press, 1928.

Cross, Russell J. *Historic Ramblin's Through Berkeley.* Columbia: R.L. Bryan Company, 1985.

Dalcho, Frederick. *A Historic Account of the Protestant Episcopal Church in South Carolina.* Charleston: A.E. Miller, 1820, reprinted 1969.

Edgar, Walter B. *South Carolina a History.* Columbia: University of South Carolina Press, 1999.

Edgar, Walter B., and N. Louise Bailey. *Biographical Directory of the South Carolina House of Representatives: Volume I: 1692–1973 and Volumes II, III 1692–1775.* Columbia: University of South Carolina Press, 1974.

Edwards, Newton, and Herman G. Richey. *The Schools in the American Social Order.* Boston: Houghton Mifflin, 1911.

Franklin, John Hope. *From Slavery to Freedom: A History of Negro Americans.* New York: Vantage Books, 1969.

Fraser, Charles. *A Charleston Sketchbook, 1796–1806.* Rutland, Vermont: Charles E. Tuttle Co.1940.

The Goose Creek Church, A Morbid Tale. New York, New York, Printed at the Sign of the Eagle, One Flight Up, 1901.

Gordon, Asa H. *Sketches of Negro Life and History in South Carolina.* Columbia: University of South Carolina Press, 1929.

Heitzler, Michael J., *Historic Goose Creek, South Carolina, 1670–1980.* Easley, South Carolina: Southern Historical Press, 1983.

Hicks, Theresa M., ed. *South Carolina Indians Indian Traders and Other Ethnic Connections Beginning in 1670.* Spartanburg, South Carolina: Peppercorn Publications Inc. 1998.

Hirsch, Arthur Henry. *The Huguenots of Colonial South Carolina.* London: Arch Books, 1962.

Hofstader, Richard. *The American Republic*. 2 Volumes. Englewood Cliffs, New Jersey: Prentice-Hall, 1959.

Hrabowski, Richard. *Directory for the District of Charleston Comprising the places of residence and occupation of the White Inhabitants of the Following Parishes to wit…St. James (Goose Creek)*. Printed by John Hobb, no.6. Broad Street, Charleston, South Carolina, 1809. The book is deposited with the South Carolina Historical Society, Charleston, South Carolina.

Irving, John Beaufain. *A Day on the Cooper River*. Enlarged and edited by Louisa Cheves Stoney. Columbia, South Carolina: R.L. Bryan Co., 1932.

Johnson, Joseph. *Traditions and Reminiscences, Chiefly of the American Revolution in the South*. Charleston, South Carolina: Walker and James, 1851.

Klingberg, Frank J. *An Appraisal of the Negro in Colonial South Carolina*. Washington, D.C.: Associated Publishers, 1941.

———. *The Carolina Chronicle of Dr. Francis LeJau, 1706–1717*. Berkeley and Los Angeles: University of California Press, 1956.

———. *Carolina Chronicle: The Papers of Commissary Gideon Johnson, 1707–1716*. Berkeley and Los Angeles: University of California Press, 1946.

Knight, Edgar W. *Public Education in the South*. Boston: Ginn and Co., 1922.

Koger, Larry. *Black Slave Owners, Free Black Masters in South Carolina, 1790–1860*. Columbia: University of South Carolina Press, 1995.

Leiding, Henriette Kershaw. *Historic Houses of South Carolina*. Philadelphia: J.B. Lippincott, 1921.

Life in Carolina and New England during the Nineteenth Century, as Illustrated by Reminiscences and Letters of the DeWolf Family of Bristol, Rhode Island. Bristol, Rhode Island: privately printed, 1929.

Martin, Margaret Rhett. *Charleston Ghosts*. Columbia: University of South Carolina Press, 1963.

McCowen, George Smith. *The British Occupation of Charleston, 1780–1782*. Columbia, University of South Carolina Press, 1981.

McCrady, Edward. *History of South Carolina…* 4 Volumes. New York: McMillan, 1897–1901.

Mills, Robert. *Statistics of South Carolina*. Spartanburg, South Carolina: The Reprint Press, 1973. The work was originally published in 1826, by Hurlbut and Lloyd, Charleston, South Carolina.

Moltke-Hanson, Michael, and David Moltke-Hanson. *Intellectual Life in Antebellum Charleston*. Knoxville: University of Tennessee Press, 1986.

Moore, Alexander. *Biographical Directory of the South Carolina House of Representatives, Columbia: Vol. V: 1816–1828*. South Carolina Department of Archives and History, 1992.

Moore, Caroline T., ed. *Abstracts of the Wills of South Carolina*. 4 volumes. Columbia: R.L. Bryan, 1960–1974.

Nevins, Allan. *Slave Trading in the Old South*. New York: Frederick Ungar Publishing Co., 1959.

O'Brien, Michael and David Moltke-Hanson. *Intellectual Life in Antebellum Charleston*. Knoxville: University of Tennessee Press. 1986.

Orvin, Maxwell Clayton. *Historic Berkeley County, S.C., 1671–1900*. Charleston: Comprint, 1973.

———. *A History of Moncks Corner, Berkeley County, South Carolina*. Charleston, 1961.

Phelps, Chris W. *Charlestonians in War, The Charleston Battalion*. Gretna, Louisiana: Pelican Publishing Company, 2004.

Pierre, C.E. *The Work of the Society for the Propagation of the Gospel in Foreign Parts in the Colonies*. Washington, D.C. From The Association for the Study of Negro Life and History, Inc. From the Journal of Negro History 1, no. 4 (October 1916).

Poyas, E.A. *The Olden Times of South Carolina*. Charleston: S.G. Courtenay & Co., 1855.

Ravenel, Mrs. St. Julien. *Charleston, the Place and the People*. New York: McMillan, 1912.

"Report of the Committee on Education," in *Acts, Reports and Regulations of the General Assembly of South Carolina.* Columbia: R.W. Gibbes, 1858.

Reynolds, Emily Bellinger and Joan Reynolds Faunt, *The Biographical Dictionary of the Senate of South Carolina, 1776–1964.* Columbia: The Senate Research Committee. The South Carolina Department of Archives and History, 1964.

Rivers, William J. *A Sketch of the History of South Carolina.* Spartanburg, South Carolina: 1856; reprinted by the Reprint Co., 1972.

Rogers, George C. Jr. *Evolution of a Federalist: William Laughton Smith of Charleston (1758–1812).* Columbia: University of South Carolina Press, 1962.

Rutledge, Anna Wells. *Artists in the Life of Charleston.* Philadelphia: American Philosophical Society, 1949.

Sass, Herbert Ravenel. *The Story of the South Carolina Low Country.* West Columbia, South Carolina: J.F. Hyer Publishing Co., 1956.

Schaper, William A. *Sectionalism and Representation in South Carolina.* New York: De Capo Press, 1968.

Sellers, Leila. *Charleston Business on the Eve of The American Revolution.* Chapel Hill: University of North Carolina Press, 1932.

Stockton, Robert P. *Historic Resources of Berkeley County.* Moncks Corner: Berkeley County Historical Society and South Carolina Department of Archives and History, 1990.

Stoney, Samuel Gaillard. *Plantations of the Carolina Low Country.* New York: Dover Publications Inc.; Carolina Art Association, Charleston, South Carolina, 1938.

———. *Plantations of the South Carolina Low Country.* Charleston: Carolina Art Association, 1964.

Thompson, Theodora J., ed. *Journals of the South Carolina House of Representatives, 1783–1784.* Columbia: University of South Carolina Press, 1977.

W.J. Townsend, H.B. Workman, and George Eayrs, eds. *A New History of Methodism.* 2 vols. 1st ed. London, Hodder and Stoughton: 1909.

Turner, Frederick Jackson. *The Frontier in American History.* New York: Henry Holt and Company, 1947.

Wallace, David Duncan. *South Carolina: A Short History.* Columbia: University of South Carolina Press, 1951.

———. *The History of South Carolina.* 4 vols. New York: American Historical Society, Inc., 1934.

Waring, Joseph Ioor. *St. James' Church, Goose Creek, South Carolina: A Sketch of the Parish from 1706–1896* Charleston: Lucas & Richardson Co. Printers and Engravers, 1897

Index

C

D

E

F

G

H

M

S

T

Y

About the Author

Michael James Heitzler was born in St. Louis, Missouri, in 1947. He is the son of Marine Corps Colonel Joseph S. Heitzler and Gentry Virginia Heitzler. He is the father of two sons, Andrew and Adam. He received his formal training in several public and private schools from Florida to Hawaii. He holds a doctor of education degree from the University of South Carolina and has served as a teacher and administrator in the Berkeley School District, South Carolina, since 1968.

Heitzler was elected to Goose Creek City Council in 1976 and has served as mayor of the City of Goose Creek since 1978. He is the author of *Historic Goose Creek, South Carolina 1670–1980*, published in 1983 by Southern Historical Press, Easley, South Carolina.

Visit us at
www.historypress.net